We Band Of Brothers

R. E. Peppy Blount

EAKIN PRESS
Austin, Texas

Photographs of aerial bombing missions appearing in this book and not otherwise credited, are from the collections of Lawrence J. Hickey, Morris J. Eppstein, W.H. Cather, John C. Hanna, William R. Witherell, Jr., Virgil E. Redd and the author.

FIRST EDITION

Printed in the United States of America
By Eakin Press, P.O. Box 23066, Austin, Texas 78735

ISBN 0-89015-443-0

DEDICATION

The following has been written in an attempt to retain, and thereby preserve, a period of time that was of ultimate importance in the preservation of this nation and our way of life. To those friends who gave the last full measure of devotion to the cause of freedom, who helped in establishing the superlative and exemplary fighting record of the *Air Apaches*, but who shall never read this account, this book is dedicated. They were our brothers!

And in memory of Alma and Boodie whose love, devotion, sacrifice, and prayers made the recounting of these experiences possible.

We few, we happy few, we band of brothers;
For he to-day that sheds his blood with me
Shall be my brother . . .

Shakespeare
Henry V

Contents

Illustrations

Foreword

The World War II record of the 345th Bomb Group, *Air Apaches,* Fifth Air Force, typifies the finest tradition that has been the hallmark of the United States Air Force since its organization. The combat record of the *Touch O' Texas,* (old *199*) its crew and their fellow airmen, is the gut-wrenching, scared-as-hell story of college-age kids who flew B-25 strafer-bombers down the gun barrels of the Japanese Imperial Navy in World War II. It dramatically emphasizes that when our nation is in trouble we call on our youth to save it! In the process, they helped establish the high standard of excellence that demanded and guaranteed the success of our space program and more recent Challenger missions. If you're interested in gaining insight into the kind of men who have made significant contributions to our position of eminence in manned space flight today, I heartily recommend *We Band of Brothers.*

ROBERT L. CRIPPEN
Captain, United States Navy
Astronaut

Captain R.E. Peppy Blount

Preface

It was a different time! It was a time of heroism, patriotism, and firm national purpose! It was a time when the American people could take much pride in having picked up the gauntlet of fear and oppression and, standing shoulder to shoulder, called the tyrants' bluff and spit in their faces! It was a time when everybody believed fervently in the cause and the task at hand. The Japanese and Germans were enemies against which there was no problem in generating a great amount of determination. These were important times, both personally and nationally, and the events that have transpired in the intervening years have not served to obliterate those times.

War was everywhere, troops with carbines slung over their shoulders proceeded in all directions oblivious of the Leyte mud that was deeper than our boots and which we would soon ignore as well. My father and uncle had been in France in World War I; I had talked to them over the years and pried as much off-guard information from them as they would divulge, so I felt I had rendezvoused with destiny, and was where I was supposed, even expected, to be.

How could a west Texas teenager, a year and a half after graduation from high school, be the first pilot of a strafer-bomber, attacking places that had been only words and foreign names in his current events *Weekly Reader* a few months earlier.

The 345th Bomb Group, (*Air Apaches)*, Fifth Air Force, was activated at Columbia Army Air Base, Columbia, South Carolina, on Armistice Day, November 11, 1942, the same afternoon the San Angelo Bobcats (who would win the Texas State Championship the next year) beat us at Big Spring 18-6, in my senior year of high school.

"What branch of the service are you going into?" I asked Bobby Boykin, my co-captain of the Big Spring High School football team. "I'm going into the Navy and be a Naval Pilot," answered Bobby, "what're you gonna do?" "I'm going into the Army Air Corps," I replied, "and if I'm not too big, I wanta be a pilot, too!"

We both became pilots. Boykin, a pilot in the Navy, and I, a pilot in the Army. We were called to active duty immediately following our high school graduation in 1943. I went through the Army Air Corps training program, flew a tour of combat, and was home in less than two years time. In the lengthy, drawn out V-5 training program of the Navy, Boykin finished his training and won his wings as a Navy pilot after the war ended in August, 1945. He never got into combat. After the war, I told him that he got the best deal!

The Bomb Group I was with, the *Air Apaches,* was a minimum altitude, strafer skip-bombing group, equipped with B-25J aircraft modified to carry two rows of four .50 inch machine guns in the nose and two package fifty caliber machine guns on each side of the fuselage. All twelve guns fired simultaneously from a button on the pilot's control wheel. Each gun, firing seven hundred fifty rounds per minute, was loaded every third round with an armor-piercing shell, an armor-piercing incendiary shell, and a tracer shell. All three kinds of ammunition giving the pilot the firepower equivalent of a whole batalion at his finger tips. The engineer gunner's top turret gave us a flying gun platform with fourteen forward-firing fifty caliber machine guns that literally melted the super structure of Japanese ships from fifteen hundred yards on in.

The B-25 had one distinction! It was, by far, the *noisiest* airplane in the Army Air Corps and that characteristic helped in subduing and freezing the enemy when more speed and maneuverability would have been appreciated. The engines roared, shook, and screamed in rage as we skimmed over the China sea, hopped hills in Formosa, flew between the trees of New Guinea and caught frantic glimpses of frightened enemy faces hiding behind the bulkheads of Jap destroyers and merchantmen in that fraction of a second as we traveled ahead of our sound. We zoomed only inches above the enemy in a rising crescendo of noise, accompanied by the angry staccato chatter of the machine guns that preceded the destructive explosions of the bombs. Smoke from the 75-mm cannon and nose guns filled the cockpit and it smelled good as we yanked, pulled, and kicked the controls of the airplane. Down on the deck it was a personal war. You could watch your tracers run deadly tracks up and into a gun emplacement that suddenly ceased firing at you; or watch the superstructure of an enemy ship dissolve as the armor-piercing incendiary projectiles melted it. You could see a Jap *Betty* bomber (a Mitsubishi G4M1 and G4M2) explode in a camouflaged revetment as your incendiaries acted like a giant flame thrower, hundreds of yards in front of your airplane! That war was immediate. You *knew* if you'd successfully destroyed your target! That was combat as the strafer-bombers knew it. And some of us, for the remainder of our lives, will never walk or ride down a city street without thinking, *What a run you could make on this town! You'd come in over those hills, six ships abreast, start your strafing when you hit that industrial area, come right down the main street between the buildings— string your para-frags from the plants, through the town and over that railroad yard— then rack 'er up to the right, over that line of tall trees, back on the deck, evasive action and get the hell out of there! . . .*

Our mission was to destroy the enemy. We used armor-piercing incendiaries .50 caliber ammunition, para-fragmentation bombs, and 500- and 1,000-pound demolition bombs with 4-10 seconds delay fuses delivered at minimum altitude. Supporting and delivering this devastation and destruction were the B-25 aircraft, their crews, and the men on the ground who worked to keep them flying month after month. Final success of a mission depended upon the crew members who flew their planes to the target, fired the guns and dropped the bombs. That was the bottom line, the payoff, but behind those few seconds over the targets was another tale and one that tells the story of the strafers! It is the story of the hours spent on the ground between missions, of the long, hot, and dusty hours working on the line, the briefings and interrogations, the games, the shacks, the rest leaves in Sydney, the bull sessions, the "prayer meetings," the chow, the weather, the songs, and all of the dust and mud, humor and sadness, comedy and pathos, heartbreak and success, dying and living that blended into our war.

How well our mission was accomplished is immortalized in the battle record of the 345th Bomb Group, *Air Apaches,* Fifth Air Force, and the pride every member had in this fighting organization. We sank 260 enemy ships and damaged 275 more, destroyed 367 enemy aircraft, flew more than 10,609 strikes for a total of 58,562 combat flying hours in eight major campaigns in the Asia-Pacific theatre in World War II — including New Guinea, Bismark Archipelago, Northern Solomons, Southern Philippines, Luzon, Western Pacific, China Defensive, China Offensive, and Air Offensive against Japan. And while the 345th became one of the most decorated units of the war, we paid the catastrophic price of 720 fatalities, and the loss of 177 B-25 strafer-bombers.

"We were the first full Air Force Combat Group sent to the Pacific in World War II and we were the best! We won the war!" said retired Colonel C. U. True, one of the 345th's Commanding Officers. He could have added that they started it but we finished it!

Starting at Moresby, in early 1943, we stopped the Japanese Dragon on the doorstep of Australia and started him backtracking. We brought about the ultimate in his defeat when, on August 19, 1945, six of our B-25s flew out to initiate the Japanese surrender by intercepting and escorting the two Jap *Betty* bombers, painted white with red crosses on their sides and tails in compliance with Fifth Bomber Command instructions. The two *Betty* Bombers were loaded with Jap peace emissaries who had left Kyushu, Japan, early that morning. The "peaceful Japs" peered through thick-lensed spectacles at the menacing *Apache* Indian Head insignia painted on the vertical stabilizers of our B-25s and the eight .50 caliber machine gun barrels protruding from the mouths of the frightening Bats painted on the noses of the 499th *Bats Outa Hell* Squadplanes. The *Air Apaches* had been honored and Major McClure had to land on Moko Strip, Ie Shima, to show the Nips where they were to land to negotiate the surrender. We had performed our last mission.

Sandwiched between Moresby and Ie Shima are most of the events that comprise this volume! Our memories are legion! The nervy Jap (described as "a mean looking bastard") who eased into formation between Captain Anacker and Lieutenant Wallace's B-25s, and less than fifty feet from either of them, coming off a shipping strike at Rabaul and the predicament of their gunners who dared not fire for fear of hitting each other; and the copilot who, while on a strike against an enemy airdome in New Guinea, went berserk and was subdued at gunpoint by the pilot while the engineer flew the plane back to base; the throwing of the proverbial "kitchen sink", rigged in a B-25's bomb bay, at a Jap airdome in the Celebes; the conversion of the B-25 medium bomber to a minimum altitude "American Kamikaze" strafer-bomber with fourteen forward firing .50-inch machine guns; sweating the gasoline, the weather, fighter interception without cover on ten and one-half hour missions in medium bombers that ordinarily were designed to fly no more than six hours, from the Philippines to the coast of Indochina, and 1,800 miles over nothing but the endless whitecaps of the China sea where loss of an engine or the shortage of gasoline resigned the fate of the airplane to ditching and death.

And while the war is over and all of those combatants who survived that hell have long since been separated from the service to pursue their lives as civilians, they have been marked for life as only combat can mark a man. It may be in a seemingly blind arrogance, or a generous tolerance of those who haven't been there, or a total disregard of the accepted morals of society and a voracious proclivity to drink until he passes out. It may be in the uncontrollable jerk of a head, a nervous twitch, an errant eye wink, an involuntary shudder or the recurrent nightmares of those who have been too close to death for too long a time — for the purpose of combat is death, and too long association with its influence, has its effects.

But after almost four decades this has started to lessen to a degree; our hands only infrequently become wings, and our thoughts and eyes have come back to earth. A church steeple has now become a church steeple instead of a flak tower; a ship once again has become something to enjoy instead of something to strafe, bomb and destroy; a train no longer poses a challenge with enemy flak cars immediately behind the engine and in front of the caboose; the trees no longer have cables strung between them to entangle and destroy unwary strafer pilots; a clump of trees is no longer an enemy gun emplacement and a rough and turbulent sea no longer the grave for a heavy-nosed, overloaded B-25 that can't fly on single engine. We're home, and mortgage payments, inflation, the aches and pains of growing old, and watching our grandchildren grow to maturity, now occupies our time and thoughts, pushing, for the most part, those nightmares of "riding the rockets" out of our minds.

The "prayer meetings," the songs, the close calls, the near misses, the combat tragedy averted by the flying genius of kids still wet behind the ears, the strafing and bombing when we punished the enemy and suffered no losses, the comic response to mortal adversity, the endless, unmatched courage and guts of those young, untested, fun-loving boy-next-door types who incessantly and unceasingly carried the war to the enemy —*I loved those moments, and the good memories far outweigh the bad.* Such feelings must be comparable to those of a mother who forgets the pain she has suffered after she observes the beautiful child to whom she had given birth!

In my memory these experiences now seem to have been a major Broadway production played out on an enormous stage in which we were all stars, and in which we miraculously were allowed to observe our starring roles! Living on the edge of life and death, massive amounts of adrenalin were secreted to assure a star performance!

Did I like Thatcher, Kenney, Bell, Warnick, Zuber, Kolodziejski, Fisher, Marcus, Cronin, Blair, Lamar, Thies, Moore, Townsley — and all the others? *To tell the truth, I loved them!* At such moments of truth, daring, fear, anxiety, bravery, despondency— nothing is ordinary. Those days and those events, mutually shared, produced a rare comradery — between men who fought, died and went to battle together — and the intensity of that association, even after all these years, still defies any rational explanation. The bond that has been created is so strong that it wipes away all the normal, ordinary barriers of class, religion, social structure, politics and race. Nothing in terms of friendship can precede it in the past, equal it in the present, nor surpass it in the future. It was and is, totally self-supporting; exists of itself! Nothing more is asked, nothing more is required.

Introduction

After induction, flight, and overseas training at Columbia Army Air Base, Columbia, South Carolina, my crew and I were sent to Hunter Field in Savannah, Georgia. Savannah was the "jumping off" overseas assignment depot for the Army Air Corps. My navigator, Paul O. "Arky" Vaughn and I, after getting billeted in the BOQ's, caught a bus across to the Officer's Club for dinner. This turned out to be old home week! Hunter Field was the assembly point for all overseas-trained personnel in the Third Air Force, which included B-25 crews, (North American B-25J *Mitchell*), B-26s (Martin B-26B *Marauder*, at first known as the *Widow Maker* due to a large number of early accidents), B-24s (Consolidated B-24 *Liberator),* P-51s (North American P-51B *Mustang),* P-38s (Lockheed P-38 *Lightning*, called by the Germans, "Two-tailed devil"), Bell P-39s (*Aira-cobra*), P-61s (Northrop P-61 *Black Widow)*, and about any other aircraft that was flown in World War II! Here we met old friends whom we hadn't seen since pre-flight days, after which we had been split up (after classification) to go our separate ways as pilots, bombardiers, or navigators. I now met some who were going overseas as radio, armorers, and engineer gunners.

Hunter Field had a lively Officer's Club that endured, if not tolerated, marginal court-martial behavior on the part of the officers assembled there awaiting shipment overseas. I felt that the permanent officer personnel fully understood the questionable behavior and antics of these itinerant visitors, knowing full well most of them were enjoying one last fling before they faced the real war and the excellent possibility they'd never get another chance.

We were sent to California, and I was appointed CO of our shipment overseas.

It was fitting that our first day at sea fell on Sunday. Of the five thousand souls aboard the S. S. *General Anderson* we probably had more religious unanimity at that time than could ever be mustered by such a group again. With everybody enroute to the same unknown destination in the same war, it made for an atmosphere of sober thought, mental preparation for whatever might lie ahead, and solid soul searching concerning a universal thought, *What if I don't come back!*

Our sleeping quarters down under on the second deck were unbearably hot, resulting in many of us taking our blankets topside to sleep on the cold steel of the deck. The first night or two proved to be a real respite, or reprieve, from the sweat box we were sleeping in. However, on the third night, we ran into a squall that fell so gently we were not awakened until we were completely wet. And then, half awake and half asleep, the water on deck finally reached such proportions that it ran from one side of the ship to the other, following the flow of gravity with the roll of the ship. The water would first come trickling, then sloshing, as the ship rolled to the low side, where I was attempting to sleep. But then, as the ship would roll to the opposite side, the water would flow away only to return a few seconds later as the big ship rolled in the other direction. Finally we were forced back into the hot, stinking bowels of the ship to escape the deluge that ultimately would build up on deck. But before that trip was completed, a few of us became conditioned, and learned to endure the quiet splashing of a little water to the extent we could sleep through a moderate Pacific squall without waking up.

Our sea excursion soon became a nightmare! The gnawing

fear of attack was ever present, and the sound to general quarters, the attack alarm, would start a mad scramble to abandon ship positions on deck to wait and watch. We would crowd the rail to scan the sea for the telltale sign of an approaching torpedo, waiting for an explosion, which fortunately never came. What we did see were porpoise, whales, flying fish, and the dorsal fins of the ever present sharks.

Seasickness, I learned, can be very contagious, and it seemed this malady reached epidemic proportions by the second day.The sickness seemed more prevalent among the ground-oriented branches of the service than the Air Corps personnel who were used to being thrown around the sky in an airplane. This nauseated agony appeared too closely akin to death itself, especially when vomiting from an already emptied stomach. Garbage cans or other receptacles were used for repositories when there was no room at the rails.

"Do you have a weak stomach?" I asked a big sergeant leaning over the rail with an artillery insignia on his shoulder.

"No, sir," he replied, between heaves, "I'm throwing 'er just as far as any of the others hanging over this rail!"

The stench of human regurgitation, mingled with the unpleasant odor of sweating bodies crammed into a space devoid of fresh air, drove me topside. Watching the eeriness of the night I found that the Southern Cross is beautiful in a clear sky. A striking phenomena was the bluish-green light that was emitted from the disturbed water in the wake of our ship. The flashes of colored light came from the phosphorescent content of the water.

To compound our problems, we were wearing heavy, green gabardine winter uniforms when we left San Francisco and, to confuse the Jap spies and Fifth Column, we hadn't been told we were going to the sultry South Pacific. The first night out we had nearly frozen to death, and that, needless to say, really fooled the enemy; but after two days at sea we were burning up. And being allowed only two changes of clothes while aboard ship, all wearing winter clothing, the smell of all personnel "ripened" quickly. This encouraged everyone to stay on deck in the fresh air as much as possible. On deck we had wall to wall people, making life topside about as unpleasant as that below deck.

After two weeks we sighted a PBY *Catalina* flying boat that circled us three or four times. These were the first non-ship human beings we had seen since we left San Francisco. We passed Guadalcanal about noon and it looked like any other island in the Solomon Group. The price we had paid for that piece of real estate made it something special to all of us. *The war was getting closer.* We watched the changing shades of green of the dense jungle of Guadalcanal, as the sun played hide and seek with the puffy cumulus clouds, until it was out of sight.

"We've crossed the Pacific — traveled seven thousand miles — and neither the Army, Navy, nor anyone else even knows we're here or where we're supposed to be," said a rather confused second lieutenant infantry officer.

"I heard we're going on to Leyte in a convoy," said another young flight officer, "and there's a guy in one of the forward cabins who's betting fifteen hundred dollars — giving five- to-one odds — that we're going back to the States!"

The rumors were running wild right up until the next day when we pulled into the harbor and through the Sub nets at Hollandia, New Guinea. The harbor was crowded with seventy or more ships of every description, with motor boats skimming the water's surface like so many water bugs, making endless trips between ships and shore. Hollandia Harbor was beautiful, with dense jungle and undergrowth starting abruptly at the water's edge, climbing to rolling hills covered with trees, and the hills sloped to towering mountains whose peaks were hidden in magnificent cumulus clouds during the day that cooled rapidly and dissipated at night, deluging us with soft nocturnal rain showers.

After three days in Hollandia Harbor and twenty-one days on the ship, we were finally "unloaded" or, as Zuber said, "rescued!"

"We're gettin' off this thing just before everybody starts to mutiny," said Zuber.

"But things haven't been too bad since the boys found out what's under our hold," he added.

"Whatta you mean?" I inquired.

"The floor of our sleeping compartment is loose planking," explained Zuber, "and day before yesterday some of the boys found out that we were sleeping right on top of canned fruit juices and all kinds of goodies!"

After being barged ashore, we were trucked twenty-six

miles inland to the Hollandia airstrip, and Vaughn and I were assigned to tent number twenty-six and restricted to the area, awaiting immediate shipment to the combat zone. We were taken off alert.

The following day we went back on alert, but by noon, after some of the guys were flown out, we were free for the remainder of the day. We had been issued shoulder holsters for our forty-five automatic pistols.

"The only place I ever saw anybody wear a shoulder holster," I said to Arky, "was in a James Cagney movie and they were gangsters and G-Men in Chicago.

"The only way I've ever seen a pistol worn — which is all my life in West Texas — is on your hip," I continued, "and I'm going to find one if I have to turn New Guinea inside out!"

Catching a jeep going in the right direction, I stopped at Base Ordnance about twenty-five miles down the road, but they had closed for the day. I hadn't found a holster but I had seen lots of beautiful country, driving along the shores of Lake Sentani.

Early the next morning I was up and on the road to Base Ordnance before anyone was alerted for shipment and having secured the holster, I caught a truck back to the strip. As I walked into camp I was met with the sight of my crew, sitting in the back of a fully-packed truck and ready to be moved to the flight line.

"Where've you been?" inquired Arky, nervously. "We've been on alert since early this morning and we're shipping out! We're already loaded and we don't have a pilot! They caught us all off guard — Zuber's got a duffle bag full of wet laundry!"

With Arky helping throw some of my stuff into a duffle bag, that was the fastest packing job I ever accomplished. We boarded a B-24 and I slouched, relaxed and dozed in the warm sunshine in the plexiglass nose all the way to Nadzab, New Guinea.

"Is the B-24 version of the Air Corps hymn really what they say it is?" I asked the pilot after we landed.

"How's that?" he responded.

Punching Arky, who was waiting for the prearranged cue, we sang together, "Off we go into the wild blue yonder . . . *CRASH!*" This was an obvious reference to the proclivity of the B-24 aircraft's failure to get off the ground on takeoff which resulted in the loss of numerous airplanes and crews during World War II. I thought he was going to hit us, but, being fast on our feet, we beat a hasty retreat to the jeep that was to take us to the staging area. We would sing this version of the Air Corps song to the *Jolly Rogers*, the Skull and Cross Bones B-24 Group of Pacific fame, at a later time and would find that they had a much more generous, friendly, and understanding sense of humor — especially after an hour or so of good steady drinking.

Our first day at Nadzab, New Guinea, we caught a thirty-five mile ride to Lae and the beach and went swimming.

We were reissued necessary flying equipment, including oxygen mask, leather helmet, earphones, A-3 bag, and goggles, the day before we flew out of the Nadzab replacement depot. As it turned out, we wouldn't need any of this equipment except the earphones.

I took communion Sunday night as the last rays of a beautiful sunset faded over the mountains, our last night at Nadzab, in a native built, grass thatched roof church. I would subsequently take communion in Westminster Abbey in London, as well as in other great cathedrals and some of the most beautiful and imposing church structures in my homeland. Never would I feel the presence of God any more strongly than in the natural surroundings of a grass-roofed, dirt floor sanctuary in the jungles of the South Pacific. "Where two or more are gathered together in my name, there I shall be also." Amen and Amen.

We were loaded on a C-47 transport the next morning at 0800 after getting up at 0200 for a 0500 takeoff.

"Why would they get us up at 0200 in the middle of the night if we're not going to take off until 0800," grumbled Warnick.

"They wanted to make sure Zuber got his laundry dry," I laughed. "They don't allow wet, mildewed uniforms in the Phillipines — it causes jungle rot!"

We landed at Pelilieu Island, one of the Palaus Island group, at 1725. We were to spend the night before proceeding on to our destination, (Tacloban, Leyte, the Philippines) early the next morning. We had hardly had time to locate a place to lay our heads for the night in the transient billet, before it was chow time. We were staying in tents just off the edge of the airstrip and only a few yards from the beach.

I asked a Seabee lieutenant, across the table at chow, about the recent battles to take the island.

"Here at Pelilieu we were fighting the Jap's first team, weren't we?" I asked him.

"You can bet your hip boots," said the Seabee officer, "and throw in your umbrella and snow shoes too!"

By this time the sun had gone down, and as we stepped out of the mess tent, the biggest, brightest moon I had ever seen was starting to ascend overhead. The moonlight was so bright you could have read a newspaper.

"You want to see something interesting?" the Seabee asked.

"Sure," I replied, "I'm not going anywhere for the next couple of years or so!" He smiled. We walked a few yards down to the beach and paused at the edge of a Jap pillbox, built just above the high tide mark. We were standing on the edge of a cove that appeared to be five- to six-hundred-yards across, and around the circular edge of the cove were four Jap pillboxes with walls of reinforced concrete, four feet thick, and all of them mutually supporting one another.

"These pillboxes must've played havoc with those troops landing on this beach," I said.

"They sure did — coupled with what happened to the landing craft about four hundred yards off shore there," responded the Seabee.

"What happened out there?" I asked.

"The landing was scheduled for high tide," he said, "but, as is so often the case, there was a *SNAFU*, and the landing craft didn't get in here after the battleship bombardment as soon as they should have. There's a big coral reef out there about four hundred yards out, that the landing craft hung up on, and they were forced to unload their troops — with heavy packs, rifles, and ammunition — into water ten to fifteen feet deep. The ones who didn't drown, were annihilated by the cross fire from these pillboxes encircling the cove, and the injured drowned when the water came in over them."

As I listened to the Seabee lieutenant's firsthand description of the battle that had ensued on this section of beach, I walked down closer to the water's edge to look at a continuous and unbroken ridge (about eight to ten inches high) of what appeared to be short, white sticks of varying length. These were piled in a perfectly-ringed simicircle, as far as the eye could see around the edge of the high water mark of the cove.

"What are all these white sticks?" I asked the lieutenant.

"Look a little closer," he said.

"These are bones — *human bones* — as far as you can see — they're — !" I stopped in amazement, as the lieutenant continued.

"They're the bones of the First Marine Division. For the most part, the bravest bunch of young American men who ever lived! They died out there in that water . . . hit first by heavy Jap mortar fire laid down on the reef, and then cut to ribbons by the cross fire from the pillboxes and other Nip gun positions further up on the beach . . . and this is all that's left of 'em, after the fish got through pickin' their bones," he added.

"This whole damn island," he shook his head, "wasn't worth the life of one of those marines. This piece of coral cost us about 2,000 American lives, and about four times that many wounded! I hope it was necessary!"

The beach was still littered with the burned, exploded, amphibian tractors, assault vehicles, and every conceivable piece of war equipment imaginable — now destroyed and no longer serviceable. Deep craters and holes in the pure white sand, made by exploding aerial bombs and high explosive shells from the giant guns of the supporting battleships and cruisers, were still much in evidence.

I thanked the Seabee lieutenant, wished him good luck, and walked slowly and pensively back to my tent in the bright moonlight. There was a slight breeze blowing in from the sea and across the cove on this beautiful night. *This was war!* This was what I had been training for, and until now, I thought, it had seemed so far away. *But this was it.*

I have written, in the Preface, that my father, Ralph Eugene "Boodie" Blount and his brother (William Granger "Billy" Blount) had been in World War I.

What would my father and my uncle Billy have thought about all these machine guns? All this firepower? The years dissolved and were lost as I looked into the blue eyes of my Uncle Billy Blount, dressed in the neat but greasy work clothes of an automobile mechanic, sitting in front of his garage in Greenville, Texas. He loved all automobiles, to which he had been introduced around the turn of the century as a mechanic's flunky in Grimes Garage in Hillsboro, Texas. As he grew older he became a race driver, racing at all the County Fairs throughout central Texas. Every Memorial Day week Uncle Billy closed his garage and made his annual pilgrimage to the Indianapolis 500. He didn't miss the 500 for over forty years. I once waited, with the impatience of youth, while he rolled a cigarette from a nickel sack of Bull Durham tobacco, licked it on both sides, popped it into his mouth, struck a match by snapping it under his thumbnail, and lit it. He had taken a deep draw, exhaled, and leaned back in the old car seat that doubled as a bench.

"Could you see 'em, Uncle Billy?" I had asked that day. "Of course you could see 'em! They were close enough to smell 'em, too!" he answered. Beneath the shade of the overhang of the garage, he had gazed across and down the street and was again in the *Meuse Argonne* and *Chateau Thierry* of France in World War I. "And you knew where they were?" I asked. "Of course, I knew where they were! You'd have had to have been blind not to be able to see the top of their trenches not more'n a hundred yards right in front of you! It was early in the mornin'. The Krauts always attacked early in the mornin'. And they came over the top yellin' and screamin' and blowin' bugles!"

"What'd you do, Uncle Billy?" "Now what would you've done?" He had answered. "I lined up the sights on my machine gun and got ready! We were the best machine gun crew in the whole 36th Division." "Did you mow 'em down?" I leaned forward in anticipation. "Just like cuttin' weeds! I raked 'em back and forth and they stacked up like cord wood! There was nothin' to it! They just ran right into my line of fire and I just kept shootin'! Thought my gun barrel was gonna get too hot and melt!" He put out the Bull Durham butt and leaned forward.

"You whipped those Germans didn't you, Uncle Billy?"

"Yeah! We finally whupped up on 'em pretty good but they were good soldiers! Wasn't nothin' easy about the German soldier!"

"Did you see Daddy while y'all were over there?" I asked. "No, and it's a good thing, too! My little brother, Boodie, shouldn't even have been in the war. Your Daddy was in the artillery and too young to be over there. When they finally found out he was only seventeen years old they couldn't send him home; so he stayed in France and fought with his outfit till the war was over. If I'd seen him I'd given him my boot where it would've done the most good!"

I said, "They sent your Grandpap Tarver home. He was a soldier, too!"

"They sent him home because he was too young. Your great grandfather Tarver was a soldier and only fourteen years old, fightin' for the South in the Civil War. He got the measles somewhere in Tennessee and they shipped him home where he should've been all the time."

"He fought the Indians after that," I said, "he told me!"

"Yeah! He fought the Indians all out in west Texas and he told me the same stories that he told you."

"Do you think I'll be a soldier someday, Uncle Billy?" I had asked.

"Let's hope not!" he replied. "We've had enough soldierin' and fightin' in this family to do us for several generations to come. If it's fightin' you want, come on back in the garage and start fightin' this broom!"

With his flair for race driving and machine-gunning, Uncle Billy would've made some kind of a bomber-strafer pilot.

Flying the strafers was the nearest thing to hand to hand combat without actually being on the ground facing the enemy with a rifle in your hands. At twenty feet you saw the expression on a face, the fear in the eyes, the frantic dive for cover, the figures sprawling and crawling in the mud all in the streaking fraction of a second's glance at an enemy taken completely by surprise. That feeling was good! It was when you had waited too long to get down on the deck, when you'd blown your surprise, the enemy knew you were coming and you felt all hell about to break loose, with no place to hide — that's when you got sick! There were many times I would get sick! I learned quickly that the ground, the trees, the natural or man-made obstacles, the topography and terrain were the best, closest, and most appreciated friends of the strafers. That was a game of the quick and the dead and only the quick were still alive.

Air Corps Tech Order "specs" on the B-25J stated that the

1750 Wright-Cyclone engines could not endure military power — that's everything, mixture, props, and throttle, to the firewall — for more than five minutes. Whoever wrote that had never flown the B-25J at mast-height level into the midst of Japanese Convoys in the China sea guarded by half the Imperial Navy, attacked heavily defended Jap airdromes at treetop level from New Guinea to the Philippines to Formosa to China to the mainland of Japan, stalked "rolling stock" just above the telegraph wires of the railroads and highways of Formosa and Indochina or made minimum altitude sweeps of Chinese waterways like the River from Canton to the sea with flak towers spaced every five miles where your only hope for survival was the element of surprise! This was achieved by flying low enough not to be observed and fast enough to be continuously out in front of the sound of those deafening Wright-Cyclone engines! I had flown those engines with everything to the firewall for fifteen or twenty minutes many times, and the fallacy of that "Tech Order" would be proven again and again, out of the necessity to save our hides! Self-preservation is a powerful stimulus that disproves a lot of things!

After the reinvasion of Bataan and the retaking of Corregidor, in early 1945, the 345th Bomb Group moved from Tacoloban, Leyte, to San Marcelino, Luzon, located thirty-five miles west and over the mountains from Clark Field and ten miles north of Bataan and Subic Bay. We had moved north, 750 miles closer to the coast of Indochina where Japanese shipping had heretofore been out of our range and had enjoyed the almost free use of the China sea. We quickly became the United States Far East Air Force specialists in minimum-altitude bombing of enemy shipping and sank in excess of 145,000 tons of Japanese ships in the first three months of 1945. We would also learn, even more quickly, that minimum-altitude bombing in the open China sea would be costly in terms of the loss of aircraft and manpower. Like the drunk who was told he could not drink the brewery dry and who responded, "but I've got 'em working at night," we lost airplanes at such an accelerated rate that we had North American Aviation working at night to keep up. We learned just as quickly that we were expendable. American assembly line production soon furnished an almost adequate number of aircraft, and the trained air crewmen to fly them, all sitting in the wings, eager to take our places. We lined the bottom of the China sea with Japanese war ships and merchantmen. The price? Grade A, top choice young American manhood and their flying machines. The best part of a successful strike against the enemy, (like winning a football game) was reliving and enjoying it together after the battle. We were winning the battles of the China sea but there were fewer and fewer players with whom to discuss and enjoy the victories. *C'est la guerre!*

During this period I was losing friends to the gunners of the Japanese Imperial Navy faster than a tourist losing nickles to the one-armed bandits of Las Vegas. Death, a subject that previously had received little attention, was suddenly my constant companion. Having lost three fellow tentmates, I would lose two more, and the odds favoring the grim reaper increased daily. My faith was in for a real test as life was now being lived hour-by-hour. I felt it was only a matter of time until the one with my name on it would show up. At age twenty, I was trapped in an impossible and undesirable situation. It was like a bad dream.

I should have been in my second year at Rice, or The University of Texas, an All Southwest conference athlete in football and basketball and a free spirit with the world ready to be conquered and awaiting my pleasure. Instead, I was sweating out every takeoff of an overloaded B-25 airplane; praying it was going to hold together until I could get it back on the ground. Every mission found the targets more difficult, more distant, more volatile, more explosive, and more dangerous. It demanded more courage to point the nose of the airplane into the flaming barrage of enemy naval guns and fly down their gun barrels. I constantly discussed flight tactics with the most experienced pilots, engine operation, limitations and gas consumption with the crew chiefs, and talked about ammunition and bomb fuses with the armorers — all in an attempt to attain the edge that might keep me and my crew alive.

The wisdom of my great grandfather Tarver, Confederate soldier, Indian fighter, kinsman and close friend of outlaw John Wesley Hardin, given to me as a child at his knee, would be put to good use.

"Whether it's an Indian fight or a gun fight," said the little gray-bearded, tobacco-chewing gentleman, "always have the sun at your back! Cousin Wes always arranged to have the sun to his back in a gun fight when he could. Said it gave him the edge, and in a fight for your life you gotta' have the edge!"

Our B-25 *Mitchell* (named for General Billy Mitchell) was a twin-engine bomber, and the most widely used US bomber of the war. The B-25H version was adapted to carry a 75-mm cannon. Its span was 67 feet 6.7 inches length: 52 feet, 10-inches, maximums speed: 284 mph at 15,000 feet, range: 1,525 miles at 233 mph; armament: up to 14 .50-inch machine guns, and up to 4,000 pounds of bombs. This is what the Tech Orders, governing safe operation, stated. In times of crises, however, — which was 90 percent of the time — the B-25J airplane flew at speeds in excess of 350 mph. The crew was usually six.

After the replacement of the bombardier's "hot house" or plexiglass nose, with two rows of four .50-inch machine guns and four package guns, the additional weight of the twelve machine guns, made this modified B-25J land at one hundred-sixty mph, or about thirty-miles per hour faster than the standard model. There were two fifty caliber waist guns, one on each side of the aircraft for the radio-gunner to fire, and a tail turrett embracing two fifties that the armorer tail-gunner manned. The waist guns would ultimately be removed (along with the tail gunner) to eliminate weight. The radio man then became the tail gunner over the target.

Ordinarily a medium bomber, the B-25, had a maximum time in the air of six hours. When we moved up to the Philippines in early 1945, typical American ingenuity had doubled the effective range of this versatile aircraft. This more effective range had first gained recognition when it propelled the Doolittle Raiders to Tokyo from the deck of a carrier in 1942. With our control of the Philippines, only one sea lane remained open to our enemy. That was from the Japanese mainland, southeast to Hainan Island (where they made up their convoys), thence south along the coast of Indochina to Borneo, Sumatra, Malaya, and the other islands of that area. This sea lane supplied the war machine of the Land of the Rising Sun. With the installation of Tokyo gasoline tanks (as used by Doolittle's Raiders) occupying half of our bomb bay, we still had room for four five-hundred-pound bombs. With extra tanks in the radio compartment behind the bomb bay, we made long range bombers out of mediums capable of staying in the air eleven hours, if necessary, and with a two-thousand mile range. Such range, coupled with the strafing and the skip-bombing ability of an attack bomber which proved 99 percent more effective than conventional high altitude bombing, made the B-25 the most versatile airplane of the United States Air Corps in World War II.

"Nobody will ever get used to this war, will they Lieutenant?" Kolodziejski said, early one morning as we made preparation to hit yet another enemy convoy along the coast of Indochina.

"No, Hank," I replied, "neither you, me, nor anyone else will ever get used to this! Tonight some of us will be back here watching the movie. Some of us will get drunk, some of us will write letters back home or just lie in the sack. And some of us will be dead. Shot down over a Jap destroyer along the coast of China, near some place we never heard of!"

Ordinarily the subject of death was avoided like the plague. We simply existed, slept fitfully and presented a cocky, *they can never touch me* attitude to each other. But I found myself constantly "looking over my shoulder," feeling the next mission would be my last. They said you'd never see the one that got you, but I doubted that. If we were still around after ten or fifteen missions our nerves were frayed, our consciences seared and our minds drawn as tight as a bowstring that could snap with the unexpected cough of an engine. I could identify with the poor devil in the song who said,

> "I gets weary and sick of tryin',
> I'm tired of livin' but scared of dyin . . . "

I understood him completely.

Group G-3 made arrangements with the Navy for our combat crews to be given one day's "Rest & Relaxation" on some of their small motorized launches at Subic Bay. So it was with an unusual air of comradery, mirth and goodwill, contrasted with the grim atmosphere, strained faces and serious attitudes of the same men who more often gathered to be ferried to the flight line and our airplane to fly a mission, that we met at Squadron headquarters and climbed into the motor pool jeep with our picnic lunch prepared by the cooks.

Kolodziejski and Zuber showed up with baseball gloves and a baseball. "I hope ya'll like to swim," I remarked. "We're going to be on a small motor launch all day and somebody just might lose their control and have to dive in to retrieve the baseball!"

"I pitched six games the year before I came into the service without one wild pitch," replied Kolodziejski.

"And I caught over thirty games one year," responded Zuber, "and only five pitches got away from me that were ruled wild pitches!"

"When ya'll are playing for the Pittsburgh Pirates after the war," I replied, "I hope you'll get free passes and autographed baseballs for all of us old war buddies!"

Subic Bay, Southwest Pacific Headquarters Base for the U.S. Navy Submarine Fleet, was bustling with activity. The navy personnel were very pleasant and accommodating; some had visited our Group at San Marcelino and been given rides in our B-25s by pilots test flying repaired aircraft damaged by enemy fire.

"Do we salute the ship or the Captain or the colors or what?" asked Cronin, as we boarded the Navy launch.

"We certainly want to be correct in our Navy etiquette," I replied, "otherwise we might be thrown overboard before we ever get on this tub. Salute the bridge! That's where the steering wheel and the CO's supposed to be!"

With everyone safely aboard the pilot set a course for the middle of Subic Bay and we enjoyed a tour of the big submarine base, getting a close look at all the ships and subs in the harbor. Sitting on the bow of the launch with our legs hanging and the wind and the spray in our faces, the relaxed and festive spirit of a day away from the war was obviously being enjoyed by all participants.

"Look how low that Submarine sits in the water," commented Warnick, "it'd sure be tough getting a bomb into her!" *We never get very far away from the war,* I thought.

We anchored in an inlet on the Bataan side of the Bay and spread our picnic lunch. There was swimming and assorted horseplay. "Look at old Vaughn," I remarked, as our navigator was poised for a dive from the bow of our launch, "there's a real 'bank walker' if I ever saw one!"

"What's a bank walker?" inquired Kolodziejski, the kid from Steel City USA — Pittsburgh.

"Yeah, what's this 'bank walker,' " inquired Vaughn, also a civilian resident of Pittsburgh.

"I can see you city boys have really led a sheltered life," I responded, "Didn't you ever go skinny-dipping in a creek or a tank when you were growing up? In west Texas, the largest and most physically endowed swimmers, like the herd bull, were the 'bank walkers' who walked up and down the bank before diving in," I replied, "to impress their friends!"

With full stomachs, after swimming and diving from the launch for an hour, everyone was stretched out dozing and soaking up the Philippine sun.

"We'd really be a sittin' duck if a Jap *Zeke* suddenly dipped over that mountain and opened up on us," murmured Warnick, half asleep but gazing up the side of the closest mountain.

"Yeah! Sittin' here like this," responded Cronin, "we wouldn't have a cut-dog's chance!"

"What would you do, Lieutenant?" asked Zuber, joining the discussion.

"I think I'd hit the water since we're so close to land — and try to put the boat 'tween me and the strafer," I said, "and hope he was as poor a shot as we are!"

"We're not that bad," chimed in Kolodziejski. Everyone agreed!

"But if it's your time to cash in your chips," responded Warnick, "that's it!"

"When it's your time to die you're going to die," he added. "So don't worry about it!"

"I don't believe that," responded Vaughn, "you're talking like a Presbyterian now!"

"It's like my Uncle Harry about twenty years ago," continued Warnick, "He drove my Aunt Holly to Fort Worth to the big hospital to see the specialists who diagnosed something in her they said was terminal and that had to be removed right then. She had to have the operation immediately, or she was a goner! Well, Uncle Harry drove her to Fort Worth, left her in the hospital, and driving home in the middle of the night he was killed when his car went off the highway between Midland and Odessa. My aunt checked out of the hospital and came home for my Uncle Harry's funeral."

"What happened to your Aunt?" queried Vaughn.

"Nothing," replied Warnick.

"Well she did go back and have her operation," continued Vaughn, "she did want to live didn't she?"

"Sure she wanted to live but it wasn't her time to die," replied Warnick, "she never went back to the hospital and she never had the operation that was going to save her life either. She'll be 90 years old her next birthday . . . if she makes it."

"If she makes it!" repeated Vaughn, "You mean whatever it was she had is finally about to get her?"

"Naw," responded Warnick again, "I had a letter from my mother last week and she said Aunt Holly fell off a stepladder trying to hang a picture early this month and she's laid up in the hospital with a broken leg!"

Little Cronin, our copilot, had been listening intently, with wrinkled brimmed golf hat pulled halfway down over his eyes. "What do you think, Cronin?" I inquired, "What's your opinion?"

"I'm just digesting right now," he responded, "but I'm not ready to *die jest* yet! But if I have to . . . what a wonderful way to go!" he replied, rubbing his stomach and trying to duck half a sandwich and the core of an apple aimed at him in response to his wit. It was a fitting and light-hearted benediction to a subject that was on everyone's mind.

When I got back to my tent at San Marcelino late that afternoon I sought the answers from the Book I had read every day of my life since I was twelve years old . . . the teachings of the same Book that had seen me through every trying and difficult experience of my young life, given me the courage and determination to survive the mental and physical pressures of Pre-flight and Flying School and which would see me through this present crisis . . . if only I would give it a chance. Why would I hesitate . . . even for a moment . . . to cast all my fears, doubts and anxieties on Him who was, is and always shall be ready to help and relieve me of any burden? First I read:

> "And do not fear those who kill the body but cannot kill the soul; rather fear him who can destroy both soul and body in hell."
> Matthew 10:28

and then:

> "For if we have been united with him in death like his, we shall certainly be united with Him in resurrection like His."
> Romans 6:5

"What then shall we say to this? If God is for us, who can be against us?"

Romans 8:31

These thoughts were not new for I had heard them taught and preached in Sunday School and church every Sunday of my life from elementary age. However, I had never been as zealous and dedicated in my search for the spiritual answers, never having considered them from a life and death concept, as at the present. Living constantly in the shadow of death, these words became more important than life itself. As the elderly black minister back home once said, "A water pump and effective prayer are a lot alike! Without water the pump don't have no suction and without trouble your prayers don't have no suction either!" The precarious and untenable situation I was in had definitely added suction to my already devoted and sincere prayers!

The clincher, the inspiration, the encouragement, the bottom line of truth, I was seeking to revitalize and strengthen my faith was Paul's Good Fight of Faith statement:

> "For I am already at the point of being sacrificed; the time of my departure has come. I have fought the good fight, I have finished the race, I have kept the faith. Henceforth there is laid up for me the crown of righteousness, which the Lord, the righteous judge, will award to me on that Day, and not only to me but also to all who have loved his appearing."
>
> 2 Timothy 4:6-8

For the first time since entering combat I was at ease, with genuine peace of mind. I could withstand any pressure, face any danger, fly any mission, undergo any test without the least equivocation, mental reservation or physical hesitation. Whatever happened to me from this time forward would be in His hands! I would, of course, never stop fighting with every mental, physical, mechanical and technical tool of war within my reach. *However,* I thought, *whether I die now, or as a gray-haired wonder at age 90, it will make no difference.* I had learned. My eyes had been opened. Death is no threat to those who aren't afraid to die! *The Lord's will be done.*

CHAPTER ONE

War Path of the Apaches

> *You are not going to get peace with millions of armed men. The chariot of peace cannot advance over a road littered with cannon.*
>
> Lloyd George

The 345th Bomb Group, *Air Apaches,* was composed of four squadrons: the 498th *Falcons,* the 499th *Bats Outa Hell,* the 500th *Rough Raiders,* and my squadron, the 501st *Black Panthers.* In any combat organization there are bound to be differences between the "old men" and the "new men" and the 501st was no exception. As we lost flying crews at an exceptionally high rate, two weeks seniority in the outfit was enough time to afford "old-timer" status and allow one to enjoy the privilege of offering advice to the newcomers. Being in the outfit for a couple of months gave one the chance to speak of the "good ole days." With our increasing losses, as we started hitting Japanese shipping in the open China sea, our crews were split up so that each aircraft would have some experienced combat personnel.

The first stop of the *Air Apaches* in their march through the Pacific, was at Port Moresby. A large cloth banner, stretched above the road, proclaimed: "Through these portals pass the best damn mosquito bait in the world." Following a double strike on Rabaul, the 345th received the following commendation from the Commander-in-Chief of the Southwest Pacific while at Moresby:

> "Please accept my heartiest congratulations for all forces involved in the superb double strike at Rabaul. It gives me a sense of great security to have such an indomitable unit in my command. Never give a sucker a break. Keep it up!"
>
> General Douglas MacArthur

The next stop for the *Air Apaches* was Dobadura, then Nadzab in the Markham Valley, then Biak, New Guinea, Dulag, and then Tacloban, Leyte, and the Philippines — arriving on D-day plus nine. While the pilots and air crew members fought the war daily, the "paddle feet" of the 345th didn't really experience the shooting war until we reached Tacloban, Leyte, and the Philippines.

The ground personnel of our four squadrons was transported in two Liberty ships (the S.S. *Thomas Nelson* and the S.S. *Morrison Waite*) to Leyte from New Guinea. The ground echelon and group headquarters personnel were crowded into the hold, jammed into and under deck-loaded vehicles, scattered under makeshift rigs of tarpaulins and some had even set up temporary housekeeping in the life rafts. Only a few of the fortunate and high-ranking squadron officers found quarters with the officers of the two ships.

The trip to Leyte was pleasant enough, with the anxiety caused by reports of the great naval engagements taking place in the Leyte Gulf and off the coast of Luzon, being alleviated with the good news that our Navy had wiped up the Japanese and sent them running back to Hirohito.

Never before had the *Air Apaches* followed so closely on the heels of the Navy and Infantry. We were intrigued by the thought of a civilized country and pleased to be so close to what might be called American soil. Overshadowing these thoughts, and more realistic, was the fact we were now putting our heads into the jaws of the Japanese lion. The lion had bases to the south of us on Mindanao, on numerous islands to the west of us, and powerful Luzon forces to the north. If the Japanese had fought so suicidally for the small bases of Pelelieu and Biak, how big an effort and battle would be mounted for the thousand islands comprising the Philippines? This would be war as we had never seen it. We would have few takers on our offer to let others crawl into our B-25s and take our places on the firing line from now on.

There were more than two hundred *Red Alerts,* warnings of enemy aircraft approaching the Leyte harbor, in the two weeks the S.S. *Nelson* and *Waite* sat waiting to be unloaded. At the first few alerts the men headed for the holds according to instructions, but as alert after alert passed with no evidence that the Jap planes were interested in attacking shipping in the harbor, our people became bolder. Only a few would retire below decks with their helmets and life preservers when the whistle sounded, and the rest would either roll over in their sacks and go back to sleep, or line the port rail to watch the *ack-ack,* tracers, and fireworks display over the airdromes ashore. All the alerts went by in this manner, and then — it happened.

On Sunday, November 12, 1944, with the harbor at Leyte filled to overflowing with the ships of our invasion forces, the hierarchy of the Japanese Imperial Air Force decided this an ideal moment to introduce their Japanese Special Attack Corps, otherwise known as suicide pilots or *Kamikaze.* For the first time in World War II, they launched a flight of forty to fifty *Kamikaze* aircraft, probably from Clark Field to the north in Luzon. Major "Bing Bang" Bong, legendary Marine pilot, and his mates, intercepted this air armada with their P-38s and dispatched thirty-six of these suicidal maniacs to their happy hunting grounds before they reached the harbor at Leyte. However, the four suicide pilots who succeeded in infiltrating our air defenses wreaked havoc and left the ignominious memory of the first *Kamikaze* attack in World War II stamped indelibly in the minds and memories of the 345th Bomb Group personnel forever.

The four *Zekes,* seemingly coming from nowhere, dove from the sky. The first Jap suicide pilot flew his *Zeke* into the S.S. *Leonidas Merritt* some eight hundred yards in front as two red streaks of tracers flashed parallel to the starboard rail of the S.S. *Nelson.* Two of the Jap suicide planes had come in low and unnoticed, and were making a strafing run on the S.S. *Nelson.* There had been no warning, and our men were caught unprepared. One of the planes peeled off and crashed into the stern of a nearby *LST*. The second plane continued parallel to the ship and suddenly banked sharply, striking the S.S. *Nelson* at the number five hatch where the majority of the enlisted men were quartered in makeshift tents. The ship shuddered from her deck plates to the keel, the violent explosion of the bomb welded to the underside of the plane knocking flat those men who were left standing. No sooner had the second plane hit, when a third screamed in at the stern, spraying the afterdeck with machine-gun and 20-mm fire. The afterdeck became a raging inferno and most of the men rushed back to assist the ship's crew in keeping the flames away from the gasoline and bombs stowed below.

Having been critically hit by two *Kamikaze* aircraft, fore and aft, during those first hectic moments, no one could be certain as to whether or not the *Nelson* would go up in one gigantic explosion. Those men who were not engaged in fighting the fire, carried the dead and wounded men to the forward part of the ship. Because the squadron medical supplies were completely destroyed by the fire and the ship's emergency equipment was rendered totally inadequate, the remaining uninjured men improvised bandages from any and everything at hand. They worked valiantly throughout the remaining air attacks until outside aid came an hour or so later.

At 1818 (6:18 P.M.) of the same day, the red alert sounded, announcing the approach of bandits, and two enemy planes were sighted coming in from the port side of the S.S. *Morrison Waite*. As the two planes came up even with the stern, one of them peeled off to make a pass at the *Waite*. The ship's guns, along with guns of every other ship in the harbor, opened fire and scored several hits, but they could neither blow the *Kamikaze* from the sky nor cause him to alter his course. As the Nip came abreast of the ship he made a deliberate suicidal dive into the side of the *Waite*. The force of the impact was so great that the Jap aircraft was carried through the hull into the bowels of the ship.

When the alert had sounded, all personnel were ordered into the hold. The men didn't care for the idea as there were only two wooden staircases for exits. They were aware of what might happen if the ship was hit. Their presence on deck, however, would have offered an attractive target but they would have preferred to have taken their chances, and at least been able to have jumped overboard. (Hindsight is always 20-20.) Nevertheless, they were ordered into the hold and there they remained.

There were one hundred-twenty men below decks at the time of the attack. The enemy plane, plunging into the hold, immediately burst into flames as its bomb exploded. The concussion blew the hatch covers from the main deck causing them and shattered parts of the aircraft to fall into the lower hold. The trucks and vehicles that were stored on the top deck were bounced around but amazingly enough, didn't fall into the hold.

The *Kamikaze* attacks on the S.S. *Nelson* and *Waite* in the harbor of Tacloban, Leyte, caused the greatest loss of personnel from any single event in the overseas history of the *Air Apaches*. With tragic accuracy these suicidal maniacs killed a total of ninety-two men and wounded one hundred fifty-six. Of those wounded, fifteen died either en route to, or in, hospitals. During a catastrophe of this magnitude, some men are giants. We had many who could qualify, and though wounded themselves, administered first aid or helped clear wreckage or lower stretchers into the holds or over the sides of the ships without considering themselves heroes. In their words, "We were only taking care of our buddies who would do the same for us!"

This being our furthest thrust from Port Moresby and Guadalcanal toward the Japanese mainland, ninety-five percent of all the American aircraft in the Pacific, heavy, medium, and light bombers, as well as fighters, were based, and operated for several months, off the "metal strips" laid down on the beach to form our runway at Tacloban. Had the Japanese only known, twenty to thirty Jap *Betty* bombers could have delivered a load of para-fragmentation bombs to efficiently destroy a major portion of the U.S. aircraft in the Pacific. As it was, they kept us pretty busy.

One night in early November, 1944, a Jap *Tess*-type transport, which closely resembled our C-47, entered the downwind leg and landed at Tacloban airstrip. An infantry guard opened the door of the plane and was shot between the eyes. Jap soldiers poured out of the ship and rushed toward one of the infantry camps, intent upon wiping it out. There was much excitement until these sons of Nippon were eradicated, but the damage to nerves was done. Later in the week a load of Jap paratroopers landed and surrounded Fifth Bomber Command Headquarters. Machine guns immediately appeared in every window to defend Fifth Bomber Headquarters. Some of us would've enjoyed seeing all that brass, (who usually flew desks and sent us out to hit targets of their choice) defend themselves as we did daily, on the firing line. The infantry dispatched the Jap paratroopers in quick order, however, and we never got to see the Fifth Bomber Headquarter personnel fire a barrel. Someone observed later, that it was "just as well, —they might've shot themselves!"

A week or so later, before the engineers had the "metal" landing strip at Tacloban completed, one of our carriers in the Leyte Gulf was sunk, leaving all its aircraft airborne with nowhere to land. They circled our strip for an hour or so, like a bunch of chicks looking for a mother hen, and as their gas ran out they crash-landed on the strip or on the beach. As they slid to a stop following a wheels-up landing for ultimate safety, the bulldozers of the Seabees and Army Engineers pushed them off into the sea to make room for the next stranded, shipless airplane to belly land. Over two hundred various and assorted aircraft crash-landed on the strip or beach that day, at least $500 million dollars worth of armed services hardware and American taxes. That was a lot of war bonds! The next day a C-46, which had just taken off, was hit by a low flying L-5 and the twenty-two passengers aboard the transport were killed in the ensuing fire. That night, a string of *frags* from a Jap bomber completely demolished a row of aircraft. We were strafed and bombed so often by the little yellow brothers (and always right at chow time en route to the mess tent), that we started wearing our dirtiest clothing. When we hit the foxholes — that never held less than two feet of water — we no longer dirtied clean uniforms.

I flew my first combat mission from Tacloban airstrip as the copilot for First Lieutenant Charles Thatcher, one of the "old-timers" of the squadron. I was as new, anxious and eager as he was cool, calm and collected. The front of Thatcher's uniform proved to be a topic of conversation that broke the ice and put two strangers at ease.

"What's all that glue-looking paste on the front of your shirt and pants?" I asked.

"That's not glue," responded Thatcher, continuing to enter the names of the crew on Form I, "that's oatmeal!"

"I'll admit it tastes better on the outside than on the inside," I answered, "but on the front of your shirt?"

"It wasn't by choice," said Thatcher, "I was eating my oatmeal, half asleep and minding my own damn business, when 'Washing Machine Charley,' the little yellow sonofabitch, strafed the mess tent, causing me to spill all my oatmeal down my front. I had to crawl in it on my belly under the table!"

"Yeah! I ate with the second group and they said they'd had a little excitement earlier," I replied, "but they said nobody got hurt!"

"Just scared everybody shitless, including the cooks! I don't know what it'll do for the food but it's got to make it better!" said Thatcher.

"How's that?"

"It can't get any worse!"

With the entire Fifth Air Force, and practically all the U.S. Air Corps in the South Pacific based on the beach at Leyte, it was a real problem getting clearance to land and take off. The eight airplanes in my first combat mission were stacked up, wings interlocking, taking up as little space as possible but still keeping the wheels on the metal decking atop the sandy beach. All of us making this strike were waiting for takeoff clearance. After a fifteen-minute wait, the tower instructed us to cut our engines. The cause for the delay was suddenly and graphically seen in the form of a huge cloud of black smoke at the far end of the runway.

The pilot of a C-47 transport, loaded with forty Army personnel, in his haste to get airborne, had forgotten to remove the chock to the vertical stabilizer which froze the rudder. Designed to prevent wind damage on the ground, the chock was routinely inserted to protect the rudder while the airplane was parked and neither the pilot nor ground crew, in their haste to get airborne, had remembered to remove it before takeoff. The pilot had violated a cardinal rule of flying: never get in your airplane for takeoff without walking around and minutely inspecting it for airworthiness from stem to stern! The C-47 had taken off, climbed to about one hundred-fifty feet and spun-in, killing all aboard and tying up all air traffic for over an hour until the wreckage could be removed from the end of the strip.

I had learned the lesson: *check your aircraft before takeoff,* from an extraordinary primary flying instructor at Oxnard, California. Even after graduating to combat flying, with eight or ten men of an engineering crew constantly servicing and checking the airplane, as well as armorers, radio and other personnel performing their daily maintenance tasks, I continued the practice of walking around the airplane to check it out before takeoff. Countless aircraft accidents were undoubtedly prevented by the excellent lessons and habits taught by this kind, considerate, and compassionate civilian primary flying instructor by the name of A.G. "Middlesnap" Middleton. One year earlier, on February 15, 1944, I was being taught to fly by this gentleman. Now a short twelve months later, I was being challenged to perform the most dangerous and difficult operational missions, demanding the ultimate in flying skill, and more expertise than any combat flying in the entire Army Air Corps. And I didn't lack confidence in my task!

With all this humidity and heat of the Philippines, I thought, as the smoke from the crashed C-47 continued to obliterate the far end of the runway, *a good west Texas sandstorm might be a welcome relief!* Once again my thoughts retreated in time to earlier, more pleasant experiences with sand storms in west Texas.

"Bite him spider!" I said half aloud. James Walker, my high school friend, addressed the ball and started his backswing on the ninth tee at the windswept country club at Big Spring on a blustery spring morning in the middle of a sand storm.

"Blount!" exclaimed Walker, losing his poise, concentration, and religion as he dropped to his knees and struck the turf with his driver. "That was a 265-yard drive right down the middle that would have sewed up this match and you ruined it all! That's not fair!"

Caddies at the country club were given the opportunity to play free on Saturday mornings and Charlie Harrell and I were taking advantage of our weekly opportunity accompanied by our friend James Walker whom we had "sneaked" on to play with us. Our match was even with one hole to play!

"Now James," I remonstrated, "when you get on the Pro tour you'll have to learn how to handle flashbulbs, babies crying, women talking, dogs barking, people running in front of you and every conceivable distraction known to man! I'm just getting you ready for your chosen profession!" Now, embroiled in a war, golf and these old friends had been fartherest from my mind until two months later in northern Luzon.

When we finally took off and were in the air, we flew approximately 200 miles into northern Luzon.

The mission was ground support for our infantry, bogged down before General Yamashita's Imperial ground forces in the mountains near Baggio, the northern capitol of Luzon. The mountainous, pine-covered terrain looked amazingly like North Carolina or East Texas. The enemy ground forces were dug in near a beautiful, scenic golf course among the tall pines with rolling greens, challenging water hazards, and glowing white sand bunkers.

"Let's land on that long Par five fairway," said Kenney, our navigator, leaning over my right shoulder and yelling into my ear so that he could be heard above the roar of the engines, "and we'll play eighteen!"

"How many strokes will you spot me?" I yelled back, never taking my eyes off Captain Musket's lead ship and jockeying for position to make the first strafing, bombing run over the enemy gun emplacements.

"We better pass today," responded Kenney as a string of Jap machine gun tracers suddenly emerged from the dense undergrowth off to the left and disappeared over the top of the plexiglass cockpit as suddenly as they had appeared.

"Those little cross-eyed bastards shoot as crooked as I hit a golf ball," volunteered Copilot Cronin.

"Or as crooked, hopefully, as you shoot that .45 automatic you're wearing!" I commented, alluding to Cronin's target practice near our squadron area at Tacloban, Leyte. He had thought he was shooting into an abandoned swamp only inhabited by water buffalo, but had scared an Infantry billet out of their soggy boots.

"Those sure aren't golf balls they're throwing at us! We better postpone the golf game until our boys have secured this area and we'll get up here on R and R," I added.

Golf! James Walker and Charlie Harrell! My high school

golf buddies I hadn't thought of since I got into this extended nightmare and now the sight of the beautiful golf course below me opened the door to pleasant . . . even cherished . . . memories of the past. "You don't miss the water till the well runs dry." I didn't realize until that moment how much I missed those friends and the events we experienced together for one spring two years before . . . A time that could never be re-created, but a time that suddenly grasped me and took me away from the smell of gunsmoke, the flash and concussion of exploding bombs and the rattling, frantic chatter on the ground-to-air radio . . . "Hello Kit Bag Leader! Oh you really laid that one in there!" "Hello River Horse! We're picking up machine gun fire near the bend of the river coming out of our gunnery runs!" "I see 'em Captain!" recognizing Kuta's voice, pilot of the trailing ship, "I'll take care of 'em!"

James Walker, Charles Harrell and I had talked Mr. J.A. Coffey, the high school principal, into allowing us to form a golf team. Mr. Gene Gardner, a math professor and golf enthusiast, had told us he would be our "watching" coach and chaperone if the school gave us the green light. We were finally permitted to form a golf team, the first and only golf team to that time, to ever represent Big Spring High School. We were to furnish our own equipment, arrange our own transportation and the school would pay for one meal . . . on out of town trips . . . and help with the gas for Mr. Gardner's car. We were ecstatic!

Charlie Harrell and I had caddied together for years at the Big Spring Country Club and Municipal Golf Courses and Charlie stayed at it. A modest, self-effacing, but responsible young man, Mr. Shirley Robbins, the golf pro at the country club, allowed Charlie to buy a matched set of Denny Shute irons and woods through the Pro Shop. Charlie was shy, slender, very quiet and retiring, always wore a golf cap in which he stuffed his long hair, had a runny nose most of the time and a pleasant and winsome smile that only left his face when he was studying a golf shot.

James Walker was puffy looking, almost fat, with dark reddish hair that made him look like a caricature of a young Arthur Godfrey. As the delivery boy for the local Postal Telegraph office, where his father was the manager, he looked like a Bill Mauldin cartoon character in his blue Postal Telegraph messenger uniform that was too small. With black leather leggins, a cap that sat on top of his head with hair sticking out on all sides and a shirttail that made no pretense of staying in his pants and flapped in the wind, he laboriously peddled his bicycle delivering messages all over town. Through his employment he faithfully saved his money and was able to buy a beautiful set of Craig Wood signature golf clubs that he cleaned and polished after every round.

The football coaches drooled after James, as they did after every young man of more than average size, and wanted him in a football uniform so badly they could taste it. He endured the insults and snide remarks of the coaches, a price he had to pay because he was a "big" boy who chose not to play.

He made only average grades and had the reputation, among his teachers, of being lazy and slovenly. He was not involved in athletics, the band or any other school activity, and I felt he was getting a bum rap from both coaches and teachers, which made me appreciate him all the more. He was simply and essentially a fine person and a good friend who didn't like to hit people and who didn't want people hitting him . . . a person not motivated to make the honor roll, who minded his own business and who didn't join every club or toot his own horn! He was a loyal friend and the kind of humble person the world needs more of. He marched to a different drummer, an able, capable young man who hadn't been challenged, or motivated, to achieve a mutually acceptable goal that met the approval and won the favor of his teachers and peers. "Every dog has his day" and James would have his.

He had an innocent, childlike, "believe anything you told him," gullibility that endeared him even more to his friends. My Dad, who never played a round of gold in his life, told James one afternoon, "I taught Craig Wood just about all he knows about golf." Craig Wood, a professional golfer of the time, was Sir Lancelot, Superman and the Lone Ranger all rolled into one as far as James was concerned.

"You really know Craig Wood, Mr. Blount? And gave him golf lessons?" James responded with awe and now a reverence for my Dad.

"It was when he was just starting out . . . as a teenager," my Dad, a real practical joker, continued when he saw that James had taken the bait: hook, line and sinker. When we finally told James the truth he was good naturedly embarrassed and enjoyed the mirth of the occasion as much as we did.

James, Charlie and I fantasized a lot about our golf. On the golf course, James was "Craig" (Wood), Charlie was "Denny" (Shute) and I was "Byron" (Nelson). We always called each other by the names of our golfing heroes and became close friends while sharing a common interest. My set of golf clubs consisted of five "Player Medalist," hammer-forged irons made by Sears Roebuck and Company for which I had traded with a friend. When we played a match, I borrowed a couple of woods and irons to fill out my set. And when I bought a Bobby Thompson signature number two wood from Montgomery Wards for $6.95, I didn't change my golfing alias, or allegiance, but remained true to Lord Byron.

Very occasionally (you might say almost never) a big name professional golfer would come to our city and play an exhibition round. During the spring of our golfing fantasy, as if by divine destiny, it was announced in the Big Spring *Daily Herald* that Denny Shute would play an exhibition at the Big Spring Country Club. The exhibition round was to be played on a Tuesday afternoon during school hours and we were concerned about getting out of school.

"I'll play hooky, even if I have to stay after school for the rest of the semester," vowed James, "if that's the only way I can get to see Denny Shute!"

"I'm going to caddy for him — free if necessary," said Charlie "Denny" Harrell, "and they can expel me . . . or whip me . . . or kill me . . . or do whatever they want to with me! But I'm not going to miss Denny Shute!"

James and Charlie got excuses and I prevailed upon my mother to write me one to see Denny Shute and, after hours of rhetoric and discussion, she relented and finally agreed. Alma wrote: "Mr. Coffey: Would you please excuse my foolish son this afternoon to see Mr. Shute play a round of golf. Mr. Shute is reportedly a world champion golf player and if Peppy isn't allowed to see him play he would be even less of an interested student than he already is if he had to remain in the classroom. Thank you. Mrs. R.E. Blount." I got to go.

Mr. Denny Shute, in knickers, tie, sweater and golfing cap, was every bit the exciting player we knew he would be, epitomizing all that the Big Spring High School Golf team knew the grand old game of golf to be. It was an exciting afternoon and provided material for conversation for weeks to come. Charlie "Denny" Harrell even changed his swing, his mannerisms and the way he walked while on the golf course after Mr. Shute's exhibition.

The following week we played Colorado City High School on their golf course, a little nine hole layout with different tee boxes to make it an 18 hole course. Leaving Big Spring after lunch we didn't tee off until the middle of the afternoon and we were tied, two matches each, with James and his opponent "even up" coming into the sixteenth hole with the sun going down. James won the sixteenth, his opponent won the seventeenth, and their match was even as they teed off on 18 in the dark. It was now so dark that we couldn't see the balls and Coach Gardner and the Colorado City coach commandeered three cars and placed them around the 18th green with their lights turned on.

James had a good drive to the right side of the fairway and his opponent drove equally as well down the middle. His opponent was away and hit first on the second shot, his ball ending up hole high but off the green to the left. James hit his second shot and it disappeared, lost in the darkness for an interminable length of time. Suddenly it emerged, as if dropped by an unseen hand from out of the darkness, into the middle of the green about fifteen feet from the pin with the accompanying whooping and hollering of his teammates. The Colorado City player chipped to within five feet of the pin and the pressure was on James to sink his putt if he was to win his round and the match.

As he lined up his putt it was evident there was a break to the right and Charlie eased forward from the crowd at the edge of the green and whispered something in his ear. James stood up, walked up to and addressed the ball, looked at the hole, back to the ball, looked back at the hole then back to the ball and stroked it with the deft skill of a Craig Wood. The ball jumped, accelerated, bounced once and then rolled in a wide arc toward the hole. Three feet from the hole the ball began to slow and it was apparent James hadn't hit it hard enough as a couple of groans of disappointment were heard, and everyone started to lean in a conscious effort to help the ball. An inch from the hole the ball seemed to stop and, rolling another half revolution, hung on the lip of the cup for a half second before dropping out of sight! We had won on James's pressure putt, after the lights and the time ran out! There was mini-bedlam around the 18th green at Colorado City as our golf team celebrated their victory.

On the way home, the shortest forty miles our golf team traveled that year, I asked Charlie, "What did you tell James before that putt?" Charlie, shyly, now back in character, had no reply. We then asked James what Charlie told him about the winning putt.

"He didn't tell me nothin' about the putt," said James. "The only thing he said was that Craig Wood had made a putt from the same spot on the 18th green at Atlanta to win the Master's by one stroke last year. If Craig could do it I could too!" The fact was, Charlie didn't know whether Craig Wood had ever won the Master's last year or *any* year!

"Is that all?" I queried.

"Well, no not exactly!"

"Well — what else did he say?" I asked.

"He said Coach Gardner said if I missed that putt I wasn't going to get any supper and I'd have to walk home."

I didn't care how, or why, he made that putt, only that he made it. This was his greatest single accomplishment and I was proud of my friend. And he had done something that every teacher and student of Big Spring High School could point to with pride. And he needed that. In fact, the golf team was the only high school endeavor that James and Charlie ever participated in and they showed the world — and all of Big Spring — that they were winners!

James graduated at the end of that semester and I didn't see him again until a year later. He came to school one day in the uniform of an Army Air Corps Cadet.

"Craig baby!", I greeted him with enthusiasm, "Where have you been and what have you been doing? — as if the uniform didn't tell it all!" Surrounded by faculty and students alike, he suddenly was enjoying all of the attention from those who had ignored him before. Former teachers now eyed him with skepticism as their manner and "you gotta show me" attitude could not be hidden. Their eyes said "I can't believe it," while their mouths said "we always knew you would do well!"

But their eyes spoke so loudly that you couldn't hear what they were saying.

"What does it feel like flying an airplane?" I asked when I finally was able to get him one on one for a few minutes.

"It's the greatest feeling in the world, Byron," he replied. "You just wait — you're going to find out," he continued, knowing how anxious, excited and determined I was to do the same thing he was doing. "You're going to make a great pilot!" James had more confidence in my future, at that time, than I did. I was well aware of the vast number of my friends who had already "washed out" of the cadet program and here was James Walker, everybody's ugly duckling, who had achieved success on a scale that had his high school nemeses agog!

The next time he came back home it was as a pilot and second lieutenant in the U. S. Army Air Corps. That was in the spring of 1943, when the Air Corps was rapidly filling its quota and building a backlog of pilots, and they were cutting back on pilot training. *Don't worry,* he wrote in a letter I received while in pre-flight at Santa Ana, California, *they'll always need pilots as good as you're going to be. Just hang in there.* I blinked and pinched myself! Was this the slow, unkempt, underachiever friend that the faculty and students felt couldn't find his way out of the high school building much less graduate from pilot school, become a commissioned Air Force officer and be assigned the responsibility of First Pilot of a three-quarter of a million dollars B-24 aircraft and the lives of 10 crewmen! And now he was giving me encouragement, telling me I could do what he had done and just don't give up! *How people are misjudged* I thought, *in the everyday scheme of things and how the cream really rises to the top when the chips are down and the battle must be won!*

The sudden sound of ripping metal was like an axe cutting through a tin roof. "We're hit in the bomb bay," came a shouted report from Zuber, who was manning the waist guns, "but it's just a hole!"

"I saw where it came from," he continued on the intercom.

"I did too," interrupted Warnick from the top turret, "and we'll burn their ass on the next pass. They're out there in the heavy rough, about halfway down that long Par five y'all were talking about a minute ago!"

"Okay, troops," I responded, "hold on tight, and don't fall through that hole back there, Zuber. We'll read 'em the riot act on this last pass!"

Kuta hadn't gotten the last machine gun emplacement and this was the thorn in our side as we came off the main target area marked by smoke bombs from the infantry who had called us in for this strike. I dropped our last 1000-pound bomb, with a ten-second delay fuse, and made a tight turn to the left instead of climbing straight out as before. The tracers, which had been coming at us out of the heavy vegetation to our left, were now coming at us head-on. I lowered the nose and answered the challenge with all twelve of the forward firing 50-caliber machine guns in the nose of our B-25. Warnick joined me with his twin .50s out of the top turret.

This was my last pass, and right then, I learned a lesson. Intent on silencing the Japanese gunners I had held the nose of *199* with her twelve lethal .50s down too long. The Nips,"dug in" a valley covered with heavy jungle undergrowth, and guarded with seventy-foot trees on top of the ridge, made our exit rather steep and treacherous. I made the fatal error of all overly zealous, novice strafers: keeping the nose of the aircraft down too long, and not allowing enough time and distance to clear any obstructions coming out of the strafing dive.

"Hold on!" I yelled, as I saw that we were not going to clear the trees. A jolt shook the airplane, (and my eye teeth) accompanied by a loud scraping and threshing sound as the airplane plowed through the tops of the trees. We severed tree limbs and leaves and cut a thirty-foot swath with our propellers.

"Can I get you to trim my trees after the war?" asked Kenney.

"I'll be glad to," I replied, "but don't expect as efficient a job as this one. I don't know if Uncle Sam will allow me the use of this tree trimmer when we get home!" We had a fine harvest of wood pulp and leaves that were matted between the cylinder baffles which Sergeant Albright removed when we returned to base. The important factor was that the windmills didn't stop turning. The B-25 was a remarkable airplane!

"That did the trick. Lieutenant," came the report from Kolodziejski in the tail gunner's turret, "nothing but smoke, fire and silence coming out of that place now!"

"That's good," I answered, "we want to keep 'em quiet and peaceful!"

"Hello, Kit Bag Leader! This is River Horse! Thank you for the help and assistance! We should be spending the night at the Baggio Country Club tonight. Over!"

"Hello River Horse, this is Kit Bag Leader," came back Captain Musket, "Send us an invitation to your first dinner dance! We're going home. Good hunting! Over and out."

We got the formation together and made the short hop back to San Marcelino and our airstrip without further incident. With no emergencies and all eight ships intact we had the squadron on the ground in ten minutes using the "fighter peel off" landing procedure.

After debriefing the jeep dropped us off at the Operations Tent and Lieutenant Ike Baker handed me three letters. "You mean we had a mail call while we were gone today?" I exclaimed.

"Neither rain, sleet, snow, fire . . . or the war . . . shall keep the U. S. Mail from being delivered," answered Lieutenant Baker, a good Oklahoman.

"Only a slight delay every now and then, Ike," I responded, "especially since this is the first we've had in a week! I'll fly another mission right now if you'll promise to have more mail waiting for me when I get back."

I tore into the letter from Mother first.

> Hi Darlin:
>
> Your Daddy says he bets you've moved again 'cause we haven't had a letter from you now in over two weeks. Everything is fine here at home and everyone asks about you and tells me to be sure to remember them to you when I write. Saw Moma Nall after church today and told her about all the rain and wet weather you had been in. Of course, she said to be sure to remind you to stay dry and if you got your feet wet to change socks immediately that this would keep you from catching cold.
>
> I have some real sad news to tell you. James Walker was reported killed in action and his airplane and all his crew lost somewhere over Europe. He was flying his 5th mission in B-24s and his plane got a direct hit and exploded. Your Daddy reminded me about your playing golf

> together and James winning the tournament for your team at Colorado City after dark and by the car lights. I'm going to see James' parents tomorrow. Do be careful, take care of yourself . . . and . . .

What a waste! But isn't that all that war amounts to? The waste of young manhood? The only good accomplished by James's Air Force experience was to provide him a sounding board whereby he showed his peers he was the very best, the epitome of success for a young man of his time, in a language they understood! He showed the coaches (who stayed stateside and taught physical fitness) he had more guts; the faculty (most of whom continued to teach school) that he had more intelligence than they could inspire and motivate him to produce; and his fellow students (most of whom would have had to salute and call him "Sir") that he had more poise and ability than they could ever display. And to us, his golf team buddies, he showed us that he could "cut it" — from sinking a fifteen-foot pressure putt to win the match, or fly a B-24 *Liberator* bomber as its commander in combat over Europe — if only given the chance! Yes, the cream always rises to the top and James Walker proved to be the "cream" of all his contemporaries . . . for whom he died!

And then we had a change of scene . . . . The move from Tacloban, Leyte, to San Marcelino, Luzon, (about 750 miles as the crow flies) took several days and involved a lot of back and forth trips. Luckily, a good bomb group is versatile. We could bomb like a B-17, strafe like a P-51, skip-bomb like an A-20, drop supplies like a C-47 and carry stoves, refrigerators (or the kitchen sink) like a C-46. Our B-25s temporarily became cargo craft instead of warbirds. We moved every conceivable item from squadron records and typewriters to canvas tents and toilet paper — all indispensable in waging war.

February 15, 1945, 5:15 A.M. found *199* loaded to 40,000 pounds of supplies — a 2,000 pound overload. Taxiing to the very end of the metal matting runway I turned so the tail was hanging over the sand with the wheels barely on the hard metal.

"You afraid you're not going to use all the runway?" yelled the navigator.

"If this big tin bird doesn't make it off the far end, I don't want it to be said that old Blount, bless his soul, just didn't use all the runway that those nice Seabees and Engineers laid down for him!"

As *199* picked up speed, a ring of fire developed in the full arcs of both propellers and danced up and down each wing in the perfect atmospheric conditions that produces the spectacular phenomena of St. Elmo's fire.

"Warnick in the top turret says we're on fire," smiled Cronin, relaying his monitoring on the intercom.

"Tell him I said to grab a fire extinguisher and jump out there and put it out, like any good, efficient engineer should do. Wheels up!"

Approaching Manila we were treated to a rare sight: the pre-invasion assault of Corregidor! There we were, flying at 5,000 feet on a clear day with a grandstand seat on the 50-yard line. Heavy naval artillery, cruisers to battleships, ably assisted by their army counterparts, were pounding Corregidor into submission. When a broadside of naval artillery struck the heavy greenery and jungle growth that concealed the openings leading into the network of tunnels that honeycombed the fortress, the little island seemed to jerk, pull back and tremble. The artillery would pause, as if reloading while the dust cleared, and waves of dive bombers delivered destruction with pinpoint accuracy.

"What if they get their signals mixed up and the dive bombers make their attack while those big guns are laying down one of those broadsides?" mused Cronin.

"I believe it would be bye bye dive bombers," answered Kenney. "Those battle wagons shoot a shell big as a thousand-pound bomb, and when it explodes you don't want to be much closer than we are up here."

"Turn on the IFF," I said to Cronin. "I don't want the U.S. Navy to think *we're* the enemy, and turn all their attention on us!" IFF was the "Identification Friend or Foe" with which all our combat aircraft was equipped, that sent out a steady, high frequency radio signal picked up by *ack-ack* crews on land or sea and identified us as friendly.

Occasionally, on the return from a mission, we forgot to turn on the IFF as we approached the Philippines; the *ack-ack* crews had fired a couple of warning rounds off our nose and tail which readily woke us up and erased any lethargy. Immediately preceding the invasion of Bataan and within sight of Corregidor a few days earlier, we had strafed and bombed from the shore to several hundred yards inland in the jungle to soften up the target preparatory to the landing of our troups. While we hadn't seen anything but impenetrable jungle, our saturation bombing and strafing had eliminated 4,400 of the enemy. The commander of the invading American forces expressed his appreciation to the *Air Apaches* for the thorough and efficient manner in which we had "neutralized the enemy defenders of Bataan, destroying thousands of the enemy, including hundreds of snipers who were found dead, and still tied to, or resting in, or falling from, jungle and palm trees where they had hidden to ambush our invading troops."

"Bataan looks a lot calmer than it did last week," said the copilot.

"Yeah," I answered. "It's amazing how you can clean up a neighborhood."

In combat an individual ceases being *I*, and, with the others with whom he daily faces death, unconsciously becomes *We*. And *we* were there to avenge the 72,000 men who had been taken captive on this ignominious piece of real estate called Bataan three years earlier. The greatest number of Americans in history to capitulate to an enemy. We were also there to help the oppressed natives free themselves from a fanatic horde of oriental soldiers who threw babies into the air and caught them on their bayonets while their mothers watched, who doused stragglers on the "Death March" with kerosene and burned them alive, who had beheaded our friends and fellow airmen when captured, and who fought the war by barbarian rules — rather than the rules of the Geneva Convention.

This was the enemy to whom General Wainwright surrendered Corregidor to save, he thought, all his wounded men from death. When the opportunity to avenge our brothers and the atrocities they suffered presented itself, we never hesitated to pay them back in the only way the enemy would understand. The combatant understands the overwhelming importance of such moments of life and death, in any generation. More importantly, it is imperative that present and future generations remember, hold onto, and even cherish, a part of what the American fighting man has been. All too often, in the assumed and "taken for granted" freedom in which each successive American generation lives, the present seeks to obliterate the past — and that must never be allowed to happen! Knowing and remembering the price that past generations paid to save our nation, future generations can understand what they must do, if necessary, to preserve it.

The time we spent negotiating the move from Tacloban to San Marcelino took the best part of two weeks, and kept flyable airplanes in the air constantly. This resulted in situations that found us all occasionally without aircraft, and compelled to hitch a ride with this or that pilot on any airplane going in the right direction.

"How about riding up to San Marcelino with you?" I asked Lieutenant Virgil Gross, slow-talking old-timer (a couple of months in the squadron) from Aberdeen, Mississippi.

"Jump in, Tex, and make yourself at home. Mighty glad to have ya, and serve the gentleman a mint julep, Shep," he said in jest to the engineer gunner. "Give him the best cigar in the house!"

"Shep," I said, "how is the mint julep?"

"A regular Louisville Slugger, Sir!"

So it was that I crawled into Gross's airplane for my first and only ride in the back of a B-25, in the radio compartment behind the bomb bay. *If only I had known . . .* Light rain was falling, dark clouds were all around us at takeoff, and the billowy mass looked like monstrous balloons filled with water that the propellers might burst if we flew into them. The airplane seemed to hit a solid obstruction; I felt I was in a submarine. Inside I started to panic. Sitting in the back of a B-25 was nothing like I had ever experienced before. I thought we were stalling and falling at the same time, and I had no flight instruments, no flight controls, nor any control of the aircraft to tell me otherwise! I was like a caged animal in a tin can, totally dependent on Gross sitting in the first pilot's seat. *I will hereafter have more respect for my crew, and appreciate their confidence in my flying ability . . . if there is, indeed, a hereafter . . .* I thought.

It became clear, in my mind if not the "ocean" we were flying through, that Gross could not coax, finesse, or otherwise persuade that overloaded lady to fly over the mountains or through the pass, freeing us of the Leyte monsoon.

"We're going back, Lieutenant," spoke the radio man in my ear, "Lieutenant Gross says he can't gain altitude and he doesn't want a game of hide 'n seek with those mountains."

"I concur! I agree whole heartedly," I replied, trying to remain calm and not show my anxiety, "and you can tell your skipper that this back seat pilot thinks a 180-degree turn would be the better part of valor and the most skilled maneuver he could make at this point in time."

We had been out of Tacloban less than thirty minutes and it was now closed to all aircraft as the tropical deluge seemed to have moved in on the beach and the metal landing strip it supported, making it an extention of the bay.

"Lieutenant Gross says we've been directed to Tanawan strip," reported the radio man. Tanawan strip was located fifteen or twenty miles south of Tacloban and was used principally as an overflow- or safety-valve for all aircraft when Tacloban became saturated with aircraft or was weathered in. Tanawan strip ran generally northeast and southwest and you could land and takeoff in only one direction and that was over water. The reason? At the southwest end of the strip was a mountain, a dead end, which required landing toward the mass of jungle that gave the appearance of an 800- or 900-foot-high green brick wall. This provided an incentive to every pilot to put his airplane on the ground in the first 100 feet of the northeast end of the runway and just out of the surf. Taking off, you put the tail of your aircraft in the jungle undergrowth of the mountain at the south end of Tanawan strip and hoped she was ready to fly when you got to the sea. Many aircraft, overloaded and otherwise, tried to become surfboards on takeoff from Tanawan.

"This looks like a flying circus," I remarked, as every conceivable type of aircraft (both Army and Navy) seemingly had been caught airborne when the weather had closed Tacloban and left Tanawan as the only port in the storm.

After twenty or thirty minutes of circling, which seemed more like two or three hours, Gross finally maneuvered our plane into the landing pattern. He was jockeying and attempting to space us in position to land behind a big lumbering C-46 cargo plan that seemed to be floating like a big kite rather than flying.

The rain was now falling in sheets, whipped by high wind

gusts, and we needed to get on the ground, not only for our own safety but to provide landing opportunities to all the other aircraft that filled the sky above this remote airstrip.

You're overloaded . . . keep your airspeed and land 'er hot! went through my mind. As we turned on to the final approach I could see the C-46 about a fourth of the way down the runway when it disappeared from view under our left wing. I stood up, peering over the bomb bay hoping to get a glimpse of where we were going, but the top turret and the navigator standing behind the pilots at the back edge of the cockpit filled the void and obstructed my line of vision. Suddenly the futility of the situation, my dependence upon someone else, came home — hitting me squarely between the eyes like a poleaxed bull at the meat-packing plant. *I didn't have to make this flight! I could just as easily have spent the night at Tacloban and flown my own plane out of there tomorrow when it returned from San Marcelino. What on earth was I thinking about!*

Gross had now eased back on the throttles. *We must be approaching — or we're just over — the end of the runway. He's kept his flying speed* — I observed, as the plane hit the metal strips of the runway and stayed there, sounding like a football game being played on the tin roof of a big barn. But that was only momentary as I heard braking tires and felt the sickening slide of the airplane to the right out of control. I started saying my prayers. You don't ground loop a B-25 and live. The motion was more exaggerated to those of us in the back of the airplane — like the last child at the end of the human line playing Pop the Whip. I felt the 40,000-pound aircraft go off the runway out of control. I was thrown to the floor against the bulkhead of the back of the bomb bay, my legs entangled with those of the radio man's, as I felt the airplane dip to the right and come to an abrupt stop with the unmistakable sound of metal against metal as the right wheel was buried in the soft sand and mud off the runway!

"Get out of here!" I yelled, my first thought being of fire and explosion, if the wing tanks had been punctured. As I jumped from the airplane I could smell burned rubber from the huge wheels. Gross had burned the brakes out of the airplane, and the right engine and wing had come to rest on top of an army truck. Down on one knee a hundred yards away from the airplane, oblivious to the rain soaking me to the bone, I've never been more appreciative of terra firma in my life! Alive . . . and no injuries. The C-46 was just turning off the end of the runway at the base of the mountain. We learned later that the C-46 was loaded with evacuated wounded, and Gross, kicking the B-25 off the right side of the runway at the last instant in deference to running up the tail of the big cargo plane, had saved untold lives and averted a catastrophe!

To miss the litter ship on the runway in front of us meant not punishing those who had been punished enough. The hospital ships were equipped with portable bunks stacked four litters high that ran the length along both sides of the fuselage, with a few extra secured to the floor to guarantee overcrowding. They stank and reeked of the vilest odors that can be emitted and eliminated from the human body including the smell of rotting flesh and disinfectant all intermingled with blood. Litter ships were reserved for those who had the most serious and recent injuries, usually only a few hours out of combat. They were on their way home even before they had time to assess their personal disasters, and the grief and remorse associated with the loss of legs, arms, eyes, and the crippling of the very young. We could be thankful that we had missed the C-46 with its precious cargo.

"Want to apologize for that landing," said Gross, a while later.

"No apology necessary," I replied, "any landing you can walk away from, I've always heard, is a good one." I was lying in my teeth, but my only flight in the back of a B-25 had taught me one thing! I'd never fly in the back of another one!

Our move from Leyte to Luzon was brought about by the fall of Bataan and Corregidor in southern Luzon, and the coordinated, successful landing of our ground forces at Lingayen Gulf in northern Luzon. We had General Yamashita, supreme commander of the Japanese forces in the Philippines in a north-south pinchers that was ready to converge and snap its jaws shut!

At San Marcelino, our infantry had secured a 3,500-foot Jap fighter strip near the small village located thirteen miles north of Bataan and Subic Bay, and about thirty miles west and over the mountains from Clark Field. The Army Engineers had added 1,500 feet, to give us 5,000 feet in which to get our overloaded B-25s off the ground, and we were in business in the dirtiest, driest, dustiest, hottest base of operations yet encountered by the *Air Apaches*. Water was at a premium and we were rationed only a helmet full for all purposes per day.

"They say you can get used to anything," said Kuta.

"I don't know," said Kenney. "I'll take the odds of flying down those Jap 20-millimeter *pom-poms* rather than have no water."

"Now doing without a little water," I added, "isn't that bad. This is just like batchin' it back home."

"Where'd you live," inquired Kuta, "the Sahara desert?"

"Not quite," I replied, "out in West Texas about halfway between Fort Worth and El Paso in Big Spring: Marvel City of the Southwest!"

"That's the Sahara desert," responded Kuta, "might as well be! I know, I'll take a PTA bath."

"What's a PTA bath?" inquired Kenney, asking the loaded question that begged for an answer.

"Pussy, tits and armpits," explained Kuta, continuing to work at unfolding and laying out the stakes for the tent without cracking a smile. Everett Thies and Richard Lathrop doubled up in laughter as Kenney got busy with raising the tent.

The hilarity set the wrong mood for a tent raising. Kenney was holding the center pole under the canvas while Thies, Lathrop, Arthur McGrane, Bill Mulligan, Kuta and I were attempting to spread the tent by pulling on the outside edge and driving the stakes to secure it. The tent had already fallen three times when the tent raisers would suddenly and spontaneously become limber from laughter.

"What're you doing under there, Kenney?" queried Lathrop, "taking a PTA bath?" Everybody turned loose and the tent went down smothering Kenney for the fourth time.

Kenney came crawling and fighting from under the tent.

"Raise your own damn tent!" said Kenney and stalked off in the direction of the operations tent.

"That takes care of the stakes," mused Mulligan.

"Not so quick," shot back McGrane, "I haven't finished the salad!"

Kenney kept walking and everyone continued in a state of comic, mirthful limbo. If somebody had brought out a bottle the whole bunch would have become passed out drunk on the spot. As it was, we didn't get the tent raised for another two hours.

Of much graver concern was our military tactical situation of which we were not appraised until Captain Jones called a meeting late that evening in the operations tent for all pilots and flight personnel.

"Our infantry reports that there are 20,000 Japs over those mountains," said Captain Jones, pointing to the mountains half a mile east of us, "and our own ground forces are trying to drive them over here on top of us!"

If anyone had been asleep or dozing, they became sober-faced and wide awake.

"They captured some enemy maps that have our infantry platted in between us and the Japs," continued Jones, "but the fact is, that there are no American ground forces between us and the enemy!"

"For that reason," he continued, "we must set up emergency flight procedures to evacuate all aircraft if we are attacked."

"In this regard all flight crews, immediately upon notice that we're under attack from enemy ground forces, will proceed to the airstrip by whatever transportation is available and take off immediately for Tacloban, Leyte, which is the nearest friendly airstrip available at this time. Should your flight crews get separated and not make it to your airplane, the first pilot or aircraft commander is instructed to take off day or night without such lost or unaccounted for crew members! Do you understand?"

These were sobering thoughts and the listeners were overwhelmed with what they were hearing.

"What do the rest of us do?" inquired Captain Lucky Holtzman, executive officer of the "paddle feet" and in charge of the Orderly Room.

"You fight a holding action," replied Captain Jones, "just like the infantry and buy enough time for our pilots and crews to evacuate the aircraft!"

"From this day forward we'll post our own sentries," said Captain Jones, "and set up and maintain our own machine gun nests on the outer perimeter of our camp there at the edge of the bush. Each tent will be issued, in addition to your own personal sidearms, a Thompson submachine gun!"

This state of readiness, comparable to front-line infantry tactics, was new to Air Corps personnel who were used to fighting the enemy in the sky and in their own backyard. Then, when the battle was over, they flew back home where they could recuperate in peace and quiet in an area far removed from the strain and pressure of the shooting war. Suddenly we were flying back to chaos, where we learned to sleep with our guns, with one eye open, and listening with ears that could hear the chirp of a dissident cricket a hundred yards away. All lights were extinguished shortly after the sun went down each evening, and my GI .45 automatic became my teddy bear.

Captain Lucky Holtzman was a typical, friendly, extroverted New Yorker from the Bronx who ran the Orderly Room and kept the records of the 501st Squadron. Since he was not combat personnel, he was not eligible for R and R leaves to Sydney. He enjoyed quizzing and listening to the exploits of the pilots and navigators when they returned from their rest leaves — to get some rest.

"How was Sydney?" Holtzman asked.

"Isn't it amazing how he can come into an alien country and alienate everyone?" asked Musket.

"We're on red alert since you left," responded Captain Holtzman, self-consciously changing the subject, "we've posted our own sentries, set up machine gun nests and we've got to fight like infantry if we're attacked."

The moment that the sun disappeared into the China sea everything got as quiet as the morning prayer in church. There were no wild drinking parties, no poker or Red Dog games to keep half the Squadron sweating in suspense after dark as everyone nervously adjusted their mosquito netting — memorizing the exact spot at the edge of their bunk — that was free to allow the body the quickest exit to a foxhole or a prostrate position on the ground in the event of emergency. During the first few days, between sleepless nights, the enlisted men and officers had moved their areas as close together as possible. It was encouraging to hear and see activity all night long, as the guards were changed each hour. With the unusual quiet you easily understood that no one could snore if they weren't asleep, and closing both eyes for even an hour might mean you'd never open them again.

After about a week of this fitful, nocturnal slumber, liberally interrupted with abrupt, nervous awakenings caused by strange noises in the night; with everyone reflecting a haggard insomniac appearance — it happened. About 2 A.M. came this blood-curdling scream piercing the quietness of the night like a hot knife in butter.

"Here they come! Here they come!" screamed the voice. "Kill the little yellow bastards! Kill the sonszabitches! Get'em . . . don't let 'em get me! Shoot 'em! Kill 'em."

I was on the ground, had thrown a shell into the chamber of my .45 Colt automatic pistol and reached for the Thompson submachine gun under my bunk before I was fully awake. Straining to see the advancing Japanese infantry, that I thought had silently disposed of our sentries, and probably were about to open up on us with our own machine guns, I wasn't fully certain that I hadn't pissed all over myself.

I heard the unmistakable sound of metal against metal as shells were thrown into chambers, the click of safeties being released as weapons were prepared to fire and then living, breathing, deathly silence again — Another scream, or a half-asleep trigger-happy individual firing at something he *thought* was the enemy, and that camp could easily have blown up like a volcano. It would have been the greatest suicide shooting gallery in history.

The ominous sound of a scuffle two tents away, and low voices in disgusted, descriptive, vintage American words (not Japanese) drew the undivided attention of the entire camp.

If we had been invaded by the enemy it appeared he had been subdued without firing a shot. I started for the tent with my finger on the trigger of the Thompson submachine gun, making a conscious mental effort to put the first burst into the lower left extremity of my adversary. The explosion of subsequent ammunition would rake upward to the right through the chest and head of my enemy. The lights came on in the tent from which the screams had emanated, and a more comic relief I had never experienced.

There was Captain Holtzman, entangled in his mosquito netting, waving a .45 Colt automatic and being wrestled to the ground and subdued by his tentmates. He was staring straight ahead — with the expression of a wild man — having the most ill-timed, ill-advised nightmare and sleep-walk of his life. The 501st Squadron slept no more that night! We subsequently learned that his automatic did not have a shell in the chamber, which probably was the only reason he didn't fire the pistol, and didn't get himself killed along with a lot of other scared, half-asleep people who could've gotten trigger happy in a hurry if one shot had been fired.

"What was wrong with him, Doc?" asked Thatcher, the next morning at breakfast.

"He was suffering from war fatigue!" Doc Marcus replied.

"War fatigue!" exclaimed Thatcher. "The roughest thing ever thrown at him is a paper clip!"

"The biggest fight he's ever been in is to get Sergeant Light to type the duty roster," chimed in Lieutenant McGrane.

"But it's how each of us approaches the war," the Doctor explained. "You fly missions, sweat out gas, sweat out takeoffs, sweat out landings, sweat out fighter interception, *ack-ack*, ditchings, worry about fighter cover, engine failure, your friends shot down, blown from the sky before your eyes and a hundred other experiences in combat. But you can take it . . . mentally you can take it! It's only when all these things, these experiences and misfortunes start piling up and finally get so heavy that you can't cope with them any longer that you'll start having nightmares and walking in your sleep, too!"

"But Holtzman hasn't experienced any of these," replied Thatcher, "except maybe the *kamikazes* in the harbor at Tacloban."

"You're wrong, Thatcher," interrupted Doc, "he has experienced all these things . . . through you and every pilot, navigator and gunner in this outfit! He's heard everyone of you tell your story at interrogation of what happened on every mission . . . every day . . . how Johnson went down, how Bell lost an engine over the target and could only make it halfway back from Formosa before going in nose first . . . how Manders flew his airplane into the Jap ship that he sank after both engines were shot out . . . and on and on!"

"Has Holtzman's little trolley fallen off the tracks then, Doc," continued Thatcher, "has his little choo-choo chugged off the cliff?"

"No," replied Doc, "he was just a little worried."

"Worried," smiled Thatcher, "you show me one guy around here who's *not* worried —"

"All of you flying people, for the most part, were thoroughly screened by the psychiatrists back in Pre-flight school and the odds were good to excellent that you could weather the pressures and strain of combat," explained the good Doctor, "you fight the rigors and pressures of the war . . . you have an escape mechanism by which you're able to fight back and not let the death, the anxiety and worry get you down!"

"Yeah, Doc," volunteered Phipps, "Thatcher can stand up under all this strain by fightin' to get in enough missions to get him back to Sydney and that sweet blonde on R and R!"

"That might be partially right," grinned Doc.

"But you see," said Doc, "Captain Holtzman finally reached the point that he couldn't cope with the pressures, the worries — he couldn't take anymore."

"Then he's not crazy, Doc?" asked Thatcher.

"No, Thatcher, if he were crazy he could sleep like a baby . . . no worry, no pain, no nothing," explained Doc, "insanity is the service of health — when you get to where you can't take anymore, you crack — go insane. It's the body's way of protecting itself!"

"Then if you have nightmares and scream and run, you're not crazy? Is that right, Doc?"

"That's right, Thatcher," said Doc, "now you're beginning to understand."

"That's it, I've got it," said Thatcher, "if you're crazy, like Holtzman, then you're not crazy!"

"That's about it," surmised Doc, "in a manner of speaking!"

What Doc Marcus didn't say was that we were all just a hair's breadth away from insanity.

A week later we were flying two ground support missions daily to ensure the success of MacArthur's return to Luzon. The morning was dark and the air was heavy with clouds laden with rain. The air mass hadn't changed in over a week and I'd begun to think that stationary fronts between Northern Luzon and Formosa were the rule, rather than the exception. Combat flying was like no other flying in the world. No radio, no beacons, no weather reports, no nothing! Just get into your "Merry B-25" and fly off into an occlusion (a front formed by a cold front overtaking a warm front and lifting the warm air above the earth's surface). And hope the weather, not to mention the enemy, didn't get you. Of course, a layer of stratus clouds (from 2,000 to 7,000 feet in altitude and stretching across the horizon), was the most welcome friend a strafer could find. Especially if you were coming off the target alone with a pack of *Zeros* on your tail. Oh, the welcome serenity of the feathery, calm, stratus that locked the *Zeros* out, and afforded an instrument return to base over the China sea — devoid of rocks and mountain tops. The catch was to shed your previously welcome cover, and pray that it didn't extend to the water's surface. This allowed an open space between the cloud base and white tops of the water in which to get your bearings,and allowed you to land on the primitive jungle path — otherwise referred to as an aircraft landing strip. When the weather moved in, (during your five to ten hours absence while seeking out and destroying the enemy) a little extra thrill was added to your day's adventure when you had a socked-in runway with mountains on three sides, the gas running out, and a couple of holes in your wing.

"The target today, gentlemen," emphatically announced Captain Musket, Operations' Officer of the 501st Squadron, pointing to a dot at the top of a big map of Luzon, "is Aparri airdrome on the northern tip of Luzon. Flying out of Formosa, the Japs are using Aparri airdrome as a staging area to fly ground support for General Yamashita and to hit other targets in support of their ground forces."

Every briefing for a mission followed the same format in the Operations tent surrounded by maps, Operations personnel and the strained faces and tense nervous bodies of the flight crews who had to carry out the strike.

"If we can knock out Aparri," continued Captain Musket, "we have effectively eliminated the enemy's air power in the Philippines. This is a relatively short mission and you should be home in plenty of time for lunch."

"What're we having for lunch?" asked Kenney, leaning over and whispering in my ear.

"Ambush stew."

"What's ambush stew?"

"It'll attack you when you least expect it," I replied. I could see he didn't appreciate the humor so early in the morning.

"If it wasn't for the honor of it I would just as soon not come back — for ambush stew!"

"Now that's no way for a fightin' Baylor Bear to talk," I replied. "Look at it this way, you've had time to enjoy breakfast, fight the enemy and recover from both before lunch! And you haven't even had dysentery yet and it comes with the package!"

"We shall make a sea to land attack," stated Captain Jones, Squadron Commander, taking over from Captain Musket, "flying out to sea north of the target about ten minutes, and then turning back toward Aparri in battle formation, all airplanes abreast, bombing and strafing targets in front of you and everybody across the target together — simultaneously!

"I don't need to remind you," he went on, "it's the airplane out front, the airplane lagging behind, or the airplane a little too high that draws the attention of the enemy! Our target is the docks, the town, and the airdrome, and we continue to fly inland right up the valley behind the town and back to base. Any questions?" There were none. "Good hunting!"

"The time is now 0614 and counting down," said Captain Musket, making preparation for a time-synchronization of the watches of all flying personnel. Everyone immediately put the minute hand of his *Hack Watch* on 0615.

"10, 9, 8, 7, 6," entoned Captain Musket, counting out the last ten seconds before reaching 0615, "5, 4, 3, 2, 1, *hack*! Good luck, gentlemen." Each watch, of every aircrew flying this strike, now had the precise, identical time. Takeoff, formation join up, battle line formation, hitting the target — lives could, and did, depend on seconds. The crews filed from Operations to the waiting jeeps and personnel-carriers to be ferried to the flight line and our waiting aircraft.

"How's she runnin', Sergeant?" I asked Albright, crew chief for *199* who could usually smell something wrong before any other crew chief could recognize it. Some other crew chiefs didn't recognize a problem even after it had happened.

"She's like a filly in the starting gate at Pimlico, Lieutenant," replied Sergeant Albright, "just waiting for the starting bell!"

"You don't have any water wings do you?" I asked.

"It looks like a pair might come in handy today, Lieutenant," replied Sergeant Albright, "but she can run on a wet track same as on a dry!"

I went through the checklist. Cronin was writing the Form I and entering each crew member's name when I glanced out the open window to my left at Sergeant Albright and yelled, "Clear One!"

"Clear One," he repeated and I started the big fan rotating. First rotating slowly, there was a backfire, a puff of blue smoke, another backfire and then all 1750-horses of the Wright-Cyclone engine caught at once and I throttled back.

Sergeant Albright moved to the right side and the procedure was repeated until both engines were purring like two giant cats. I hit the brakes, allowing *199* to roll out of the revetment on to the taxi strip — which wouldn't pass for a good country road in west Texas — and started bouncing my way to the south end of the single runway. I throttled back as the aircraft began to roll and pick up speed. Eight airplanes were making the strike and we worked our way to takeoff position with Captain Jones in front, Kuta, number two, and I filled the number three slot; there were five ships behind me. We were stacked like sardines on the very end of the runway, wings interlocked, with 38,000 pounds of airplane ready to be launched into a gray and foreboding sky.

"She ought to be ready to fly a little quicker this morning in this cool moist air," said Cronin, leaning over and yelling about six inches from my ear so he could be heard over the increasing roar of the engines.

At that moment Captain Jones was given the green light, straight up 0700 hours, and his airplane responded to the full throttles of takeoff.

Exactly thirty seconds later Kuta started to roll as I was saying, *Move it, Kuta; get it out of here,* to myself under my breath.

Another thirty seconds: the green light. With firm dispatch I eased both throttles all the way to the firewall. Old *199* responded with rumbling, grumbling noises as we hit chuck holes that were too shallow to fill but not deep enough to lose an airplane in. Halfway down the 5,000 foot strip we had enough airspeed so that I could feel the rudder and elevators coming to life. Until that moment I was keeping the B-25 rolling straight with the brakes. Now, just as suddenly, we had passed the point of no return! With a full load of bombs and ammunition, it was *fly or die* — there was no turning back. The airspeed indicator showed 115–120 mph; the end of the runway flashed underneath the left wing as I pulled the 38,000 pounds of payload from an earthly hand that didn't want to let go. Simultaneously I gave Cronin a thumbs-up signal to retrieve the landing gear and remove that massive drag.

The airplane controls were mushy, but quickly became more stable as the airspeed increased. A second sense had me ready to respond to the prop wash of the airplanes ahead of me. There was an immediate problem of monumental proportions resulting from the airplanes ahead of me stirring up the air — much like a giant mixmaster. That kind of turbulence will cause an aircraft to fall off on a wing, either to the right or left. For every advantage there is usually a disadvantage. While thirty second takeoff intervals conserved gas, shortened the time of assembling aircraft in formation, and cut time to the target, it didn't allow enough time for the prevailing wind and/or conditions to correct themselves naturally, before another airplane was flown into the same area of disturbed air. An unsuspecting, novice pilot, would reflexively attempt to right his airplane with aileron, but the experienced flyer instinctively picks up the wing with the opposite rudder. Prop wash, right on the deck following takeoff, could release the flight of an aircraft just as quickly as it bound it in its grasp. For that reason, if the aileron, which imparts a rolling motion to the aircraft, was wound into the control mechanism, when the troubled air released — the pilot just as suddenly was left with an airplane on its side at minus zero altitude. This condition was almost always 100 percent fatal. By picking up the falling wing with the opposite rudder (which controlled the direction of flight in the horizontal plane) the prop wash was suddenly dissipated. The aircraft then maintained level flight, averting an almost certain catastrophe. Particularly in a fully-loaded, combat-bound aircraft.

Captain Jones held a course straight off the end of the runway, climbing to 1500 feet, and started a slow turn to the left. Kuta began a slightly tighter turn, and I started a turn even tighter than that to catch up and establish my plane in number three position on Captain Jones's left wing. By the time Captain Jones had made a complete 360-degree turn, all eight aircraft were in formation and headed for Northern Luzon and the target.

The weather, with the dark, rain-laden clouds, became more foreboding the further north we flew. *What if the weather is ceiling zero at the target? That's Captain Jones's worry*, I thought. *My only job is to fly his left wing; but what if he flies us into one of those mountains in this area* . . . I quit thinking and started looking for those mountains.

Flying the number three slot, I had to look across Cronin to maintain my position in formation. The expression on his face had changed as the rain squalls and the dark clouds worsened. He leaned forward as Captain Jones made a turn to the left, into us and down, causing me to advance my throttle setting to keep the airplane in formation. We were losing altitude at 500 feet per minute as we caught the full force of the rain squall Captain Jones was trying to circumnavigate.

"Now I know what it feels like to ride in a submarine," said Kenney. For the moment he had left his navigation charts and was standing with his hand on the back of my seat, searching intently the void in front of the airplane as he looked through the plexiglass.

"I don't understand how those engines can function under water," Cronin said to nobody in particular.

Rain was pouring through the side windows, around the edge of the plexiglass windshield, and from somewhere in the fuselage above our heads.

Just as quickly as it had begun, it stopped. We broke out at 900 feet into light rain with nothing but whitecaps below.

"Hello Aircraft Commanders," came Captain Jones's voice through the wind and rain, breaking radio silence for the first time, "this is Kit Bag Leader. Assume battle formation!"

I could see Captain Jones through the right window, his left hand on his throat mike as he issued the command from his cockpit only seventy feet away. I moved out and down about ten feet, then moved up even with Captain Jones's airplane. Kenney began to put the fifty pounds of flak suit over my front and the flak helmet on my head. Cronin charged four package guns manually by pulling up on the cables from the floor. I charged the other eight guns with the automatic button on my control wheel.

"Pilot to crew," I spoke into the intercom after switching my radio from intership, "we're ten minutes from the target. Check your guns, keep your eyes open and be alert. The copilot will call any *ack-ack* positions he sees from the cockpit so you Zuber and Kolodziejski can answer in protecting our rear! Let's get 'em!"

We now had eight B-25s flying abreast toward the coast of northern Luzon at about 500 feet — through rain squalls and whisps of clouds that look lost, they're so out of place.

"We ought to get combat pay for just flying in this weather," grumbled Cronin, leaning over and hollering to be heard above the roar of the engines.

"I know," I responded, continuing to fly battle formation, and fighting the wind and rain. I looked across the cockpit, past Cronin, in order to maintain my flight interval to the left of Captain Jones. "Some people just don't belong in combat! But we must keep trying to learn to love it!"

Cronin had a sick look on his face as I smiled at him.

We were down to a hundred feet and I increased the propeller pitch to 2100 rpm, and moved the mixture control from cruising lean to rich. I signaled Cronin to open the bomb bay. We weren't sweating the gas and I could afford to pamper the engines — the best friends we had in the whole world at that moment. Suddenly the coast of Luzon loomed ahead and it looked as if it were being guarded by a gigantic, billowing, mass of black thunderheads. We were going in under this umbrella of swirling cumulus clouds.

The Squadron navigator in Captain Jones's lead ship had done a miraculous job of navigating, for there directly ahead through the wind and rain squalls, was Aparri. The jetty and docks located in the mouth of the river along the sea coast rose to meet us and we raked them with the .50s. The nose of Captain Jones's airplane was a solid mass of fire with all his guns firing. I dropped three demolition bombs into the jetty and docks and the remaining seven in the town — strafing all the way. The airdrome was on the inland side of the town and a Jap *Betty* bomber was readying for takeoff at the end of the runway. Through the wind and rain squalls the *Betty* became an instant casualty, and no longer of service to the Emperor. Due to the rain and inclement weather the Japanese were either asleep or they didn't figure we'd be flying, as the *ack-ack* was very light.

The feeling of elation, inspiration and relief from the tension that mounted before, during, and immediately following a combat strike took hold of us. This was particularly true when a check of the crew revealed little or no serious damage from the enemy. I felt like I was nine feet tall and could have whipped King Kong. The adrenalin glands can do funny things to the human body at such times. But my elation was short-lived.

Flying up the valley behind the Aparri target, the ceiling dropped and the weather began to close in. Five minutes later the eight airplanes of our strike force found themselves flying in circles at the end of a box canyon. Fortunately, the valley was wide enough to accommodate our eight aircraft flying in circles, but the only way out was the way we had come in — and nobody was about to fly out of the trap and over that airdrome and the city after waking them up.

"To all Aircraft," came Captain Jones, now breaking radio silence, "this is Kit Bag Leader. The only way out of this trap is straight up through this soup. We are surrounded by mountains and locked into what appears to be a box canyon on the map. I suggest that all aircraft start a spiraling ascent out of this box canyon. Repeat! All aircraft will start a spiral ascent out of here. Be sure to maintain a spiral. Flying for over thirty seconds on any one heading could be disastrous! Everyone is on their own. Good luck and out."

What the captain had forgotten to tell us, however, was that we shouldn't all try to climb out of the valley at one time.

"Pilot to crew," I switched from the intership radio to the intercom of our airplane. "We're trapped in a box canyon with a ceiling less than 700 feet. We're going to climb through the soup above us and get out of here. Relax. We're going home. Over and out!"

Leaving the prop pitch at 2100 rpm I stuck the nose of old *199* into the soup and started a slow climb to the left, out of the valley. Increasing the throttles to maintain 165 mph I set the rate of climb at 500 feet a minute. The cloud mass was so solid and thick that it gave the feeling of a dead void. We were suspended in space. The roar of the engines told us that we had to be moving but for all practical purposes we seemed to be spinning our wheels in a mud hole that wouldn't release us. I gazed at the dials; the altimeter told me we were ascending and that we'd just passed 3000 feet. The radio and magnetic compass reflected a slow turn to the left, the wings of the airplane on the gyro were above the horizon with the left wing down in a climbing turn, and the needle and ball were perfectly centered, indicating a perfectly coordinated turn. But something in my gut told me all was not right in Mudville!

Cronin was apprehensive as he squirmed in his seat. Changing position he looked first through the plexiglass above us, then out to the right through his side window. Then he leaned forward as if straining to see something, *anything,* in front of us.

The altimeter now read 4,300 feet and my head was like a universal joint as my eyes strained to pierce the opaqueness of the surrounding and endless cloud mass.

"I wonder how thick — how high this stuff is?" Cronin finally broke the silence. "I don't know but I'm glad to find out that we're not climbing up through a thunderstorm with all the attendant turbulence. That could be just as bad as the mountains if we should hit a 300- or 400-mile per hour down draft, or up-draft, at this speed and under these conditions!"

At 4800 feet the cloud cover surrounding us started to brighten and all at once we appeared to be in a fairyland — or heaven! The apprehension that had seemed to have a stranglehold on our minds and movements a moment before seemed slowly to be abating. Our speed was now 168 mph, we were climbing at 450 feet per minute into this heaven-like brightness. We had completed our mission! I doubted if we had any holes, doubted much less we had lost any airplanes, and we were evidently reaching the top of this soup at close to 5800 feet. In my own uneasiness I thought about the failures of pilots in the past who somehow failed to exercise good judgement under stress or emergency and how, if they hadn't the failures, would still be alive today. The brightness became more luminous, indicating a close proximity to cloudless and clear skies. Our flight egos soared in direct proportion. But if something happened to aircraft *199* on instruments and in all this soup, no F.A.A. check, no analysis, no investigation would find out what happened. The crashed airplane would never be found. We would just vanish from the face of the earth and a "missing in action" notice would be all that our families would ever receive. Captain Jones would say that we went across the target side by side, strafed and bombed, and that we were seen in the box canyon, (maybe) but we'd never be accounted for if we didn't make it out of this impenetrable soup.

I switched to intercom to see if the crew was talking. Silence. I switched back to intership. Silence there too! My eyes went back to the control panel and at a single glance, all the instruments were exactly where they should have been. We were at 6300 feet, I had no vertigo, the airplane was operating smoothly, perfectly, and we should have been breaking out on top of the stuff.

I wound in another half-turn of rudder trim to hold the 450-foot rate of climb, looked at the instruments again, examined all the knobs and switches above and below me and to the side of my seat. Then I moved my eyes up to the windshield, straining to see the first patch of clear blue sky. Then it happened! A dark, olive drab object *whooshed* across the top of our airplane not missing us by fifteen feet! For a heart-stopping moment I saw the underside of a B-25, and two flashes of exhaust fire from its engines. Then it flew off— above and to our right— just as quickly as it had arrived, disappearing into the cloud mass that enveloped us. Cronin had his nose pressed against the window to see if he could see the airplane that had been above us. We had just missed a mid-air collision by inches. Cronin pointed to the intercom. When I switched on, I heard Warnick in the top turret, who had been closer to the near midair disaster than anyone on the aircraft.

"Lieutenant! Lieutenant!" he yelled, "did you see that airplane?"

"I saw it Warnick, and I'm thankful I can say it and still be climbing out of this pea soup!" I took a deep breath. The first officer pilot must outwardly exhibit coolness and composure under all situations, particularly those endangering the aircraft and the lives of his crew. No matter how scared he might be! Inside I was jello.

In another three minutes we burst through the cloud cover at 7,475 feet like a cork popping to the surface after being submerged. We were the third airplane out on top of the 7,500 feet thickness of stratocumulus cloud formation. I continued to climb and set a course back to our base at San Marcelino in southern Luzon. I did not want to be close to any other cork-like B-25s who might come bobbing out of the soup and surface under old *199*. One near miss was enough for one day.

My diary entry following this strike included a special prayer of thanks to an ever present God who delivered us from this near catastrophe. I would never know why I had readjusted our rate of climb from 500 to 450 feet per minute or made other minute adjustments on the elevator trim climbing out of that cloud formation! Why had we been spared? I had learned a lesson. We were not only fighting the enemy but the weather was also a treacherous adversary. The threat of death from being shot down was only the tip of the iceburg of danger. Those dangers were faced daily by the air crews of the 345th *Air Apaches*.

Ninety percent of the whole, cold iceburg, (taken for granted and never mentioned by those involved) was flying overloaded aircraft that caused pilots and crews to sweat out takeoffs. Shot-up aircraft called on personnel to sweat out landings. And we flew in the worst weather conditions in the world, without benefit of radio, and meteorological or weather reports.

"That instrument flying, when you're sharing the same cloud with seven other planes, sure takes your mind off the enemy *ack-ack,* doesn't it?" Cronin said, as we walked from the interrogation tent carrying our parachutes.

"Yeah," I replied, "they only ask us about how we hit the enemy — and don't show a bit of concern in how we nearly hit each other."

"But no casualties," said Cronin, "that's the important thing."

"Just Warnick," added Kenney. "He's gotta change his pants!"

CHAPTER TWO

And There Was Class

Nothing endures but personal qualities.

Walt Whitman

The Fifth Air Force was a class organization from the moment General George Kenney flew into Brisbane, Australia, in early 1942. He was there to organize the "Fightin' Fifth," and this he accomplished in record time with few men and fewer aircraft. Air Force scuttlebutt, off of the third hole of the latrine, rated the General as anything but your ordinary Regular Army officer.

"General Kenney is not your ordinary regular, regular Army officer," insisted one of the old-timers, "he never asks any of us to do anything that he wouldn't do himself!" That was a good recommendation!

Time proved the truth of this statement. Reports floated down through the chain of command that General Kenney was flying over Papau without fighter escort, observing the enemy operations and mapping our future strategy. The next landing for the Japs, at that time, was Australia.

The flip side of that record was General Douglas MacArthur, who would follow Kenney shortly thereafter with a similar excursion over southern New Guinea. This was followed by a four-column picture on the front page of the *Brisbane Telegraph* showing the photogenic Supreme Commander of the Southwest Pacific Area checking out the situation from the waist gunner's position of a B-17 *Flying Fortress*. The difference between the Generals' flights was that "Glory Mac" was escorted by ten fighters!

In my mind, Captain Jack Jones, graduate of West Point, class of 1942, and the Squadron CO of the 501st, measured up in every respect to either of those two Generals. The only factor that kept him from sharing the supreme leadership and responsibility of those two gentlemen, I felt, was time and age. The Captain was United States Army, the son of a West Point General. His father was serving on MacArthur's staff in the Philippines when the Japs overran Manila, Clark Field, Bataan and Corregidor in December, 1941, following their sneak attack on Pearl Harbor.

"Dad was taken prisoner by the Japanese," the Captain said, "my senior year at the Point and I immediately made application to be sent to the Pacific where I thought I would avenge him. But before my request got through channels, I was sent to Europe and flew a tour of combat in B-26s. When I got home from Europe, my request had finally gone through Air Force channels in Washington and I was sent immediately to the Pacific!"

Jack Jones was an inch or two shy of six feet and chubby. One wondered what he might have looked like in those high collared West Point cadet uniforms. He was fighting his own "battle of the bulge" and his belt divided that bulge evenly. His neck and shoulders would have looked good on an Army nose guard but I got the feeling he hadn't played football. He had a good face, a head topped with wavy blond hair with a mustache to match.

Jones's face was appropriately expressive but you felt he was older than his years — due no doubt to his previous tour of combat in Europe. He had the eyes of a gentleman not only at war with the Japanese but with the world around him, yet he loved it all. He was always in control, whether leading the Squadron in combat or as the guest of honor at a prayer meeting. He was gracious but dogmatic, stubborn but reasonable, and brave — but modest to the point that others might have to report the details of his success on a strike.

Except for an occasional swim at the beach, he seemed to hate all forms of physical exertion. I always thought his main sport might have been avoiding calisthenics — if we'd had any. When he sat down he was ready to stay there a spell. When he stood up he had a definite purpose and reason for doing so with no lost motion. His eyes were never still and you knew that he was continually evaluating his personnel and command. He had the respect of every individual serving under him and particularly those of us who flew with him. When things were going smoothly you hardly knew who the commanding officer was, but let problems, or troubles, surface, and it was amazing how quickly matters got straightened out.

Once a month the 345th Bomb Group *Air Apaches* dispatched a special plane. It was a stripped down B-25 (called *Fat Cat*) with everything taken out, and off of it (including the removal of camouflage paint) that reduced it to nothing but a hull with two engines. It was flown to Sydney, Australia, to pick up a load of fresh lettuce, tomatoes and eggs. The perishable foodstuff, plus all the booze that could be stacked into the bomb bay, provided a tomato and lettuce salad and fresh eggs for the troops for only two meals each month. But no single event was anticipated and appreciated any more than the arrival of the *Fat Cat* bearing its culinary and alcoholic delights. Immediately upon landing, the contents of the craft were equally distributed among the four squadrons of the Group.

On one occasion a full case of the precious hen house gold, allotted to the 501st, came up missing. Nobody could really blame any enterprising member of the Squadron for pilfering the cackle fruit. With a case of fresh eggs you could trade and/or barter the army supply people, not to mention the native Filipinos, out of the whole island of Luzon. When Major Jones learned of the theft, the eggs, you might say, hit the fan! With the help of Captain Holtzman and his paddle-feet assistants making the inspection of the officers' tents, Jones satisfied himself that no officer had taken the case of eggs. This is not to say that any of several officers, notwithstanding their appointment as an "officer and a gentleman" by the President, wouldn't have purloined the eggs had the opportunity presented itself. The fact was: no officer living in the officers' area with Captain Jones would have even *thought* about stealing a case of hen fruit, or anything else that brought such universal joy to the squadron. They would never have risked arousing his wrath. They would sooner have risked courts-martial!

Jones then proceeded to the enlisted men's area. "A case of eggs is missing from the mess tent," stated Captain Jones to all of the assembled enlisted personnel of the 501st.

"I'm giving the person, or persons, who stole those eggs exactly one hour to bring them back to the mess tent," he thundered.

"And if they're not returned within the allotted time, I can promise every last member of this Squadron that you'll be confined to this area until you rot! Do you understand me?"

Did they ever understand! Those eggs were back in the mess tent within fifteen minutes.

Our Squadron Commander could be even more emphatic, volatile and intense if he thought those in his command had failed to carry out their duty, particularly when it pertained to combat. Upon the return of the squadron from a strike to the China coast, Captain Jones learned that the squadron strike force had chanced upon a Japanese cruiser and destroyer — not their primary target — in an inland bay. Only one airplane had made a halfhearted pass at this prize target with no success. Notwithstanding the excellence and prestige of hitting such a target, all of us recognized the outright suicide associated with such devastating naval firepower, particularly when supported by heavy shoreline antiaircraft positions. Calling a special, private meeting of all the officers who had manned the aircraft on the mission, Captain Jones didn't mince any words.

"Gentlemen, I am aware of the optimum enemy target you located in an inland bay along the coast of China today. I am keenly disappointed, for whatever reason, that you did not attack and destroy those enemy warships. In the future, no matter what your assigned target may be, you will attack without hesitation any target of this magnitude and importance. This is your duty and you shall be expected to carry it out! This target was, by far, more important than anything you might have been assigned or expected to find on or near the China coast today, and you will never — I repeat — you will never make this mistake again. The loss of your lives and aircraft would have been a small price to pay for such a disastrous blow to the enemy. And if you survive, there'll be other targets for you to lose your lives over! But should you ever fail to attack another target of this nature, I can promise you'll wish that you had gotten shot down compared to what you're going to get when you get back to this base! Do each of you understand?" Everyone understood!

"I just hope a Jap battleship doesn't come steaming up the coast of Indochina," said Thatcher, after hearing what Captain Jones had said, "we're gonna sink it — "

"Or get our asses shot off trying!" interrupted Kuta.

When we moved up to San Marcelino, Luzon, the Squadron went through a couple of weeks of intense training in strafing and skip bombing, attacking the beached hull of an old enemy ship below San Antonio. We were making preparation for the all-out assault on Jap shipping to the coast of Indochina that would require round trip missions of 1,500 to 1,700 miles with maximum time in the air of nine to eleven hours.

"You've all been schooled in how to squeeze every last minute of flying time out of a drop of gas," stated Captain Jones.

"Flying to the coast of Indochina will test the ability of every crew member," continued the Captain, "and without every man doing his job we won't be able to make the trip, much less strafe, bomb and sink Jap ships! When we come home the gas will be gone or we'll have so little left that we'll be flying on fumes! For that reason we've got to get the airplanes on the ground in the shortest time possible and we're going to utilize a fighter peel off to get the job done."

He then went to the blackboard and drew the squadron fighter peel off maneuver.

"The key to this maneuver is the number three man in the lead element," said the Captain, pointing, "this man right here, flying the left wing of the Squadron leader. And how fast he can get back on the ground! Starting from a shallow dive at 5,000 feet, we'll hit the end of the runway in squadron formation at 800 feet. On my signal number three peels off, up and to the left, and hopefully can get on the ground in five minutes. I follow, as do the remaining aircraft in the squadron, every fifteen seconds, each of us spacing ourselves in the landing pattern so that we land at as close to thirty-second intervals as possible. Do you understand?"

All pilots nodded their heads.

"Then let's get to the flight line and try it!"

After five days of practicing the fighter peel off Captain Jones was still not satisfied with our performance. We shot landings until we could have put the airplane on the runway blindfolded but we still couldn't get all the squadron on the ground in the time the Captain wanted us to do it. He had tried several of the older pilots in the number three position in the lead element but they just weren't doing the job.

"How about giving me that number three slot tomorrow, Captain?" I asked as we rode back from the flight line after yet another training session. "If I can't get my airplane on the ground in half the time of any other pilot in this outfit, I'll check in my wings!'"

"You're on, Blount!" came the Captain's reply, "and you better get out of the way 'cause I land second and I might be flying up your ass!"

I couldn't wait, and the next morning enroute to the flight line, I tipped off the crew we were flying a new position in the squadron line up.

"The Captain has retired and you're leading the Squadron?" asked Kenney.

"No," I replied, "but we're on the Captain's left wing,which makes us number one in the hearts and minds of all the fans and personnel on the flight line!"

"We're not playing football now," said Cronin.

"Now you tell me!" I replied, "and just when I thought I'd run a 'down and out' in old *199* and go all the way!"

As we lined up on the end of the runway, stacked six deep with wings interlocking, Captain Jones looked over the sixty-five feet that separated us and gave me a skeptical grin as he poured the coal to his airplane and started rolling on takeoff! In thirty seconds I was right behind him and a brisk wind blowing off the beach removed the turbulent air stirred up by his props. We had a smooth takeoff and joined his warm side in nothing flat. Joining up and flying formation can be a perilous experience if performed by a novice. Needless to say we were the cream and, in my own mind, I was better than any other pilot in the outfit. Not a cocky, extroverted confidence but a deep, self satisfying feeling that was its own reward in what I could make the airplane do. The confidence built on hundreds of hours of formation flying allowed me to put the tip of my right wing in the Captain's ear as we swung out over the sea. He wouldn't even look my way, much less give me an approving look, but you could bet your hip boots he knew where I was and how I got there.

Having climbed to 5,000 feet the Captain started his shallow dive toward the end of the runway with the lead, three-ship element stacked twenty feet above the second three-ship element, and with all the airplanes now indicating 275 mph as we approached the end of the runway. This was the moment of truth, and how I loved it!

As we began the shallow dive, I had started rolling in elevator trim tab with my right hand on the wheel at the base of the island between pilot and copilot that held the throttles, mixture and prop pitch controls. I had to hold forward pressure on the stick with my left hand to keep the airplane from going straight up and standing on its tail. When the Captain gave me the peel off sign with his left thumb, I turned the wheel loose, simultaneously kicking left rudder, and the plane shot up to 2000 feet faster than a skyrocket.

At this point I had to do some things that my instructors would have washed me out for doing in a B-25 back in Advanced Flying School at La Junta, Colorado. But this was neither La Junta nor was it flying school. This was combat where you didn't get a second chance — where lives and aircraft were lost if you couldn't cut it. There were no washout check rides here! Only death, swift and sure, took up the tickets at this performance. So you learned to deliver the difficult, the unexpected flight maneuver in spades, in order to stay alive!

At 2000 feet I was at the top of a chandelle! The instructors in flying school and the tech manuals said that landing gear, and flaps, were never put down while the B-25 airplane was in a turn, much less on its back! I did both — maintaining that any maneuver, any change in the flight surface of the air foil that could be accomplished in straight and level flight could also be accomplished in a turn or upside down — if necessary. At least as long as the turn, or changed flight position was a well-coordinated maneuver, with the needle, ball, centered and the airspeed perfectly coordinated. In addition, you never let your wheels and/or flaps down with an indicated speed in excess of 160 mph. At 2000 feet on my back, with my airspeed at precisely 160 mph, my airplane was in perfectly coordinated control as evidenced by all flight instruments on the panel. I cut the throttles, let the wheels down, and let down thirty-degrees of flaps as the airplane started falling toward the ground. I came over the end of the runway at 165 mph, kicked the airplane out of the turn, levelled the wings, and then I lined up with the runway, as my wheels touched down. When I rolled off the far end of the runway and had retracted my flaps, Captain Jones, the number two ship to land, was starting his turn into the final approach. From peel off to touchdown we had consumed sixty-five seconds! There was a five-minute delay from the time we touched down until the Captain got his airplane on the ground.

Taxiing to our revetment, I completed the Form I and joined the rest of the crew sitting on their parachutes in the shade of the wing waiting for transportation back to the Squadron area. In a moment we saw a jeep coming toward us leaving a vast cloud of San Marcelino dust in its wake, with Captain Jones in the passenger seat. Upon arrival the Captain jumped from the jeep and, striding toward me, hit me in the stomach with his fist.

"Damn it, Blount!" he exclaimed. "If you don't tarnish my brass! You made me look like a Primary Flying Student who hadn't soloed on that landing!"

"But how was it for gettin' it on the ground, Captain!" I asked.

"It was so good that you've won yourself a permanent spot in the number three slot of the lead element!"

That was good news, particularly when handed out by the Squadron CO in open recognition of your ability in front of your peers. With that kind of reputation I felt compelled to make every Squadron landing one of those never-to-be-forgotten — you-ain't-seen-nothin-yet type of peel off and I was successful. Everyone, flying- as well as ground-personnel, started coming out to see the 501st peel off and land. All of us need a little of that in life, no matter what our chosen endeavor!

"What does it feel like, riding with Lieutenant Blount in the back of that airplane during his peel off?" a tail gunner of another crew asked Kolodziejski.

"It's the best roller coaster ride in the U.S.Army Air Corps," replied Hank.

A week later our names were posted on the Squadron bulletin board for a strike on Formosa. Captain Jones was leading the strike and the target was the town of Mato and a sugar factory.

"The town is about ten miles inland," said Captain Jones at the briefing. "The sugar factory is located on this side of the town and everyone, particularly the pilots, should take a look at these aerial photos, to get the location of the factory in your minds!"

"Think we'll have time to pick up some sugar candy?" whispered Cronin.

"Candy . . .

"I always call my sugar, Candy," volunteered Arky Vaughn, adding, under his breath, "cause she makes my peanut brittle!"

"Cool it you guys!" came a voice from the row behind us. "Some people just don't have a sense of humor," said "Wilky" Wilkinson, "you'd think we were fightin' a war!"

"We're carrying a special kind of bomb today," said Captain Jones, "and this will be the first time it has been dropped on Formosa, It's a napalm, or fire bomb, that hits, splatters and burns with intense heat. Each airplane will be carrying five bombs and we're to skip 'em in just like we were dropping free-falling, 500-pounders!

"We'll fly to this point," indicating a spot on the map, "down on the deck here, strafe and bomb the target in a southeast to northwest pass, all six ships abreast over the target. Then stay on the deck and strafe targets of opportunity all the way back out to the coast. Any questions?"

"What's the *ack-ack* concentration?"

"The gun and *ack-ack* emplacements are marked on the aerial photos," replied the Captain, "and they're concentrated at the edge of the town and particularly around the sugar factory!"

"Following the strike and strafing targets of opportunity," continued Captain Jones, "pay particular and close attention to the location of these Japanese Prisoners-of-War Camps. They tend to blend into the other buildings and can be easily mistaken for army barracks or concentrations of Jap troops. Whatever you do, don't bomb or strafe these POW camps — they're our people! Understand? I want no mistakes on this!"

"What's he so fired up about the POW Camps?" Cronin asked, leaning over and whispering into Lieutenant Ike Baker's ear.

"His dad, General Jones, is in one of those camps and he wants to make sure that we don't strafe or bomb our own POWs by mistake," he replied.

As long as we flew missions against the enemy on Formosa you can rest assured that every pilot and crew knew the exact location of the POW camps and no airplane of the 345th Bomb Group ever flew over, much less strafed, any of them. In later years I have had occasion to visit with some of those who were held captive in those POW camps on Formosa, and the greatest lift of spirits and joy they experienced was when we attacked and bombed targets in their vicinity. Particularly did they appreciate the B-25s with the big Indian head painted on their tails: all dipping their wings, and acknowledging their presence when they flew near their camps.

"We knew that you knew we were there," I was told by one good friend who was in one of the POW camps, "and after three years behind the Japs barbed wire, you'll never know the encouragement or understand the boost you gave our morale. You gave us the first hope that we were winning the war and that there was a definite possibility that we might be liberated to return home to loved ones and friends!"

Captain Jones continued his briefing. "Our navy submarines, will surface for thirty minutes after our strike and their coordinates are: *Filthy Filly,* 25° 108 min, north 121° 55 east latitude; *Forlorn,* 23° 45′/119° 36′ east; and *Flat Failure,* 24° 51′ 120°, 55′ east, and they can be contacted on Emergency Channel Two. *Playmate* and *Juke Box* Eight will also be available if you lose an engine and the navigators will list their locations and call-signals in their logs." *Juke Box* was the code name for the PBYs that would land (if they could find us and the sea wasn't too rough), to pick up any survivors following the ditching of an airplane. *Playmate* was the code name for a PBY that carried a twenty foot boat, strapped underneath, with engine and emergency rations that could be dropped to survivors when the sea was too rough to land.

Lieutenant Baker then briefed us on the weather:

"Our latest weather report is good, with eight to fifteen miles visibility, scattered cumulus clouds and occasional hazy spots. The weather over the target should be good as well, and you should have no trouble seeing the town of Mato, and the sugar factory!"

"That's our trouble," grumbled Johnson, they won't have any trouble seeing us either!"

"Takeoff is at 0655," added Captain Jones. "Good hunting!"

Six planes were flying this mission and our preparation had been detailed and intense. After being delivered to the flight line, every man immediately took his position and went through his check-out routine. I took my walk around *199* and ended up in front of the airplane with the crew chief, Sergeant Albright. He had changed the plugs and tuned the engines. I couldn't have had more confidence in any other individual who could possibly have been assigned the responsibility of taking care of the airplane. I climbed up the ladder, leaned around the top turret, stepped up to the flight deck and squeezed into the pilot's seat. The cockpit couldn't have been any smaller and have been comfortable for my six foot-five-inch size. I began a rundown of the checklist, checking toggle switches, adjusting controls, and reacquainting myself with over one hundred-fifty different knobs, handles, instruments, lights and switches, so that each of them felt like an old friend. I had a feeling of confidence in every man who rode that rocket and they had confidence in each other, which resulted in teamwork that was hard to beat!

The airplane seemed eager to fly, as I had to brake it all the way in and around revetments, taxiing to takeoff position. Excitement was in the air and my adrenalin was flowing as the six airplanes stacked up: roaring, belching, coughing, backfiring, and straining at the bit to be turned loose. The end of the runway behind us had been cleared of dust and rocks for one hundred-fifty yards, by the blast of the twelve Wright-Cyclone engines revved for takeoff. The airplane was alive, shaking, vibrating, rattling and ready to free itself from the earth that held it.

"Kit Bag Leader to squadron," came the voice of Captain Jones over the command radio, as I looked at him over the short sixty feet that separated us, "I'll circle a half turn to the left at 5,000 feet; follow me!"

We joined up at 5,000 feet and headed for Formosa. I asked

Kenney about the time-lapse from takeoff to the coast of Formosa and he told me we were two minutes late.

"Little more head wind than we anticipated," he said.

"You didn't allow for the time we expended climbing to altitude!"

"Yes I did," hollered back the navigator, feigning insult that I'd questioned his calculations.

"Okay," I said, "that's just two more minutes they've had to sit there and get ready for us!"

If they knew we were coming, an additional two minutes wouldn't make any difference, and Kenney knew it.

As Formosa came into view on the horizon, I called for my flak suit and Kenney and Cronin obliged. I charged my nose guns with the electric charging button on the panel. There was a massive *thud* as all the nose gun mechanism went off simultaneously throwing the first shells into each chamber. The two package guns, on either side of the fuselage, Kenney charged manually by pulling the handles located between the pilot and copilot.

"Two guns on the right are charged and ready," reported Kenney, who added, "just wish you'd let me fire one of 'em!"

"Now why would you want to do that?" I asked, this being the one hundred sixty-first time we had covered this point.

"I want to shoot a gun, or drop a bomb, or fly the plane," complained Kenney, getting worked up over the prospect. "You don't understand how tough it is to have to stand here and look over your shoulder when we get to the target — mission after mission — and never do anything!"

I knew his answer as well as he did, and I responded in unison with him. Cronin was about to crack up!

"Gettin' us to the target and then back to that tiny strip at San Marcelino, in *SOUTHERN* Luzon," I added, "is about the most important job on this airplane! But you're going to get your chance. Just hang in there."

Flying around the mountains at the southern end of Formosa, Captain Jones started taking us down on the deck at a 700-feet-a-minute descent. In five minutes we were streaking over the Formosan countryside. Skimming above the treetops, or below them when there was an opening in the forest, was the most exhilarating flying I ever did. It was like opium on which you could become addicted. The danger was forgotten as efficiency and ability in minimum altitude flying was increased with the continued, day in, day out, use of the airplane. The only manner in which the true speed of an aircraft can be physically and visually appreciated is to fly it in close proximity to the earth where all objects are stationary. Ordinarily, such freedom with an airplane by a novice pilot is a prelude to disaster with a high percentage of all aircraft crashes credited to buzzing at low altitude. The manner in which we flew minimum altitude missions was a way of life, a planned maneuver in which we engaged in many hours of practice and rehearsal until the blur of trees, buildings and other objects became natural to us. Just as the *modus operandi* of the medium and heavy bombers, holding steady at 7,500 to 15,000 feet until *bombs away* sounded, and then diving right or left to miss the *ack-ack,* was to them. Beating the enemy by flying ahead of my sound, at minimum altitude, attacking, strafing and bombing any target for no longer than fifteen seconds and then getting out of there in the same manner in which I had entered, was intoxicating. The sobering aspect of such intoxication was when the enemy was waiting for us, knew that we were coming and then having the enemy stick the barrels of their antiaircraft cannon in our guts!

All six ships flew as one, hitting 275 mph as we flew formation on Captain Jones's airplane in the middle. The town of Mato loomed up ahead and so far not one single solitary puff of *ack-ack* had been sent our way. The sugar factory was across town and appeared as large, brown, frame buildings with smoke billowing out of two big smoke stacks. The airplane strained and vibrated as I opened up with all twelve guns at the edge of town. I watched my tracers and incendiaries race right up into and through the town and toward the sugar factory. Captain Jones, Kuta, Lamar and I straddled the factory with the two outside planes across the far edge of each side. Halfway through the town a large flock of black birds appeared as if from nowhere, and were caught up in the whirling propellers. At the same moment there was an explosion in front of me as the left half of the nose of my airplane suddenly disappeared and I only had three guns firing straight ahead.

"Pilot to top turret. We're hit and I've lost most of my firepower in the nose. Strafe straight ahead but keep your eyes peeled for fighters."

"Roger! Wilco!" came Warnick's reply, as seemingly thousands of empty shell cases came falling to the floor of *199* under the top turret as he delivered the hot lead treatment to the factory and gun emplacements that had come to life.

I kept our nose on the deck ten feet above the ground all the way out to the coast. There, all six planes arrived simultaneously, spread out over an area of one-half mile.

"Kit Bag Leader to squadron. Let's join up. Check your damage and let's head for the house!"

"Any damage in the back?" I asked on intercom.

"Everything's all right in the tail," said Kolodziejski.

"Same in the waist, Lieutenant!" responded Zuber.

"What does the target look like?"

"The whole town is burning, and that factory is nothing but brown sugar now! I've never seen anything burn like that napalm!" reported Kolodziejski.

Upon landing, Sergeant Albright and all the ground crew gathered around the nose of our airplane.

"Did you get any metal through the plexiglass windshield when you lost the left side of the nose, Lieutenant?" asked Sergeant Albright.

"Didn't feel a thing but the explosion," I told him, "and I apologize for bringing her back so messed up!"

"That's all right," he replied, "we don't care how you bring her back, just as long as you bring 'er back!"

"We did fly through a big flock of black birds," I added, "right over the target!"

"Here's all that's left of one that you caught in the right engine nacelle, Lieutenant," said a mechanic holding up two bird feet and a few feathers.

"I'm glad we caught 'em in the engine and not through the plexiglass."

"Looks like three barrels melted this time, Lieutenant," said one of the armorer sergeants responsible for the machine guns.

"Let's see, I burned out three the last mission, too, didn't I?"

"I don't like to do that," I replied, "but with all the time and trouble it takes to get to these targets, I sure don't want to bring any ammunition back! I want to deliver every round as long as I've got one barrel firing and today I only had three after we lost the left side of our nose!"

"I agree, sir," replied the Sergeant, "we've got more barrels than you can burn out and there's nothing that gives me more pleasure than replacing burned-out barrels!"

We didn't lose an airplane, the *ack-ack* was light — compared to most targets on Formosa — there was no fighter interception, and aerial photographs showed the sugar factory completely destroyed.

Three weeks later the CO of the 500th Squadron flew two war correspondents, one Associated Press and one United Press, to Mato to show them the total obliteration of the sugar factory and the devastation resulting from the first napalm bombs dropped on Formosa. As was so often the case, public relations sometimes got out of hand, and that trip ended in tragedy. Forgetting, or overlooking, the danger, someone failed to realize that the place was still a live and volatile target. The sight-seeing trip ended in disaster when the plane was shot down near Mato with the loss of all aboard.

Our names were posted on the bulletin board the day before we were to fly a most memorable mission. Seldom did we know what the target would be, until the early morning briefing before takeoff, but my thirteenth mission was the exception. Word leaked out that we were going after shipping in the harbor at Hainan Island where the 500th had lost three airplanes earlier in the day.

"If the 500th went in there and got the shit shot out 'em," exclaimed Thatcher, "why in hell are they sending us back in there to commit suicide too? We've got plenty of time! Let those mothers come out of that mountain fortress, into the open sea and give us a chance!"

Thatcher, of course, had the one hundred percent support of all the flying personnel surrounding the bulletin board and one hundred-fifty percent support of those of us who were scheduled to fly the strike.

Right before evening chow I dropped by Captain Jones's tent. He was washing his hands and face at the showers so I sat down to wait. As he came in, a towel draped over his shoulder, I started to get up.

"At ease, Lieutenant," he said, "don't get up. Let me pretend you're in charge of this nightmare!"

"I've got a question! Why are they sending us into Yulin Bay tomorrow? Particularly after what the 500th got today?"

"Ours not to reason why . . . ours but to do or die!" he replied.

"Yeah! Emphasize the die!" I added.

"I didn't mean that," he shrugged, "it was a poor attempt to be funny!"

"I'm as concerned as you are and quite frankly I can't understand why we need to go into Yulin Bay after that shipping, except, militarily speaking, we have 'em all in one barrel. The possible destruction we can do the enemy far outweighs what it will cost us in manpower and airplanes! Someone in Fifth Bomber Command, or even in the office of the Supreme Commander of the Southwest Pacific, has decided this strike is necessary and we've been assigned the job!"

"That doesn't make me like it any more," I replied.

"Nor me either," responded Captain Jones, "but we'll fly it and we'll do all right too!"

"Fifth Bomber may order the strike, but I determine how it will be flown," he added, "and I think you'll like what I've planned!

"Let's go to chow!"

Hainan Island lies just off the China coast about halfway between the mainland of Japan and Sumatra, Malaya and Borneo. It was one of the principal sources of fuel, fiber and food for the Japanese war machine. The merchant ships and tankers came down from Japan, were made up into convoys at the big Jap naval base on Yulin Bay, and were then escorted by Jap cruisers and destroyers south — to be loaded with oil, rubber, iron ore and food stuffs, and returned to Tokyo. The Japanese had occupied Hainan since 1939 and during that time had developed their naval base at Yulin Bay into one of the strongest in the Orient, and the equal of Saigon, Hong Kong, Shanghai or Formosa. The shoreline of Yulin Bay was lined with heavy antiaircraft guns. One of the survivors of the 500th strike earlier on that afternoon had described it as being shot at like a fish in a barrel! If they didn't get you in the cross fire from the antiaircraft guns on shore and all around the circular harbor, the destroyers, cruisers and other war ships in the harbor would!

"Captain Jones will have us in and out of there faster than

a cat can lick his ass," spoke up Arthur McGrane. We all knew that was wishful thinking. Most pilots, I thought to myself, should only fear the elements such as ice, thunderstorms, rain, snow, fog, and perhaps poor radio and weather information. Those were the logical, sane and ordinary worries of pilots, but I'd never given the weather and other ordinary problems encountered in a purely flying environment a second thought. If I could lift it off — I could get it down! My concern was: could I fly far enough on one engine to make it to that friendly submarine — could I ditch it in the perennially rough and turbulent China sea? Could I go in on *top* of one of those whitecaps and not in the *valley* between two of them that formed a grave . . . and swim away from it? Flying, no matter what the weather conditions, was absolutely no sweat! It was being a daily, constant, clay pigeon for all the Jap gunners of the Imperial Navy and their little brothers that was making me nervous in the service! The antiaircraft revetments around every land target filled me with a fear that I could hardly endure! A fear that, like every other pilot, I never admitted to anyone. It was a fear that gnawed away at my psyche and my mind until I broke out in cold sweat and couldn't sleep. I rolled, tossed, and turned all night long! I prayed to be relieved of my agony and anxiety, to be allowed to sleep. It seemed I hadn't slept fifteen continuous minutes the entire night when the OD punched me with his flashlight to wake me.

"That's not necessary, I'm already awake."

"Everybody's awake this morning," he said, "they must really be ready for this one."

He didn't know the half of it, or maybe he did, but neither of us would attempt to explain it to the other.

"What's for breakfast?" I inquired of Theron Lyman, who was coming out of the mess tent.

"It's okay — " he replied, "just remember me in your will — and write it before you eat that stuff!"

"Look at this tray! It still has dried potatoes on it!" complained Hardeman.

Don was from San Angelo, Texas, and probably as nervous that morning as I was. "Something's dried on it," he repeated.

"Did you say somethin' died on it?" I asked. "Eat it! It's probably better than what they're serving this morning!"

"I don't care how bad the food is — "

"You don't? I do!"

"But they can give us somethin' clean to eat it out of!"

"Don't criticize our sanitary conditions! Say anything you want to about the food but we change the filth here every day!"

It was a relief to break the loneliness of the night and be back among friends, leading a normal life, bitching about the food and the service. There was still some sanity left in the world!

"Why do we have to go to war so damned EARLY?" demanded Townsley, stumbling out of the mess tent in the dark after breakfast.

"In the next war Vernon, we're only gonna fight after lunch," I replied. "That way we can sleep in, have a leisurely breakfast, an enjoyable lunch, fly our strike and be back in plenty of time for a hot shower, formal dinner and a show, before turning in!"

"Our strike is the shipping in Yulin Bay and Hainan Island," announced Captain Musket, Operation's Officer, as if he really needed to tell us at the briefing session to the crews flying the mission. "And we have a harbor full of Jap naval and merchant vessels. Captain Jones will tell you how the strike is to be flown!"

Captain Jones stepped forward. "This is the first time our Squadron has gone after this target and in light of the experience of other squadrons, who've hit this heavily defended harbor, we will attempt the unexpected and hope to accomplish two things: deliver the maximum destruction to our enemy with the minimum loss of personnel and airplanes to ourselves!"

Had somebody stood up and yelled "Let's hear it for the Captain!" all the personnel of the 501st still asleep and not making the strike would have come out of their sacks wondering how they'd missed the prayer meeting!

"That's the most encouraging word I've heard since I found out what the mission was for today," said Lieutenant Vernon Townsley, flying copilot on this mission. "Two hips and a hooray for Jones!"

"Hainan is about the same size, and has a coastal plain and mountains just like Formosa," said Captain Jones, pointing to a large map superimposed on the blackboard.

"In the northern half are the Five Finger mountains and

other assorted ranges that vary in height from 5,000 to 7,000 feet. Between these mountains are valleys of the same depth, most of which drain into and form Yulin Bay. Thus far, all other attacks on this target have been mounted from the open China sea with the airplanes flying through the mouth of the harbor or slightly to one side. We shall fly down one of these deep valleys up here in the northern part of the island and hit Yulin Bay from the opposite, and least expected side. Hopefully, we'll catch the enemy sleeping on their guns. Our only problem will be in selecting the right valley, but I trust our navigators will direct us down the right one! We're carrying five hundred-pounders with four-second delay fuses and the hunting should be good, with ten to fourteen ships reported in the harbor!

"We'll have a friendly sub, code name: *Kleptomaniac,* monitoring emergency channel two on your radio, approximately fifty nautical miles at 21°18' North latitude. Should you lose an engine try to make it to these coordinates and the Navy will pick you up."

"I don't need to tell you about the quality, or the quantity, of the enemy *ack-ack* in and around this target," reminded Captain Jones.

"The shore batteries, not to mention the warships themselves, will make this as well defended a target as we'll hit outside of Tokyo. The element of surprise is paramount. Over the target nine ships abreast. Don't ever stop strafing, and turret gunners, keep your eyes peeled for fighter interception from above."

As we arrived at the airplane in semidarkness, the *Touch O' Texas,* with guns protruding from her nose, her back, sides and tail, was an awesome sight. The bomb bays were still open as the armorers winched the last five hundred-pounder into position. Mounted on a sixty-seven foot wing, with two Wright-Cyclone powerhouses containing a combined 4,000 horsepower thrust, this was the "flying battleship," the most feared weapon of destruction in the Southwest Pacific. This was also an old and intimate friend whose hydraulic system, with its innumerable relief valves, pumps, and lines; its electrical system with circuit breakers, switches, fuses, and knobs; and its fuel system with a normal twelve tanks which, with the addition of "Tokyo" and "Radio" tanks, doubled our range. I knew these systems like the back of my hand and could draw them from memory.

My ground school instructors in engine theory and maintenance had insisted that I be thoroughly acquainted with the complexity of the Wright-Cyclone engine. At the time, like so many things, I hadn't understood their devotion and insistence, but now I did. Flying the PT-17 Stearman bi-wing trainer, you looked for the nearest pasture or open area if the engine stopped. The B-25 was a lady that operated only on reasonably flat, well-prepared surfaces although she had shown her tougher nature in operating off the "metal beach" and jungle, chug-hole runways. The Army Air Corps didn't care if you killed yourself but you damn well better protect and take good care of its aircraft.

Such mature thinking was difficult for some of us who were only nineteen years of age and who looked upon the airplane as our personal hot rod and an instrument of fun and frolic. The war took away our stripped-down Model-A's and T's, but replaced it with the B-25. When skillfully and artfully rolled, spun, dived, looped, or flown as a slashing, cutting, devastating instrument of destruction, an airplane could provide endless excitement and delight. We forgot the hot rod back home. We also fell in love; seized with the passion few other activities could ever equal. There would be few callings in our lives to muster or demand the personal interest, courage, devotion, or dedication that was necessary to win the wings of an Air Corps pilot. We were being paid to indulge ourselves in this intoxicating love affair — while enjoying the universal respect and highest esteem of our peers. To be totally honest, any one of us would have paid the Air Corps to allow us to fly their aircraft!

These are retrospective, peacetime feelings. The shadow of death and combat placed a real burden upon the love affair — much like a third party of a triangle that upset, and destroyed, the perfect marriage.

The "old" pilots looked skeptically at the "new" pilots who inexorably made their appearance to fill the sacks of those who fell before the enemy guns daily. They were braced with a fixed set of standards and flying protocol from which, in self-protection, they never deviated. This carried over into their informal, social, and non-flying time on the ground between strikes, and prevented some of them from becoming friends with anyone. They were hard, tough, skilled, combat wise, and suspicious men, navigating constantly on the edge of disaster much like the top gunslingers of the old West. They played the odds, never making close friends because their own longevity meant most of their friends were gone. They tried being a friend to everyone, never forcing their views or opinions, and never giving life-saving advice or making voluntary suggestions unless they were asked.

Since they'd assisted in gathering together the personal effects of too many good friends to be sent home to wives and parents, they now looked at each new pilot and tried to size him up as to flying ability . . . under combat pressure. They tried to picture him flying on their wing at three hundred miles per hour on the deck, wing tip to wing tip. Tried to imagine what would happen if a massive shell shot an engine right out of his wing! How would he behave? Would he rise to the occasion and fly the airplane through the hell of the target, or would he peel off into the dead engine and take two or three of his own squadron with him? What would he do when he got his hydraulic system shot out, a live bomb stuck in the bomb bay, his airplane on fire, half of his controls shot away, when a quick decision or a quicker movement must be automatic to prevent a tragedy? The old pilots did not look for heroes! They much preferred a certain intangible stability, which in moments of crisis was found more often among the more reckless, mad dog, "hell bent for leather" type of individual who exhibited a spontaneous, reflexive response to skillfully kill and silence the enemy before the enemy disposed of him. It was: *Do it to them before they do it to you.*

The 499th, Bats Outa Hell Squadron (so named at a wild prayer meeting by Captain Julian B. Baird, with the insignia designed by Corporal John Michalowski) was flying this mission with us. The *bat* likeness that covered the entire noses of their B-25s, was an awesome and fear-inspiring spectacle — even before the pilots hit the gun buttons that released 9,000 rounds of fifty caliber ammo per minute out of those *bat* mouths.

"I'm glad we've got company," said Zuber, "if only to draw some of the Jap *ack-ack* away from us!"

As the weapon's carrier vehicle stopped to let our crew step out under the wing of *199*, the Sergeant driver said, "Good luck today, Lieutenant!"

"Thank you, Sergeant," I replied, thinking to myself it looked like we'd need it. The Army said that for every man actually attacking the enemy with a gun in combat, it took ten noncombatant personnel supporting him (behind the lines and in the states) to perform vital functions of supply, training, armament, transportation, intelligence, and a hundred other jobs to just get him out there to kill the enemy. At that moment I wondered how I got to be that one in combat instead of one of those ten who were supporting me back there out of sight!

Walking around the *Touch O' Texas* I saw that maintenance had repaired and covered the jagged holes in the fuselage (from the last strike) with large squares of bright new aluminum. Our airplane was needed so quickly for this mission, the painters hadn't had time to paint and blend the new aluminum squares into the overall camouflage design.

"Looks like our baby's got the bright measles on her bottom," observed Kenney.

"I'm sorry, Lieutenant, but the painters didn't have time to get to it," responded Sergeant Albright, crew chief *extraordinaire,* "we barely had time to make the necessary repairs to make her flyable!"

"That's all right!" I quickly added. "Those who see us from the front ain't gonna be around to tell their children about it; and those lucky enough to see us depart, will only see us with our rear in gear and lightin' a shuck."

As I climbed into the cockpit Townsley asked me if I had any special instructions for the copilot.

"Just don't forget the toggle switch that turns on the camera as we go over the target. You can forget just about anything else, but we might salvo you, if you don't get the pictures!

"Of course, if you think I'm about to fly this baby into the ground, or a ship, you pull us out of it. I haven't yet, thank the Lord, but I think Cronin has thought I've come close a couple of times."

The ground crew, two men on each engine, manually pulled the three-bladed propellers through to force out any oil that might have drained into the lower cylinders following Sergeant Albright's pre-flight check a couple of hours earlier.

With the props pulled through I set the throttles at one-half inch, pushed the prop control all the way forward, advanced the mixture control to 'full rich,' adjusted the Supercharger to low blower, opened the cowl flaps, turned the 'carburetor air' to full cold, closed the oil coolers, turned the 'Battery Disconnect Switches' to on; checked the 'Booster Pumps' on, turned the Ignition Switch and the Ignition Safety Switch to the left engine to on; hit the energizer and prime, yelled 'Clear Left' and start! After the engine started, I immediately checked the oil pressure and then repeated the same procedure to start the second engine.

To "start engines" in combat means to kill or be killed! The adrenalin started pumping. We were off down the runway.

Hainan Island, appearing first as a dark line on the horizon, loomed up out of the China sea some three hours later and Kenney and Townsley assisted me with the fifty pounds of flak suit.

"I've grown so used to this flak *zoot suit* I might just wear it home after the war!"

"You'd be the rage at the prom," replied Kenney.

"Whatta you know about a prom?" I asked, "Pat Neff would no more allow a prom on the Baylor campus than he would allow an atheist to speak in chapel."

"You're right," replied Kenney, "but some of my friends at that liberal Christian school up in Dallas . . . SMU . . . told me about a prom once."

"What does that E6B confuser tell you about our ETA to Hainan?" I asked.

"It says we're gonna be about three minutes early."

"That's good. Maybe we'll slip up on their blind side even more."

Captain Jones had "Arky" Vaughn, originally a member of our crew, as squadron navigator, and they were searching for the right valley that would guide us into Yulin Bay. After passing two, the Captain turned into a third chasm 5,000 feet deep and from three to five miles wide. The mountains on each side were almost perpendicular and covered with dense growth of indescribable beauty. Looking up at the mountain tops on either side, it was as if we'd been swallowed up by the earth! The nine ships of the 501st are stacked in three-ship flights, one above the other. The 499th, with their nine *Bats Outa' Hell* bat faces gleaming from the noses of their airplanes in the spotty sunshine, were a sight to see! The sun was shining in and around the little puffs of cumulus clouds floating in the great valley, and the *Bats* were stacked in three echelon flights below us. Framed by the steep mountainsides, the eighteen airplanes in close formation, with the bottom flight separated from Captain Jones's lead flight by only five hundred feet, was a spectacle of aerial beauty. The sides of the mountains got closer as the valley got narrower, the further we flew toward our target. A few isolated natives on the mountainsides, at eye level to our aircraft at four thousand feet, seemed close enough to shake hands. They were aborigines, and, like their Filipino and New Guinea counterparts, probably hated the Japs!

"Hope one of those natives doesn't have a radio transmitter to alert the Jap navy in Yulin Bay," I said to Townsley.

"Ain't it the truth; but you can bet I'd have some kind of observation post up at this end of the island to protect my shipping in the Bay if I were the Japs!"

We had eaten the Japs' lunch in the early days of the war when they'd sent their troopships and barges unescorted into New Britain, Buna, and New Guinea, and our Aussie and French Planter spotters would tip us off. Our first B-25 bomber-strafers made their debut, and established our reputation, at the beginning of the war with such help.

"Look at that view! Have you ever seen anything that beautiful?" exclaimed Townsley, pointing to a waterfall that plunged a thousand feet, almost straight down.

"And look at that sky! Have you ever seen anything as beautiful as that deep, clear blue with those little marshmallow puffs of cloud," sighed Kenney, as he left his navigating, and got ready for the target. "Why would they waste it here in the middle of a war?"

"I think it's a giant mural painted by the Japs to throw us off," I grinned at him over my shoulder.

As the mountains started to fade and the southern coastal plain of Hainan Island appeared, it was instantly obvious that we had taken the wrong valley and had missed Yulin Bay. There was no wailing or gnashing of teeth in aircraft *199* — or in any other of the eighteen airplanes making that strike. Just one of those little military *snafus* that saves your life!

"Kit Bag Leader to all aircraft!" came Captain Jones's

voice over the intership radio, breaking radio silence for the first time, "Split up and hit secondary targets! Watch for enemy fighters!" Having blown our cover, and having lost the element of surprise, we had no alternative.

I needed no further prompting. Sweating from the heat and fear generated from the anticipated, but now aborted, suicidal attack in the fish barrel of Yulin Bay against the Jap Imperial Navy, I breathed a *Thank you, Lord.*

Hugging the top of a mountain, I slipped over the edge and streaked down the other side of it toward the open sea. A very large red brick factory on the nearest edge of a town received my full attention. The nine thousand rounds per minute from my twelve .50 caliber machine guns ate through and disintegrated the red brick target like a giant termite might do away with a rotten log. The water tower for this community, rising forty feet in the air, was directly in my line of flight so I perforated it liberally, destroying the water supply and creating a giant shower. Standing at my shoulder, the now excited and impetuous ex-Baylor Bear, Nat Kenney, was pointing out targets.

"Let me fire a gun! Let me drop a bomb!" yelled Kenney, caught up in the moment, "let me fly the airplane!"

At that moment we heard the unmistakable sound of ripping, tearing metal, like an axe slicing through the side of the airplane, and *199* shuddered. I glanced down the left wing to see a clean, round hole, the size of a volleyball, about five feet from where I sat. We also saw tracers that looked as if they were coming right into the cockpit, but which vanished over the top of the plexiglass at the last instant.

"Check to see if they hit one of the wing tanks!" I yelled at Kenney, as I put the nose of the airplane into the source of our aggravation, and shut it down as quickly as it had started.

I turned my attention to the courthouse, a three-storied building in the center of town, and in the top turret, Warnick joined me in a crescendo of destruction that left the building in shambles and burning. I pushed the nose of the airplane down, into an opening below the trees for our protection as we got out of town.

Later, and coming from behind a hill on the coast at 275 mph, we saw a heavy gun emplacement right in front of us with about fifty Jap soldiers lined up in three ranks for inspection. I gave them the last instructions most of them would ever receive as the .50s littered the sand with enemy. This was the mouth of Yulin Bay and this gun emplacement, had we found the right valley, would've been waiting to ambush us as we came out of the harbor. As it was, fate turned the tables and the ambushor became the ambushee, *c'est la guerre!* This was the original logic expressed by General Kenney, first Commanding Officer of the Fifth Air Force: to destroy and kill the enemy from above and thereby reduce the number of Japs our ground forces would have to kill on the ground.

"They are vermin," the General had flatly stated, "that must be exterminated!"

I kept the airplane so close to the water that we threw up a cloud of spray behind us for a hundred yards or more. Water temperature was constant so the air was smooth and it was like flying on a velvet carpet. Staying that low was doubly beneficial to our cause: the enemy *Zekes* couldn't dive on us without going into the water, and the Jap gunners had a much more difficult time trying to hit targets that were moving away at minimum altitude and that were taking evasive action.

"Pilot to crew. Do you have any damage in the back? Over!"

"Just a couple of holes in the fuselage," reported Zuber.

"We have a beautiful large hole through our left wing between the left engine and the cockpit," I reported, "and we can thank the Lord it wasn't an explosive shell that detonated on contact! I don't think it hit any of the three main gas tanks in the immediate area of the wing. What does it look like from the top turret, Warnick? Over."

"I can't see any evidence of a gasoline leak, Lieutenant," replied Warnick, "but I'll keep an eye on it! It's a miracle that a shell that big could go completely through the wing in that location and not hit a gas tank."

"Keep your eyes peeled for fighters. Some of the others have stirred up a hornets' nest and they're battling 'em right now!"

We climbed to 5,000 feet and Kenney gave me a heading back to the Philippines. I reduced the propeller pitch to 1,750 rpm and the manifold pressure to twenty-six inches of mercury. I had already leaned out the mixture control to cruising lean, and now lowered it even more.

"You got it runnin' on the fumes now," said Townsley.

"I know, but we've got a long way to go and what we do now might just keep us from getting our feet wet!"

I pulled the mixture control below cruising lean; the next notch was *off:* the position to kill the engines when we got on the ground. As the engines received less fuel, the cylinder head temperature began to rise, which, if I reduced the amount of gasoline going to the cylinders any more, would burn the engines up. I locked the mixture control into its position just below cruising lean, and left it there, back to the Philippines.

"Kenney," I asked, turning halfway around in the pilot's seat, "how's our heading?"

"We're doing fine! Our ground speed is one hundred eighty knots and the fuel consumption, while close, is all right!"

"You've been wantin' to get in on the action!"

"You betcha I have! Nothing is more frustrating than having to stand here behind you while we're over the target and do nothing!"

"Well, we're gonna remedy that today! Townsley is gonna slide out of his copilot's seat and we're gonna let you fly it for a while. How about it?"

"Hot Dog!" exclaimed Kenney, "I'm ready!" With us well on our way home, and surely we could not miss something as big as the Island of Luzon, I felt it safe for Kenney to get the flying time he wanted so much.

"Now you know how important it is to maintain that heading and this altitude?"

"Yeah! I got it!"

"She's all trimmed up. She's all yours," I said.

Rather than letting the airplane fly itself, Kenney made the mistake of all novice airmen by trying to force his will on the ship in an uncoordinated manner. He would lose two hundred feet altitude, then he would gain three hundred feet of altitude. As he gradually got back to our cruising altitude of 5,000 feet he lost our heading when he looked at the cylinder head temperature. As he looked from the compass to the big hole in the wing, back to the needle and ball, or the artificial horizon, the airplane would start to lose altitude. He couldn't do it all at once. You would've thought we were in an elevator! Up four hundred feet, down five hundred feet! Five degrees off heading — back on heading. After fifteen minutes of this mental and physical struggle the sweat was pouring off his forehead, down his cheeks, and into his eyes. He was starting to sweat through his flight suit.

"Here, take this thing!" he said, "I've had enough! It's time for me to check our position anyway!"

"Pilot to Warnick. Have you checked our fuel consumption with the navigator? Over!"

"I transferred the last of our gas out of the radio tanks just before we turned down the valley through the mountains of Hainan. I think we've got enough to make it back to base but don't go the long way around!"

The shortage of fuel, with every mission demanding we fly to the farthest reaches of the China sea to seek and destroy the enemy, caused a constant nervous stress. The prolonged thoughts about coughing, stuttering and then silent engines, with props rotating in the wind without power to turn them, "could give you nightmares and provide a trip to the funny farm" in Lyman's words. My fears didn't surface immediately, but usually came about an hour after we'd hit the target, and had resolved the worry set aside for taking a direct hit, losing an engine or having to ditch. Only when you could shift your worry to the lesser dangers of not enough fuel to get you home could you relax. Worries had their priorities!

We landed at San Marcelino nine hours and thirty-five minutes after we had taken off, with forty gallons of gasoline left for each engine. We could only have stayed in the air another twenty, twenty-five minutes! *God was with us and I am indeed thankful* was my diary entry after the strike to Hainan. We were among the lucky ones. The 345th *Air Apaches* would line the bottom of Yulin Bay with our aircraft before the war was over.

"We took the wrong turn," I said to Captain Jones, coming out of the interrogation tent, "we didn't hit the correct valley through the Five Finger Mountains!"

"Yeah. Something like that," he said, winking at me.

"I still think the best strategy against Jap shipping is to let 'em come out of those harbors and bays into the open sea where we can get at 'em without all those gun emplacments and shore batteries to help 'em out!"

"I like that approach, too," he replied, "and our subs along the China coast keep us advised of every enemy ship movement for five hundred miles, all within our range!"

"Well, those who missed today at Yulin Bay, will live to fight another day!" I said.

"So true! So true!" replied the Captain.

That evening at chow I ran into Arky Vaughn who had been the Squadron navigator with Captain Jones earlier that day.

"Did you take the wrong canyon today, or did Captain Jones?" I asked.

"We took the wrong canyon together," replied Arky. "There are four canyons shown on the map, two of which lead to Yulin Bay. We didn't have time to fly up and down the coast of Hainan looking for the right canyon and, from the map, we thought we'd taken the right one!"

"For whatever reason we missed the canyon," I said, "I'm appreciative and thankful to be enjoying the exquisite cuisine of the 501st famous restaurant here tonight instead of being fish bait in Yulin Bay!"

"What's for chow?" I asked Lum Lamar who was coming out of the mess tent.

"I couldn't stop it with my fork but it came to me when I called it!" he replied.

"Eating here is a bear we've all got to cross!"

And while the chow barely rated zero on a scale of one to ten, the opportunity to eat it, compared to the earlier fatal alternative, made it taste like a ten-course dinner at the Waldorf-Astoria!

CHAPTER THREE

The Prayer Meeting

Wine and youth are fire upon fire.

Fielding

We *homo sapiens* deal with worry, pressure, frustration, depression, and fear in strange and startling ways. The fighting, flying and fearless cadre of the 345th Bomb Group, Fifth Air Force of World War Twice chose to meet the enemy with a bottle in each hand. And while they were absolutely without equal in the realm of courage, they were the most dedicated assemblage of drunks with whom I've ever been associated, easily surpassing the Texas Legislature, a minority number of the Texas Longhorn football team, and the Alpha Tau Omega Fraternity on the campus of The University of Texas at Austin. There were circumstances and conditions that contributed to, even aided and abetted, the inebriation of these undiffident knights of the sky.

There were those days, and they came often after we started hitting Jap shipping, that we had nothing to do because of the shortage of serviceable aircraft. These days were spent doing nothing, waiting for the next strike — and the longer we waited — the bigger the blow off. It was on these occasions, particularly on soggy afternoons, when the jungle downpours had all sacks filled with sore and sagging bodies reclining in real or imagined mental pain and battle fatigue, that an idea, suggestion, reason or excuse would appear, germinate, and spread faster than crabs on a latrine seat. Soon an all points bulletin was being broadcast. Heads would poke through tent flaps, confirmed sleepers who looked more like mummies would turn over, and the most dedicated Squadron project was on, prayer meeting tonight!

"Attention, please! Testing!" from the Orderly Room tent came Lieutenant Fisher's voice over the scratchy public address system. "Are you bored, bored, bored . . .? Hello, man overboard!"

"Get on with the announcement," came a disgruntled voice in the background.

"A prayer meeting will be held in Captain Jones's — pardon me — *Major* Jones's tent tonight, right after chow. The occasion is to celebrate Major Jones's promotion to Major and the promotions of other and lesser lights. Bring your own liquor and anything else you might have to drink. Over and out!"

And while (as leading theologians of the time openly stated) there were no atheists in the foxholes of the battlefields or in the cockpits of the strafers, you could never have proved it by the actions and conduct of the participants at a squadron prayer meeting. In those gatherings, I'm sorry to say, religion was neither the main theme nor was it ever mentioned.

"To put it bluntly, Blount," said Chester Kuta, "the main idea at a prayer meeting is to get pissy-assed, passed-out drunk!"

"But I don't drink," I responded, "I don't have anything against those who do, but I simply do not drink!"

"That's good," replied Kuta, "that'll mean that there's just that much more for me . . . and the more I drink the more I enjoy it!"

Prayer meetings were usually held to celebrate promotions but they could just as easily and mysteriously evolve to celebrate a new baby, a "Dear John" letter, the passing of the hundred-combat point mark, the arrival of the Group's *Fat Cat* (with a load of fresh eggs and booze), someone going home the next day, or the arrival of a PX ship laden with a bountiful supply of beer and liquor. The mere fact that it had been four or five days without a prayer meeting was reason enough to call such a gathering.

The Squadron immediately got busy with duffle bags, footlockers and other hidden gear being pulled out of hiding, unlocked, and precious bottles, long-hidden from sight, suddenly and miraculously made their appearance.The intoxicants ranged from three-two beer and Jack Daniels brought from stateside, to rotgut, Australian squeezings, hospital brandy and confiscated Jap rice *saki.* Most of the foreign potions didn't taste too good but "When you're out on your ass, or on your knees, how do you know how anything tastes anyway?" asked Bill Mathews.

There were two types of prayer meetings. The early prayer meetings and the later prayer meetings. The early prayer meetings were staid affairs that took place for the most part in one pyramidal tent. The later prayer meetings, starting about the time we were based at San Marcelino, found the troops wandering around and getting drunk all over the area. The later meetings involved carrying your friends out of mud puddles, foxholes, pulling them out of trees, and in every condition of limbo, and putting them to bed from two o'clock in the morning on!

The promotion prayer meeting of Major Jones, *the granddaddy of all prayer meetings,* started out in the true, and time-tested manner of the "old boys" — particularly since it was to honor our Squadron's Commanding Officer. He viewed with scorn and disgust the drunken meanderings of the newer, untrained, younger, drinking personnel, who couldn't hold their liquor in a stationary, sitting, and cultivated position. Everyone started gathering right after chow with the sun in the China sea and dusk beginning to fade into night. Everyone came bringing a chair, his canteen cup, any liquor he had or could find, and most important of all, a loud and lusty singing voice. The Air Corps had taught all of us to sing from Cadet School — where we never marched in formation without a marching song — to the present drinking celebration, where we could exhibit all the music we had ever learned. It was around the risque drinking songs that the prayer meeting revolved, and the more inebriated the participants, the more obscene became the songs.

Those songs provided a psychological release; an uninhibited chance to be wicked with no one to be shocked. With chastity enforced by geography, there was nothing left to do in the Pacific but fight, drink, and die. So we sang on the way.

"There's not enough *ooo's* in *smoothe* to describe this," announced Major Jones in response to a shot of Canadian Club poured from a long-hidden bottle, the property of Captain Musket.

The early arrivals burst into *Bell Bottomed Trousers,* with additional voices joining in as they entered the tent.

Early in the morning before the break of day,
A five pound note he handed her and this to her did say,
If you have a daughter, bounce her on your knee,
But if you have a son, send the bastard out to sea!
Singing bell bottomed trousers, coats of navy blue,
He will climb the riggin' like his daddy used to do!

"Where did you find these peanuts and cookies?" inquired a smiling Captain Holtzman in a put-on voice with a questioning look on his face.

"From the PX," replied Major Jones, "and I appreciate your helping get them here tonight, Lucky."

"The pleasure was all mine," responded Holtzman, who knew better than anyone else how the Major had gotten the *hors d'oeuvres*. He hadn't been in supply with the 500th and made captain as the Executive Officer of the 501st without knowing how to brown-nose and produce whatever a superior officer needed.

"To get ahead in this man's Air Force you have to practice the three W's," stated Lieutenant Lyman, a past master of the art.

"What's the three W's?" inquired Kuta.

"Thought you'd never ask," replied Lyman, "it's What, Who, and When — to kiss it!"

It was the general consensus that Lyman and Holtzman were champions in the art of brown-nosing.

Spontaneously, two voices started to sing and everyone joined in:

"Bless 'em all! Bless 'em all!
Bless the needle, the airspeed, the ball;
Bless all those instructors who taught me to fly—
Sent me to solo and left me to die,

If ever your plane starts to stall,
You're in for one hell of a fall!
No lilies or violets for dead strafer pilots so
Cheer up my lads bless 'em all!

Bless 'em all! Bless 'em all!
Bless the long and the short and the tall,
Bless all Lieutenants and their bloody sons,
Bless all the Sergeants who never had one,
For it's flak and not flies at Rabaul
That shoots off our ass, makes us fall,
Now boys won't you listen, don't fly any mission,
Till the peashooters cover us all!

Bless 'em all! Bless 'em all!
Bless the young and the short and the tall,
Bless all the Generals and all Colonels too,
Bless their poor judgment that kills me and you,
We bombed and we strafed Rabaul
And we really were on the ball,
But there'll be no promotions this side of the ocean,
Fifth bomber has frozen them all!"

The party was in full swing and gathering momentum when Doc Marcus, flight surgeon of the 501st, made his appearance bearing irreplaceable, unmatchable gifts. The sudden eruption of sound from the assemblage when they saw what the good Doctor was waving in the air, would have done credit to the response of Texas partisans to a Longhorn TD against Oklahoma in the Cotton Bowl.

"I thought the best thing I could do for this occasion would be to contribute three fifths of Old Grand-Dad 'medicinal-purposes only' whiskey," he announced to the continuing swell of cheers and appreciation.

"If this activity is not in the best interest of the health and mental well-being of this unit, the purpose for which I dispense this prescription," he continued, "then I'll go back and write another prescription!" The only time we ever saw Old Grand-Dad smiling at us from the wrapper on the bottle was when we returned from a mission and we were at the interrogation table. Doc Marcus personally dispensed the whiskey, (which he kept under lock and key) to all combat personnel after each strike. The effectiveness of the enemy resistance encountered, the roughness of the mission, all determined how much Old

Grand-Dad you got — which ranged from a stiff shot to half a canteen cup.

"Did you bring the grapefruit juice, Doc?" I inquired when the party settled down and the rush for the "medicinal prescription" had subsided. The grapefruit juice, also provided by the good Doctor, was used as a chaser for the Old Grand-Dad by the imbibers.

"I just happened to bring along a can of grapefruit juice," he said, "kinda thinking you might want your special brand! Besides, under the laws of the state of New Jersey, you're too young to drink intoxicants anyway!" he said.

"Thanks, Doc, you're the greatest," I replied, "and I'm too young to drink in Texas, too! Do you reckon I'm too young to fight?"

"I'll pass on that," he laughed, "and take the fifth! No pun intended!"

Captain John F. Marcus, flight surgeon of the 501st, openly maintained that drinking and relaxation was the greatest mental and physical therapy for flying combat personnel, a medical theory in which he enjoyed the unanimous support of the squadron he served.

"I'm predicting a Squadron state of drunkeness that will reach epidemic proportions this evening!" was the way Doc Marcus put it. That was an understatement. The entire 501st was tanked! The whole Squadron didn't ordinarily get plastered simultaneously, although there were pockets of dipsomaniacs that met nightly. But the chemistry, as well as the reason, was perfect for a rip-roaring drunk! And if the promotion of our Squadron CO wasn't enough, the persistent and constant prospect of not surviving tomorrow's mission encouraged everyone to fill and refill their canteen cups.

The 501st was a study in intoxication. There were crawling drunks, crying drunks, confessional drunks, laughing drunks, stubborn drunks, pleasant drunks, complaining drunks and, in the words of Thatcher, "knee-walking, commode-hugging drunks!" There were drunks who talked about the good old days, after-the-war-is-over drunks, sexual conquests drunks (actual and imagined), flying drunks, none of whom, perish the thought, would ever drink alone. There were argumentative drunks, belligerent drunks, fighting drunks, but, because of their training, they were all *singing drunks,* which prevented riots, curbed tempers and saved untold lives.

"Statistics last year show that freight car loading went down eighteen percent," said Stiles, the intellectual, "but during that same period, whiskey sales went up twenty-six percent, which shows that more people are getting loaded than freight cars!"

"Like a little Bible belt, Chaplain?" offered a well-soused Chester Phillips.

"You don't offer the Chaplain a drink," reprimanded Thatcher. "Excuse him, Father!"

"That's all right, my son," replied Father Kozlowski, "I'm joining Lieutenant Blount in some of that fruit juice chaser."

"The meek may inherit the earth, Chaplain," said a drunken, ordinarily reserved Fisher, "but ish the horshish assish who get the promotions!"

"There's much logic in your statement, my son," responded Father Kozlowski.

Lieutenant Lyman had impressed me from the moment I had first met him as a replacement pilot. He had a twinkle in his eye that indicated, correctly, that he was full of it, would try anything, and was cut from the same cloth as the Ensign Pulver character of *Mr. Roberts* fame. In retrospect, Lyman could have given Jack Lemmon a run for his money as the devilish, ingenious Ensign Pulver in the movie version of this naval classic.

"Can you get extra points for going home by giving blood?" asked Lieutenant Lyman, who was feeling no pain.

"No, I'm afraid we have no facilities for taking your blood, Lieutenant," replied Doc Marcus.

"I think you better seriously start getting rid of me, Doc," continued Lyman, "that is, I mean, you better *seriously* start thinking about getting rid of me, Doc! I'm crazy! I'm out of my skull!"

"Lieutenant Lyman, if I got rid of all the crazies in this outfit I'd be the loneliest man in this camp!"

"Aw . . . come on, Doc, gimme a Section Eight!"

"You're not crazy, Lieutenant," argued Doc Marcus, "a little inebriated, yes. But crazy? No!"

"Then how about a Section Four!"

"Because you're half crazy — right?" Marcus laughed out loud.

"Okay! How about a Section Two to Sydney, and I'll swim home from there!"

Doc Marcus threw his head back and laughed even more, and the small circle who had been listening to the conversation was equally entertained.

"War is like chess," said Major Giese, "Losing a pawn doesn't mean anything! Winning the game is what's important!"

"Horseshit!" responded an uninhibited Thatcher. "It all depends on whether you're the pawn!"

As if by spontaneous combustion another favorite tune of the 501st suddenly burst forth:

"I used to work in Chicago in a department store,
I used to work in Chicago, I did, but I don't anymore.

A woman came in, she wanted some hose,
And then she wanted some more,

I laid 'er down, and hosed her I did,
I did but I don't anymore.

"Was that spam hash we had at chow tonight?" asked a new pilot.

"Yeah," replied McGrane, "and what we don't eat we drop on the Japs tomorrow!"

"What're you doing with that whiskey, Major?" asked Jay Moore.

"I'm savoring the nectar of nature. You inhale it, entice it up through your nostrils, savor its aroma, allow it to float around your head, then treat your palate to a luxurious taste fantasy. Such an intoxicating experience is only fit for a king," replied Major Giese.

"No booze for me," I cracked, "it offends my palate — not to mention my co-palate!"

"It doesn't offend me," answered Cronin, my copilot, "in fact, I'll take all you want to get rid of, Major!"

"All right, gentlemen," shouted Lyman, waving his canteen cup in the air, the *Strafer's Song*! The group needed no further prodding, if indeed, they needed anything but the suggestion, and we were off — with all forty-five airmen singing at the top of their lungs to the tune of *Man on the Flying Trapeze*.

Once I's a Gadget, an innocent lad,
The Chaplain did teach me the right from the bad
Of all his advice, these words were his last
Don't fly too high and don't fly too fast!
So I joined the strafers with these words in mind
And off to New Guinea did go
But when I arrived, what did I find?
That the strafers fly too fuckin' low . . . Oh-h-h-h!
Chorus:

We fly o'er the trees with inches to spare
With blood in our eyes and gray in our hair
Our tracers look fine as a strafing we go
But look out there brother, you're flying too low!

Lyman, who was a connoisseur of our drinking songs, once wrote them all down, "because they'll be important someday." He broke right into another favorite:

Roll me over, in the clover,
Roll me over, lay me down, and do it again!

"How about some of Uncle Ben's perverted rice?" offered Kuta.

"You mean *saki*?" inquired Everett Thies.

"Thas right," responded Kuta, raising a green bottle of the pure white liquid and speaking in thick-tongued, halting speech.

"Where'd you get that stuff, Kuta?" asked Thies.

"Shum of our infantry boys brought it in," explained Kuta, "and it tashe pretty good!" He didn't know or care how it tasted, in his condition.

"And you don't use a chaser," chuckled Cronin. "Nothin's fast enough to catch it!"

"It's my pleshur — gimme your attention!" Holtzman was rapping with a bottle on the table in the center of the tent.

"Holtzman, you bastard, you're drunk!' shouted Lieutenant Pallotta, "but I give you my personal, standing ovation!" As he attempted to rise to his feet in his inebriated condition, he lurched forward, and landed face down on top of two of his buddies who were already on their knees on the dirt floor of the tent.

"Cover that stinkin', garlic eating Italian with a blanket!

Give me your attenshun, please!" Holtzman was still trying to get the drunks quiet.

"Ish my pleasure to present First Lieutenant Blount who was a *second* lieutenant until this afternoon, who is goin' to make the first speech tonight! Lesh have a big hand for First Lieutenant Blounsh!" Wild applause!

"Thank you, Captain Holtzman. Since our host and honoree, Major Jones, is from *Texas*, (Bronx cheers) I thought I'd just say a few words about Texas." More Bronx cheers!

"My Mother always told me never to ask anyone where they came from. She said "If they're from Texas they'll tell you and if they're not, there's no sense in embarrassing them." More boos and cheers.

"In my vast, world-wide travels —," I tried to continue, "I — "

"You've traveled your West Texas ass all the way from Muleshoe to Manila and from San Angelo to San Marcelino," interrupted Don Hardeman from San Angelo, Texas.

" — as I was saying before I was so rudely interrupted by the uncouth gentleman waving the bilious orange and blue pennant of the San Angelo Bobcats, in my world-wide travels I have found there are only two kinds of people — Texans, and those who want to be." More boos and cheers.

"Now you're probably thinking I'm going to get strung out here and tell you a lot of funny things about Texas," I said.

"Yeah," responded Major Giese, "you're going to tell us whether we want to hear 'em or not!"

"Now that's not right, Major," I replied, "back home we tell 'em to each other and we love to hear 'em. It's just 'cause we're so danged proud of our dirt, cactus, rocks, ticks, chiggers, buzzards, mosquitos, and rattlesnakes that we never get tired of bragging about 'em! We don't brag much on ourselves but we can dang sure brag on Texas.

"You think we've got weather here in the Philippines," I continued, "but you ain't seen nothin' until you've seen Texas weather. We had a mule team headin' west a few years back on a mighty hot day in September when a blue norther came up. The lead mule froze to death and the mule at the other end of the team died of sunstroke. Simultaneously.

"We have some funny things in west Texas, too, and one of these is the loco weed. The scientists down at Texas A&M have never been able to isolate the active ingredients of this drug, but they've been trying for years. It's as harmless and innocent looking as a grass widow, but if a horse or cow gets a mouthful they become addicted and start acting like we're acting here tonight. In fact, if any self-respecting rancher saw y'all acting the way you're acting tonight, he'd castrate, worm, dip and dehorn every one of you!'

"You tell 'em, Blount," exclaimed Lieutenant Bell, the raucous Oklahoma cowboy, who waved his hat in exuberant support, "no self-respectin' cowhand would ever get this drunk without goin' to the jail and payin' his fine in advance! Turn out the lights and call the law!"

"You've gone too far," exclaimed Major Giese, "and you're stone cold sober, too!"

"Somebody has to chaperone this shindig," I replied, "and tell it like it is!" This didn't win any friends, but did influence some people!

"You're getting ready to have a drink, with all of us, right now," stated the Major, "isn't that right, boys?" Of course when the Major spoke people moved and they all came in my direction. Once again I had been talking when I should have been listening as six assorted Lieutenants, all inebriated, grabbed me and held me upside down while Giese tried to pour Old Grand-Dad down my throat.

"Why do you want to waste that Old Grand-Dad," I asked Giese from a completely immobile horizontal position on the dirt floor of the tent, "you guys love that stuff so much I don't understand why you want to waste it." I hardly got another word out as the whiskey went in my eyes, ears, hair, and down the front of my shirt with a minimal amount getting in my mouth. The other forty or so members of the prayer meeting were beside themselves as they fully enjoyed the wrestling match. I didn't struggle or put up much of a fight to thwart the Major's determined effort to have me drink with the Squadron. With six assistants (two of whom were sitting on my chest) I figured I might as well relax and enjoy it as much as possible.

"What's a kid like that doing in combat?" inquired Major Giese, perhaps the oldest person present with the exception of Doc Marcus.

"Maybe there was no opening on the Joint Chiefs of Staff!" volunteered Major Jones.

"They had to make him a First Lieutenant," replied Giese, "he's too young to be an enlisted man!"

"Another song," volunteered Lieutenant Chester Phillips from Akron, Ohio "let's sing "Hardships You Bastards" and with feeling!" At that stage of the evening Chester couldn't feel anything. He was numb, and doing well to remain ambulatory.

> *Flying up to old Wewak, 10 to 1 you don't come back*
> *Singing Hardships, you bastards, you don't know what hardships are!*
>
> *Flying up to old Luzon, you look around and your wing man's gone,*
> *Singing Hardships, hardships, you don't know what hardships are!*

On such occasions arguments always ensued and differences of opinion surfaced between individuals that would have never been mentioned had those involved never bent their elbows and gotten under the influence.

"They're gonna get you for an Air Force military violation, Esty," said Johnson, a fellow pilot.

"I'm military and I've never been violated," chimed in Phillips during a lull in the conversation, "but I'd like to be — hic!"

"What kind of military violation, Johnson?" asked Esty.

"Loitering at the controls of a B-25!" replied Johnson. I stepped in between the two principals of the conversation as traces of temper flared.

"Hold it, gentlemen!" I said.

"You've got to be a man first before you can be a gentleman," said Esty, "and he misses on both counts!"

"Differences!" said Lieutenant Baker, "I presume you'll settle it like children!"

"Shay, Lyman," said a now well-embalmed Thatcher, "you know how a limber dick and a rattlesnake are alike?"

"How ish a limber dick like a rattlesnake?" repeated Lyman.

"You don't fuck with either one of 'em!" replied Thatcher, doubling up in convulsive laughter at his own joke.

"How about another song, Chester!" I said, "we need another good song."

"Okay, First Liueutenant Blount," he mumbled, rising to his even less stable feet, "Okay, old buddy! Let's do it!"

"Sounds good, Chester! Anything you say! Let 'er rip!"

"All right, everybody . . . with feeling!" and Lieutenant Chester Phillips smiled at me with drunk, unfocused eyes that were open, but didn't blink, and that stared straight ahead, but didn't see! I knew that he couldn't see me! He was only speaking and answering in the direction of my voice! (The now totally uninhibited inebriates burst forth to the tune of *Bless 'em All*)

> *Fuck 'em all! Fuck 'em all! Fuck the long and the short and the tall,*
> *For we're off hedge hoppin' with one gun a poppin' so cheer up now boys, fuck 'em all!*
>
> *Oh, it's bombs and not bullshit we throw,*
> *As after the Japs we go,*
> *For we're off hedge hoppin' with one gun a poppin'*
> *So cheer up now boys, fuck 'em all!*

Lieutenant Phillips's legs gave way at this point in the melody and he fell back into a drunken stupor leaving the remaining eight or ten conscious, ambulatory singers he was directing without a song leader.

"Why all this preoccupation with sex?" asked Thies to nobody in particular..

"Cause there's no occupation like sex!" stated Lyman, coming up for air and then going back to sleep in his chair.

"Sexual freedom is a partner of the war," added Thatcher, philosophically, taking a long draw on his cigarette followed by a sip of the Old Grand-Dad he was nursing. "The moral decay of the weaker sex is directly proportionate to the intensity of the war!"

"And the shortage of male companionship in Sydney!" added Doc Marcus fully aware of Thatcher's conquests in the Australian R and R city of the 345th.

"That might be a factor all right, Doc," added Thatcher.

"All the sex and this excessive drinking — I don't worry about it," continued Doc, "when the war is over and we get out of this hell and all get back home, everybody will forget their drinking, everything that caused it, and we'll be back to a normal life!"

"You're mighty damn right, Doc!" said Kuta, "Yesh shir, you're right as rain! After this war is over, I'm never gonna take (hic) another drink! But *pussy*, Doc, pussy is . . . *Roll me over in the clover, Roll me over lay me down and —* " and he sang himself back to sleep, leaning against the center tent pole.

The prayer meeting was in overdrive, some of our fearless warriors were sleeping soundly in positions of contortion that would have done honor to a Walt Disney cartoon and everyone was out, or nearly out, of control.

"I gather you drink?" said Lathrop to a bleary-eyed, reeling, Don Hardeman.

"Only to excess!" replied his friend, staggering to stay on his feet.

"Your attention, please," I said, at the top of my voice, "give me your attention." I was experiencing as much trouble as Holtzman, or more, in my attempt to hold down the noise while trying to tone down the grossly uninhibited, and completely saturated revelers.

"We've come to that part of the program where we recognize the honoree, the gentleman for whom this festive occasion was organized, planned in detail, and has now been carried out in dedicated, devoted, efficient, and excessive drinking!" Wild applause, Bronx cheers, and obscene gestures followed this announcement.

"From the ornate, canvas Arrogance Ballroom of the Jungleland Hotel in downtown San Marcelino, Luzon, Philippines, it has been our pleasure to bring you the sweetest music this side of heaven from the *Black Panther* Squallers' chorale ensemble, singing obscene, never-heard-before, pornographic ditties. And to our honoree, formerly Captain, but now *Major* Jones, our fearless leader, as a reward for your appearance on our show this evening you shall be flown at our own United States Combat Airline's expense, 1,263 and one-half feet to Colonel Coltharp's double canvas, mosquito proofed, and Japanese beetle-eradicated tent where you will enjoy totally free, and at government expense, the Olive Drab Room, which overlooks the beautiful, refurbished Enlisted Men's latrine, which emits beautiful sounds and continuous odors for your enjoyment and entertainment. You will dine in sumptuous splendor at the Philippine gourmet's delight in the Southwest Pacific's most famous restaurant, Tommy's Tantalizing Ptomaine Terror Restaurant, featuring powdered milk, powdered eggs, dehydrated and diced carrots, beets and potatoes, that all taste amazingly alike. You will feast on that rare, succulent delicacy of Roast of Spam, Brisquet of Spam, T-Bone Spam, Strip Sirloin of Spam, Club Spam, French Fried Spam, Filet of Spam, Broiled Spam, Spam Hash, and Cold Cuts of Spam — served pied, dyed, fried, laid down on the side, and topped off with that famous gastronomic Southwest Pacific dessert of selected flour-filled chocolate bars from a dinner K-Ration!"

Much applause, yelling, and "Speech! Speech!" came from the imbibers.

"Some men are born to greatness," Major Jones began, still in control and carrying through the theme of the occasion, "some men have it thrust upon them . . . and a very . . . yes, but only a very few men are ever given the honor to lead the finest outfit in the entire U.S. Army Air Corps . . . the 501st Bomb Squadron!"

Much applause, more yelling, waving of canteen cups, bottles, and assorted intoxicants.

"And since it's now three A.M.," continued Major Jones, "and even the roosters are comatose, I'd like to offer one last toast: Here's to longer lives and shorter wars!"

"Hear! Hear!" responded Doc Marcus and Major Giese.

Everyone still on their feet, (and there weren't many) and several who were sitting in the dirt, raised their canteen cups and drank together.

"If we had a whispur of moral character, Major," said Kuta, "we wouldn't be standin' . . . uh, sittin', here drinkin'! We'd be soberin' up for that mission in the mornin'!"

"That mission is in three hours, Lieutenant! Let's put a cork in it," said Major Jones. "We fly at 5:30!"

"That's only two and a half hours from now," said Hardeman, suddenly coming wide awake with the realization that the night was gone.

"That's why we've got to put the cork in the bottle," replied Major Jones. The now docile and inebriated *Black Panthers,* by ones and twos, leaned, fell, staggered, crawled, and stumbled back to their separate tents.

"Yes, shur! They should throw all the guns away," said a tanked and philosophical Thatcher, "I mean *all* the guns, and invite all the soldiers on both sides to a prayer meeting! *The last man on his feet wins the war!*"

"Very commendable," replied Doc Marcus, trying to assist Thatcher to his feet and get him pointed toward his tent, "but that's too much logic and common sense for the warlords of Japan and our Joint Chiefs of Staff to comprehend."

It was one of those brilliant, full moon nights by which you could read a newspaper — if you had one. As we neared our tent we heard a human voice howling, emitting a sound much like the mating call of a wolf in heat.

"What is that?" exclaimed Lathrop.

"Sounds like somebody is in big trouble — or great pain!" I replied.

Stepping behind the tent for a look, the mystery was quickly solved. Lieutenant Phillips was down on his hands and knees and with his head thrown back was howling and baying at the moon in a most persuasive, hound dog fashion.

"What are we gonna do with him?" Lathrop asked.

"We could put wheels on him and enter him in the Soap Box Derby," I suggested. I picked him up, threw him over my shoulder and carried him to his tent. Taking off his boots, I put him in his bed and tucked in the mosquito netting around his sack. I wanted him to sleep off as much booze and get as much rest as he could possibly cram into the next two-and-a-half hours. I was selfish, as well as benevolent, in my charitable assistance. He would be flying my left wing on the eight-hour strike against the Jap's mammoth Toyohara Airdrome in three hours, and that would demand all the flying skills a stone cold sober individual could muster, much less one who had been a passed-out drunk only two hours before. Toyohara Airdrome promised to be an interesting mission.

"Lieutenant! Time to rise and shine!" came the most irritating voice I had ever heard, arousing me from a deep and sound sleep. The Officer of the Day, shining a flashlight in my face through the mosquito netting, gave me a friendly nudge in the ribs to make sure I was awake.

"I'll rise," I answered, sitting up and feeling with my feet for my boots on the ground, "but after last night I won't shine very much! Besides, I don't recognize but one 5 o'clock per day! The one at 1700!"

"Why do you always turn your boots up and shake 'em before puttin' 'em on?" inquired Lathrop.

"If you ever slept on the ground in west Texas," I replied, "and crowded a scorpion or a rattler by puttin' your foot in a boot that's been on the ground all night, you'd shake your boots too!"

"How do you fly in those boots?" inquired Thies, making reference to my infantry combat boots. "They can't give you a very sensitive touch on the rudder controls!"

"He wore those things on a strike to the coast of Indochina last week and they gave him the DFC," said Blair. "If he'd walked in 'em they'd probably given him the Congressional Medal of Honor!"

"It's not parlor slippers and Stearmans we're flying, men," I replied, "it's more like cowboy boots and Sherman tanks when it comes to kicking twenty tons of airplane around below the treetops at 300 mph!

"And if we crash-land, I'm prepared for the long walk out. I'm using my kidney!" I added, pointing to my head. What time is it?"

"Nearly half past the twentieth century," came a smart retort, "but specifically it's 0500 and breakfast is served in the main dining room."

"We only went to bed a couple of hours ago," responded Thies.

"Think how good that sack's gonna feel tonight!" said Blair.

"If General MacArthur wasn't countin' on me — if I wasn't so indispensable to winnin' this war — I'd just crawl right back in that sack," said Kuta. "But because it's my patriotic duty, I'm gettin' up to help you boys out, up there at Formosa today!"

"Your hemorrhoids and all?" inquired Lathrop.

"Yeah! My bleedin', bloody hemorrhoids and all!" replied Kuta.

"Now that's damn nice and mighty thoughtful of you, Kuta," responded Ed Bina, "and it'll keep you from gettin' a court-martial, too!"

"It's too early for that true red, white and blue," I said, "save it for the Toyohara homecoming about noon today."

At breakfast that morning the fighting 501st was the sickest, most hung over group of non-aggressive looking human beings I had ever observed. Although ambulatory, you wondered if they could make it to their airplanes, much less fly them.

"Good morning, troops. How's the cuisine?" I announced in something louder than a normal tone of voice as I entered the mess tent.

"Shut up, Blount!" growled Johnson, placing both hands over his ears as if trying to hold his head on, "don't underestimate your power to be a pain in the ass."

"Obviously there are those present who do not appreciate abstinence," I responded, "and the physical exhilaration associated with throwing off the shackles of slumber, to observe a Philippines sunrise that comes up like thunder out of the officers' latrine!"

At that moment, the haggard, drooping, and stumbling Lieutenant Chester Phillips, who only a short time before had been on hands and knees baying at the moon, made his subdued entry into the mess tent.

"Get your platter and watch it splatter," I said, handing him a metal tray.

"Now I know who invented the blind staggers and the DTs," said Kenney.

"Whatta we have for breakfast?" he asked, squinting through bloodshot eyes, trying to see what the cooks were putting on his tray.

"It'll fill you up if you can keep it down," I answered, "in honor of our CO's promotion, the special for today is called 'His Majorosity on a Shingle.' " Lieutenant Phillips gagged and I thought he was going to throw up.

Chester Phillips was lean of build, wore a thin hairline mustache and had worked in radio stations in Ohio and Pennsylvania in civilian life. The language he spoke came out in round dulcet tones that you could readily associate with American radio. "We should make arrangements to share you as the announcer for Tokyo Rose," I said, "it would sure 'liven up her broadcasts!

"You were down there bayin' at the moon last night," I continued. "You were something — great sound effects for a radio presentation of *The Hounds of the Baskervilles.*"

I was interested in seeing Chester consume several cups of

hot coffee, since he would be flying my left wing during the strike in the next couple of hours.

"Make the tent pole stop swaying," sighed Chester, "and if the tables keep dancing around, I'm gonna crawl outa here."

"You can't crawl out of here," I replied, "you gotta be sober to crawl! Roll? Maybe! But crawling is out!"

"I think I've got a problem," continued Chester. At least he was facing up to the responsibility he had in flying the mission, I thought.

"What's that?" I asked, "flying today's mission?"

"No," he replied. "Just sittin' in this chair!"

He sat there, looking into his cup. "What's in this coffee?" he inquired.

"Coffee beans from Brazil," I replied, "salt peter from New Jersey — "

"Salt peter! I don't need anything to curb my masculine desire," he said, "what I need is something to clear my head and bring everything back into focus."

"I didn't think you were old enough for the menopause," I replied, "you're obviously experiencing a hot flash and a shot of hormones from Doc Marcus will bring you around pronto!"

"Tell Doc to make that another shot of Old Grand-Dad!" he replied.

An hour later all flying personnel were seated in the Operations tent, being briefed for our strike to Formosa.

"The target today is Toyohara Airdrome," explained Captain Musket, "and we're hitting the target in conjunction with the 38th Bomb Group. The 38th will go in first and soften 'em up! Hopefully, while they're licking their wounds, we'll slip in right behind the 38th and give them another dose of the same!"

"I don't like it," said Kenney, leaning over and whispering in my ear, "all the 38th is gonna do is stir up that hornet's nest so they'll be ready for us!" I was inclined to agree with him and would've much preferred to be the first group over the target.

"We're carrying para-fragmentation bombs and you have to be at least sixty feet high before releasing the bombs to make them operative," continued Musket. "The chute opens, pulling the firing pin on the bomb, and it detonates on contact with the ground or with whatever it touches. Major Jones will give you the details on how you will attack the target."

"We'll fly regular formation to the south end of Formosa,"

said Major Jones, "and north along the west coast, about five miles out to sea, until we get to approximately here," pointing with a stick on the big map of Formosa.

"At this point we will turn inland and hit the coast on the deck to avoid detection," he continued, "and following this valley move into a nine ships abreast formation with 100 to 200 feet between airplanes. Toyohara Airdrome is located on a level plateau at the head of this valley. We come up out of the valley, over the airdrome, strafing any aircraft, buildings or other targets directly in front of us and releasing our para-frags simultaneously. Your bombs are set to be released at 100 foot intervals and these are mean little firecrackers that will destroy everything on top of the ground for fifty yards in all directions. We should be over the target and out of there within ten seconds time, nine airplanes dropping a continuous string of 250 para-frags, 100 feet apart, over an area about 1,500 feet wide and 3,000 feet long with overlapping saturation."

"Let me emphasize again," he continued, "fly straight ahead, don't swing left or right to strafe or bomb a target. You could easily fly into another airplane and wipe out half the squadron. Should you get an engine shot out, concentrate on flying your airplane, holding it straight, and forget bombing and strafing. The remainder of the squadron will cover you and we'll be with you to help you out of the situation!"

"Also remember not to lag behind, get out front, or fly higher than the rest of the Squadron. We must all go across the target simultaneously at the same altitude; otherwise, you invite the extra attention of the enemy gunners to go after your airplane! Are there any questions?"

I wanted to ask if we had oxygen bottles, or other medical or therapeutic assistance, for all those suffering with hangovers from the prayer meeting of the night before. Particularly Lieutenant Phillips, who would be flying my wing, but I controlled my inquisitiveness. I thought about suggesting that Doc Marcus intervene, but he would never suggest anyone, particularly a pilot, not fly a mission just before takeoff. Excuse one and the whole mission would have to be scratched as every pilot instantly succumbed to whatever infectious malady was capable of keeping a throttle jockey from his flight duty. Especially after the target had been announced. Toyohara Airdrome was heavily defended with antiaircraft bunkers two and three deep on all sides, with a string of gun revetments down each side of the runway. Our only hope would be that we maintained the element of surprise.

"Being able to surprise 'em," said Cronin, in the jeep to the flight line, "is all that we've got! If they know we're coming we might as well borrow their swords and commit *hari-kari!"*

"We're going over the target at 300 miles an hour," I replied, "and I intend to keep every Jap gun emplacement we fly over silent until we get out of there! We might not be high enough for those parachutes to open to arm the bombs to explode on contact, but that's the Jap's problem. I don't intend to hang around long enough to sign autographs, but we'll be low enough to preserve our safety!"

"And our asses," added Cronin.

"And they'll keep their heads down after we go over 'em, too," added Kolodziejski, who was manning the tail turret.

"So there you have it, Cronin," I said, "you've got nothin' to worry about. Now, what're you gonna do?"

"Just sit there and wait for you to take a piece of shrapnel," he replied, "so I can fly the airplane!"

"While I'd love to see you check out as first pilot," I answered, "to accomplish it in this manner is asking too much of this pilot. All you have to do is remember to turn on that toggle switch to start the cameras, just what you forgot to do last week on that shipping strike. Ain't nobody in this crew gettin' a scratch today! Do all of you understand?"

Everybody nodded approval.

"Did you see Phillips?" I asked Cronin, and before he could answer, "And how did he look walking? — *was* he walking — ?"

"He's got a good copilot," answered Cronin, "if he gets sick over the target, the copilot can pull him through!"

"He still looked a little green around the gills after briefing," I said. "Maybe his copilot can fly him to Formosa and the fresh air 'tween here and there might have him back in focus before we get to the target!" I said this facetitously, but thinking about it, decided that buying a little time from San Marcelino to Toyohara, Formosa, might be just what the doctor ordered to aid and assist old Chester.

"How does Lieutenant Blount feel?" inquired Zuber, engaging Kenney in conversation off to the side.

"Great, as far as I know," replied our navigator. "Why?"

"I heard the Lieutenant singing louder than anybody else at the Major's promotion party last night," continued Zuber, "and he sounded stronger than anybody at two A.M. I figured he'd drunk 'em all under the table!"

"Would you believe he didn't have a drink of anything?" replied Kenney.

"Kolodziejski owes me five dollars," exclaimed Zuber. "He bet me the Lieutenant was drunker than an old cooter!"

Warnick topped off the gasoline tanks while I walked around *199* in the pre-flight check with Sergeant Albright, the crew chief. Climbing aboard, Kenney retrieved the bottom door with sliding ladder that sealed the opening into the airplane. I started the engines, increased the throttle of the left engine and simultaneously released the left brake, lightly holding the right, so the aircraft turned slowly to the right, out of the revetment. We started rolling toward the end of the runway and takeoff position. The 500th Squadron was joining us in the strike and they would follow us to takeoff. Once we were airborne, ship-to-ship communication was held to a minimum except in dire emergency, until a strike was completed and we were off the target.

After a half-climbing turn to the left by Major Jones, the other eight airplanes of the 501st joined the formation and we were on course to Formosa much like a giant formation of geese. Upon a hand signal from Major Jones all the aircraft tested their guns and you could see the gunsmoke emitted from the gun turrets of all the airplanes to the sides, above and below as the guns fired, raising little geysers where the projectiles hit the placid water.

The most distinguishing feature of the Island of Formosa, which the Japanese acquired after the Sino-Japanese war in 1895, is the prominent mountain range which occupies the central and eastern parts of the island reaching heights of 13,000 feet. Having had the island for fifty years, Formosa had been developed into a vital military and naval base that more nearly resembled the Japanese mainland than any other area. To fly a mission over Formosa was like hitting the mainland of Japan. We were attacking the enemy on his native soil, where he was more prepared, more dug in. They would fight more stubbornly and fanatically than ever.

To gain the edge and strengthen my hand, I immediately

faced the problem of trying to decide what I would do if I lost an engine over Formosa. We had never recovered an airplane or crew that had an engine shot out over this Japanese island stronghold. It is 242 miles in length and varies from nine to eighty-seven miles in width. All of our missions were flown on the western side of the island, the heart of the economic life, and the situs of all military and industrial targets. This placed the mountain range between us and the nearest friendly landing strip in the Philippines. If the Jap fighters didn't get you as a straggler on single engine, as you flew the length of the island to circumnavigate the mountains, then ditching in the turbulent China sea would automatically seal your fate. As we were the most hated and feared of all enemy forces, delivering our destruction from minimum altitude where the little yellow men could taste, feel, and see the devastation of our flying incendiary and exploding steel barrage, we refused to even think of the torture, and our fate, should we fall into the hands of the Japanese particularly near or in the vicinity of a target we had just annihilated. All of our friends, taken captive under such circumstances, had been beheaded on the spot. For this reason I carried a single .45 caliber shell in my pocket. Should I successfully crash-land or bail out over enemy territory, this last round of ammunition from my pocket would quickly dispatch me beyond the torture and inhumanities a lot of five foot orientals would otherwise enjoy practicing on a six foot five enemy pilot! And while we were instructed (if taken prisoner by the enemy) to tell Hirohito's emissaries everything we knew about our military strength in addition to our name, rank, and serial number, these little yellow bastards had never heard of the Geneva Convention. I'd never heard of humane treatment in any degree for the strafers.

I quickly determined that our only alternative, if we lost an engine, would be to bail out or crash-land on the western plain as close to the mountains as possible, and hope to join the guerrillas who were reportedly operative in the mountains, and who opposed the Japanese. Every time I flew a strike to Formosa I thought of the scripture *I shall look up to the mountains from whence cometh my strength, but my strength cometh from the Lord,* and I gained strength as I studied every detail of every peak and valley. These thoughts were going through my mind as Major Jones started a turn toward the west coast of Formosa with the high range of mountains in the background.

As we hit the coast we were on the deck under their radar. Trees and other features of the topography were blurs under my wing. We expected to hit our target so quickly that the enemy would not have time to get to their foxholes, much less have time to man their guns to return our fire. However, if they were *not* surprised and were waiting for us, following the 38th Groups's attack, then we were sitting ducks and prime candidates to "buy the farm!" Flying at treetop level, and below, allows the foliage and the natural topography of the land to muffle the noise of the Wright-Cyclone engines.

The fifty pounds of flak suit and steel helmet with the steel hinged ear plates had me plastered to my steel molded pilot's seat and sweating. Only my hands and feet were free to fly the airplane, drop the bombs, and fire those twelve .50-inch, air-cooled machine guns that literally chewed up and disintegrated anything and everything in their path.

The air over the land became bumpy, causing the airplane to bob slightly up and down. Over the water the airplane had flown as smooth as silk, as the temperature remained constant. Now over land, the temperatures were constantly changing, causing the nine airplanes of the 501st to look like the horses on a giant merry-go-round going up and down. We observed a few oriental farmers in their fields and rice paddies who remained motionless as we thundered fifteen feet above their heads. They might as well because they would have been dead before they ever saw or heard us, had the gunners chosen to squeeze their triggers, or had I depressed the button on my wheel. These were only farmers. That was good. We did not want to see anyone who might have given us away.

"Pilot to top turret," I said over the intercom, "fire straight ahead with me when we reach the target, Warnick, unless they've perched some *Zeros* up there in the sun to welcome us!"

"Roger, Lieutenant!"

"Pilot to crew, I see the target just over the ridge at the far end of this valley. We will be over the target in about two minutes. Rake 'em good and hose 'em down! Make every shot count and cover us on the way out, Hank!"

"Roger! Roger! Roger!" acknowledged Warnick, Zuber, and Kolodziejski. I increased the prop pitch to 2100 rpm as the airplanes came up nine abreast and were in battle formation. Chester was up on my left wing, flying with his left window open (so he could get plenty of fresh air!) And Major Jones, in the middle, and on whom the rest of us were flying formation, was hunched down in his pilot's seat buried in his flack suit and helmet.

"Gimme the bomb bay doors," I hollered to Cronin, never taking my eyes off of Major Jones and glancing over to Chester who had momentarily fallen behind eight to ten feet. A forward motion with my left hand, across the one hundred feet separating us, brought him up even with me. We were now streaking over the trees and the stream in the valley at 285 mph and picking up speed, and Chester needed only a minute throttle adjustment to bring his airplane up the recalcitrant ten feet.

We could see some smoke ahead but being below the level of the ridge and the trees we couldn't tell if it was Toyohara Airdrome or a Formosan farmer burning his weeds. It had to be the result of the 38th's attack, and I hoped and prayed we'd caught the Nips licking their wounds, putting out fires, or doing anything but sitting behind their guns, with the guns pointed into our bellies, with their fingers on the triggers.

As we popped out of the valley and over the ridge, the Airdrome, with its beautiful runways, aircraft hardstands, and revetments — a far cry from the jungle path we were operating from — was exposed like the bare backside of a skinny-dipper. Mechanics were working on airplanes while other airplanes were being refueled. A variety of human forms were trying to extinguish fires which were a result of the 38th Group's attack a few minutes earlier. All guns exploded simultaneously and the airplane recoiled from the jolt. The edge of the Airdrome came up to meet us and the rising sun markings of the airplanes on the ground (all those brilliant red meatballs) shone like party decorations. They made perfect targets as I watched my tracers, followed by incendiaries, disappear into a two-engine, *Betty* bomber that exploded, throwing smoke, fire, and junk a hundred feet into the air. There was no turning left or right and my heart skipped a beat as we barreled through the smoke and aerial booby trap of our making. Somehow we missed the pieces of exploding Jap bomber thrown into the air. Toyohara Airdrome was under us, the planes were scattered over the area, Japs that were standing in small groups were now dispersing in confused, almost comical behavior, running wildly in all directions. The smoke we had observed on approaching the target came from burning aircraft — three enemy and two B-25s from the 38th Group.

"The toggle switch!" I shouted at Cronin, to make sure my copilot had performed the only function required of him over the target — to flip the toggle switch and start the camera pointing out the back of the underside of the airplane, taking picture after picture of everything we'd strafed and bombed. While I was strafing, dropping bombs, flying formation, and trying to avoid flying debris, the copilot sometimes failed to remember to do the one thing that must be done to record the degree of success of our mission. I found that the more I did, the more I could do, including reminding the copilot to flip the toggle switch for the camera. He had the toughest job — sitting there doing nothing!

The Jap gunners weren't asleep as we had hoped. Every gun emplacement and revetment was alive, and steady streams of *ack-ack* came directly at us, and from each side. I continued to release a steady stream of para-frags, and the little chutes popped open to arm their floating destruction as I zeroed in my fifties on a string of gun emplacements directly in front of me and evenly spaced down the left side of the main runway. The smell of hot steel and gunsmoke filled the cockpit — a familiar and welcome odor of *strength*. The gun emplacements became silent as quickly as they had come alive. The tracers and armor-piercing incendiaries ravaged the enemy bunkers. In a brief three seconds I had fired several thousand rounds of death and destruction into those enemy gun emplacements and the pictures from this mission would show what was eradicated and neutralized.

Two revetments, camouflaged and with an airplane in each, appeared dead ahead toward the end of the enemy runway. The aircraft burned and exploded before I got to them, my incendiaries having performed the task better than a flame thrower. For the first time, since we hit the edge of the Airdrome nine airplanes abreast, I looked over at Major Jones. The nose of his airplane was a solid mass of fire power and so was Chester's on my left. The scathing, intimidating, devastating firepower of our airplanes provided protection for all of us.

The ground, in front, to the sides and behind us, was a maze of arcing tracers as friendly and hostile ammunition crossed in an attempt to silence each other. Diving, running, sprawling Japs, trying to escape our guns and bombs, were so close I could have knocked them down with a baseball bat.

Out of the far corner of my eye I saw one of our B-25s working over Jap gun emplacements. I was used to observing my fellow pilots miss their targets by inches with their airplanes, as they followed the hot lead and incendiaries pouring from their nose into an enemy target. I was not surprised until I saw one airplane continue to follow his tracers until my own depth perception told me he was going to hit the revetment.

"Pull up!" I shouted into the intership radio but it was too late. He hit the revetment and it looked like he put the whirling, twelve-foot props into the enemy gun emplacement much like one might put a giant lawn mower into a ditch. The airplane hit the sandbags atop the emplacement and was thrown back into the air. *Miracle of miracles, it continued to fly. . . .* With propellers that were bent back on the ends. We had obliterated their Airdrome. Acrid, billowing, black smoke shot thousands of feet into the clear blue sky from our para-frags that had found their ammo and fuel dumps. It was the most inspiring and exhilarating sight I'd ever seen, defying all description.

As we came off the target, Warnick swung the top turret aft and opened up a new crescendo in harmony with Hank and Zuber in the tail turret and waist (respectively), continuing to pour death and destruction into the target area behind us. With the nose and package guns silent for the first time since the attack began, the remaining six guns on the ship made for minimal vibration.

"Pilot to radio. Is the bomb bay empty, Zuber?"

"Roger, Lieutenant!"

"Bomb bays closed!" and Cronin pulled the lever closing our belly.

"We're hit! We're hit, Pappy!" The most fearsome and distressing message from someone in the 500th Squadron came through the earphones to all pilots monitoring the intership channel.

"We took a direct hit in our right engine! We're going down!"

"Hold her steady," came the reassuring voice of Pappy, the 500th Squadron leader, "lighten your load! Jettison and throw out everything that's loose or that you can tear loose! We're going home!"

I recognized the voice of the pilot who had been hit as a friend with whom I had gone through the Replacement Training Unit (RTU) at Savannah, Georgia. The futility of his situation suddenly and completely overwhelmed me. He and all his crew were lost.

The converted B-25, the most devastating war machine of World War II, was a flying paradox! Those fourteen forward-firing .50-inch machine guns gave it the most destructive and feared reputation of any allied weapon in the Pacific. But, with the extra weight of the guns and ammo in the nose, lose an engine and you had a flying coffin. Fly the airplane as a medium bomber as it was designed (with an empty plexiglass nose) and lose an engine, you could fly to Hong Kong and back. If you respected the odds, feared for your life, and had any sense, you shouldn't fly strafers!

All he had to do was fly the length of the island, around the mountains, hope the *Zeros* didn't take him, or that his buddies could stay with him in sufficient numbers to protect him from the enemy fighters, and then fly across the perpetually rough and windswept China sea to the northern tip of Luzon. Like so many others, he did make it to the China sea, and ditched, but none of the crew were ever heard from again.

"Pilot to crew! Do we have any damage? Over!"

"Nothing from the waist!" responded Zuber.

"We have a nice big hole in our right vertical stabilizer," said Kolodziejski from the tail turret, "it's making a whistling sound but I don't think I could ever get used to it!"

"We don't want you to," I responded, "over and out."

I stayed on the deck, five feet above the ground and below the trees, and throttled back to 250 mph looking for targets of opportunity enroute to the coast. Dead ahead, flying up to meet us, appeared a bridge with a little house at each end; obviously an enemy check point for rolling stock.

"Pilot to top turret. Bridge coming up with house on each end. You take the house on the left!"

"Roger!"

At 500-yards, and closing at 250 mph, Warnick and I released the devastation at our fingertips. Ignoring the red prism gun-sight that was projected on the plexiglass in front of me and relying completely on my seat-of-the-pants feeling to aim the guns (which was simply aiming the airplane,) my first burst of hot steel and flame-throwing incendiaries ripped into and exploded the little house. I now had only three guns firing, the remaining nine were either out of ammunition or I had burned the barrels out. Air-cooled .50-caliber machine guns were made to be fired in no more than two-to three-second bursts; however, targets like Toyohara Airdrome needed considerably longer bursts from the faithful .50s and we had plenty of extra gun barrels at San Marcelino. Warnick enjoyed the same success with his twin .50s from the top turret on the inspection house at the other end of the bridge.

"We probably messed up a couple of good poker games," volunteered Warnick over the intercom.

"I feel kinda sorry if we did," I responded, "that'd be the closest thing to supporting an American institution the Japs are doing in this war!"

As we hit the coast I climbed to a thousand feet and started looking for the rest of the squadron. I recognized Major Jones's airplane to starboard about five hundred yards, then Chester Phillips came up aft and to my left. Then there were four, five, six, seven — *where are the other two?* Noboby reported fighters, but even if there had been any, they would think twice about attacking us on the deck. We'd taken away their advantage of diving at us. Far too many of them had flown into the ground while making passes at us on the deck. *Maybe our last two have joined up with the 500th Squadron going home . . .*

Back on the ground, the waiting jeep whisked us to the interrogation tent and I started plotting my bombing and strafing run on a blowup picture of Toyhara Airdrome.

"We came down the left side of the big runway," I told the interrogation officer, "I started releasing my *daisy cutters* right here and never stopped until they were all expended. We strafed, heavily, the gun emplacements and bunkers — here — and here — the *ack-ack* was heavy — and too accurate. How many did we lose?"

"Five ships. The 38th lost two and we lost three. Every ship in the strike was holed!"

"I saw one of the 38th's ships about here. He must've taken

a direct hit, otherwise he would've been able to get farther away from the target."

"I think our pictures will confirm two *Bettys* that I strafed right here and here; they won't do any more flying in this war!" Thirty-six airplanes from the 38th and 345th Bomb Groups had fired over 300,000 rounds of armor-piercing, incendiary and tracer ammunition, dropped three thousand para-fragmentation bombs that scattered jagged, cutting, death-dealing shrapnel, leaving neither man nor manmade object standing; destroyed twenty-three airplanes, fuel and ammunition dumps, and killed several hundred of the enemy at the largest enemy Airdrome on Formosa — all within thirty seconds. The price: five B-25s and the thirty men who flew them. In war, they were expendable, and the scales of military success weighed heavily in our favor. But nobody polled the thirty who died.

"Pardon me, Lieutenant Blount!" interrupted Flight Surgeon Marcus, "Lieutenant Phillips has requested your ration of medicinal whiskey!"

"Chester has what?" I asked in amazement and surprise, looking down two tables to where Lieutenant Phillips was toasting me with his canteen cup raised above his head.

"By all means, Doc," I replied, "give him every drop I have coming today. And for your medical records, Phillips flys better drunk than most pilots do stone cold sober. And I'll take a double-shot of that grapefruit juice, if you please!"

"I saw you ram that Jap gun emplacement up there today," I said to Flight Officer Bill Matthews from Indianola, Iowa, a new pilot at the next table, "but you gotta remember that's not a Sherman tank you're flying out there!"

"I didn't do it on purpose," came the half apologetic, half thankful reply, "I saw all the *ack-ack* coming out of that hole, and I was in there on top of 'em before I knew it!"

"You were using the prism gun-sight weren't you?" I asked.

"Yeah! How'd you know?"

"That lousy sight has killed more pilots and lost more airplanes than the Japs have shot down. You get to concentrating on that gun-sight and you fly the airplane into the ground or into your target. At minimum altitude you don't need a gun-sight! At twenty feet just aim the airplane — your guns will take care of the target, and you'll have your head up so you can fly the airplane!"

"Thanks for the tip," he replied, "I'll never use that gunsight again!"

"Of course," I suggested, "if you can improve your act, you can become the top performer in Buffalo Bill's Flying Circus after the war and do somethin' like that every day!"

"That would be too much,"he replied, "I never repeat my aerial acts!"

"You're wise," I said, "nobody would believe 'em anyway! I *saw* it and I still don't believe it!" In addition, four *Zeros* had jumped him when he became a cripple, leaving him a ventilated airplane with over 200 holes! He learned a valuable lesson, and he was lucky to fly away from the experience.

"I understand you had doubts concerning my flying ability earlier today," said Chester, as we were walking from the interrogation tent.

"Naw, Chester," I replied, "nothin' like that . . . that fifth cup of black coffee I helped you get down at breakfast this morning was 'cause I own stock in a coffee company."

"How did you like the way I cuddled up to your warm side as we went over the target today?" he asked.

"Had you been any closer people would've begun to think we were going steady! And when that heavy stuff opened up about halfway across the target, and I glanced over there and saw your nose on fire, I could've kissed you!"

"How do you think we got home?" asked Major Jones, walking by and eavesdropping on our conversation. "We didn't need a beacon light! We just followed the glow of Chester's nose in from Formosa. After last night, his nose was the brightest glow this side of San Francisco!"

"A couple of more of these," said Chester, "and I qualify for leave in Sydney!" Actually, that's what nine-tenths of the flying personnel of the 345th were flying, and living for — R and R in Sydney!

CHAPTER FOUR

A Full Baptism

When the ancients said a work well begun was half done, they meant to impress the importance of always endeavoring to make a good beginning.

Polybius

"Now hear this! Testing! Announcement coming through! If the war's over I'll meet you in Dallas at the Baker Hotel in ten years and we'll go to the movies. Will you please give me your attention!" I spoke into the scratchy Squadron PA system, backed up by Nat Kenney, Donald Hardeman, John Hammner (three good boys from Texas), and Bell, from Southern Oklahoma.

"Today is March 2nd, an international holiday all over the world" I said, "it's *Texas Independence Day,* the day when all of Texas, and part of Southern California, flies the Lone Star flag of the great State of Texas, partakes of a few bottles of beer, and pays honor to great Texas heroes, both past and present, and the men of the Alamo, such as Colonel William B. Travis, Davy Crockett, and Jim Bowie, *and* General Sam Houston, who won our independence at the Battle of San Jacinto when he caught General Santa Anna with his pants down taking a siesta!"

"Shit! Taking a shit!" corrected Hamner.

"Who gives a rat's ass?" yelled an obvious malcontent two tents away who failed to appreciate the history and the heritage he was hearing.

"Why did Sam Houston jump on that poor little Mescan boy anyway?" came a raspy voice from another direction that was easily recognizable as Thatcher's, "why doncha give Texas back to Mexico? That would make everybody happy!" There were cheers from isolated tents.

Unperturbed, I continued on the loudspeaker. "In honor of this occasion," we have assembled the Four Hits and a Miss, the world famous singing group that has performed before kings, queens, potentates, three wild cow milkings, two hog callings, four joint sessions of the Texas Legislature, the inauguration of a justice of the peace, a constable, a notary public in Muleshoe, Texas, and other world titular heads! In keeping with the indomitable spirit of those brave and dedicated defenders of Texas freedom who yelled: *Remember the Alamo! Remember Goliad!* at San Jacinto, we dedicate this rendition of our national anthem to all of you, the friends of Texas.

With that introduction, the hastily assembled, ill-prepared and untalented Four Hits and a Miss broke into *The Eyes of Texas are upon you,* evoking a spontaneous response from every clear-witted, sober individual in the camp.

"Blow it out your ass!"

"Only two things come out of Texas! Steers and queers!"

"We want to lose you — like a bad habit!"

"What is Texas? The asshole of the universe!"

"Blow it out your barracks bag!"

. . . *Till Gabriel blows his horn,* we finished. "We want to thank you for your respect, your rapt attention, your generous and flattering comments upon the occasion of the celebration of this important date in history and your unselfish and devoted willingness to share in and be a part of it," I continued.

"In further celebration there'll be a prayer meeting in Admiral Root Hardeman's tent this evening immediately following chow, beginning at 1900 hours!"

"Admiral?" came a retort, "Admiral of what?"

"Admiral Hardeman of the Texas Navy, Sir! Front line officer of the Texas Naval Department now on temporary duty to this group to lend prestige, inspiration, and example to an array of numbnuts who otherwise would be lost without his sterling Texas leadership."

At 1900 hours Hardeman's tent looked like the Chez Paree. Obviously some of the heavier drinkers had skipped the evening meal and started drinking the main course a little early.

"If I owned Texas and Heaven," paraphrased Hardeman, host extraordinaire, "I'd rent Heaven out and live in Texas." Only a few of the native sons showed any emotion at Hardeman's pronouncement.

"Thatcher!" inquired Hardeman, "do you know where to find a naked frog?"

"No, Root!" responded Thatcher, "where do you find a naked frog?"

"Under a 'horny' toad!" replied Hardeman, laughing uncontrollably at his own brand of west Texas humor.

"Lyman!" shouted Major Jones, "come over here!"

"Coming your most Imperial Majorosity!" answered Lyman. "We have a finely tuned system! He hollers and I jump!"

"May I speak to his Highness?" asked Lyman.

"I always have time for the little people!" answered the Major.

" . . . and further more," Thatcher was saying, as he stood on a chair across the tent and waved a cup in one hand and a bottle in the other, "when there's nothing to lose, let's go out in a blaze of glory!"

"I believe the flying that'll kill him keeps him alive!" remarked Doc Marcus.

"The woman said, 'If I were your wife I'd put poison in your coffee!' to which Sir Winston replied 'Madame, if you were my wife, I'd drink it!' " and Holtzman went into uproarious laughter.

Palotta had been trying to get the singing started with a stirring rendition on his concertina.

"Do you take requests?" Vincent asked him, in a gentlemanly and courteous manner.

"Yes, I do," smiled a pleased Palotta.

"Then take that squeeze box and cram it up your ass."

"Do you hate the Japs, Thatcher?" asked Phillips, rather philosophically.

"No, not particularly!" answered Thatcher.

"Well, I do." responded Phillips, "it won't make you happy but it'll keep you going."

"Now remember the rules," Moore was telling a new pilot, "the first one to make a mistake doesn't get a chance to make another!"

"The army feeds you, clothes you, gives you a place to sleep, gives you a career, and it's the best friend you got. What you need is an anchor, something that won't run out on you — the Army Air Corps!" announced Major Giese.

"You remind me of a horse trader who tried to sell me a dead mule one time," responded Kuta, "he said it wasn't hard to feed and it didn't kick!"

"They want you to go out there and fight!" said Palotta.

"How's that?" asks Vincent.

"Like a man!"

"Who said that?"

"The Colonel!"

"Screw the Colonel!"

"He's not my type!" answered Palotta.

"I hope not!" added Doc Marcus, overhearing the conversation.

"A toast," shouted Hamner, "here's to Montgomery Ward — and his orchestra!"

"Here's to Harry Truman!" said Bob Jones from Missouri, "the best damned vice president since the last one!"

"No matter who the guy is, don't get too close to him!" said Lamar to Burg, a new pilot, "don't get to likin' anybody too much! He'll get killed just when you feel he's your best friend — when you need him the most! Enjoy everybody but don't get too friendly! Purr me . . . uh . . . pour me another round of that Aussie rum, old buddy!"

"My Aunt Sabrina is psychic, Doc! She has premonitions about things!" said Caskey. "She even had a premonition of the Japs hitting Pearl Harbor!"

"Did she tell anybody about it?" inquired Marcus.

"No," replied Caskey, "she didn't have the premonition until December 9th."

"Doc! Doc Marcus!" yelled Lyman. "Ask me to make a sentence with disaster!"

"All right, Lyman. Will you make us a sentence with disaster?"

"Thought you'd never ask, Doc. She backed into an airplane and it disaster!"

"That stuff is too smooth!" said Musket, "I'm used to putting my fist through the tent to get it down!"

"That's Seagram's Five Crown! I paid a hundred dollars for that bottle!" said Phillips.

"That's too much money!" said Steele.

"Nope! Money's like cow manure. You gotta spread it around to make things grow; and I'm growing a beautiful, happy, inebriated drunk!"

"Ladies and Gentlemen, and those of you who are in between. There'll be one more toast," said Major Jones, "and then let's put the cork in the bottle!"

"I'll make the last toast," said Phillips. "May we all be with our loved ones before long."

"Hear! Hear! I'll drink to that," came several responses.

"And may nobody's husband or wife find out about it!" added Phillips.

After three missions as a copilot I had been checked out as a first pilot and qualified to get moved up to the left seat, as the aircraft commander, instead of in the right seat as a copilot who was compelled to go, do and be subjected to whatever whim, decision, judgement, or lack thereof, the gentleman in the left seat decided was expedient and necessary. Riding in the right seat I was not the captain of my fate, which was directly opposed to my theory of survival. This was implanted in my mind at an early age and quite innocently by my great grandfather, George Y. Tarver, an old Indian fighter, who placed total and unrestricted emphasis on obtaining "the edge" in any fight, particularly when your life was riding on the outcome.

"In a showdown fight for your life," he had told me as an impressionable child, "always seek to gain 'the edge,' and give yourself every opportunity to come out on top! If it's a gunfight or Indian fight, try to have the sun at your back. If it's playing poker in a saloon, Cousin Wes [John Wesley] Hardin always sat with his back to the wall so everybody in the whole place was in front of him. Having the edge in a fight means you're gonna stay healthy and live longer!" At the time I thought his advice interesting, but now it was a formula for life and survival itself.

At the moment I was one of the most skillfully trained, efficient executioners in the United States armed services' stable of specialized fighters. My crew had been trained equally well, and together we could not only deliver the death and destruction to the enemy for which we had been trained, but we were eager and anxious to do the job. And while we had been split up and assigned to other crews for the purpose of gaining combat experience, on my seventh mission we had been brought together for the first time to do the job for which we had been trained as a team.

The Air Corps emphasized the importance of the leadership role. I had seen a wide variety of experts in the trade. Some who kicked butts and took names, some who delegated authority, some who low-keyed it, some who led by example, and some who did it the way John Wayne did it in the movies. I could not be the ranting, raving, threatening, butt-kicking maniac, and I disliked those who commanded through tricks and techniques. As the youngest man in the crew, I decided I'd try to run that crew and fly that airplane in the same manner I'd observed my Dad run his line crew all of my life: quietly, and with confidence in every man until someone failed to do their job. They would respect rank, but I had to earn their respect as the first pilot and CO of that rocket. I had already learned that rank had nothing to do with the confidence and respect a flight crew had, or didn't have, for the person occupying the left seat in the cockpit.

"I've called us together," I began, "because we start our first job together tomorrow morning. It's shipping up along the coast of China, and you've learned they shoot back. Unlike that friendly convoy we flew up on in the Gulf of Mexico during overseas training. I have total and complete confidence in each of you, and I know you to be the best in your jobs, bar none, of any men in this outfit! I know! I've seen 'em and flown with 'em and I've prayed for the day we'd finally be brought back together. I'm dedicated to flying that airplane in any manner — upside down if necessary — to get us out of any danger, and back to this base in one piece following every mission. Even if it means flying down every gun barrel in the Japanese Imperial Navy and through Hirohito's Palace on the way back here.

If you ever have any questions don't hesitate to ask me, and that includes family, military and anything pertaining to your job. You can rest assured that I reserve the same right, and I hope that none of us will ever hesitate to give suggestions or constructive criticism about how any crew member's job can be done more efficiently. We're all dependent upon one another for our well being — for our lives — so let's operate our airplane in that manner. Are there any questions?" There were none and we never had another crew meeting during our entire tour of combat. A leader, I decided, could never lead looking over his shoulder! To the contrary, I didn't have time to be looking over my shoulder, I had to be looking forward at all times, exuding the utmost confidence in the men who were flying and fighting behind me. Not to my surprise, the confidence was quickly reciprocated as our crew busted their butts to show they were as good as I believed them to be. In all modesty, we were the best.

Accompanying my promotion to first pilot came the assignment of my own airplane and the authority to oversee and manage its maintenance and service. Our 12 fixed strafing (nose) guns were ordinarily depressed six degrees and vortexed to come together at 600 feet in front of the airplane, each gun firing 750-rounds a minute. Working with my armorer sergeant, I had my guns raised to three degrees depression, and vortexed at 800 to 900 feet.

"As low as I fly this baby," I told the sergeant, "six degrees depression would put all that hot steel in the dirt about fifty feet in front of the airplane! I don't intend to strafe any target from higher than twenty feet!" After seven missions we removed all the depression, mounting all the guns straight and level, and vortexed them at 1,000 feet. I still had the feeling I was shooting *up* into most targets! With this concentrated firepower I could bust a building, neutralize and sink a ship, wipe out a gun revetment, disintegrate a train or rolling stock and give myself the edge of that critical fraction of a second when I could reach out to silence or out draw the guns of the enemy. Two B-25s, wing tip-to-wing tip, strafing and bombing could take an enemy destroyer. One B-25, with its guns vortexed at 1,000 to 1,500 feet, cutting, slashing and flying like a "bat outa hell" could, with a little luck, hold its own! But like drawing to an inside straight, I would never push my luck in a one-on-one confrontation with a destroyer except in self-defense or under circumstances where I had no other choice. I found it to be an unhealthy situation!

Our test under fire came quickly. The next morning at 1130 hours, Lieutenant Julius Fisher, Squadron Leader for the strike, sighted — through broken clouds at 5,000 feet — four unescorted merchant freighters in convoy moving in a northerly direction up the coast of China.

Tallyho! came Squadron leader Fisher's announcement over the Command radio. Fisher was a gentleman from the northern climes of the United States where fox hunting was pursued in the gentlemanly fashion of red riding coat, horses, and dogs. This was the first time radio silence had been broken since leaving San Marcelino, and then this *Tallyho* floated over the airwaves.

"Hello Kit Bag Leader! This is *199! Tally Ho* to you, too; Over!"

My west Texas ignorance of the cry of a huntsman at the sight of the fox had not penetrated my mental perception until I looked across the one hundred feet into the cockpit of Fisher's plane and saw his hand signals to look beneath us. Sure enough — there was a four-ship Japanese convoy a mile off the coast. They reminded me of four large elephants in a circus parade, each holding the tail of the one in front in perfect line.

The Squadron continued over the coast and on into China — hoping to lull the convoy into believing we hadn't seen them through the cloud cover — if, in fact, they had sighted and identified us as a foe and not friendly aircraft. Behind the mountains and the other natural terrain of the China coast Lieutenant Fisher made a 180-degree turn and signaled for us to form into attack elements of two ships each. Flying the number two slot in the first flight, I dropped back and became the wingman for Blair, leader of the second flight. As I pulled in close on his right wing, he gave me a thumbs up signal and a broad smile, knowing full well that this was my first mission as first pilot, and wanting to do anything that would relax me, and give me confidence. I knew what he was doing and appreciated the gesture.

I increased the prop pitch to 2100 rpm and maintained twenty-six inches of throttle, which, coupled with our rapid descent from 5,000 feet, had us skipping across the tops of the small mountains at two hundred eighty-five indicated airspeed. Making a land-to-sea attack against shipping gave the airplane a big advantage, particularly since we had mountains with lush green vegetation as a backdrop that blended with our green-camouflaged aircraft. That gave the Jap gunners an even more difficult target. *They gotta find us before they can shoot us!* went through my mind as I mentally gave Fisher a pat on the back.

We were streaking toward the coast and the last ridge of mountains, trying to escape detection. The convoy, a mile off shore, loomed up a short mile away.

"Pilot to crew! Keep your eyes peeled for *Zeros* in the clouds — Warnick! Cover us on the breakaway. Hank, you and Zuber! Let's take 'em!"

"Roger! Roger!"

At that moment we broke over the ridge, our bomb bays popped open and we dove another four hundred feet to level off five feet above the water's surface. The entire airplane shook and vibrated as all guns fired simultaneously, and our incendiaries climbed up and into the third ship in line. We were fortunate indeed to find four merchant ships alone, unescorted by warships. Ordinarily, there would be at least two destroyers and a couple of gunboats assisting merchantmen of this class; but maybe we had caught them before they rendezvoused with their protection.

Their gunners had not been caught napping. Two arcs of tracers, from the bow and stern of the ship, started to converge on our airplanes. Making a broadside attack, I was limited, as was Blair, in the fantailing I could do in raking the ship with my fifties. Before I could silence the aft gun, we were hit in the right engine, but I continued, and dropped two five hundred-pounders in tandem with Blair. Over the ship I pulled to the right and dropped back to the surface of the water as a string of enemy tracers passed over the cockpit. The right engine was smoking as I took violent, evasive action until we were out of range of the enemy guns.

"Pilot to crew. We're hit in the right engine! Warnick, you and Zuber check the right engine from your positions and give me a report."

"I can't see anything but smoke, Lieutenant," reported Warnick from the top turret.

"Me, too," reported Zuber from the waist.

"Do you see any fire?" I asked.

"Fire, negative," reported Warnick.

"Same from the waist," parroted Zuber.

"Are we hit anywhere else?" I asked.

"Two holes in the right vertical stabilizer," reported Kolodziejski from the tail turret, "but not big enough to hurt anything!"

We had sunk one ship and left the other three sinking, disabled, and dead in the water. As we joined formation to return to base, the right engine continued to smoke, and as soon as we were out of range of Jap fighters, I asked Warnick, the engineer, to join me in the cockpit. Warnick loved those engines like most men love a woman, and I wanted his evaluation of the situation.

"The oil pressure is staying within operational limits," I said, "whatta you think?"

"We haven't lost any power in that engine have we?" asked Warnick.

"No," I replied, "and the oil pressure is still normal and the oil temperature is not excessive!"

"We've probably got an oil line shot out that's bleeding oil on to a hot cylinder that's causing the smoke," said Warnick, "let's keep watching that oil pressure and temperature. Even if we lose pressure and the temperature starts to go up, we've got to keep her running as long as we can. Let's just pray the hole in that oil line doesn't get any bigger!"

"Kit Bag Leader to *199*. Over." It was Lieutenant Fisher.

"*199* to Kit Bag Leader. Over."

"You're smoking pretty good. How're the vital signs on your bad engine? Over."

"Oil pressure and temperature are holding steady and no change so far! Will appreciate your keeping a lookout from your vantage point and letting us know pronto if you see any change in the amount of smoke! Over!"

"Roger *199*! We'll keep a close lookout for you. In addition, we'll soon be getting within radio range of the base and we're alerting them that you're hit and to stand by. Over!"

"Roger! We appreciate all the help we can get at this point. Over and out."

My first combat mission with all my crew! Is this what all those hours of strafing, bombing, navigation, instruments, cross-countrys, night flying, formation, staging, training procedures ad infinitum were for? To get shot down on our first lousy mission?

Lousy! I didn't want to disgrace the pilots in an outfit who were expected to fly their airplanes without ailerons, rudders, engines, or under any other adversity if necessary. Erickson made his run over the target, dropped his bombs and then flew his plane back from Formosa with the entire left rudder shot off. He landed at 170 mph without flaps, and with the help of a parachute dropped from the rear hatch at the last moment to stop the airplane! And there were Anacker, Wallace and Peterson at Rabaul. Jumped by fifty fighters coming off the target, without fighter cover, Wallace got an engine shot out by *Zeros,* and Anacker and Peterson flew escort for him until Peterson got shot down. At Cape Gazelle they were hit by yet another fifty *Zeros,* and had a running battle on the wave-tops that lasted for over an hour and ten minutes. With leaking gas fumes filling the airplane, Lieutenant Hicko, a copilot, *shot at attacking Zekes with his .45 through the right window of the cockpit,* until he took a fighter's bullet through his gut, Wallace met head-on attacks from his antagonists four separate times by climbing into them and then turning into his dead engine to get back down on the waves. In spite of the loss of one engine, forty-one gaping holes in his airplane, and his gunners shooting down five Japs, Wallace baited four more *Zeros* into diving at him at minimum altitude. These *Zeros* were lost when they crashed into the water. Wallace finally landed at Kiriwina. Anacker ditched, with only two survivors (Sergeant Henderson and Lieutenant Migliacci). Both planes were credited with fourteen enemy fighters for the mission.

And what about Manders, I thought. On a strike against Jap shipping in Hansa Bay, New Guinea, Manders was hit by heavy, acccurate *ack-ack* as he started his run on a large freighter. Ditching near enemy troop concentrations was spelled d-e-a-t-h, so rather than be taken alive by the Japs, he dove his airplane into the ship and sank it. *And you're feeling sorry for yourself with a smoking engine*? Fisher's voice brought me back to the present! The smoking engine, while still respected, had been placed in proper perspective.

From where I sat I could see only the top of the right engine and the propeller and the cowling on the front of the engine. Even if we started to lose oil, the life's blood of the engine, I couldn't see it under the wing. Zuber or Kolodziejski or one of the pilots in another airplane in the formation would have to tell me. Without the oil the engine would have frozen solidly within a few seconds. The propeller would probably have torn itself away, and the possibility of a fire would have been excellent. I was ready at a moment's notice to kill the engine and feather the propeller to the right engine, should the oil line completely sever and release all the oil.

"Pilot to crew!" I spoke into the intercom, "This is my assessment of our situation. Chances are good that we're gonna lose this engine! Take all your guns from their mountings and stack 'em, along with all ammunition and anything else that's loose in the airplane, and be ready to throw everything overboard to make this airplane a flying hull on a moment's notice!"

"Does that include Saint Christopher?" inquired Zuber, from back in the waist.

"Saint Chris can stay," I answered, "but empty his pockets! You can empty your pockets, too, and start peeling the paint off the inside of the fuselage."

When the horizon defined itself as three mountains surrounding an airstrip, about three hours later on the southern coast of Luzon, we all breathed a sigh of relief. While the right engine was now emitting a much larger volume of smoke, I felt as if we could make it to shore if the whole engine fell off that airplane.

"Give us a red flare from the back, Warnick," I said on intercom, simultaneously turning on the IFF, "we want everyone to know this is an emergency landing! We're making a straight in approach!" Everyone backed off and gave us the right of way as we put the *Touch O' Texas* on the ground. I cut the right engine (now belching smoke without the slipstream to carry it away) the moment we touched down, and took the first exit, clearing the runway for the remaining birds to come in to roost.

"We were sweating you out," said Blair, as we sat down in the interrogation tent.

"I wasn't sweatin'," said Doc Marcus, distributing canteen cups and pouring from a fifth of Old Grand-Dad, "I knew you would make it!"

"You didn't even know I was flyin' today, Doc!" I answered.

"Oh, yes I did!" he replied, "I knew this was your first mission as first pilot!" Thatcher had said Doc Marcus huddled with Major Jones and Musket before a pilot was turned loose as an aircraft commander. Maybe he was right.

"And it sounds like you got the full baptism!" added Doc.

"If that's not all I don't care to go back for the rest of it," I answered.

There would be more, but I'm glad that I didn't know about it then.

There were dog days in combat, just as there were always days with nothing to do, no place to go, time on your hands, and boredom up to your eyeballs. On such days we slept in until at least 0900 and enjoyed a late breakfast. And, like the postman who takes a walk on his day off, I flew practice skip-bombing missions against the old beached freighter down the coast. Efficiency and expertise, in anything, from shooting a basketball or kicking a football to strafing a target or skip-bombing an old ship, should be done as often as possible to sharpen your edge. It had been raining for a couple of days and, with so much moisture in the air, I left vapor trails over my wing tips at ten feet. Returning from the flight line I saw Thatcher was lounging in his usual skimpy attire, the ever present beer bottle in his hand. His fresh laundry delivered by the Filipino native women was still laying on his sack where it had been placed two hours earlier.

"How're things?" I asked.

"Quiet as a church!" he replied.

"That bothers me!"

"Why?" he asked.

"I don't think you've ever been in a church!"

"We did have a little excitement this morning," said Townsley, "you might say it was an explosive situation!"

"What happened?" asked Harrah, who had entered the tent behind me.

"Oskea went to the latrine after chow," said Townsley, "with his usual cigar and the month-old sports page from his *San Francisco Examiner*. Today being Saturday, and unknown to Oskea, the latrine orderly had poured two gallons of 90-octane gasoline down the latrine to burn up the excess paper."

"Didn't anybody tell Oskea what he was sitting on while he smoked that cigar?" asked Harrah.

"Naw! It all happened so quick!" replied Townsley. "After the latrine orderly poured the gasoline in the latrine, he spied the inspectors making their rounds so he grabbed his broom and *vamoosed.* As Oskea was enjoying his cigar and reading about the baseball spring training camps, he casually lifted the cover of the hole next to his to flip the ashes off his cigar. You shoulda' heard the explosion! Latrine covers flew in all directions!"

"What happened to Oskea?"

"A few things got singed but other than that nothin' was hurt," said Townsley, "but his feelings!"

"Did you say his butt?"

"But his feelings."

"Noboby else in the squadron will ever flip ashes in the latrine again," said Townsley.

"We all move from one disaster to another around here," remarked Thatcher. "The important thing is to keep moving!"

"You want to set an example for the men?"

"No. Actually I want to set an example for the women," responded Thatcher.

"I'd sure like to see my wife," sighed Harrah.

"I'd like to see *anybody's* wife," replied Thatcher.

The day I had entered Big Spring High School, I'd had a meeting with George "Cap" Gentry, the principal, and we had planned my curriculum to prepare me for the entrance examination to West Point. Our Congressman, the Honorable George Mahon, was contacted regarding an appointment to the Military Academy the summer I would graduate in 1943. In the meantime Pearl Harbor and World War II came along, changing a lot of plans; my name, however, had stayed in the pot, and in April, 1945, I received a letter from my mother telling me that my name was under consideration for an appointment from the Congressman's office. The moment I received the news I made a beeline for Major Jones's tent.

"Major," I said, bursting through the entrance of the pyramidal, "guess what?"

"Let's see, Blount!" he replied, "you've designed a more daring peel off whereby you land eight minutes before I do?"

"No," I replied, "this is serious! I've just received a letter from my Mother and she says I'm in line for an appointment to West Point. Whata' you think?" I could see my news came as a surprise to the major, and the furrows on his brow deepened.

"That would send you home!" he said, "but if it comes through I hope you'll think about it."

"Whata' you mean think about it?"

"I mean think it over before you make up your mind," he replied.

"What's there to think about," I said. "I've been planning this ever since I entered high school!"

"You've already been through Cadets and you know what that was like! Now you're a first lieutenant. You'd have to resign your commission, put in four years of that pressurized spit and polish military life, and then finally graduate as a second lieutenant. You don't want to do it. You won't like it!"

"I came down here to share this wonderful news with *you,* an old West Pointer, and you're talking like a Navy Midshipman at the Army-Navy game."

"I'm sorry," replied the Major, "but I just don't think you'd like it. Notwithstanding your age, you've experienced too much combat, you've seen too much action, and been exposed to too much war to ever go back to the life of a West Point cadet. The first time one of those little smartass eighteen-year-old second-year men puts you in a brace and dresses you down, you'd be ridden out of the service for breaking the jaw of an upperclassman."

"Do you really think so?" I drooped.

"I'd bet my next leave to Sydney on it," he replied. "The military life at West Point is programmed for seventeen- and eighteen-year-olds who've never experienced any form of military discipline before, with the exception of a few private military schools where parents send their kids when they can't control 'em."

"Besides," he continued, "you're about ready for a promotion and if you stay I can promise you your captain's bars. You won't find many twenty-year-old captains in this man's Air Corps."

You've really got me confused now," I replied, "when I came in here a minute ago there was no doubt what I wanted to do but now you've really confused the issue!"

As I walked back to my tent I tried to sort out my feelings and separate the truth from the fiction. I remembered Paukovich and Sawyer, and the personal dilemma that was created when they allowed their names to be put in for captaincies instead of going home when they completed their tours of duty. They then sweated it out in reverse. They both (only too late) were hoping desperately that their railroad tracks [Captain's bars] wouldn't come through. When Sawyer's promotion bounced, the hopeful, expectant look on Pauk's face, waiting to learn his fate, would never be forgotten. Equally unforgettable was his sorrowful, downcast countenance, when he learned that he was now a captain — and Sawyer was going home.

"If he gets shot down," said Kenney, "he won't even be buried in those railroad tracks, much less be alive to wear 'em." A point well taken.

And then there was Major Robert Canning, CO of the 500th Squadron, who was shot down on a shipping strike to Formosa the day his Majority came through. A gentleman truly admired by those who fought beside him, he had experienced a meteoric rise from second lieutenant to major. He was taxiing for takeoff on his last mission when word of his promotion reached the squadron and he could not be notified. "I'll betcha he'd trade that gold leaf for a ticket home today if he had the chance," Moore had said.

There had to be a limit, I decided, on how far any of us could tempt fate. When my time, or chance, to go home presented itself, I made up my mind I was going to accept and take advantage of it! Even if I was nothing but a private in the rear rank. A live private would ultimately be a higher rank, I decided, than a dead general!

"How can I make a request to see if an appointment to West Point has come through the chain of command from Washington out here to the Pacific?" I asked aloud, after I got back to my tent.

"You start here in the Squadron," answered Kuta.

"And then where does it go?"

"It goes to Group Headquarters!" said Lathrop.

"Then who? *God*?" asked Lyman.

"No, Fifth Bomber Command!" said Kuta.

"That is God!" said Thatcher.

"I remember sending my request through channels to get married!" said Major Giese.

"What happened?" asked Doc Marcus.

"By the time it got through our son was in junior high school."

The following day I drew standby duty, which meant I was on alert to fly to the rescue of any of our planes that might get an engine shot out on the strike against Jap shipping on the China coast. As I came from chow Sergeant Franko intercepted me near the Operation's tent.

"Squadron radio reports they've received a message that we have a ship down in the drink, Lieutenant," he said, "I've alerted Lieutenant Cronin and they have your ship ready on the flight line. They report three survivors in a raft!"

"Tell 'em I'm on the way!" I replied, as I ran to my tent to pick up my flying gear. Lieutenant Frank Born, from Chicago, was the navigator on standby and the moment he got the coordinates of the downed ship we were on our way to the flight line. Cronin, Warnick, and Zuber had arrived ahead of us and in twenty minutes from the moment I had received the word from Sergeant Franko, we were aloft and flying to the spot in a vast sea of nothingness where the plane was last seen and reported ditched.

"I just hope there's something, or somebody, left to find," said Warnick.

"Me to!" I responded, thinking how much I would appreciate someone coming to my rescue if I were in the drink.

"Crank in the *Gibson Girl* frequency," I said to Zuber over the intercom, "maybe they were able to salvage the emergency radio to lead us to them!"

The *Gibson Girl* was the little orange emergency radio that was standard equipment on all aircraft and came complete with kite and balloon to stretch the antenna while the "rescue" cranked out an emergency radio signal.

We could then fly to the coordinates given on the radio as the location of the downed airplane, and start a search consisting of flying a pattern of ever increasing squares at a thousand foot altitude.

As we approached the spot everyone became silent, and I overstated the situation once again as I said to Zuber on the intercom "Now listen closely." *What else could he be doing?* In the cockpit we were absolutely silent as I flew the first square of one minute legs; then a minute and a half; then two minutes, carefully watching the gyrocompass to make sure we covered every inch of the ocean under us. We continued this pattern for two hours and found only an empty dinghy and the expended wing tank from one of our fighters.

"I'm sorry to say but this is like hunting for a needle in a haystack," said Cronin.

The clock on the panel told me we'd been out for four-and-a-half hours, two-and-a-half of which had been spent flying in circles. With the sun starting to go down, I was wondering if our navigator knew where we were.

"I think it's about time to head for home," I said to Born, "has all this flying in circles sufficiently confused you?"

"I think I know where we are, but we've got to find this big reef," he said, pointing to a big mass, painted in on his navigation map, "then I can give you a heading back to San Marcelino."

"That sun is getting mighty low," I answered, "I hope the reef isn't too far! It might be kinda hard to find in the dark."

"You're right," replied Born, "take a heading of ninety-two degrees and let's see what happens." I put the airplane exactly on ninety-two degrees and started climbing to twenty-five hundred feet. If it got dark, I didn't want to be so high that we couldn't see the reef. On the other hand, if it was dark, I wanted to be low enough to be able to see the reef by the last rays of light, or whatever light might be left.

After ten minutes flying at ninety-two degrees (and no reef) I asked Born, "how high is this reef — how high does it stick up out of the water?"

"It doesn't stick up out of the water at all," came his reply, "it's completely covered by water but it's a very prominent feature which we won't have any trouble seeing from above!"

"If we fly over it," I added.

"Yeah! That's right,' replied Born, "when we fly over it!"

"If we fly over it while we can still see? If it's still daylight," I added.

"That's right!" said Born, "if it's still daylight!"

"What if the sun is all the way down and it's dark when we get there," I asked, seeking more detail, "can we see it?"

"It might be kinda hard to see under those circumstances," admitted Born.

"Do I need to ask what we do then? Under such circumstances?" I asked.

"I'll figure something out!" came his reply.

I had already figured it out! Flying in circles for two and a half hours, our navigator — any navigator — would be hard put to know exactly where he was, particularly flying around in the middle of the China sea. The big reef was his point of reference, the nearest and most prominent feature on his map, and if he could find the reef, he could get a bearing, and determine a compass heading that would direct us back to San Marcelino. But the reference point, or reef, was completely under water. As the sun started to descend into the boundless waters of the Pacific, a feeling of futility and apprehension started to well up inside me.

If we fail to locate the reference point, I said to myself, *then we're lost, short of gasoline, and little short of a miracle will keep us from getting our feet wet!* The sun had disappeared, and dusk, on the open Pacific, was rapidly turning into night. Only the whitecaps of the ever present waves of the China sea were now discernable below us!

We had flown for seventeen minutes on the ninety-two degree heading, and Cronin was once again peering, (pointing like a bird dog) his nose practically against the plexiglass, staring into the void ahead of the airplane, trying to see a reef that was completely submerged. I'd grown used to this little copilot, seat-belt unfastened or adjusted very loosely, leaning on elbows that were resting on top of the instrument panel in a partially standing position, peering straight ahead trying to see through fog, rain, clouds, or like then — darkness!

With the last glimmer of dusk, just before it gave way and capitulated into the darkness of night, Cronin yelled, "There it is! There it is! The reef! The waves are breaking up over it — it's white, cause the water's so shallow!"

"You're right!" answered Born, showing a certain relief in his voice. "That's the reef! Our heading is ten degrees."

Now we could steer a course from our known position to the island of Luzon. We were flying directly into the five thousand-foot mountains that surrounded San Marcelino airstrip on three sides. I climbed to six thousand feet and into a buildup of stratocumulo-form clouds. I turned on the landing lights, hoping to see what was ahead. This, of course, was more for peace of mind than doing any real good, because the airplane traveled so fast that we had flown through whatever might have been ahead of us before the beams of light could illuminate, and allow our eyes to focus.

"I'd stay and fly an extra two weeks of combat, past my tour of duty, for a radio beam and a full range of ILS radio facilities down there to bring us in," I said out loud.

"I'd almost stay an extra month myself," answered Cronin, trying to see through the clouds with his same previous concentration, "for that same radio range!"

I'd never really appreciated the responsibility of the first pilot, aircraft commander before. Every man on the crew had his duties and each had to perform them well for the aircraft to operate. But the first pilot was the captain and, regardless of the circumstances, he could never shift or share the responsibility as the leader, with anyone. He was held responsible, and readily accepted the tradition that whatever misfortune occurred on any mission was basically his fault. Having forgotten the concern generated by our failure to find the reef before darkness hid it until morning, a short time before, I gladly accepted the full responsibility for putting this airplane and its occupants on the ground, under instrument conditions, but without any radio navigational aids whatsoever.

We were picking up some turbulence as we approached the heavier built-up cumulus which had to be the result of cooling factors and warmer air from the sea against the mountains. *Luzon and San Marcelino shouldn't be too far ahead.*

"If anyone sees anything below us," I said on the intercom, "let me know immediately. A light — or anything!"

The turbulence stopped abruptly as we burst out of a large cumulus cloud and when I looked down, I nearly dropped my teeth. There below us, six thousand feet straight down, was our valley and San Marcelino airstrip.

"Turn on the IFF before they shoot us down," I shouted to Cronin, pointing straight down at what I'd seen.

The opening in the clouds was no wider than the valley and those mountains on three sides of the runway were still occluded; hidden in the cumulo build-up. Under ordinary circumstances, back in the States, I would have ignored such a hole and stuck with the ILS radio navigational aids. But this was *seat of the pants flying,* and even if we had to circle inside those three mountains, we would have been in an even worse situation if we had stayed at that altitude.

Instinctively I chopped the throttles and held her nose high in an ever-tightening circle until I had dissipated our airspeed to 165 mph, then I wrapped the airplane in a near vertical, banking turn, staying within the cloud-free portion of the valley.

"Put the landing gear down," I yelled to Cronin.

"The gear won't go down!" he screamed back.

I looked at the hydraulic pressure and my heart jumped into my throat! No wonder it wouldn't go down, there was no hydraulic pressure to force the wheels down! That meant there would be no hydraulic pressure to force the flaps down either!

"Warnick!" I screamed into the intercom. "You've got to manually pump the wheels down! The hydraulic system is shot!"

"Roger!" came Warnick's voice. I heard activity in the well behind the cockpit as Warnick went to work.

We were still spiraling down and only the erratic backfiring of our engines broke my concentration. At three thousand feet the opening in the clouds widened so that I could see we were not as crowded; not sandwiched between heavy cumuloform clouds, as we had been at six thousand feet. We were descending at one thousand feet per minute, and I could reduce the rate of our descent with the increased visibility and space to fly in. At fifteen hundred feet I could make out the tents, the movies that were being shown in each squadron area, and the outlines of planes being overhauled and repaired in the service squadron. *The havoc I could wreak if I were the enemy,* crossed my mind. But now I needed room to maneuver while breaking away from the tight spiral while giving Warnick time to manually pump down both landing gear.

"How's Warnick coming with the landing gear?" I asked Cronin.

"He has one down and one to go," Cronin said.

"Let me know the moment he has both in place."

"Roger Wilco!"

We were down to six hundred feet and I turned back toward the open sea, the only direction that was free of rocks and mountains. I held the airplane at six hundred feet, awaiting the final word from Warnick that the wheels were down and locked. The minutes seemed an eternity! Finally Cronin gave me the thumbs down sign signifying *wheels down*. We were ready to land.

I had already started a slow turn back to the south but pulled it up tight as I saw the few lights in and around the runway beginning to disappear. Also, that big mountain was there on the edge of that gloom and ooze, and I wanted no part of that mountain!

"Call the airspeed! And don't stop!" I yelled at Cronin. I had the wheels down and I was indicating 165 mph! I was about a mile south and thirty degrees off the side of the south end of the runway.

"One sixty — one sixty — one fifty-five — "

I eased over and lined up with the runway. "Warnick, can you find me fifteen degrees of flaps?" Our engineer had anticipated our need and at that moment I felt the airplane balloon slightly as he cranked the flaps downward, changing the shape of the airfoil and slowing us down!

"One fifty-five — one fifty-seven — one-sixty . . . "

I had to maintain 160 mph to control the heavy-nosed airplane when I leveled off previous to setting her down.

"Gimme some landing lights!" And Cronin hit the lights that illuminated the runway as we swooped down. The landing gear touched and I held the nose wheel off until the speed was dissipated. Cronin switched the lights off quickly, knowing the intensity of their heat on the ground would quickly burn through the transparent plastic material that protected them. A jeep suddenly appeared out of the darkness and we followed it to our revetment.

As I stepped down into the well behind the cockpit, I found it full of hydraulic fluid. The line had broken during our flight, releasing all the pressure and destroying the capability of operating our landing gear and flaps.

"You came through again," I said to Warnick, "and landing with the wheels down, in preference to the wheels up, sure makes it easier to walk away from the airplane!"

"It sure does," said Frank Born, our navigator, in agreement.

"I appreciate the way you found the reef, Frank," I added,

"the point of reference from which we got a heading to make it back here. That was a nice piece of navigating."

"We almost stayed out too long, though, before we started looking for that reef," he responded.

"That was my fault," I said, "I should've insisted on our starting back a little sooner!"

"Yeah! But we didn't know that we wouldn't find those poor devils in another two or three minutes!" said Born.

"But we tried and that's all any of us can do!" I said. The crew we were looking for was never seen or heard from again.

When we got to the mess tent, a short time later, a couple of Born's navigator buddies were waiting for him. After we were seated at the table they made their grand entrance and presented him with a little box containing an aircraft compass with this poem attached:

"Next time you fly, take plenty of gas
Just in case you lose your ass!
But if you're lost, and start to stray
Let this little compass point the way!"

It was a fitting climax to an otherwise tense and tedious flight and we all enjoyed the fun and laughter of the living.

This would be the next to last flight Lieutenant Frank Born, from Chicago, Illinois, would ever make. His airplane was shot down on a strike to the China coast the next day, with the loss of the entire crew.

<u>CHAPTER FIVE</u>

Never To Sydney For Love

> *Conscience—that vicegerent of God in the human heart, whose still, small voice the loudest revelry cannot drown.*
>
> W. H. Harrison

> *I only know that what is moral is what you feel good about and what is immoral is what you feel bad after.*
>
> Ernest Hemingway

"Blount!" exclaimed Thatcher, bursting into my tent, "you're on the list! *You've made it!*"

"Made what?" I asked, rolling over in the sack and still half asleep.

"We're going to Sydney for R and R! Land of the free and the home of the sexually depraved!"

After ten missions, if you were still alive and in good health, flying personnel became eligible for Rest and Relaxation leaves to Sydney, Australia. Paradise of the world! It was the most immediate reason for any red-blooded, patriotic, horny male to stay alive.

"I'll get you lined up with the most beautiful blonde you've ever seen," he added. I didn't doubt his veracity because he had been there twice and the stories of his sexual conquests were legend in the squadron.

"I've had you lead me before," I replied, "like taking me in unannounced on a Jap destroyer without my guns charged or my bomb bays open and then crowding me off the target to boot!"

"Now I couldn't help that," replied Thatcher, "you know your radio was out and there was no way of telling you otherwise!"

"You still have hands — you could've waved, waggled your wings, or anything!"

"I know, but I'm gonna make it up to you in Sydney! We're gonna have a hell of a time!"

According to the old-timers who were veterans of at least one R and R experience to Sydney, all the Aussie women were tall, blonde and beautiful, sharing an ancestry common to our own. But while these young ladies looked like American girls, the Aussie lassies had a "better understanding for what their bodies are made for and their purpose in life" as one old-timer put it. Being a part of the British commonwealth, the mother country had given the Australian fighting men some rather tough assignments. Most able-bodied males were in Europe and Africa fighting for England. Under great odds they had acquired the nickname of the "Rats of Tobruk," in stopping the German *Panzers* in Africa. Like the popular song of the time, the Aussie women could sing with feeling and understanding:

They're either too young, or too old,
they're either too gray or too grassy green . . . .

and those that were left fought for their homeland in the jungle hell of New Guinea, "leaving thousands of unsatisfied and sexually deprived women who'll tear your clothes off of you right on the street" — according to Thatcher.

"How do you go about this? I mean what do you do, Thatcher?" I asked.

"Whatta you mean what do you do?" he replied, "You don't have to do nothin' but pick the woman you want! Just remember never to end a proposition with a sentence. And if you're wise, you won't pick the first one but work the crowd before making a choice!"

"Well, you don't just walk up to a girl and say 'Howdy do, Ma'am, would you like to go to bed with me?' do you?"

"Blount, for twenty years old I know you must not've had much experience in the ways of the world, but you can't be that dumb!" exclaimed Thatcher.

What Thatcher didn't know was that he was talking to a novice. There before Thatcher stood the guardian *extraordinaire* of the chastity of the girls of Big Spring High School I had been encouraged to escort by doting, matronly mothers. They had regarded me as a highly respected and moral young gentleman who could be trusted to protect the virginity of their high school daughters. Always too busy playing football and basketball to have time for girls, my invitations to high school proms, presentations, and coming out parties came complete with the name of the young lady I was to escort already selected for me by a zealous mother.

Charles T. Thatcher was a slender one hundred forty-seven pounds on a five foot nine-inch frame. He always wore shorts and the typical Air Force Pilot's cap with the thousand hours crush, and if you hadn't known better you would have sworn that artist Milton Caniff had used him as a model for the hero of his popular cartoon strip *Terry and the Pirates*. His skin was a yellowish bronze, the result of a combination of atabrine and Philippine sun. A wisp of blondish-white hair protruded from under his pilot's cap that framed a face with a mischievous smile and dancing brown eyes. When it was available, regardless of the hour of the morning, afternoon, or night, he had a bottle of beer in one hand. With no ice or refrigeration at hand, he drank his beer hot, after allowing it to sit in the open sun for a few hours.

"I'm never going to drink a cold bottle of beer again,"he vowed, "drinking it hot is the only way you can really taste it!

"You've got to give in to your feelings! If it feels good do it! There's not a man alive who's twenty-nine years old that hasn't had 'satchel fever' and the 'sweet ass' at least once in his life!" said Thatcher.

"You say that," spoke up Kuta, "because you've had 'em both and you're twenty-nine years old! But what's 'satchel fever?' "

"Satchel fever's like you and me gettin us a couple of gals in Sydney and goin to Mansion's Bar or some other Pub and drinkin' and just saying anything in front of 'em we want to without being careful of our language at all. Then afterwards hustlin' the women back to the apartment with some more drinkin' and fuckin', and then maybe we'd switch gals in the middle of the night! But the sweet ass is when you think you've done found that virgin, that one and only dream woman who hasn't been touched by any other male member of the human race! And you wouldn't stand still, you wouldn't *tolerate* anybody saying anything out of line, or the least bit off-color around her, or within her hearing. And then after you've kept her up for about six months or a year you come to find out she's got somebody else just like you. And that's when you start walkin' the floor cause here's the sweet ass that you *knew* was a virgin, the only woman besides your wife, that you ever really loved — and then you walk the floor all night long!"

"Who gets that involved with these Sydney women?" asked Lathrop. "Everybody knows, including the women, that R and R, for us, and all those like us, is only a one-night stand!"

"You'd be surprised! Half of these bastards who sleep with a woman think they own her, and that she won't sleep with anybody else!" responded Thatcher.

"That's what McDearman down in the 500th thinks about my little blonde in Sydney! He thinks he's the only sonofabitch gettin' in her pants, and that's all right, if it keeps him happy! I'm for keeping the morale high and the sexual desire appeased among all the fighting men in the U. S. Air Corps, particularly in the 345th!"

"What if McDearman finds out about you?" asked Mathews.

"My little blonde's not gonna tell! She's having too good a time! And the odds of us going on R and R to Sydney together are practically nil!"

"If that was me, and with my luck," said Kuta, "the other guy would be in Sydney on R and R, unknown to me, and we'd both be gettin' in bed at the same time from opposite sides — and meet each other with the woman in the middle!"

"But how do you make contact with these girls? What do you do?" I asked.

"Well, you've got to realize that we're looked upon as conquering heroes. We've driven the Japanese from the doorstep of Australia and removed the threat of the oriental dragon.

American movies and the favorable press and radio down here have created an image that all the women simply swoon over, and they are anxious to do anything — and I mean do anything — to please us!" explained Thatcher.

"It's our patriotic duty to relieve the war tensions of our female allies," he added, "and I'm just the one to do my patriotic duty!"

"Don't you listen to anymore of this, Blount! You're contributing to the delinquency of a minor," Bell said to Thatcher, "and back in Oklahoma that'll get you two to five!"

"That's not delinquency," replied Thatcher, "that's education!"

"You need to be educated like I educate my bull calves back home," said Bell. "I change their minds from ass to grass!"

"You do what?" asked Thatcher, with a perplexed look on his face.

"With a couple of helpers," said Bell, starting toward Thatcher across the tent and brandishing his jungle knife, "we spread the calf's legs, pull his balls out to about here and then make a jagged cut which holds the bleeding to a minimum! Dob him with a little blow fly ointment and he grows into a fat handsome steer like Blount, thinking only of grass, instead of a little ole scrawny, dried up, skinny, emaciated, scrub bull like you, thinking only of ass!"

"Just because I'm a little younger doesn't mean I'm impotent," I responded, "when do we leave, Thatcher?"

"It better be pretty soon," said Kuta, "every morning for a week when Thatcher wakes up and rolls over on his back, it looks like the circus has come to town!"

"Whatta you mean it looks like the circus has come to town?" asked Blair.

"The tent pole's up!"

"Oh, you mean he pole vaults out of bed!" said Blair.

"Monday," continued Thatcher, ignoring his detractors, "day after tomorrow morning. I have us an apartment at Bondi Beach and we'll go from there. We'll go to King's Cross, where most of the single working girls live — although we won't discard any married women if they catch our eye — about 1700 at Mansion's Bar or the Roosevelt. They're so thick you can't stir 'em with a stick! Of course, we must sign up at the Leave Bureau to get our liquor cards and ration tickets. I'll trade you some extra ice cream and milk for your liquor card — maybe we'll go to the Australia and pitch pennies up at the big glass chandeliers while we're looking for suitable women.

"Is Thatcher that good with the women?" I asked Bell in a low voice, off to the side.

"Yeah, he's that good," answered Bell, the Oklahoma rancher, "I've seen him operate! Women — perfect strangers — cuddle up to him like a sick kitten snuggles up to a hot brick!"

"I don't know whether Sydney is for me or not," I sighed to Thatcher later.

"I can't believe what I'm hearing! Say that again!"

"I really don't know whether Sydney is the place for me right now." I continued. "To go down there for a week knowing that I still have to come back here and fly more combat — I don't know that it wouldn't be best to just stay here till I get through, be done with it, and go home."

"I can't believe this," said Thatcher, "there's not a man in this outfit who wouldn't give his left testicle and an arm to go to Sydney and you're hesitating! That's why they send us to Sydney, Blount! To get us out of combat, get our minds off of killing and being killed — give us some rest so that we don't go crazy — so we can come back and keep on killing Japs, after we eat, drink, and make Mary."

"That's what I'm talking about," I replied. "I think I'm an average Joe when it comes to facing up to the risks we take on every mission, every day that we fly up to Formosa, the China sea, or the coast of Indochina. There's an empty sack right there that had a buddy in it day before yesterday who's not with us now, and the odds of our making it are gettin' smaller for all of us with every strike we make."

"Don't give me that shit! What does flying more missions have to do with gettin' to Sydney — except the more missions you fly the more reason you need, and the more you get to go to Sydney." He looked at me with his head to one side. "And being a good, righteous Christian, ain't gonna save you. I've seen the good ones as well as the bad ones get it. That Jap flak makes no distinction between the good and the bad, and it doesn't make any difference if you're a saint or a sinner!"

"That's where you're wrong," I said, "you don't know what you're talking about!"

"Don't tell me," he replied, "the good, the religious, they

get shot down just like the atheist, so what difference does it make if you're religious or not?"

"All the difference in the world," I said, "it comes down to how you accept adversity, live with failure, and accept death. There are some people whose faith is so strong that they think they'll be better off when they're dead. They're the ones I'm trying to understand — the ones I'd like to be like!"

"When you understand 'em you let me know about it!" he replied with a puzzled look on his face.

"What I'm trying to say, if I don't make it back from that strike to Formosa tomorrow, and on Monday I've got to rendezvous with my Lord instead of with you in Sydney," I reasoned, "my conscience tells me it will be clearer if I stay here and keep flying and fighting rather than going to Sydney and — "

"Fucking and fornicating!" Blair broke in.

"Now Blount might have something there, Thatcher," spoke up Lathrop, "he reads his Bible and I was wondering how he was going to reconcile Sydney with what he was reading."

"I read my Bible, too," said Thatcher.

"When it opens it falls open to Sodom and Gomorroh!" added Kemp, one of Thatcher's tentmates.

"Aw come on, Blount," said Thatcher, "rotten up with the rest of us. We're gonna trade our boredom for a fine Bordeaux! Trade celibacy for a bouncy bordello!"

"We'll see, I've got a couple of days to make up my mind!"

"Lieutenant Blount! Lieutenant Blount! Report to Operations!" came the announcement over the PA system.

"Whata you need?" I inquired of Sergeant Franko, reporting in.

"Captain Musket wants to see you, Sir. He's right over there," said the Sergeant, pointing to the other side of the Operation's tent where George Musket stood in front of the board containing the Squadron maps, charts, and duty rosters.

"You want me?" I asked Musket.

"The Service Squadron has a ship with a new engine in it that needs to be test flown," he stated, glancing up from his paper work, "can you give it a test hop? This one will give us eight good airplanes for the strike tomorrow if it checks out!"

"The pleasure's all mine!" I replied.

"Tell Franko to get hold of whoever you want to fly with you!"

"Call Warnick and tell him to meet me here at Operations in fifteen minutes," I said to Franko, "tell him we're test hopping an airplane just out of the service squadron and to be ready to fly!" Even on test hops or a flight over the mountains to Manila we always took along survival gear and side arms. Three minutes in any direction by B-25 from our airstrip, we would be so far back in enemy country that it would take days to get back to San Marcelino and/or friendly forces if we crash landed or bailed out . . . and survived.

By the time I changed clothes, got into my infantry combat flying boots and back to Operations, Warnick and our jeep were waiting.

"Kolodziejski wants to go along, too," said Warnick, "and he said he'd meet us on the flight line!" Hank was already at the airplane when we arrived, talking to three submarine officers who had driven up the ten miles from Subic Bay, Southwest Pacific Headquarters for our submarine fleet in the southwest Pacific.

"Lieutenant Blount: Lieutenants Johnson, Blake, and Allen," said Hank, introducing the submariners all around, "they'd like to go along for the ride if it's all right with you."

"We'd be delighted,," I responded, "for the many favors you people have done for the men of the 345th bomb Group, inviting us down to Subic Bay as your guests for those T-bone steaks and ice cream, test dives in your submarines, not to mention all the crews you've fished out of the drink when we've been shot down along the coast of Indochina. We're permanently in your debt! In fact, I'll ride in the back and let y'all fly the airplane if you'd like!"

"No, Sir, no way." responded Lieutenant Johnson. "We know about as much about an airplane as one of these Philippine natives knows about brain surgery! We'd appreciate just going along for the ride!"

"Do you have some ammunition in the turrets?" I asked Warnick and Kolodziejski.

"Yes, sir," came the response.

"All right, let's combine some business with pleasure and go down to the beach and make some practice gunnery runs on the old Jap ship that we use for skip bombing and gunnery practice! We can give you some idea of what we do in tactical combat maneuvers!"

Our new eager friends climbed the ladder into the rear of the airplane with their host, Hank Kolodziejski.

After completing my inspection tour of the airplane, going over the work sheet and discussing the repairs that had been made by the service squadron and the installation of the new number one engine, I climbed into the cockpit, started the engines, and rolled the airplane out of the revetment and toward the end of the runway for takeoff.

"Pilot to tail gunner. Over!" I said on the intercom to Hank.

"Tail gunner to Pilot," answered Hank.

"Give our guests a set of headphones and throat mikes, Hank, and put 'em on intercom so they can ask any questions and communicate in flight if they'd like."

"Roger wilco," answered Hank, as I continued to run the checklist while rolling toward takeoff position.

Turning the airplane at a forty-five degree angle at the south end of the runway, I revved each engine and checked the mags. As I turned the ship down the runway and looked for an all clear, ready for takeoff signal from the primitive, native wood tower, I checked with our guests.

"Everything secure in the back?" I asked.

"Roger," came the combined response from all four voices.

"Then hold on," I said, "I'm going to rev the engines, we need to check this new engine anyway, and when the airplane feels like it's coming apart back there, have no fear! We haven't lost more than three or four airplanes that fell apart from excessive vibration since we've been over here!"

With that admonition, I increased the throttles on both engines and held them there long enough to give our guests the full Mixmaster treatment of the massive shaking and vibrating of the airplane! After twenty seconds of noise and tantalizing turmoil, I released the brakes and the empty B-25 literally jumped down the runway. I gave Warnick, riding in the copilot's seat, the thumbs up signal as we hit the end of the runway and the wheels retracted, adding an immediate surge of thrust and airspeed. I didn't bother to gain altitude as I remained on the deck, exploded out of the jungle over the open sea, and dropped down so that only ten to twelve inches separated the end of the props from the water. We left a giant spray behind us as the whirling props picked up the sea water and threw it a hundred feet into the air.

"Tail gunner to Pilot. Over!"

"What cha' got, Hank?"

"Lieutenant Johnson says to put up the periscope, Sir!"

"Tell the Lieutenant to watch this, Hank!"

Dead ahead lay a sampan, the native sailing craft of the China sea and South Pacific, in full sail and moving at a right angle to our path of flight. I continued in a straight, bee-line for the little native outrigger and precisely at the last moment pulled up and over the sampan and right back over the water on the other side. Our prop wash and spray blew the native boat over on its side!

"I don't believe it!" came the voice of Lieutenant Johnson over the intercom, "that sampan is at least forty feet in length and its sails are a good thirty feet high!"

"We have a Sampan tournament going on in the Squadron right now," I replied, "and the first pilot to get fifteen, wins!"

"How many do you have?" came the question from the submariner.

"That's nine for us! Or is it ten, Warnick?"

"That's ten, Lieutenant!" came Warnick's reply over the intercom, "we got number nine last week when you were checking Lieutenant Lyman out as a first pilot!"

"Get in your turret, Warnick, and you do the same in the tail, Hank," I spoke into the intercom, "the target is about three minutes down the beach and we'll make a straight in approach on the first pass! You get it head-on from the top turret going in, Warnick, and you pick it up going away, Hank! I'll be fantailing the airplane taking evasive action just like it was a live enemy ship, Hank, so be ready to adjust your fire accordingly!" You could never get too much of this kind of practice and it was nice that the gunners could impress the passengers. On the first pass I pulled the airplane up to five hundred feet and dove on the target! Warnick raked the entire hulk of the ship from bow to stern and the incendiaries disappeared into the old ship hulk. At the last moment I pulled up and over the ship, fantailing the airplane in an evasive maneuver as I heard Hank's guns start their staccato chant! It was beautiful music, even in practice!

I racked the plane up into a chandelle to 1,000 feet at 300

mph that I knew had plastered our guests to their seats and began another pass at the ship.

"Pilot to gunners," I said into the intercom, "I'll take you by the ship on the seaward side to give you a side shot. As I get to the ship I'll lay it over on the right wing so that you have a shot right out of the top of your turret, Warnick. Got it?"

"Roger!" came the two voices.

I put the nose down and the empty B-25 responded with all 3,500 horses trying to jump out of the airplane. At 300 mph I put the ship into a steep bank, laying it over on its right wing about fifty feet off the water and Warnick and Kolodziejski had a field day. Their tracers and incendiaries described a huge arc, or a giant C, as they had to fire several widths of their gun sights ahead of the target to get their projectiles into the ship.

"Good shooting men! How are our guests, Hank. Over!"

"They say you're about to kill 'em, Lieutenant!"

"Tell 'em to hold on! We're going to fly straight and level now so they can enjoy the flight!" But I didn't say at what altitude!

Continuing on up the coast of Luzon I dropped down below the palm trees growing along the sandy beach as Warnick crawled down from his top turret and back into the copilot's seat. As soon as he was seated, I racked the plane to the right, putting the right wing between two big palm trees, and turned up a little stream just wide enough to accommodate the sixty-seven foot wing spread of the airplane, and dropped down on the water so that we could look up at the tops of the trees. I had never had a hot rod. Being a product of the great depression, I never could have afforded one. Uncle Sam, however, had given me a B-25, which more than made up for such deprivation. In my attempt to impress our guests, however, I made an almost fatal mistake: never fly minimum altitude over an unknown area where you're not familiar with the topography and surface features. On every land target that we hit on Formosa and along the coast of Indochina we knew the height of every hill and mountain, and were intimately familiar with the details of every foot of ground over which our strike would take us. No one had ever told me about the jungle mountains north of our San Marcelino base, but I was about to find out, and suddenly.

Our sight-seeing tour was over Japanese infested jungle and we turned inland at treetop level, cruising at 250 mph indicated airspeed. A small range of mountains suddenly appeared. I took the north side of the range, remaining on the deck, and flew the meandering, changing path of the mountains without noticing their increased height the further away from the sea we flew. We had flown inland, and made several long, arcing turns around the base of various mountains, when the last turn found us flying into a box canyon at minimum altitude. Looking up quickly to see the height of our obstacle, I made my second mistake. Strafer pilots must be able to make immediate, corrective action in flight. On instantaneous impulse I pushed the props to 2300 rpm, advanced the throttles to full power, and started my climb straight ahead out of this situation, pointing the nose of the airplane at what appeared to be the lowest rim of the natural vessel that had me boxed in.

I glanced quickly at the instrument panel and the airspeed indicator was dropping alarmingly fast. I judged the mountains to be 2,000, maybe 2,500 feet, but we were about halfway to the top and still a good one hundred-fifty feet in altitude above the trees. *What's wrong now?* Everything appeared all right, but the seat of my pants told me otherwise.

There are moments of truth in the life of a pilot when intuition, instruments, or the immediate understanding of the problem allows him to decide within seconds what must be done. I started to second-guess my decision to climb out of this trap, but it was too late. I was fully committed to fly that airplane out of there, and straight ahead too. Even the slightest turn, at stalling or near-stalling speed, was the quickest and surest way to finalize a stall and wipe us out.

One hundred seventy! I started to pull back on the elevator controls simply to check, to feel. It was mushy. The memory of all those airplanes trapped in the box canyon and circling with a 500-foot ceiling on my first mission to Aparri, the airplane that I missed by only fifteen feet climbing out of the soup there, flashed through my mind! *How many chances does a man get before time runs out?*

One hundred sixty! That was the stalling speed of the airplane that I had learned the hard way, that nearly washed me out in advanced flying school at LaJunta! *Maybe I should've been washed out to survive this war! Maybe graduating and ending up in combat as a strafer pilot only prolongs the destiny and agony that eventually comes to all bomber-strafer pilots caught up in this insanity! I can't clear this mountain, I can't even clear the trees! But I'll make it if it can be made.*

One hundred fifty! That was the slowest I'd ever flown a B-25, and what held it in the air could only have been the hand of God! I could count the leaves on the trees. I had *everything,* props, throttle, and mixture, to the fire wall — as on takeoff — and I anticipated the deathly shudder that would tell me the airplane had stalled and we were almost dead on a mountainside in Luzon! Fright most often is an instinctive physical reaction, that causes the adrenalin glands to secrete their marvelous potions that some times inspire people to survive situations which should by all reason have been their end. On such occasions a man becomes oblivious to his hands, arms and legs as they function in a harmony of mental and muscle instinct. Fright creates fear, but confidence, bolstered by training and discipline, dispels it!

When the airspeed indicator dropped to 145 mph my hands, legs, and mental processes were entirely engaged in trying to satisfy the physical demands of flight. The airplane was light, thank the Lord, with Warnick, in the cockpit with me, and Kolodziejski and the three submariners in the back. Our total weight was 33,000 pounds and composed a mass which must be kept moving through the air at an absolute minimum of 160 mph. At any airspeed less than this we would stall and the law of gravity would write finis quickly and absolutely. The Tech Manual said so. There were two sources of life-saving speed and acceleration in that airplane: power from the engines, which we were utilizing at peak efficiency, and putting the nose of the airplane down and diving, which meant a loss of altitude. The airplane was only twenty feet above the tops of the trees.

What a way to go! went through my mind. Of all the combat, danger, explosions, bomb concussions, single engines, flak, close calls, and near misses I had been involved in, to finally have bought the farm test hopping a refugee airplane from the service squadron on a joy ride! What a stupid jackass I felt like.

There were eight basic engine controls in a B-25 with sixteen ancillary switches, knobs, and handles by which the functions of each engine was controlled. In addition, there were sixteen instruments with figures and red lines, to mark the limits of operation, which apprised one of the health of each engine. In a moment like that, the orchestration of the symphony of levers, knobs, gauges, instruments, and switches had to be directed with the hand of a Toscanini. An incorrect reading, a wrong movement, and there would be instant disaster.

The airspeed indicator needle quivered at one hundred-thirty. *Never had I observed one hundred-thirty airspeed on a B-25 in the air.* I lightly pulled back on the elevator controls. Nothing there. I dared not think, much less touch, the ailerons. To commit the aerial *coup de grâce* at that moment would have been to bank the airplane ever so slightly, and lose a trifling, minimal airspeed that would have been the difference between flight and disaster. Suddenly I was consumed by, but oblivious to, my own sweat, with large, salty drops flowing off my forehead and filling my eyes.

Then I could see the top of the mountain; I saw every crag, every crevice, and every rock. Could it be — ? Dead ahead was an opening, free of trees and exposing only jagged rocks. That would give us an additional thirty-foot edge between life and destruction.

One hundred and fifteen! It was now a race between the distance of 500-yards to the crest of the mountain, a final precipitous five hundred feet above us, and the disastrously diminishing airspeed necessary to keep the airplane flying. It would take nothing less than a miracle. A miracle of synchronization of all the factors of distance, height, speed, rate of climb, wind, and the peak mechanical efficiency of the Wright-Cyclone engines of that airplane, one of which was new and providing the purpose of this flight! Never would an engine receive a greater, more important test.

My last glance at the airspeed indicator was enough to bring on a heart attack. One hundred-ten! I didn't even know what was holding the airplane up. Was it the updrafts, a weather phenomenon peculiar to mountain crests that can suspend hawks motionless in the air? I had observed that countless times, lying flat of my back on South Mountain as a boy in west Texas. Glider pilots always sought mountain crests to gain altitude. *Heavenly Father, hold us in the hollow of Your hand.*

Instruments showed the cylinder head temperatures creeping into the red line area. With the most difficult hurdle ahead of us I made up my mind not to look at the instruments again. The engines were already beyond their endurance and had exceeded their normal operative heat limitations. One hundred and ten miles per hour, and we needed a minimum of one hundred-sixty.

The futility of my choice to climb out of that trap now haunted me in nightmarish proportions. I was grasping, mentally, physically, spiritually, for help that would avert our certain destruction. And it came to me in a flash — how to obtain additional or maximum lift from an airfoil! You change the shape of the surface to make the air, sliding over it, give you more lift!

"Full flaps, Warnick! Quick! Give us full flaps!" I yelled hysterically.

He slammed down the lever and we experienced the most debilitating, but stimulating, elevator effect, as the airplane shuddered and lost even more airspeed. However, we had ballooned straight up like a helicopter a good fifty feet and we were atop the mountain — our engines still at full military power, the airplane hanging on the propellers, but the mountain top was flat and we'd missed the rocks by inches. The top of the mountain was narrow, like the slender humped back of a wild boar hog, and I lost no time in easing the nose of the airplane down the backside, slowly milking the flaps up and picking up airspeed. We flew straight and level at 2,350 feet altitude, out of the mountains, out of the jungle, and out over the placid open sea where the air was smooth, each one of us contemplating deeply, our brush with disaster. Not a word was spoken for ten minutes. Warnick and I could only weakly look at one another.

"That was a great exhibition of *manual* dexterity!" said Warnick, finally breaking the silence

"Old *Manuel*!" I replied, with a nervous laugh, "I thought he died with all those other Mexicans at the Alamo!"

"He almost did!" said Warnick. "Had you thought that maybe what we thought was the top of that mountain might not've been the top at all? That there might've been more that we couldn't see?"

"Yeah," I answered, releasing a great sigh of relief, "that entered my mind when we were about two-thirds of the way to the top! But the embarrassment of such a situation, if there really was more mountain for us to climb, was too much for me to even consider!"

"I never knew that a B-25 could fly that slow," said Warnick.

"I didn't either," I replied, "and I hope I never have to fly one that slow again!"

"You know that our airspeed got down to ninety-five miles per hour?"

"Did what?" I asked, starting to feel faint and sick again.

"Our airspeed got down to ninety-five miles per hour indicated!" he repeated.

"When it got down to one hundred and ten I made up my mind that I wasn't going to look again," I replied, "there's nothing I could do about it anyway!" I had pulled empty B-25s off the ground at one hundred-fifteen miles per hour within six hundred feet, simulating an aircraft carrier-*Thirty Seconds Over Tokyo*-takeoff, but that was the first, and the last time I would ever fly the airplane at less than one hundred miles per hour.

"That just proves what my Aunt Jake always said!"

"What's that?" asked Warnick.

"That when the Lord closes a door, He always opens a window." I answered.

"He almost put the window a little too high!"

"Yeah! But He knew we were gonna make it!"

I flew directly back to San Marcelino and put the airplane on the ground. Taxiing into its revetment, I cut the engines and finished the Form I as the *whir* of the gyros spun down. When I climbed down out of the airplane our three submariner passengers were openly showing the effects of our flight. They had unsteady legs and ashen-gray faces.

"I thought for awhile there my mother was gonna get those two additional rooms she wants to add to our house back home in Virginia," said Lieutenant Johnson, the submarine officer.

"Two rooms on your home? I don't understand," I replied.

"My mother is the beneficiary on my service insurance policy!"

I grimaced, but said politely, "Sure enjoyed having you fellows along for the ride today, hope you'll come back. You're welcome anytime!"

"Thanks, but I think that does it for us," said one of the lieutenants, "I don't plan to ever get back in an airplane again. I'm gonna stay in a submarine."

I had learned my lesson. I would never go buzzing in an airplane again, where I did not know every inch of the countryside over which I was flying. I fully understood, for the first time, the old adage plastered on every pilot's ready room I flew out of in World War II:

There are old pilots and there are bold pilots,
. . . but there are no old bold pilots.

I brought myself back to the moral task of making a decision on R and R leave in Sydney. Why this gave me such a hard time, I don't know. There were two voices within me: one said "go," and the other said "no."

I told myself I could go to Sydney, see the sights, eat steak, lettuce and tomato salads, fresh vegetables, and all the ice cream and milk I could hold. I could see the shows, get away from this living hell, and relax! I'd earned it! There were other guys who'd give a year's pay just to have the opportunity to get to Sydney, and I'd never been there.

I didn't have to go with Thatcher and the other guys to pick up any women. And *really,* this was the first chance I'd have to wear all those brand new, fancy, dress uniforms the Air Corps had bought me. It had been a *really* dirty trick to send me overseas right after graduation from advanced flying school anyway. I *really* deserved a little vacation — and my country owed it to me!

The other side of the coin was that if I went to Sydney, I might not have control of every situation I might get myself into with my friends. Just because I had been scared a few times, away from home and halfway around the world, was no more reason for me to go to Sydney or anywhere else to do something I'd never do back home. I couldn't betray the confidence of family and friends. And what about that girl out there somewhere? The one I would marry. She deserved as morally sound a husband as I'd expect her to be as my wife.

I was still thinking about it when Warnick and I drove to the Field Hospital after chow that evening, about six miles down the road, to visit friends. Lieutenant Chester Kuta, one of the older pilots in both age and experience and with whom I had flown many misisons, had been admitted for a hemorrhoidectomy and Warnick's friend, an engineer gunner, had caught a piece of shrapnel in the leg on a strike to the China sea.

"Hold on to those bottles!" I said to Warnick, as we hit a chug hole in the road which made the Jeep try to become airborne. We had fifteen bottles of beer that had arrived the day before on a PX ship from the States. We had my ration of nine bottles for Kuta, and six for Warnick's friend. In addition, I had "requisitioned" a couple of cans of grapefruit juice from Doc Marcus and some cookies.

"I'm looking for Lieutenant Chester Kuta of the 501st Squadron, *Air Apache's* 345th Bomb Group," I said to the nurse at the reception desk of the hospital, "where is he, please?" Locating Kuta on the hospital records, the nurse gave me directions, and I proceeded to the tent ward where he was hospitalized while Warnick proceeded to locate his friend.

"Whatta you doin?" asked Kuta, as I walked down the aisle between two long rows of beds containing patients in various states of physical pain and suffering, with bodies rigged to tubes, bottles, and IVs.

"Come to see you," I replied, "how're you feeling?"

"I'm great! Pay no attention to the buzzards circling this hospital tent."

"Because of your good conduct, splendid cooperation, and devotion to duty, you've won yourself an all expense paid vacation here in the Southern Luzon General Hospital," I responded, "and Major Jones sent me down here to tell you about it, and to help you anyway I could while I was here!"

"The bedpan has already been emptied," came a smart retort.

"Watch your language or I'll smear your bedpan seat with airplane glue not to mention taking what I brought you right back to camp!" I said.

"What'd you bring me?" he inquired, looking interested.

"Nine bottles of beer. My entire beer ration for the next three months," I said.

"Gee, thanks," said Kuta, changing his tone of voice. He quickly tucked the bottles, the grapefruit juice, and the cookies out of sight under his bed.

"You know I was on that list to go to Sydney for R and R with you!" said Kuta, "And look what I've got in its place!'

"Aw, this isn't such bad duty," I responded, "all you gotta

do is lie here, eat, and go to the latrine a couple of times a day! Can I bring you anything from Sydney?"

"Yeah! One of those hot water bottles about 37-24-37!"

"From what I see running around here in nurse uniforms," I replied, "it looks like you've already got several of those hot water bottles!"

"They give you such a sponge bath that you want to take a cold shower!" said Kuta.

"Oh, we're angels of mercy," said a smiling nurse lieutenant, coming to take Kuta's temperature and overhearing our conversation.

"How're you doing, Lieutenant?" asked a bird colonel Doctor who followed the nurse and took Kuta's chart from the end of his bed.

"Just fine, sir! answered Kuta, "but I'll really be glad to leave."

"We'll try not to keep you here too long, lieutenant, no longer than is absolutely necessary," the colonel said, "we need every bed we've got, as soon as we can empty one there's always someone waiting to fill it!"

The hospital was still full of wounded infantrymen and allied units that had absorbed a lot of Japanese lead and steel in the Luzon reinvasion that had wrested the control of this real estate from the enemy!

"Don't leave anything out or take any shortcuts on this guy, Colonel," I said.

"Rest assured Lieutenant Kuta is to receive our Sunday Special Hemorrhoidectomy," replied the Colonel, "in fact, while we have him under, I plan to give him a new racing cam, universal joint, and dual exhausts, not to mention a whole new rear end!"

"You know, Kuta, you're in here for the wrong ailment," I said.

"What's that?" asked Kuta.

"Now if you were in here for an ulcer the Colonel would have no alternative but to sign your ticket back to the States," I replied.

"Is that right, Colonel?" asked Kuta.

"The Lieutenant knows what he's talking about," responded the Colonel, "that's right because we have neither the means nor the personnel to operate on and treat an ulcer patient!"

"I think maybe I've got an ulcer, Doc," said Kuta, "you should see what they feed us! They say food will win the war, but I don't know how we can get the Japs to eat it!"

"We'll check out your ulcer symptoms while you're here, Lieutanant," said the Colonel as he walked across the aisle to check his next patient.

"Is there anything I can do for you before I leave?" I asked.

"Not a thing," answered Kuta, "just have a good time for me while you're in Sydney. That's a wild place!"

"So I've heard! Let us know if you need anything." I took my leave without further comment about Sydney.

That night, after I got the mosquito netting tucked in and used the aerosol bomb to clean the netted enclosure of any stragglers, I reflected on Bible teachings, lust, goodness, and my indecision. I remembered "watch and pray that you may not enter into temptation; the spirit indeed is willing, but the flesh is weak." Was it ever!

The following morning was Easter Sunday and I was up at 0600 for the sunrise services held in the Bomb Wing Chapel about a mile down the road. And although seven of us overloaded a Jeep, it was a "Mountain Top" experience that I shall never forget. The chapel was made of native bamboo with a thatched roof, and the pew seats were metal bomb finboxes turned upside down. The bamboo chapel was decorated with hundreds of the largest, most exquisitely beautiful orchids in varied colors that I had ever seen. They had been picked by native Filipinos in the jungle. Orchids outlined the pulpit, the communion table, the sides, and every vacant spot in the chapel. By the time the service started, the little chapel was full to overflowing as military personnel continued to drift in by twos and threes from every branch of the service. They came in every imaginable form of attire, nurses with telltale blood stains on white uniforms, and infantrymen with helmets in their hands and carbines slung over their shoulders. They stood in the doorways and just outside the perimeter of the roof overhang, forming human walls of the chapel that had no walls. Every face was taut, tense, and rigid from the rigors of war. But their eyes, expectant and anxious, told you they were believers who had come of necessity, in response to the promises of Christ's love.

One of the things the Chaplain, a major with a deep voice, said:

"Dawn is the best time of the day. Birds know it; they start chirping at the first glow of light. Doctors know it; their favorite night-call expression is *Things will look better in the morning*. Most of us in the military know it because most of the fighting, and its preparation, starts at dawn. On Easter morning, God's morning glory of faith really blossomed into reality. The end of this body is not the end! There is another place and another dawn for those who have found another life in Him who is the Bright and Morning Star.

"One of the best known missionaries of Biblical history wrote a letter to the Christians at the Church at Phillipi just before his death. Paul wrote from prison, in Phillippians I: "God's greatest concern at this point is that we do not fail to give God our all, and to risk our all, that His purposes might be accomplished through us. It means that we be willing to put our lives on the line, to live and, if need be, to die, to fulfill our commission as God's soldiers and servants. We have nothing to lose and we have nothing to be afraid of."

After all, when you know that you are going home, there really isn't anything of which to be afraid, is there?

That Easter Sunday afternoon we played a softball game against the Troop Carrier, Air Transport Command from down the road, and beat them three to two. Afterwards we came back to the squadron area and Thatcher's tent, where there was a spirit of Mardi Gras as the lucky "Sydney Specialists" were packing and getting ready to fly out in the Group C-47 the next morning for "paradise."

"Sydney! Ah, Sydney!" said Roman Ohneumus, "I loved a girl there once — no three times."

"What were you doing?" asked Stapley, "taking a course in how to get your face slapped?"

"Sex is a misdemeanor in Illinois," said Thatcher, "the more I miss the meaner I get!"

"I can understand that after showering with you for the past month," replied Bell, "just bending over in the shower to pick up the soap could be a crime and injurious to your health!"

"I'm going to Sydney 'cause I don't like my steak and sex the same way!" said Walter Johnson.

"How's that?" queried Thatcher.

"Rare!" answered Johnson.

"What did you decide, Blount," asked Blair, "you going to Sydney?"

"Naw, he's not going," answered Thatcher, "he's got religion."

"That's about it," I replied, "but each of us has to dance to our own tune, and our own faith! Give Sydney my love!"

So, I didn't make the trip to Sydney, but I did have Lieutenant Lincoln Grush of the 500th Squadron purchase an Eisenhower battle jacket for me. I did get a memento from Sydney! One that I could wear and continue to enjoy while retaining a clear conscience!

There would be numerous and unlimited opportunities and situations in my future which would allow me to fall from grace. I wouldn't fair nearly so well as when I told my friends to "give Sydney my love."

CHAPTER SIX

Odd Man Out

A superior man is modest in his speech, but exceeds in his actions.

Confucius

"Superstitious? For the last three missions that we've put up an odd number of airplanes," said Lamar, "we've lost an airplane and crew!"

"That doesn't mean nothin'," replied Blair, turning over in his sack, "the guys who got it were just in the wrong place at the wrong time!"

"But the fact remains that every mission we've flown with six or eight ships, for the past two weeks, we haven't lost an airplane," continued Lamar.

"Who do you get those statistics from anyway?" I asked.

"Sergeant Franko in operations," replied Lamar, "I've checked 'em out and there's a definite pattern!"

I winked at Blair and he smiled. We both knew that each of us was looking over our shoulders and straining at every superstition from numbers to rabbits' feet to Saint Christopher medals to steel-jacketed New Testaments, to find that elusive answer to the perplexing problem of how to stay alive.

"That's just superstition, Lum, trying to say that when we have an odd number of airplanes flying a strike, we lose one," I stated, "and there's no place for superstition in fighting a war! It'll make you do silly things!"

"Like what?" he asked.

"Like me not flying a mission without wearing my red leather hunting cap," I replied. Lamar threw the towel hanging over the end of my sack at me.

"That superstitious crap doesn't bother me!" said Wild Bill Bell, the Oklahoma cowboy.

"Yeah," added Thatcher, "I saw him lie down with a witch in Sydney and go sound asleep!" Bell reached for a boot under his sack while giving Thatcher a menacing look.

"What would you do if a black cat ran across the runway on your takeoff to hit the Jap navy in the harbor at Hainan?" I asked.

"Just what any average, ordinary, red-blooded, bull-dogging, calf-roping, bull-riding, bronc-busting, steer-wrestling, Grade A, U.S.D.A. approved, young American citizen would do!" he answered.

"What's that?" I asked.

"Spit over my left shoulder, then spit on the middle three fingers of my right hand and stamp 'em in the palm of my left, followed by a closed left fist punched into the palm of the right hand three times with feeling! That's guaranteed to remove the spell of any black cat anywhere in the world, even here in the Philippines!"

"What in the hell does spittin' and rubbing your hands in it have to do with anything involving a sane, rational and civilized human being?" asked Esty. "Whatta you think, Doc?"

Doc Marcus, the infallible flight surgeon, seemingly dozing quietly with eyes closed and apparently oblivious to this verbal banter, answered without opening his eyes, "Bell might have something there! I've seen some strange, miraculous and unexplainable cures in the field of medicine. And while I'm no psychiatrist, who knows that some good solid spitting and patting it in your hands doesn't remove the evil spell of a black cat?"

"Aw, c'mon Doc!" said Esty, while Doc Marcus winked at Bell.

The fact was, there was a lot more than superstition that

had all of us looking at our hole cards! Pilots were beginning to use any excuse to return to base after taking off on combat missions. So many, in fact, that Colonel Coltharp, Group CO, set up a Board of Inquiry. Every pilot and crew had to appear before this Board if they returned from a combat mission before hitting the target.

"I don't care how many Boards of Inquiry they make me appear before," I said, "if there's something wrong with my airplane, we're coming home!"

"That's bullshit, Blount!" said Jay Moore, "you'll fly that mother without a rudder if old Fuzzy Balls tells you to."

He was right, of course. This was the kind of talk reserved for tent bull sessions. Things were different when we were faced with serious aircraft operation problems. I had returned from a strike against enemy shipping near Hong Kong a couple of weeks earlier. After being out for an hour, excessively high fuel pressure built up in the right engine and the transfer system on our right auxiliary fuel tank failed to function. Warnick had tried everything in the book — and some things that weren't. He tried various combinations of crossfeeds, valves and pumps, without success; so I made a 180-degree turn and came back to San Marcelino. I wondered if I'd return in light of the new Board of Inquiry Regulations? With the pressure on us to proceed, no matter what the engine or flight instruments or our common sense told us, it would take an engine falling off the wing to make any of us return from a strike, after once taking off. Despite all of my big talk I knew very well what I'd do in the face of Group's new decision to have a Board of Inquiry investigation and interrogation of pilots and crews who turned back! "I'll fly it if it harelips the son of a bitch!" said Lamar.

"The mission today is a Jap convoy proceeding north along the China coast," stated Captain Musket, pointing to the general area where we could reasonably expect to make contact with the enemy.

"This is a twelve-ship convoy, seven merchantmen escorted by five warships," he continued, "and all the warships are thought to be destroyers, although one of them might be a cruiser. The warships are our targets. If we can sink the warships, our subs can get the merchantmen."

"Stay away from that cruiser," whispered Kenney, "if we find that convoy!"

"Don't have any choice," I replied, "we're flying Thatcher's wing in the third flight and if he gets the cruiser, we get it too!"

"If we get the cruiser we'll be the loser!" said Kenney under his breath.

"Shut up!" came the irritated response from two or three men nearby. I gave Kenney a hard look.

"Lieutenant Baker will give us the weather," concluded Captain Musket.

"There has been a front moving north over the China sea and up the coast of China for the past two days, and that's where this Jap convoy has remained," said Lieutenant Baker.

"They're hugging the coast and staying up under the low ceiling provided by this massive weather disturbance. If you locate the convoy, you'll more than likely have to fight the weather as well as the enemy! Good hunting!"

"We're the ninth ship and we're last to take off today," said Cronin, leaning over and yelling to be heard above the roar of the engines.

"Yeah!" I answered as I watched the seventh ship start its takeoff roll as the sixth plane became airborne at the far end of the bowling alley. "What difference does that make?"

"Oh, I was just wondering if you were superstitious!" he added.

"The master of superstition is the people, and in all superstition wise men follow fools!" I replied.

"Who said that?"

"Bacon!"

"How do you know?"

"Used it in a theme I wrote in Mrs. Gentry's senior English class year before last!" I replied.

"What does it mean?" he asked.

"It means we're wise," I replied, as I started to advance the throttles driving *199* shaking and trembling down the runway, "following a bunch of fools into a thunderstorm along the coast of Indochina trying to find a Jap cruiser and destroyers that want to shoot us down!"

"Gimme ten degrees of flaps," I hollered about halfway down the strip, "and let's see if we can pull this ruptured duck off the ground!"

As I joined formation I checked my radio.

"Hello Kit Bag Leader! Do you read me? Over!" Silence!

"Hello Kit Bag Leader! This is *Touch O' Texas!* Do you read me? Over!"

Still no response.

Looking across to Thatcher's cockpit I got his attention, and held up my earphones with a palms up signal indicating my command intership radio was out. He repeated my signal, indicating he had no suggestions to correct the situation, and went back to flying his airplane.

"Pilot to Radio," I said on the intercom, "we have no intership radio communication, Zuber! Do you have any suggestions? Over."

"Radio to Pilot. I sure don't, Lieutenant," came Zuber's reply, "the command radio is in a sealed box back here. I can't even get into it. That's something that the ground crew has to work on. I'm sorry."

"Thanks Zuber." He didn't know how truly sorry I was! Without contact with the rest of the squadron I imagined a hundred emergencies that all spelled disaster.

"What you gonna do?" inquired Kenney, who'd been listening on the intercom and spoke to me over my shoulder, "you gonna turn back?"

"Not on your life," I hollered back to be heard over the roar of the engines. "Not even if I have to wave semaphore flag messages out the window!"

"Pilot to crew," I announced on the intercom, "our intership radio is on the blink. We can neither send nor receive a radio message from the other airplanes on this strike. However, we're going to proceed as planned and fly the strike. The radio won't make that much difference. Are there any questions?"

I had several of my own, but there were none from the crew! I had never felt so isolated and alone. We always maintained radio silence after the first hour anyway on the way to a target. But there was a difference in having the radio and not using it, as compared to not having it and needing it. How would we know when to go into battle formation if we found the convoy? How could I receive any instructions from Captain Musket or Thatcher, my flight leader on this strike? I would just have to fly close formation and watch Thatcher for hand signals. I hoped that he would let me know in plenty of time before we made contact with the enemy convoy.

The next two and a half hours were spent in dodging,

weaving, turning, and circumnavigating the attendant thunderstorms along the path of the front we were flying into. That was good, in a way; at least it kept my mind off the dead radio. Captain Musket was doing a masterful job of picking the way, leading the squadron through the turbulence that was getting worse the farther we flew toward the China coast. With the increased bumps of turbulent air I moved out and up on Thatcher's wing. I could see him hunched down in the cockpit so low that I wondered how he could see over the instrument panel and through the windshield.

Light rain hit the plexiglass. For a moment it increased in intensity and hissed like that den of rattlesnakes Frank Webb and I found on South Mountain two summers before. Then it stopped, just as suddenly as it had begun.

"Give me the carburetor heat," I called to Cronin. He pulled back the two red knobs without hesitation, and adjusted them to maintain the proper temperature. That was the paradox of the weather we flew and fought in. It was so hot on the ground we'd perspire, but in the space of a few hours, it would be freezing only 2,500 feet above the China sea.

"How long we been out?" I asked Kenney over my right shoulder.

"Four hours and fifteen minutes," came the reply. I had noticed nothing but the eccentric, devious and erratic flight of the squadron. I constantly stayed glued to Thatcher's left wing; turning hard left and descending, then flying straight and level, only to turn back to the right and gain 300 feet of altitude with wind and rain gusts playing games with the controls.

It came as no surprise when we turned hard left and started to lose altitude at 500 feet per minute. Just another maneuver in this rotten weather that provided a moving pocket for that Jap convoy to hide in as it moved north along the coast of Indochina. We would never find our quarry today, I thought, and it was time to start thinking about turning back, if we were to have enough gas to make it back to base.

"How much gas we got left?" I asked Kenney.

"Warnick has just transferred the last gas out of the Tokyo and Radio compartment tanks!" answered Kenney. "We can't stay out here much longer and make it back to San Marcelino."

So it was a rapidly diminishing fuel supply, and this continued pattern of flying, demanding acceleration and constant throttle-setting changes to circumnavigate thunderstorms, was not conducive to obtaining maximum fuel consumption.

Those were my thoughts as we rounded the edge of a dark, billowing mass, and burst into a clear area, much like an amphitheater with a 500-foot ceiling. We had the first full view of an angry China sea that was churning whitecaps thirty to thirty-five feet high, blown by massive winds. The first full view of the angry waters, obscured before by the nasty weather until that moment at 300-foot altitude, didn't excite me nearly as much as the angry Japanese destroyer in front of us!

The destroyer was laying a screen of heavy black smoke from its smokestack directly ahead of us about a half mile, in a belated and useless attempt to screen the heavy transports of their convoy from our sight. We had caught them completely by surprise. They never thought, even suspected, that any rational, sane, human being would attempt to fly in that kind of weather — much less attack their ships during weather approaching typhoon conditions. Not even birds flew in that kind of weather. But the Japs didn't know the *Air Apaches,* or the men who sent us to sea in our flying machines. For that matter, and flying under those conditions, you could say that we also didn't know the men who sent us out there. Ours not to reason why!

"Pilot to crew! Charge your guns! Jap destroyer dead ahead! Everybody get with it!" I shouted into the intercom as I advanced power and prop pitch to 2300 rpm and pulled up close on Thatcher's wing, hitting the gun switches to arm the eight guns in the nose, and simultaneously opening the bomb bay doors. It was too late for flak suits and helmet! It was too late to tell Warnick to strafe straight ahead into the guns and superstructure of the destroyer and to tell Zuber and Kolodziejski, in the tail turret, to cover us from the rear as we went over the ship. Cronin and Kenney were pulling the manual cables between the pilots' seats, charging the package guns, as I opened up on the destroyer.

The airplane shook and trembled, the cockpit filled with gunsmoke as the .50s did their stuff. The firepower of both Thatcher's guns and my own guns obliterated the destroyer. We could see the superstructure start to melt. Warnick and Thatcher's top turret gunner were pouring a steady stream of armor-piercing incendiaries into the ship, and we had neutralized the destroyer's firepower momentarily, as there seemed to be mass confusion on the enemy man-of-war. The deck was alive with running, scrambling, or lifeless Japs, from the moment we started our attack until we leveled out to drop our bombs.

What are you doing Thatcher? I said to myself as he crowded me off the stern of the destroyer on the first pass as the enemy took evasive action. Being on the left, and on the outside, I kicked my airplane into a bank and threw a bomb that missed the stern of the destroyer about forty feet. The destroyer was mobile and could move surprisingly fast! I fantailed the airplane over and off the other side of the Jap ship, careful to keep the props out of the whitecaps and taking evasive action going away, as the tracers from the enemy ship passed over and under my airplane. For the first time I was appreciative of that rough and angry sea. It spoiled the aim of the Jap gunners. Thatcher was making a big turn but the longer we waited to resume our attack, the more time the enemy had to regroup and replace dead gunners. I noticed other airplanes, to the sides and further back under the dark and dismal canopy of black clouds, attacking other ships in the enemy convoy. I had stirred up my own hornets' nest and it was every man (and every airplane) for himself. *I can't wait for Thatcher!* I thought.

"Hit the toggle switch," I yelled at Cronin, to get him to activate the camera for the pictures that would record the effectiveness of our attack. I racked the airplane up in a tight turn, no more than five feet above the water, and carefully avoided the churning, giant waves with my wing tip as I began another run at the destroyer. The Jap commander had turned his ship in a wide arc, and as I started to close, he turned his bow to me with all the guns aft opening up simultaneously. Our withering .50s, with their armor-piercing incendiaries, ate the deck and superstructure like an army of termites in an abandoned barn. I dropped two bombs on the second pass and got a direct hit with the first, while the second hit amidships on the steel deck and bounced harmlessly into the sea on the other side. The first bomb opened a hole in the side of the ship big enough to drive a truck through and, moments later, sent the destroyer to the bottom. There was nothing to equal the (personal) satisfaction of seeing an enemy ship turn end up.

"I smell smoke!" I yelled into the intercom. The cockpit

was full of the smoke of gunpowder from our guns, but this was another kind of smoke. It had the distinctive smell of something "different" burning in the airplane.

"Find the smoke!" I shouted back over my shoulder as I wheeled to start another run. One of the enemy merchantmen, that had been protected by the warships (and who were now receiving the full attention of our Squadron) loomed dead ahead like a sheep strayed from the flock. I felt the elation that the wise and canny wolf must feel when he has eluded the shepherd, separated the sheep from the flock and is ready for the kill! The smoke inside the airplane continued to thicken with the smoke from our guns and the acrid smoke that was coming from an unknown source. I fantailed the airplane, spraying the deadly .50s like a giant firehose of destruction over the decks, and straightened the airplane at the last fraction of a second to skip my one remaining bomb into the side of the enemy ship. I could see the Japanese, huddled in fear and seeking any protection only twenty feet below me, as we passed over the ship!

Four seconds later, as the delayed fuse exploded the bomb, Kolodziejski reported from the tail, "The bomb raised 'er about ten feet out of the water, Lieutenant! She's going down!" Tracers from the enemy ships wove a web in front and to the sides of the airplane as we were then in the middle of the convoy. I saw two ships burning, another sitting idle and smoking in the water, while another was smoking and going in circles with its controls destroyed. We had sunk five ships, and left three more burning as we started for home on the tops of the waves.

"What was the smoke?" I asked into the intercom, as we started to assess our damage.

"It was the radio on top of the bomb bay, Lieutenant!" replied Zuber. "We took a hit in the radio and it caught fire. Lieutenant Kenney took care of it!"

"What did you do Kenney?" I asked.

"The thing was smoking so I just threw it out of the airplane," he replied. What he *didn't* say was that the radio, about the size of a bread box, was *bolted* to the top of the bomb bay by three-quarter inch steel bolts, metal to metal. Kenney had performed a herculean, superhuman feat by pulling the smoking radio from its bolted position, physically impossible for any human being under ordinary circumstances. And he had thrown it into the China sea! It couldn't be explained, but he did it.

"Did you drop it on that last Jap ship?" I asked.

"It was so hot I had to let it go a little early," he replied.

"Pat Neff would've been proud of you today," I said, referring to the revered and venerable president of his alma mater, Baylor University.

"Yeah," replied Kenney, "I hope so!"

"I think he'd even approve of that strong shot of Old Grand-Dad Doc Marcus is going to give you when we get back home," I said, "to settle your nerves!"

"Now I wouldn't go that far," replied Kenney, knowing the official position of aggressive disapproval of alcohol by the Baptists of Baylor.

While we hadn't lost an airplane on that strike, every ship had been holed and suffered damage. That could be expected everytime we hit Japanese shipping, particularly in the open sea. We had part of our right aileron shot away, a hole in the left wing, and, of course, the radio atop the bomb bay shot out. For the umpteenth time, old *199* went to the service squadron for repairs that would make her flight-worthy and ready for combat.

"We're going to have a new airplane before long," said Zuber, as we looked at the half-missing aileron on the trailing edge of the right wing, "if we keep this up."

"Whatta you mean?" asked Sergeant Allbright, the crew chief who was going over the airplane like an anxious mother.

"Everything on this ship will be replaced with new parts if we keep getting it shot up the way we have the last few missions."

"Nothing I enjoy more than putting old *199* back into flying order," replied Sergeant Allbright, "all I ask is that you bring it back and I'll take it from there!"

"Now that's a deal we can't refuse!" I added, as we all loaded into the jeep.

"It's times like this that I wish she were a horse!" I said.

"So you could pat her and rub her down?" asked Allbright.

"Yeah," I replied, "and give her an extra bucket of sweet feed for the way she took us in and brought us out up there today."

In spite of the adverse weather we had sunk four merchant

and five war ships for an estimated total 50,000 tons. We had expended twenty-six- and-a-half tons of 500-pound bombs and 74,000 rounds of .50 caliber ammunition.

"Why didn't you let me know we were starting to make a run on that destroyer this afternoon?" I asked Thatcher, going into chow that evening.

"What'd you want me to do?" he asked, "send up a flare? Wave my hanky out the window? I'm just a pilot!"

"Yeah! A Pontius Pilot!" interjected a disturbed Cronin.

"It was embarrassing, you know," I continued, "when all of us in the front of the airplane pissed in our pants!"

"That's really being scared!" added Kenney.

"None of us are perfect, Blount!" replied Thatcher, "particularly those of us who aren't perfect!"

I couldn't argue with that. I talked to Lamar later that night after chow.

"We had nine ships in the strike today," I said, "and we didn't lose an airplane! Kinda ruins your superstitions and doomsday statistics doesn't it?"

"Naw, we just had eight ships on the strike today," he replied.

"Lum, whatta you mean?" I said, "I was the ninth and last ship out of the chute this morning and I counted eight ships take off ahead of me!"

"You lost your radio didn't you?"

"Yeah!"

"Well, while we were flying in and around all those thunderstorms, you didn't hear Hardeman when he turned back with engine trouble," he replied, "eight ships made the strike and we didn't lose an airplane!"

"You can't believe that, Lum!" I said.

"The facts don't lie; an even eight airplanes and we didn't lose a ship!" he replied, "and that makes eight missions in a row without a loss! It's only a question of time," he continued, "we're all going to get it!"

"Get what?"

"Get shot down . . . buy the farm . . . cash in your chips!" he stated, in the blaśe, matter-of-fact tone of voice of a man resigned to death. "Premonition of death," he said, "could be God's way of telling me I'm gonna die!"

"So you've got it all figured out."

"Yeah! All my buddies — all the pilots and crews I came into the outfit with about five months ago — are gone. And all the signs are there. First, I've had five airplanes flying my wing on my last ten missions, shot down! Why not me? How long can this keep up without them getting me? Then if I had been on that mission to the coast of China earlier this week, in Van Scoyck's place like I was supposed to've been, that 20-millimeter shell would've blown my head off — "

"You keep talking like that and this 20-millimeter fist is gonna bust your jaw," I replied.

"But when I came to, nothing would have changed!" he responded.

"You're not going to get killed in the air — ," I grabbed him by the shoulders and turned him around so that we were toe to toe with noses only a foot apart. "Not up there where you can come in low, ahead of your sound, be on top of 'em, strafe and bomb, out fly, out fight 'em, and then get the hell out of there."

"I don't know," he said, "I hope you're right!"

"You bet your last dollar I'm right!" I added, "and don't you forget it!"

The Group went right back to the coast of Indochina the next day after the same Jap convoy and lost two airplanes. Lieutenant John Walker, pilot of one of the planes from the 498th Squadron, was a good friend. We had gone through the Replacement Training Unit (R.T.U.) at Savannah, Georgia, and had gone overseas together. The report said that he had hit the water going full speed, and there were no survivors.

The next week Captain Musket led a nine-ship strike to the coast of Indochina. They found a Jap convoy of four big tankers guarded by two destroyers and a destroyer escort. As our squadron returned from the strike we were playing the 500th in a softball game. The game stopped as we watched them straggle in by twos and threes. One airplane was either badly shot up, had wounded aboard (or both) and red flares illuminated the sky giving the "cripple" priority to land ahead of the rest of the squadron.

"How many ships did we put up today?" asked Esty.

"Nine!" replied Riehius.

"And I only count eight!" I said. Nine airplanes up and we had lost one.

We soon learned that Lieutenant Lum Lamar and his crew

had been lost to the gunners of the Japanese Imperial Navy. His copilot, Lieutenant Everett Thies, was my tentmate, and Lieutenant Frank Born, his navigator, had flown with me on the search mission the day before.

After chow that night Captain Musket, who had led the strike and had sunk one of the enemy destroyers, was in the Operations tent.

"Can you tell me what happened up there today?" I asked.

"Lum was leading the third flight and went in on the second destroyer," said Musket.

"He must've gotten both engines shot out or was hit in a vital spot because his plane lost power immediately. He ditched about a quarter of a mile from the good destroyer and another airplane reported seeing four survivors in a life raft. We got hit by about twelve *Zeros* after our first pass and we don't know what happened after that. Somebody did say that the Jap destroyer was making for the life raft as we left the target. Just wish we could've sunk that one too!"

"Yeah," I said, "that might've helped!" But we both knew that survivors in a life raft in the middle of a Jap convoy had about as much chance as the proverbial snowball in hell.

Musket went silent, staring at the pilot chart and removing Lum's name. I suddenly needed some fresh air and a drink of water. The lister bag, holding the Squadron's drinking water, was only a few steps in front of the Operations tent. A couple of the pilots who had flown the strike that afternoon were filling their canteens.

"Did you see Lum after he got hit today, Herb?" I asked Lieutenant Herbert Denny, from San Antonio, Texas, whose airplane sustained the most damage of any on the mission, and who had shot the red flare to make an emergency landing.

"Lum was off to my right but I think it was the second destroyer that we didn't get a bomb into, whose gunners got both of us," he replied.

"Captain Musket got the first destroyer," continued Denny, "but we just didn't get that second destroyer like we should have. You couldn't see the destroyer for the fire from their guns! That was the most helpless, exposed and frightening situation I've ever been in!"

"I know," I said quietly.

"But it was kinda funny," he continued, "we didn't hear a

thing from Lum's airplane! There wasn't a 'We've been hit' or even a 'Mayday' call! It was kinda like maybe he expected it and already knew what he was going to do!"

"Did you or anyone on your crew see any survivors?" I asked.

"I don't know! The fighters hit us about that time and we were lucky to get out of there with our skins."

"I understand," I said, "and we're sure glad you made it!"

As I started back to my tent I could hear muffled laughter coming from Kuta's tent with a piercing, loud and uninhibited "I Win!— I'll play any man from any land, any game he can name for any amount he can count!" from Captain Richard Burg announcing to the world that he had beaten the card off the top of the deck, and won his bet in the Red Dog game that had Townsley, Milton Esty, George Vincent, Heath Steele and Wendell Opdyke huddled over a table with the light of a 40-watt light bulb making them all look like mannequins except the winner. A couple of tents down, Lyman and a couple of his friends were playing records on a record player that had to be continually wound by hand to keep it playing. An Aussie pop tune they played night and day was being wafted on the night air for everyone within a hundred yards to hear:

I can tell by your knees that your folks
climb coconut trees,
Oh you're bound to look like a monkey
when you grow old!

Lum and Thies and Born would be in the Red Dog game, or listening to Lyman's monkey music if they were here, I thought, as I walked on toward the flight line, enveloped now in the quietness of the night. I stopped and gazed into a sky full of sparkling stars. And I thought of the advice, the things I'd said, the encouragement I had tried to give Lum only two days before. Had I been talking to myself, and for my own benefit as much as his? Yes, absolutely! How can death be a loss to someone for whom life seemed to have no meaning? I hoped he had understood the arrogance of my being so outspokenly alive, but I was at war with death. I was determined to win the battle as long as God permitted me to draw a breath and as long as anyone survived to listen to my plea. The very least I could do was to continue my personal war with that impostor by continuing to fight fear, pessimism, and discouragement — the cowardly allies of death. At least I would make the enemy take me by force and never by capitulation!

"Lum finally got to be the odd man out didn't he?" asked Blair the next morning. "There were nine ships in the strike yesterday and we lost one ship! It's almost prophetic isn't it?"

"I guess we're all superstitious to a degree," I answered, "but I can't buy that philosophy!"

Neither Lum, nor any member of his crew, was ever heard from again. I helped gather the pictures, the letters, diary and personal effects of Lieutenant Everett Thies, my tentmate, to be sent home to his parents and family in Arlington, Massachusetts. His clothing, sheets, pillow cases, boots, shoes, underwear, soap, all those items that made existence in the jungle a little more bearable but which were so difficult to come by, were spread out on his sack for anyone to take who had the need. These items soon disappeared, quietly and quickly, as the empty sack became immediately ready to receive a new personality.

"Thies would've liked that," said Blair, "he would've wanted his friends to get as much good out of those things as they could."

More new faces, — replacements — took their places the next morning as the olive drab army truck stopped in front of the Operations tent to disembark its bright, eager passengers. There were no "You'll be sorry!" salutations that had greeted all of us at earlier times upon arrival at Sheppard Field for Basic Training or Pre-Flight at Santa Ana. This was the end of the line where you really *could* be sorry. And that's why noboby said it.

At mid-morning, a couple of days later, Kenney and I were checking the bulletin board when a weapon's carrier pulled up in front of Operations and let out a pudgy, pipe-smoking individual carrying a B-4 bag and a typewriter.

The gentleman had been flown in by the Troop Carrier outfit down the road and they had been kind enough to deliver him to the 501st. Lieutenant Ike Baker, intelligence officer, subsequently introduced him as a war correspondent with the Associated Press who would be visiting us for a few days and who would like to talk to as many of us as possible.

"Send him over here and let him help carry my Purple Hearts," said Thatcher.

"You're drunk again, Thatcher," said James Harrah, "never saw a man yet who could hold his liquor like a bottle."

"Whiskey for me and beer for my horse!" responded Thatcher.

The Correspondent was introduced and we all shook his hand at evening chow. "You got here at the right time," said Kuta, "Cooky's pulled out all the stops, and is serving a culinary delight in your honor this evening, Spam A la Commandant or Spam Hash re-hashed!"

"Thank you," replied the polite, courteous journalist, "I appreciate this thoughtfulness!"

"Don't believe, or take seriously, everything these people tell you," explained Lieutenant Baker, leaning over and whispering in the guest journalist's ear, "they've been known to stretch the truth considerably when they think they've found a pigeon!"

"My mannerisms and appearance probably obfuscates my true nature," replied the correspondent, quietly, "but it's pretty hard to bullshit an old bullshitter!"

"I think you'll do all right," replied Ike Baker and they moved on through the chow line.

"Bet you'd like a good breakfast!" said Bell to the visiting journalist the next morning.

"I sure would but I'll settle for what you boys have to eat," came his reply.

After breakfast the journalist engaged Kenney in conversation.

"What's your name, Lieutenant?" asked the newspaper reporter. "Nat Kenney." "Where you from?" "San Antonio, Texas!" "What were you doing before the war?" "I was a student!" "Where?" "Baylor University." "What's your job?" "I'm a navigator." There was a pause. "Who's crew are you on?"

"Blount's! That big tall fellow over there."

"He's from Texas, too, isn't he? Is that why you two got together?"

"Naw! But it helped. We've lost so many crews that they split us up a lot — trying to give each crew as many experienced crewmen as they can. But I'd fly with Blount on every mission if I had my choice."

"Why is that — because he's the youngest pilot in this outfit?"

"Age has nothin' to do with it! He's the best pilot in the 501st and I asked to be assigned to his crew," replied Kenney.

"How do you know he's the best?"

"Mister, I was a navigation instructor before I got to combat and I've got over 3,000 hours in the air. I've navigated B-17s, B-24s in combat training, and C-47s, C-46s, and C-54s in the Troop Carrier and Air Transport Command! I've flown with every kind of pilot Uncle Sam has put through flying school — good, bad, in between, and otherwise — and none of 'em can make an airplane do the things Blount can do with a B-25!"

"Who's your closest friend?" asked the man from the AP.

"Lieutenant Claude J. Stiles from Louisiana, my tentmate! We've been together for a long time!"

"How long?"

"I met Claude Stiles in Carlsbad, New Mexico, in November, 1943. We were instructors teaching bombardiers to navigate B-25s and B-26s. We got on the bus together to go to Hobbs, New Mexico, to teach B-17 pilots how to navigate and how to check up on their navigators."

"You mean B-17 pilots couldn't trust their navigators?"

"With as many of 'em that were gettin' lost between Berlin and London somebody figured we better have somebody who could check on the navigators. We were stationed at Hobbs for only a month when I took Stiles and a couple of more of my buddies to San Antonio for Christmas. Well, we couldn't get out of San Antonio until after Christmas because of the weather, and in the meantime we had been put on orders and our outfit had been shipped out to combat with the 490th Bomb Group at Mount Home, Idaho. Stiles and I hitchhiked, rode a train all night, and ended up riding a bus through Wyoming and Utah; finally arriving at Mount Home, Idaho, two days later."

"Did you catch up with the 490th Bomb Group?" asked the journalist.

"No. The 490th had already shipped out when we got there. Then we were reassigned."

"How did you and Stiles get back together here in the 345th Bomb Group?"

"When I got to Kearns there was a list of one hundred-fifteen ex-navigator instructors on the bulletin board who were going to combat. Really old men by Air Corps standards! Claude Stiles was one of the names on the list so I got a room in the B.O.Q. for us together. We shipped out of Kearns on different planes to Nadzab, New Guinea, replacement depot for flying personnel in the South Pacific. They lined us up after we got there and we were sent to different outfits. But, somehow we ended up not only in the 345th Bomb Group, but in the 501st Squadron together."

"How did you end up on Blount's crew?"

"The first night here the officers had a prayer meeting — "

"The officers had a what?" interrupted the correspondent.

"The officers had a prayer meeting — they threw a party for us, that's what we call a party, you wouldn't know that, naturally."

"I was thinking this was a very religious approach, actually out of character for most of the personnel I've seen thus far!"

"That's a correct observation," replied Kenney. "The prayer meetings of the 501st really have very little, if anything, to do with religion, although our Chaplain does attend at times. At any rate, the officers threw a party for us seven old navigators the first night we arrived. Lieutenant Rico Pallotta, a little Italian pilot from Ohio, was playing his accordion, everybody was singing, and it all looked like something from a movie set. Anyway, I remember seeing this big, loud Texan who was singing louder than anyone so I stepped up to Captain Musket — "

"That's your Operations officer?" the AP man asked.

"Yeah, our Operation's officer, and I said to him, 'See that long, tall, Texas Joker? How about letting me fly with him?' "

"What has impressed you the most flying with the *Air Apaches?*"

"The minimum altitude. I mean *below the trees,* where everything is a blur at 300 mph. Our navigating is all dead reckoning flying *for hours,* and never seeing land from the time we take off until we get back to base. On one of our early missions, I saw this young Lieutenant Colonel come down to the flight line just before takeoff and bump the copilot on Captain Jones's airplane, and take his place. I learned later it was

Colonel Coltharp, our Group's CO. I was impressed. And, my first mission with Blount made a believer out of me!"

"What kind of a mission was it?" he asked.

"We were hitting a Jap convoy off the coast of China. According to the bearings given us by our submarines, through Fifth Bomber Command, we were supposed to intercept the convoy about twenty miles off the coast, but instead we caught them eighty miles off the China coast earlier than expected, and due west of where they had last been sighted the day before. We were flying Thatcher's wing behind Captain Jones. When we came out over the convoy, Captain Jones and his wing men took a sharp turn to the left to look things over. Not us! Blount found one of the escorting warships, a destroyer, and opened up with all twelve of those .50s. He put the tracers across the bow of that destroyer and then raked the whole ship from bow to stern clearing all the deck of Japs. We missed with our first bomb because Thatcher crowded us off the destroyer, but Blount flipped the bomb out of the bomb bay when he put the airplane in a tight turn — but the bomb went over the fantail. We made another tight turn to the left and made our second pass before the others had completed their first. This time our bomb hit behind the bridge. We were being shot at by the sister destroyer of our target ship and I saw a big black burst of *ack-ack* in front of us. Blount dove low under the *ack-ack* and I patted him on the back and said 'Atta boy, Blount.' We got all our electrical system shot out. The smoke was so thick I was choking and I thought this was my first and last mission with Blount. I told him to fly east and a little later we saw one of our own planes and flew back with them."

"I guess it was pretty much touch and go getting back?" asked the writer.

"Naw! Blount let me fly the airplane awhile coming back which was my first time, and probably my last, as the pilot of a B-25. I enjoyed flying with Blount so much that Musket has let me fly every mission with his crew ever since!"

"Do you know what he said to me after he let me fly the airplane?"

"No! What?" asked the Correspondent.

"Blount said, 'You create the illusion of flight admirably, Lieutenant Kenney!' "

When Major Jack Jones was interviewed by the correspondent, the interview was intelligent and long. But there was one thing I'll never forget:

"Incidentally, there's a Congressman who's talking about letting women into West Point! Do you have an opinion?" said the journalist.

"Well," said Jones, "it'll give a whole new meaning to lights out!"

"You're Lieutenant Blount, I believe?" asked the Correspondent, a rather pudgy individual whom I judged to be in his mid-forties. He had a brown mustache, smoked a pipe, dressed in fatigues, had pencils and tablet on the table, and a portable typewriter still in its case in the dirt beside him.

"Yes, sir," I replied.

"I just talked to Lieutenant Kenney," he said, "your navigator, I believe!"

"That's right!"

"What do you think of him?"

"Best navigator in the United States Army Air Corps, bar none!"

"How do you know?"

"He's never wrong! We fly out of here and see nothing but whitecaps and flying fish for four hours and I say 'When do we hit the coast of Indochina?' and Kenney will say 'Four- and-a-half minutes or 1047.' Mister, you can set your watch by it! And when he tells me we've only got forty gallons of gasoline left in the airplane after being in the air for ten hours and thirty minutes, I start looking for a place to set her down, because he knows! I know he knows, because I've checked him out after we got on the ground. He's the best fuel consumption man we've got in the Squadron, and out here that's life and death every day."

"You and Kenney sound like a mutual admiration society," said the correspondent, "he said the same thing about you!"

"That's good, we just believe in each other. I guess we have the same attitude!"

"How's that?"

"We always give our best, always do whatever is necessary

to carry out a strike against the enemy, and bring the airplane home, no matter what shape it's in!"

"What do you think about the rest of your crew?"

"I put my life, willingly, in their hands every mission! Does that answer your question?"

"Who are they and where are they from?" he asked.

"Staff/Sergeant Harold Warnick is a fellow west Texan and our engineer-gunner. He loves those Wright-Cyclone engines.

"Staff/Sergeant Joe Zuber, our radio gunner from Turner, Michigan, is as solid as the rock of Gibraltar. He possesses that quiet, retiring confidence that is deceptive. Once, the armorers failed to clean his guns on a night mission, and when he tried them, enroute to the target, he found they'd stuck. He took those twin fifties completely apart, fieldstripped them, cleaned each and every part, and reassembled those guns in total, pitch-black darkness so that they functioned perfectly for our strafing run on the target! Staff/Sergeant Hank Kolodziejski, from Pittsburgh, Pennsylvania, is the same caliber personnel as the others. So you see, we have the best team in this man's Air Corps!"

"What about your copilot?"

"I've had Ken Cronin, from Sheffield, Alabama, perhaps more than any other, but I've also had Townsley, Harrah, and a few others. They try to give copilots as much experience as possible, trying to get them ready to be checked out as first pilots. We need them. We're losing so many first pilots and crews! When the CO finds a potential first pilot among the copilots, he wants to put him in the lineup as soon as he can get him ready!"

"Lieutenant Kenney says you're from west Texas! I've done some writing for a paper or two in Texas, including the *Dallas Morning News, Houston Chronicle,* and the *Fort Worth Star Telegram.*"

"We get the *Star Telegram* every Sunday at home," I replied. "I grew up on the *Star Telegram!* But I never read anything except the funnies and the sports page!"

"They tell me you're the youngest man in this Squadron," continued the correspondent, "if not in the entire 345th Bomb Group! Twenty years old! Is that right?"

"Yeah, answered Kuta, passing by, "Doc gives him an antipuberty pill everyday!"

"You're a little young to be over here fightin' a war, aren't you?"

"I agree," I answered, "put that in your story and maybe a Congressman or the PTA somewhere will read it and demand the President and the Joint Chiefs of staff send me home for moral reasons! The things going on over here sure are a bad influence on a minor!"

What do you think about it? Being the youngest man in your outfit, a first pilot, and the CO of your airplane?"

"My Dad was in France in the First War when he was seventeen and my Great Grandfather was fighting for the Confederacy in Tennessee when he was fourteen. So I think I come by it naturally!"

"You have a gun-sight and a bomb-sight, don't you?" inquired the journalist.

"Yeah! But we've lost too many pilots and crews who used them. Do you know what you'd be doing to fire a howitzer, or drop a torpedo, or even drop a bomb if you were in B-17s or 24s? You'd have to spot your target, feed the speed into the computer along with the direction, and wind drift, wait for the answer, which you'd then crank into the weapon or bomb-sight and five minutes later pull the trigger or the toggle switch and hope you hit the target! By the time a bomb falls 20,000 or even 5,000 feet, a moving ship can be in the next ocean! If the target changes direction before all the calculations are in, you've got what the little boy grabbed at as the chicken went over the fence. With us, we see what we're coming in on, and in a split-second decision we decide how low or how high we wanta' come in, how much strafing, roll the airplane in, and aim it at the target with bomb bays open. If we're worth our salt we put the first burst of those .50's into the target neutralizing it, and setting it up for those 500-pound firecrackers to follow! And all of it is done without the help of one computer, gun-sight, bomb-sight, or any other mechanical aid except the one I've got in my head!"

"Or in the seat of your pants," added Kenney, walking back into the tent after getting a drink of water.

"Do you think anything good will come out of this war?"

"Yeah. Me!" I said, "if I get out alive!"

"Good luck, young man!"

"Thanks," I replied, "we're sure going to need it!" I stood up."One more thing," I added.

"Yes?"

"Say a prayer for us! All of us! And tell the people back home, too!"

"I will!"

"Thanks! That's the only thing that can bring us through!"

"What's your name, Lieutenant?" asked the war correspondent, catching Kuta after chow in the mess tent.

"Chester Kuta!"

"Is it all right if I sit here and visit with you while you finish your lunch?"

"You mean before this lunch finishes me?" replied Kuta. "Drag up a bench!"

"Those powdered eggs we had earlier weren't too bad," said the journalist.

"Not unless that's all you've had for breakfast for the last six months! We call 'em Eggs Benedict Arnold! They're nourishing but treacherous!" said Kuta.

"You're the Flight Surgeon, Captain Donald Marcus?" inquired the journalist. "That's right," replied Doc Marcus.

"Where you from?"

"New Jersey."

"Do many of your people get sent home because of nervous breakdowns or on your recommendation as a Section 8 discharge?"

"Hardly any! These people are the cream of the crop! You would expect them to be able to take more pressure, withstand more heat and perform their duties more capably under duress than the average GI!"

"I've noticed most of the personnel in this Squadron seem to be drinking a good part of the time, no matter the hour or time of day! Is there too much drinking going on?"

"It's all in the eyes of the beholder! It's all relative! When you take into consideration what these people are doing, the casualty rate, their prospects for being alive day after tomorrow, whatever they do — drinking or otherwise — can be understood when you know the unbearable pressures they have to live under just to exist; the things they've got to do to stay alive! If they didn't have an occasional R and R excursion to look forward to, I'm convinced we'd soon be running a funny farm instead of a fighting squadron!"

"I've heard about R and R leaves to Sydney! Sounds like most of 'em need to get back here to get a rest?"

"That's true and it's good! Almost without exception I've seen our flying personnel leave for Sydney on R and R, one step away from the little room with the rubber wallpaper, and come back normal human beings! I don't know about their escapades other than boys being boys, girls being girls and war being hell, but the leaves to Sydney probably make for situations that a young man wouldn't ordinarily run into if he was growing up on a farm in Iowa before the war!"

"The survivors, those who live through this experience, will there be any mental — personality scars?" asked the newspaper man.

"Yes and no! It will vary from individual to individual! Some will probably have bad dreams for years to come. But most of them, if this war will hurry up and end, are young enough that they will get back into their civilian pursuits and forget this nightmare! At least I hope so. If the young didn't heal so well there'd be fewer wars!"

"I agree, Doc. Thanks for visiting with me!" said the journalist.

"Thanks for coming to see us. We seldom get to see or talk to anyone from the outside world. Tell 'em our story back home!"

"I will," said the correspondent, "I surely will!"

"Hello, Lieutenant! Can I buy you a cup of coffee?" The war correspondent was addressing Lieutenant Charles F. Thatcher, in flying boots, pilot's cap with a thousand-hours crush, shorts, dog tags, and swigging on his ever present bottle of beer.

"Do I look like I need a cup of coffee?" asked Thatcher, in a stilted, sarcastic tone of voice. "If I drank any of that stuff I'd need an antidote! Don't drink it until your spoon dissolves!"

"I just thought beer at 0900 hours in the morning was a little early!" protested the journalist.

"If you never went to bed last night, it's still late in the evening, wouldn't you say," answered Thatcher, "and it's never too late for a bottle of beer!"

"Do you do a lot of drinking?"

"I guess you could say it's a lot of drinking if we were just sittin' around the house back home doin' nothin. But we don't do enough drinking for what we're doin' and goin' through over here!"

"Heck, if you — " started the Newspaper Reporter.

"You can say hell here!" interrupted Thatcher. "If you can't say hell in hell where in the hell can you say hell!"

"All right," answered the reporter, "how in the hell is your morale?"

"It's not allowed over here," answered a half-inebriated, totally frank and completely honest Thatcher, "it was real good for awhile, until it got so bad, then the colonel declared it off limits and we don't have any anymore! If we did have it, it would be lower than a gopher's basement!"

A pleased smile crossed Thatcher's face, indicating self approval of his answer as he took another draft of the hot beer from the bottle in his hand.

"The Colonel runs a tight ship so we're all pretty tight!" added Thatcher. The newspaper writer grinned as he took notes. Obviously he was beginning to enjoy Thatcher.

"Ask him about his Australian women!" volunteered Lieutenant George Foy, passing by.

"Do you ever get leave? R and R? Where do you go?"

"Sydney, brother! Beautiful Sydney!"

"Are you ever afraid?" asked the Journalist.

"Just at night when I start to fall asleep, and then just before dawn," replied a suddenly serious Thatcher. "When I realize where I am and what happened to my buddy — and I see the empty sack next to me where he slept last night but sleeps forever today — how I missed death yesterday, but will it get me tomorrow? And then you notice your sack is shaking; you have a chill although you're so hot you're sweating. Then you realize it's your heart beating, pounding so hard it makes your bed shake!"

"Do you want to see any of these people after the war?"

"If I live through this hell, and any of these nuts make it back; yeah, I'd like to see 'em! These guys aren't soldiers! They're misplaced civilians. But they're the fightin'-est bunch of bastards I've ever seen — and it's an honor to have served with every man in this outfit!"

"Then you respect your fellow combat pilots?"

"What kind of question is that? Politicians, whores, and strafer pilots all get respectability if they last long enough! All those that are still alive around here, and those that aren't, have my *undying* respect! And I emphasize undying!"

"What would be the nicest thing I could say to you if I had the opportunity, and possessed the authority to carry it out?"

"Congratulations, Thatcher! You're going home! *Alive!*" Thatcher took another long, comtemplative swallow from the beer bottle.

"Dress, military courtesy, and the usual spit and polish atmosphere of a military unit seems to be lacking here! Does this have any affect on the military proficiency of this Squadron?"

"Don't judge a book by its cover! You won't interview or talk to a braver, nicer, more talented, more skilled, more efficient group of killers in this man's Air Corps! And don't get your ass in front of one of their airplanes on a combat mission if you don't want it shot off quicker than a dog can tree a cat! Any pilot in this outfit would strafe his own grandmother — if she were standing on the bridge of a Jap destroyer! You don't pull Superman's cape, tug at the mask of the Lone Ranger, say a disparaging word about Hudson High in the presence of Jack Armstrong or question the efficiency, or the ability, of the gentlemen of this Squadron! We're informal, you might say, but we fight like hell!"

"After the war do you think you'll look back with pride on these days of combat? Do you think the people back home will appreciate your sacrifice?"

"When the war's over, nobody is gonna give a shit if you were a hero or a fuckin' 4F! If you shot down all the Japanese Air Force and sunk every ship in the Imperial Navy it wouldn't make a bit of difference! Remember! Life is the only thing that's important! Just stay alive!"

"The effects of your beer are beginning to show, Lieutenant."

"You might be right! You might be right!" replied Thatcher, ducking as he bent over to walk out of the tent. The war correspondent looked after him until he passed from sight around a tent.

"Is he good?" asked the Correspondent.

"The best!" replied Lieutenant Baker.

"He doesn't look big enough. Mean enough. He doesn't look like the kind of personality that'd be doing this kind of fighting!" said the journalist.

"If he wasn't mean, rotten, and crazy he wouldn't have any personality at all!" said Lieutenant Foy, passing by again and overhearing the conversation.

"He lets his airplane and his guns do his talking," said Ike Baker, "they're great equalizers when he comes up against a Jap convoy."

"I guess they are," said the newspaper reporter, "I think I can understand how they could be when in the hands of Lieutenant Thatcher!"

There were a hundred more or so of us who would've told him the same thing if he'd have asked us.

Staging out of Dobadura, the Air Apaches, *joined by two squadrons of the 38th Group, bombed and strafed Vunakanau airdrome just outside Rabaul. This picture shows three sitting ducks at Vunakanau getting the* daisy cutter *treatment. Returning home from Dobadura, thirty-six* Air Apaches *wreaked havoc on Wewak and Boram (New Guinea) Jap airdromes, being attacked by twenty experienced and aggressive* Zeros, *ten of which were shot down by our gunners. We lost Lieutenant Stookey and his crew of the 500th, last seen in a life raft three miles from shore.*

— M.J. Eppstein Collection

We would emphasize that this picture of a smoking Jap Betty *bomber at Clark Field was not taken on the ground. It was taken by an* Air Apache *that climbed to ten feet to snap the picture before returning to the safety of minimum altitude.*

A Jap destroyer escort meets an Air Apache *quarter-ton demolition bomb with a 4-second delay fuse. Bomb skips into enemy ship.*

Debris flies high as enemy vessel is obliterated. Conclusion: Jap destroyers could not carry USAC 500-pound bombs!

— Courtesy of W.R. Witherell Jr. Collection

There was heavy ack-ack *at Boram. Lieutenant Hyder of the 499th bombed and strafed these six 105-mm gun positions. Coming in at sixty feet, instead of 6,000, confused the Jap gun crews as they hugged the sides of their revetments.*

Hitting Clark Field, just north of Manila, on January 1, 1945, we wished the Nips a Happy New Year by dropping 2,000 para-frags on enemy planes widely dispersed around the four runways. In this picture a heavily camouflaged twin-engine fighter is placed on the enemy's inoperative list.

Traveling up the coast of Indochina under foul weather on March 29, 1945, an enemy convoy of 17 vessels was badly mauled by 31 Air Apaches. *In spite of the extremely adverse weather, we sank four merchant and five naval ships, for a total in excess of 24,000-tons. We expended twenty-six and a half tons of 500-pounders, and 74,000 rounds of .50 caliber ammunition. In this series of three pictures, (1)* An Apache *swoops in on one of the naval escort vessels, (2) a 500-pounder thuds into the starboard side and (3) the result is another lost ship in Hirohito's dwindling shipping.*

Another Apache *run, another bomb . . .*

— Courtesy the L. J. Hickey Collection

. . . And the deck of this Jap destroyer escort gets the cleanest sweepdown, both fore and aft, than it ever otherwise received in World War II.

— Courtesy The J. C. Hanna Collection

Yet another Japanese destroyer is sent to Davey Jones's locker by the Air Apaches. *Unlike some land targets, it was impossible to surprise enemy ships in the open sea. The* Air Apaches *understood it was kill or be killed, depending upon the ability and quickness of the gunners on both the ship and the airplane. Such confrontations brought out the best in an individual's quickness and reflexes. The desire to continue living was a strong stimulus.*

Another tanker fell prey to the Air Apaches *under the very nose of the Japs at Tourane Bay on the Indochina coast. Attacking enemy shipping in landlocked bays was the meanest and most costly of combat flying. Not only did the attacking* Mitchells' *have to contend with the ship antiaircraft—fire but the shore batteries also had a field day. We traded one* Air Apache *crew, six men and their airplane, for this tanker.*

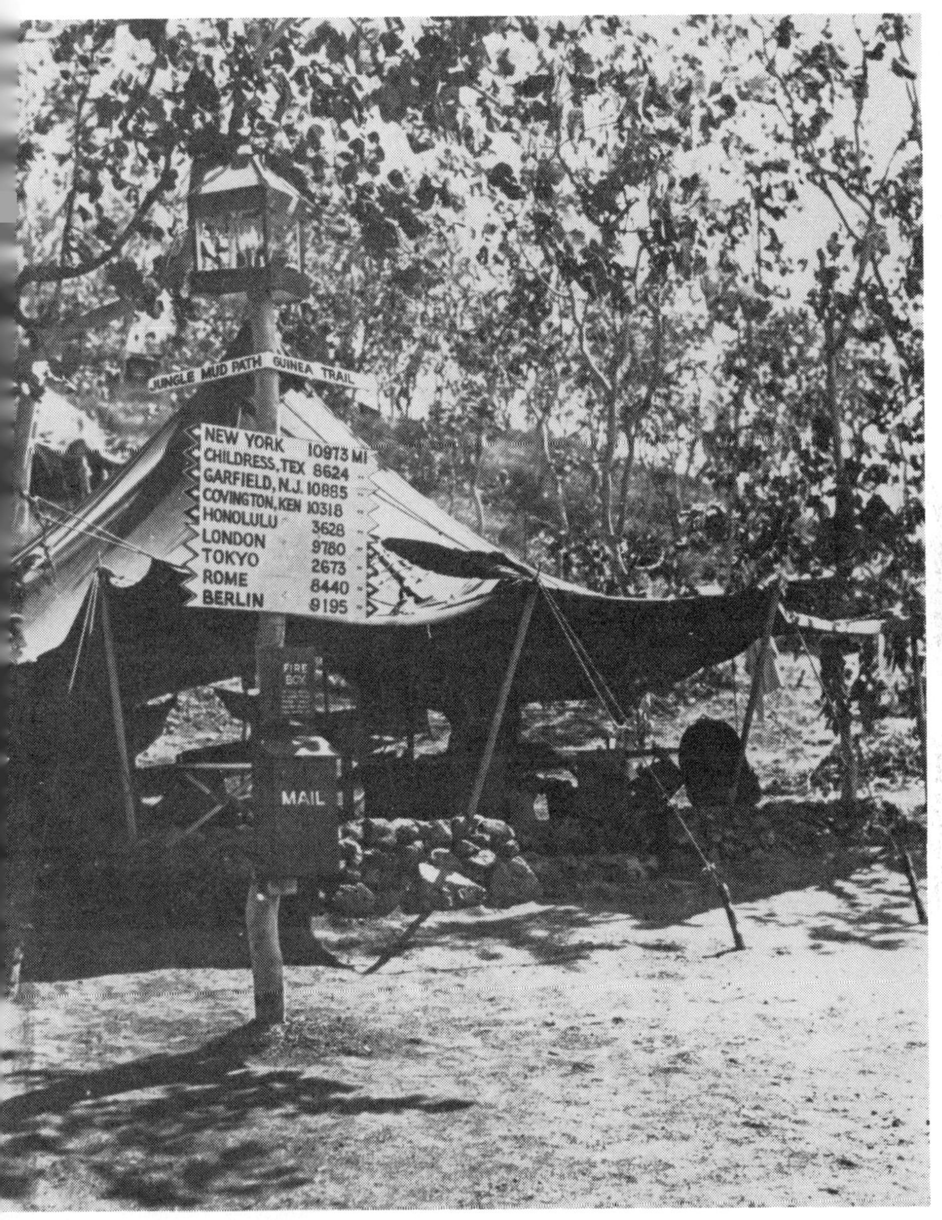

The first full Air Force Combat Group sent to the Pacific in World War II, the 345th Bomb Group, Air Apaches, *Fifth Air Force, started at Port Moresby in early 1943. A large cloth banner, stretched above the road, proclaimed, "Through these portals pass the best damn mosquito bait in the world!"*

Three Air Apaches *attack the Japanese Dagua Airdrome through dense smoke billowing up from thirty-five of the sixty enemy aircraft that were destroyed. Parked in neat rows on this important fighter and bomber base, our* daisy cutters *(parachute fragmentation bombs) made neat rows of junk for the enemy.*

An enemy tanker of 8000-tons, as well as the Jap submarine it was refueling, explodes in the background from two 500-pound demolition bombs with four- to five second delay fuses that allows the Air Apache *time to extricate the airplane from his own explosion. One of the tanker's escorting corvettes is under attack off New Hanover.*

Father Kozlowski, Group Chaplain, conducts first overseas Easter Sunday Catholic services at Nadzab, New Guinea, in open palm leaf-roofed hut built by natives. The pews are metal boxes in which 500-pound bomb fins were shipped overseas to prevent damage.

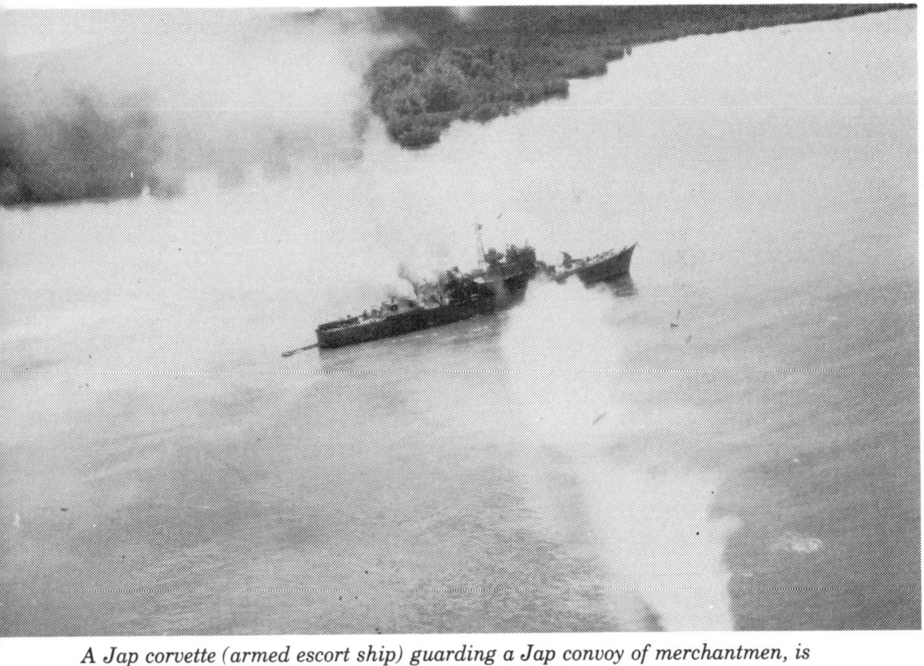

A Jap corvette (armed escort ship) guarding a Jap convoy of merchantmen, is knocked out first by the Air Apaches. *No longer able to evade our attack with rudder and steering mechanism destroyed, it sits burning in the water as a 500-pound bomb drops toward the bridge.*

Staging out of newly-won Middleburg, fourteen Air Apaches *dropped demolition and incendiary bombs on closely-packed warehouses at Gorontalo, NE Celebes. Twenty-one Jap warehouses and smaller buildings, stacked with enemy war materiel, was destroyed.*

Jap Betty *bomber, No. 783-13 ignites warmly to strafing with incendiary ammo by Lieutenant Mosser of the 499th's* Bats outa Hell *Squadron at Padada Airdrome. The* Air Apaches *definitely destroyed in excess of 260 Jap planes on the ground before the end of the war.*

A Betty *bomber and twin-engined Jap fighter fall prey to the* Air Apaches *at Aparri Airdrome, northern tip of Luzon. In early 1945 this was the last operative enemy air base on the largest Philippines island. Flying out of Formosa, the Japs used Aparri as a staging area to fly ground support for General Yamashito's Japanese ground forces.*

Part of the 189,143 total tons of Jap shipping sunk by the 345th Bomb Group, Air Apaches, *goes down to the bottom of the south China sea off Swabu.*

One of twenty interceptors that rose to meet us on a strike against Samah Airdrome is photographed by an Air Apache. *The Jap slipped under our attacking formation, head-on, and was caught in this unusual photo as he tried to land on the well-bombed runway.*

With nose guns still blazing, a 500th Squadron Rough Raider *pulls away from Samah airfield. Two* Air Apaches, *hit by* ack-ack, *collided and were lost over the target. Another* Apache *ditched and sixteen of the thirty-four planes were damaged. We destroyed several hangars and other large buildings, leaving twenty-five enemy aircraft* permanently *grounded. From twenty miles out to sea we could see sixteen separate columns of smoke as warm evidence of our visit.*

An even dozen Mitchells *fought off fighter interception by ten enemy fighters definitely claiming four kills. The remaining six* Zeros *could not prevent the sinking of this prized enemy merchantman at Nha Trang.*

The large Jap white brick and glass railroad facility at Phan; Rang, Indochina, was hit by Musket, Blair and Blount of the 501st Black Panther *Squadron on March 28, 1945. In the first photo the bombs are in the roundhouse. (2) The building is illuminated by bomb blasts as the metal roofing starts to buckle; (3) The building disintegrates as the other bombs explode and (4) nothing but the ends of the facility are still standing. Blair had an engine shot out over this target and, with nothing but 800 miles of China sea between him and our base in Luzon, he was lost. The heavy-nosed strafers of the* Air Apaches *seldom flew on one engine.*

Plane #192 of the 498th Falcon's *failed to return from this May 26th, 1945, Byoritsu oil refinery strike. This Formosan target was well defended and this aircraft, trailing smoke after dropping two 250-pound para-demolition bombs, crashed and exploded. The excellent record of the 345th was not attained without high cost. Losses were particularly heavy during Moresby and Luzon periods.*

A 499th Bat Outa Hell, Apache, *makes a run on a frigate off the coast of Indochina. This ship was sunk by subsequent attacks of the 498th and 501st.*

The Air Apaches *flew their last big mission on August 19, 1945, when they were honored to fly out and escort the Japanese peace emissaries who had left Kyushu in the early morning. Major McClure, of the 499th, had to land on Moko Airstrip in Ie Shimo to show the Japs the way in. We had performed our last mission.*

The Manila conference over, the homeward bound Japs once again peered through thick-lensed spectacles at the familiar Apache *Indian Head insignia of their escorts. Captains Naas, Tatelman, Bannister and Tech Sergeants LeBlanc and Gaylor flew in this 499th ship on August 21st, 1945.*

And while the Japs didn't see our jeeps, weapons carriers and trucks, they saw too much of the Apache *Indian Head on the vertical stabilizers of our 345th B-25J aircraft. The gentleman in this picture is not identified but the comparison of his height shows the size of the* Apache.

A 499th Bats Outa Hell *comes in with his hydraulic system shot out. For a last, solitary moment it retains the beauty of a proud bird, nose high and tail down, assuming the landing position.*

It has now skidded its underbelly into the choking dust of San Marcelino, Luzon, watched over by the cumulo-type cloud build up off the mountains each afternoon that protected the landing strip.

A destroyer escort attempts to lay a smoke screen off Tsu Shima, on August 8, 1945. Parts of the ship and debris flies from starboard quarter as Air Apache *bombs rip into hull. Taking evasive action in circles, three Japs man forward gun. Nine planes were holed on this strike.*

This series of aerial photos taken by the author show this 5800-ton Japanese freighter being destroyed. At the top is the freighter with the bombs inside seconds before the explosion....seconds later as the bomber moved away from the target, the camera shows the exploding ship and other exploding bombs. Below is a high altitude photo classified "secret" and made previous to the Saigon mission dated April 26, 1945.

One of the most spectacular air photos of the war was taken by a 498th Falcon *a member of the third squadron to attack this Jap destroyer. Captain Musket, leading the Group and the 501st Squadron, was the first element to attack this enemy naval vessel and Blount led the second two-ship element attack. The 498th cleaned up the task and obtained this picture of 100 Japs, scared shipless!*

My original combat crew that was formed at Columbia Army Air Base, Columbia, SC. This picture made in November, 1944. From left to right (standing): R.E. Peppy Blount, Pilot, P.O. "Arky" Vaughn, Navigator; Harold Warnick, Engineer-Gunner; and squatting in front: Henry J. Kolodziejski, Armorer-Gunner and Joseph Zuber, Radio-Gunner. We were a B-25H crew which was the B-25 with the 75-Millimeter cannon in the nose and no copilot. By the time we got overseas, a couple of months later, they had done away with the B-25H and replaced it with the B-25J which had fourteen forward firing .50 caliber machine guns and a copilot.

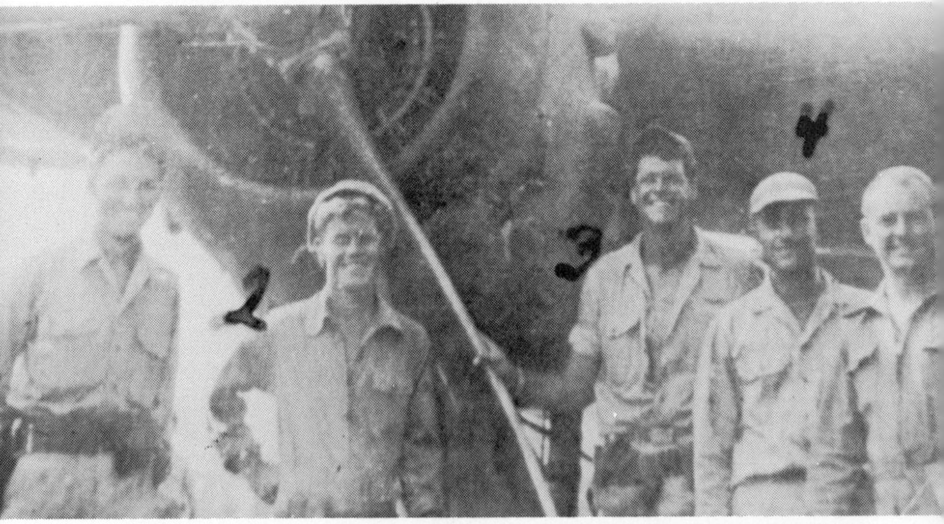

This photo taken immediately after landing from Saigon mission April 28, 1945. Right elevator shot off, hole in right engine nacelle caused from hitting mast of Jap ship and right horizontal stabilizer nearly severed. Identified (left to right): Warnick, Engineer-Gunner; Cronin, copilot; Blount, pilot; Zuber, Radio-Gunner; Kenny, Navigator.

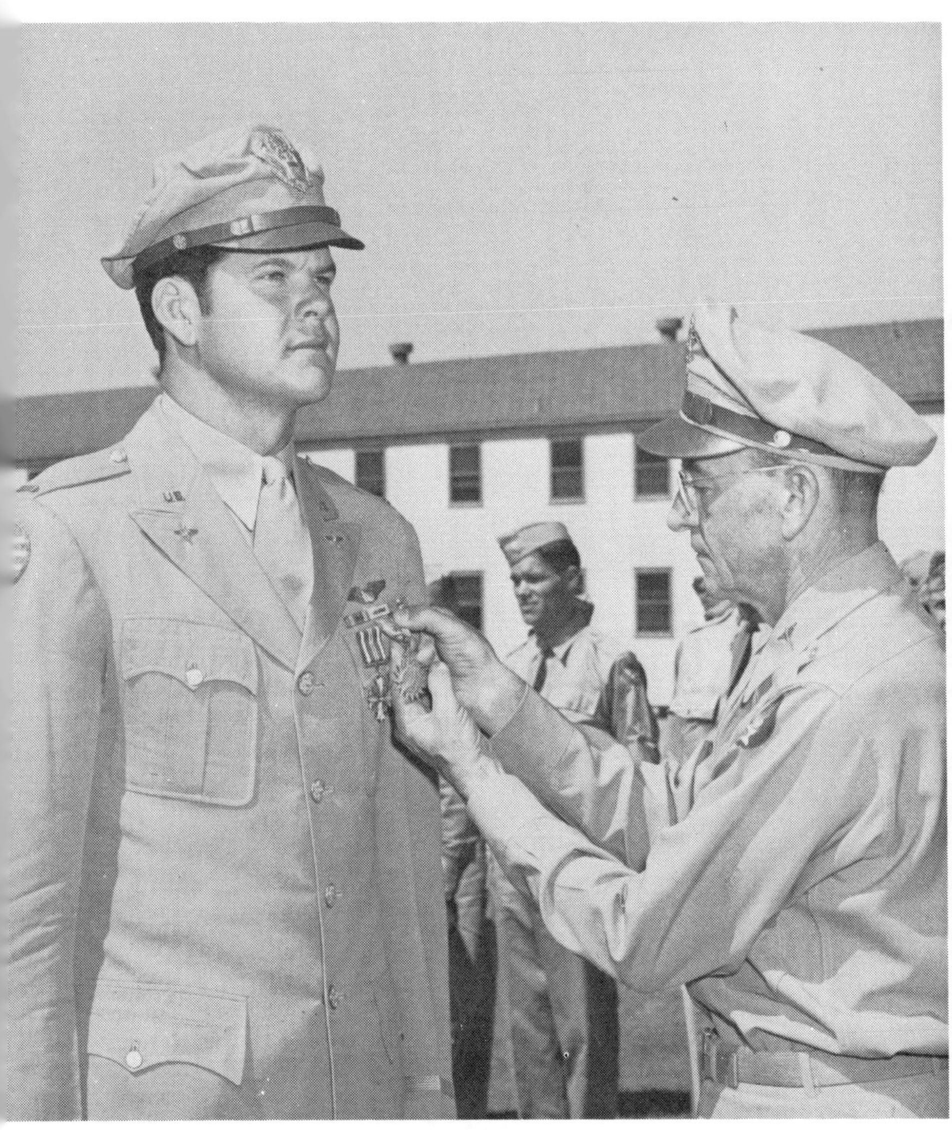

R.E. Peppy Blount being presented the DFC and Air Medal (3 Clusters) at Goodfellow Air Base, San Angelo, Texas. This picture appeared on the front page of the San Angelo Standard Times *(Newspaper) previous to Blount's election to the Texas State House of Representatives, the youngest person ever elected a State Representative in the history of the State of Texas. He served three terms and was subsequently elected County Judge of Gregg County, Texas, on a write-in ballot in the general election of 1962, the highest elective office ever attained by write-in ballot on voting machines in Texas history.*

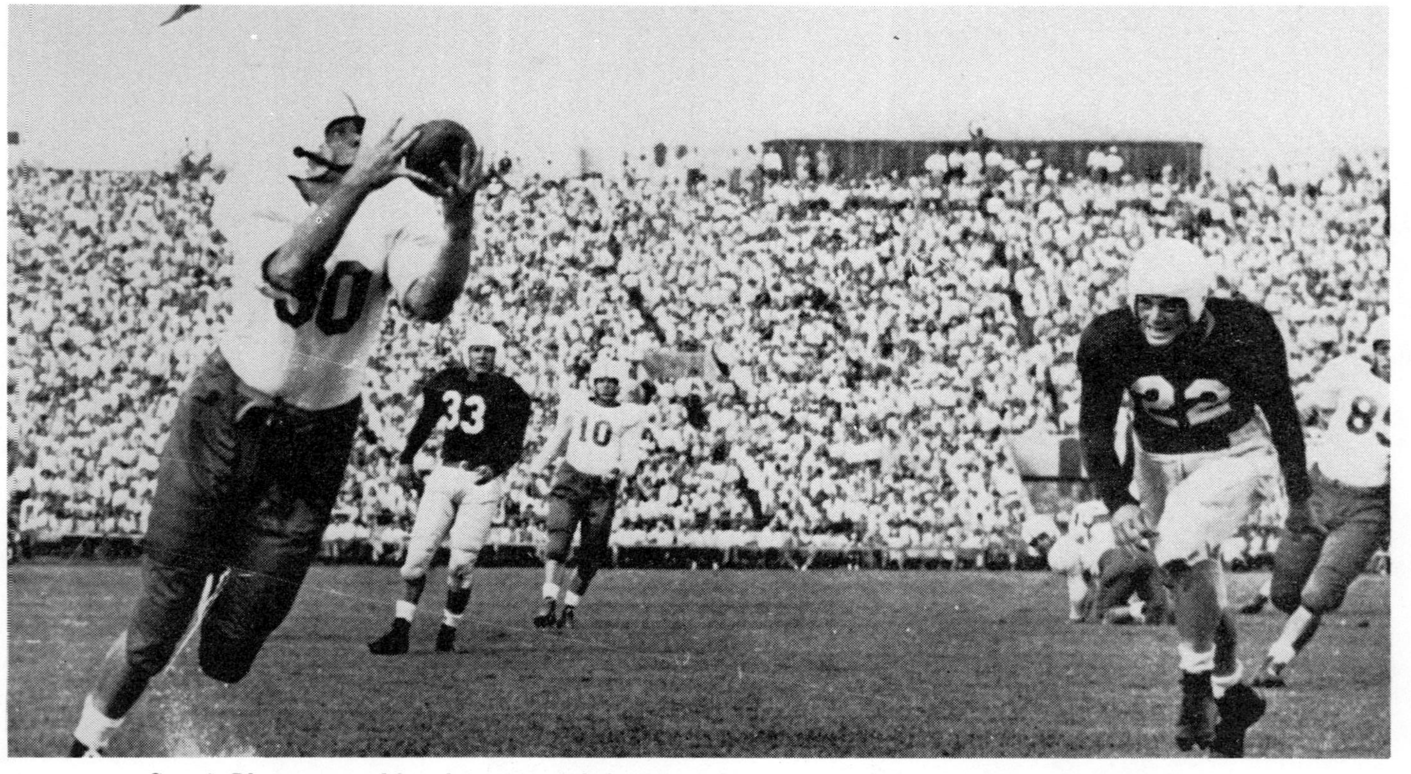

Captain Blount returned from his service with the Air Apaches *to another kind of war on the gridiron for The University of Texas Longhorns. Here he makes a miraculous touchdown catch from Bobby Layne to help defeat the North Carolina Tarheels 34-0 in 1947. Choo-Choo Justice, North Carolina's Heisman Trophy candidate, is beaten on the play. "This is the greatest game The University of Texas ever played," wrote Jinx Tucker, legendary sports writer of the* Waco Tribune-Herald.

Five months after flying his last combat mission for the Air Apaches *in 1945, Peppy was catching passes and winning football games for the Texas Longhorns. Trailing SMU in the last thirty seconds, Blount takes a 33-yard touchdown pass from Bobby Layne to win the game, 12-7, the Southwest Conference Championship, and put Texas in the Cotton Bowl. This was the first of many passes Peppy caught from Layne at Texas. Matty Bell, legendary coach of the Mustangs, said, "That was the greatest catch I've ever seen in football. We had him covered by three men — Doak Walker, Paul Page and Dick McKissack — and they were at the right spot but he just out jumped everybody!"*

This picture, made in September, 1944, on my last leave home before going overseas in December, 1944. This is the only group photo ever made of the R.E. Blount family. Left to right are: R.E. (Boodie) Blount, Alma H. Shipp Blount, Helon Jacqueline Blount and R.E. Peppy Blount Jr. My dad, R.E. Blount, Sr., died in January, 1975 and my mother, Alma, died in 1966. Helon [Kaldenberg] (little sister) has been on the Broadway stage in New York for twenty-seven years and is still going strong . . . currently in Woman of the Year *with Lauren Bacall.*

CHAPTER SEVEN

We Were Expendable

He who controls the skies controls the war.

Herman Goering
Air Minister, 3rd Reich
World War II

In early April, 1945, the 501st Bomb Squadron, *Air Apaches*, had only six airplanes in flyable condition, with two in the Service Squadron being repaired and rebuilt to fly again. The twenty-four aircraft we had three months earlier had now dwindled to eight. We lost nine airplanes in a twelve-day stretch, establishing a record that was not broken until we moved up to Ie Shima and lost ten in the same period of time. Ill-omened fate, ominous and inevitable, was on a rampage, taking the highly skilled as well as those more hopeful than able.

"I sure wouldn't want to be the insurance company carrying the coverage on anybody in this outfit," spoke up Clair Casky.

"In a manner of speaking," said Earl "Wilky" Wilkinson, "it's not bad to have just eight airplanes left. If you don't have airplanes you don't have to fly missions."

"Will you volunteer to fly one of the last eight and get your ass shot off so the rest of us won't have to fly any more?" asked Chealander, listening to the bull session. Jerry's question settled the issue.

Fifth Bomber Command, for official dissemination, told us to be positive. Tell them that we sank 145,000 tons of Jap shipping in our blockade of the China sea! But when we started equating the number of men that it took to sink a single ton of Jap shipping, the price we paid was more than the collective consciences of fellow warriors, grieving families and civilized society should be called upon to bear. The bombs of Hiroshima and Nagasaki would be a good eight months too late.

If there was a hatchet man in a combat flying unit it had to be the Operation's Officer. It was he to whom the Engineering section reported the number of Squadron aircraft ready to fly; a real trick when the Japs were knocking us down faster than we could be replaced. And it was he who named the pilots whose names went up on the bulletin board to fly the missions.

"A better trick is to find enough pilots ready to fly the airplanes that are ready to fly," said Blair, upon learning the service squadron had performed their task and repaired enough aircraft to put us back in the Japanese exterminating business!

"How does old George choose his 'hit list,' " asked Vincent facetiously, "does he draw our names out of a hat or does he just assign those of us he doesn't like?"

"Naw! He does it like playin' Russian roulette," responded Stone, "but he gives you the six-shooter with bullets in five chambers!" Our odds of making it back from any mission against Jap shipping in the China sea were decreasing every day. The first mission Lieutenant John Stone flew after joining the 501st Squadron was enough to have driven him to a Section 8! "Stoney" had been assigned as copilot of the plane that was to fly the Squadron leader's right wing on the strike. The squadron was lined up on the end of the runway, all engines running, awaiting the signal to takeoff when a last minute decision was made in Operations and Captain Hilding Jacobson (now a retired Major General) made a frantic jeep ride to the aircraft stacked up on the end of the runway. Lieutenant Stone was ordered to switch copilot positions with Lieutenant James Waldo who was already in the lead ship, had run the checklist and was ready for takeoff. Three hours later Stoney watched Waldo's plane catch a massive shell in the left engine over the target that caused it to catch fire and explode with no survivors. Stoney would subsequently survive the crash of his B-25 and the burns he received in connection therewith would send him home.

Captain George Musket was our Operations Officer, a little older at twenty-nine or thirty years, I judged; clean cut features with the movie profile of a William Holden. His face was pocked with peculiar indentations more like the aftermath of an allergy than a souvenir of earlier chicken pox. These minute craters, easily covered with a heavy beard, were never visible until he shaved. With a pencil behind his ear he looked like he might have been the neighborhood druggist, and the type a movie producer might cast as the good old boy next door. He was friendly to everyone but a close friend to no one. He was pleasant, quiet, stayed in the background, had a nice smile, was very low key, and kept his drinking under control at all the prayer meetings! His desk was everybody's and nobody's in the Operations tent, and he ran his job, seemingly, out of his head. He could easily have been a father confessor to apprehensive and scared pilots, which included all of us, had he ever indicated that he would listen to a gripe or give an encouraging word. But he kept rather to himself, and close to our CO, Major Jones.

Musket's job had no counterpart; there was no other like it, in the operation of our squadron. It was his function to schedule the combat flights of all the pilots and their crews. That might seem a rather ordinary routine accomplishment. But he knew that going after the Imperial Japanese Navy in the shoreline-to-shoreline *ack-ack* batteries of Yulin Bay was a rougher mission (fraught with more danger) than say, dropping leaflets for propaganda purposes over Formosa. And if he assigned a pilot to fly through the impenetrable fire power of Toyohara Airdrome on Sunday, would he skip the same pilot, and assign another pilot and crew to fly Wednesday's mission against a convoy guarded by two Jap cruisers and six destroyers? Actually, it was an incredibly complicated, difficult, and heartrending task. It required a deep appreciation of human nature, oriental patience, advanced psychiatry, a knowledge of the breaking point of the human animal, the shrewdness of a merchant, the wisdom of a Solomon, and the religious conviction of a Paul. For all of these virtues, which I judged he possessed in various degrees, the job he had to perform could never have been adequately compensated.

Musket knew every one of us in his depleting stable of pilots, by name, face and flying ability. He was studying us at chow, playing softball, swimming, at prayer meetings and could tell you at the drop of a 500-pounder how we flew our airplanes, and how we met the challenge of an enemy target. We were his family so he considered it his job to know as much about each of us as one man can know about another under the most trying of circumstances. When one of us got a Dear John letter, received bad news from home, or returned from a wild and wooly leave in Sydney, he found out about it, and ended up with all the details, computerized and stored in his memory bank for future reference. Musket, in cahoots with Doc Marcus, figured out how often and how much we should fly.

"Why does Captain Musket put me up on that board so often?" I asked the flight surgeon, strongly suspicious that he was helping call the strikes, (and I didn't mean baseball).

"Now Lieutenant Blount," began the able and wise doctor, "why would you address such a question as that to an old and weary sawbones like me?"

"You know why I'd address such a question to you, you old fox, because I want to know why I seem to fly so frequently! I could pass out, or go bananas with war fatigue, get the Hirohito flashes, the Yamashita dysentery — I could get real nervous in the service with malaria in the area and have a complete break down!" I replied.

"Blount," he looked me straight in the eye, "only that every pilot in this outfit could be as war weary as you! We'd never lose an airplane and the Japanese would capitulate every time they got word we were about to hit them!"

"Flattery will get you everything, Captain," I replied, "but it won't help me fly down those gun barrels or through those cobwebs of tracers those Japs throw at us." I strongly suspected he would've told any pilot in the outfit the same thing but I approved of his psychology and, naturally, would continue trying to prove him right.

Musket listened to what I had to say as if it were the first time a troubled pilot had ever come to talk to him one on one.

And though he was busy, pouring over the pilots roster of the 501st in deep concentrated study, he put the pencil behind his ear, leaned back in his chair, cupped his right knee in the clasped palms of both hands, smiled and said, "How're things going Blount?" He talked so easy and relaxed that you'd never know, even suspect, that he had flown a strike that afternoon, sunk a Jap destroyer and watched two of our pilots and their crews shot down.

"I'm concerned — ," I began, and the expression on Musket's face didn't change a fraction.

"No, I'm worried!" I said as I changed my phraseology.

"Listen Blount," Musket said, "there's not a one of us flying these twin-engine death traps, day in and day out, who isn't worried but — "

"You don't understand, George," I cut in and interrupted his speech.

"Don't get me wrong — I'm plenty worried about myself but it's somebody else I'm worried about."

"This is different then! Who're you worried about?"

"It's another pilot. I've watched him as we've flown together, that fraction-of-a-second hesitation before he makes his move, the way he doesn't quite go right over the center of a ship he's strafing and skip-bombing, the kinda. . .mechanical, I guess. . .way he flies the airplane. I'm just afraid for him and I know he's going to get it! He's ripe for those Jap gunners and I feel that it's only a question of time before he'll be gone — and he's gonna take five other good men with him!"

"You really think so?"

"I do, Captain," I said earnestly.

"Have you gotten to know him very well" he asked, "since you started feeling this way?"

"I'm afraid I have, he has a beautiful wife and the most adorable little girl with long blonde curls you've ever seen. He carries their pictures in his billfold, and he's never without that picture. I guess that's a lot of the reason I feel the way I do about him, even watch him as much as I do, because of that beautiful little girl. She really needs a daddy like him!"

"If it helps any," said a now mellow, sober Operations Officer, sitting straight in his chair, "I feel the same way about him — Oh I know who you mean — and you're very observant in your analysis of him and his flying. And while I'm just as concerned as you are about his future in the squadron, he's got to take his turn when his name comes up — just the same- Otherwise we're doing the other pilots an injustice.

"I kept — him — a copilot longer than any other pilot in the outfit, and it was almost against my better judgment, and the CO's, that I finally allowed him to check out as a first pilot and get his own crew," he continued. "And while I might put him back as a copilot, for his own good, he couldn't take it. It would be a professional insult. Knowing him, he wouldn't be able to look any of us in the eye, and he would want to be transferred."

"Can he be transferred?" I asked, thinking this might be the solution.

"Transferred where? And to what?" This is combat, the end of the line. There's no other place to go and besides, he's not checked out in any other airplane even if I could transfer him.

"Group Headquarters, not to mention Fifth Bomber Command, would want to send a psychiatrist down here to talk to me if I asked permission to transfer a pilot," said Musket, "particularly in light of my continuous request for more pilots to fill the shoes of all those we're losing."

"I guess it's one of those *catch* situations, but if I ever saw a loser, if I ever saw a guy looking to get shot down, that pilot is it!"

While we never said his name, we knew him well. He was a gangling, almost skinny, long-armed individual who was almost too tall to be a pilot in Uncle Sam's Air Corps, and looked as if he'd have been much more at home on a basketball court in his native Iowa. He was a quasi-extroverted, nervous individual, too old to be doing this kind of flying at thirty-two or thirty-three years of age. He had a lean face that always produced a smile when someone was looking at him, but a countenance that changed to a rather grim, if not downright scared, expression, when he thought he was alone. His blond hair was thinning and he had been in the training command, where he still should have been, before being shipped to combat as a copilot. I had flown a couple of missions with him, had an opportunity to observe him under fire and felt he was lucky to be alive.

My conversation with Musket was a result of observation,

intuition and a gut feeling acquired after having flown and been associated with hundreds of pilots. I saw many fellow Air Corps cadets wash out in flight training because they were secretly afraid of the airplane. The mental anguish, physical pain, and nervous seizures those pitiful individuals suffered as they anxiously nursed their dread and fear until the day they died or the war was over, must have bordered on the unbearable.

Experience wore them out, instead of hardening them to their task; leaving them afraid of themselves and afraid of the airplane. Their existence, particularly at the times they were called upon to fly the airplanes, was a half-frightened daze. They might go into a trance that not only placed their lives in jeopardy, but was a formidable threat to the lives of the crew who must fly with them, not to mention the other airplanes that must fly wing tip-to-wing tip formation next to them.

It would have been better for all of those types, if they had washed out in primary, and, contrary to what General Patton said, "counted socks in the Quartermaster depot in Kansas City." In so doing, not only their own life but the lives of all their crews would have been spared as well. It's no disgrace to admit that you can't, and shouldn't, do that special something that will prove disastrous not only to yourself, but particularly to others. The disgrace is to pursue such an endeavor that might prove fatal, not only to yourself, but to the innocent, who, by chance, and through no choice of their own, are forced to die with you and because of you.

A couple of days later my name appeared on the bulletin board to fly a strike with Captain Musket leading the squadron.

"I don't know whether I'm happy or disappointed to find out we've finally got enough airplanes ready at one time to fly a mission," I told Musket as we came out of the mess tent.

"Only three of 'em are really ready to fly," he answered, "the other five are just stuck together with glue and baling wire. And nobody but me knows which three ships are truly in sound flying condition."

"My crew chief will tell me that I'm flying one of the good ones," I answered, "or it'll be written up for repair and grounded."

"Yeah," responded Musket, "I think you would. And you should."

"The target today is shipping," announced Musket at briefing the next morning, "and this is a group strike with all four squadrons putting thirty-six airplanes in the air. The 501st will lead the strike and we'll be looking for a big Jap convoy of ten to twelve ships. The 499th is behind us, the 500th behind them and the 498th brings up the rear. The weather looks nasty and Lieutenant Baker will tell you what he knows."

"The weather is bad, with rain squalls that extend from northern Luzon to the coast of Indochina. This information is about eighteen to twenty hours old, and maybe the worst of the winds and rain have already blown through to the east. On the other hand, it could be stationary and just as bad as it was yesterday when this came in!" Lieutenant Baker said.

"Get your coordinates for the friendly subs along the coast of China and west of Formosa. *Kleptomaniac, Dill Pickle* and *Silly Filly* are our subs on this trip. Any questions?" There were none and we were off to the flight line.

"That weather sounds like we don't want to lose an engine and have to ditch in that kind of a sea," Kenney said to me, holding on as the jeep hit a chuckhole.

"You ain't just whistlin' *Dixie,* and if you did have to ditch in that kind of weather, the people on those subs could never find you if you got out of the airplane alive."

In my inspection walk around the airplane, I found a fourteen-inch screwdriver in the left engine nacelle. Sergeant Albright had won my confidence long ago as the finest crew chief in the Air Corps, and I trusted him implicitly. This was the first time I had ever had reason to doubt the expertise of what I considered the premier B-25 mechanic-engineer in the United States Army Air Corps. I didn't have to explain or discuss the ramifications, or potential dangers, associated with a loose, fourteen-inch screwdriver, rattling and bouncing around between the props and the cylinders of a 1750-horsepower Wright-Cyclone engine.

"I don't know how it got there, Lieutenant," stated the apologetic crew chief, "or why it was not discovered by me or one of my crew. I check this airplane personally, from nose to tail, before and after I pre-flight it, and I just don't know how I could overlook something like that."

My silence was more eloquent than anything I could've said to the Sergeant.

As I completed my inspection and climbed into the airplane, Zuber had crawled over the bomb bay and was waiting for me.

"I think I know how that screwdriver got overlooked in the left engine nacelle, Lieutenant" confided Sergeant Zuber.

"How?"

"Sergeant Albright got a Dear John letter from his fianceé yesterday that has hit him pretty hard. They were to be married as soon as he got back from overseas. A couple of his friends have been talking to him, because he's really been down and dejected. He didn't even go to sleep last night; I think he stayed down here with the airplane all night long."

"I can certainly appreciate his troubles, but he was about to stack the deck against us a little more — when the hand we've got to play is already bad enough!" I said. "I'll tell him to take the next twenty-four hours off when we get back. That's Doc Marcus's standard prescription for a broken heart." And while I was truly sympathetic to the crew chief's personal problem, I was relieved to know there was an open and obvious reason for what could have been a fatal oversight.

During the business of setting our altimeters, fastening seat belts and running the checklist, I looked down at Sergeant Albright on the ground, and gave him a smile of understanding. He returned it with a hurt, apologetic, humble smile that made me feel like a dog. I was a good ten or twelve years younger than the man, and I hoped I hadn't acted like a complete ass.

It had been raining for two days and had settled the dust of San Marcelino. It looked like all the airplanes in that end of the world were making for the end of the strip for takeoff. Thirty-six airplanes trying to roost on the end of one runway, as narrow as the path from which we were operating, was a spectacle in itself. Musket poured the coal to his airplane, and off he splashed down the runway. By the time he hit the end of the strip the second plane had started its forward roll. I started revving my engines as he hit the midpoint of the runway, and the tail section vibrated, shook and rattled as I released the brakes. The aircraft literally jumped forward like a filly out of the starting gate. With the heavy moisture in the air, I left vapor trails off my wing tips as I rocketed into the air at the end of the strip, accompanied by configurations of vapor along my wing and about the propellers that described a perfect, swirling demonstration of the basic principles of what makes an airplane fly. As the landing gear retracted, we picked up flying speed rapidly, and I quickly overtook Musket and slid into the number three position on his left wing.

"Kit Bag Leader to Group!" Musket's voice sounded hoarse coming over the command radio as I watched him place his fingers over his throat mike, a short sixty feet away, to assure a solid contact and more legible radio transmission to the other thirty-five airplanes, "I'll make one slow, wide circle to the left. Everybody join up! Over and Out."

At 5,000 feet, Musket had completed his circle and we were pointed toward Formosa at 0650. Notwithstanding the bad weather we were already in, I couldn't imagine a more thrilling way to go to war. Every time we made a strike at group strength, a full four squadrons of thirty-four to thirty-six airplanes, I felt a surge of confidence. *We could sink the entire Jap Imperial Navy in the morning, and bring the mainland of Japan to its knees in the afternoon of the same day, if we wanted to!*

"Don't let your bulldog mouth overload your hummingbird ass!" I'd heard one of the old pilots tell a younger, less experienced birdman one day when the latter had expressed the same feeling of confidence, with the sky full of the 345th Bomb Group at full strength.

"They'll shoot your ass off just as easy with fifty airplanes on a strike as they will if there are only five!

"The only advantage with more airplanes is you've got more targets for the enemy to shoot at, lowering the odds on how many can concentrate on you. And with all the heroes flying twenty feet too high or lagging twenty feet behind, they'll draw the fire away from me while I strafe and bomb the target flying lower and less exposed than they are, and cross the target right in line with the majority of the squadron!"

The memory of these words of wisdom from one who had saved his skin, his crew and his airplane for thirty-five missions brought me abruptly out of my daydreaming and back to the reality of what we were doing.

The weather became increasingly turbulent, fraught with rain squalls, as we rounded the southern end of Formosa and started up the western coast. As the weather got rougher, I eased another fifty feet off Musket's wing to relieve some of the tension associated with close formation flying in such turbulence. Reaching the Pescadores Islands, the whitecaps, forty feet high, were crashing upon the beaches as we turned west across the China sea to Hong Kong, and there was still no convoy in sight. Turning down the coast from Hong Kong we intercepted two Jap destroyers coming up the coast directly in front of us. These were the newest antiaircraft destroyer escorts, displacing 3400-tons and equipped with multiple, triple-banks of 3.9-inch, .65 caliber high-velocity antiaircraft machine guns, capable of firing twenty-five rounds per minute. Their single-trunked smokestacks made them look like scaled-down models of the newest Japanese cruisers.

Captain Musket, leading the squadron and the group, was the first ship in on the attack, taking the first destroyer. Both destroyers turned in opposite directions, but neither had a chance as all thirty-six airplanes jockeyed for position to make their strafing and bomb runs. Musket's first bomb found its mark and a cavernous hole suddenly opened in the side of the ship as the explosion lifted the vessel ten feet out of the water and threw it down again.

We were the second element to attack, the number three airplane in the second flight moving up on my right wing to fly shotgun, as we peeled off and in to the second destroyer. The strafers' odds-on best maneuver, affording the greatest protection from enemy gunners and presenting the most difficult target for them to hit, was a change in airspeed, altitude and direction. This was accomplished by making a steep, diving turn into the ship, raking it from stem to stern with my twelve fixed fifties spitting out 6,000 rounds of armor-piercing incendiary ammunition per minute. The superstructure on the ship started to melt as the deadly streams of fifties meted out their destruction. The tracers from both ships were now arcing in a cross fire above and below us, as I released a 500-pounder just off the stern of my target, that made a sharp turn to port. As I pulled up to clear the mast of the destroyer, I could see the expressions of fear on the faces of the Jap sailors and gunners, as well as the backs of others hiding behind bulkheads, trying to escape the continuing wrath of the fatal .50s!

As I dropped down on the water, taking evasive action away from the destroyer to escape the enemy fire and present as difficult a target as possible, the first destroyer turned head-on into its tormentors. I came up even with the ship, and their forward guns fired a broadside in my general direction, but above and slightly to the side of my airplane — and into the trailing 499th's squadron of B-25s preparing to make their attack. The flames out of these heavy naval guns made a solid wall of flame thirty feet in front of the end of each barrel, and, in a reflex motion, I involuntarily ducked, although I was not in the direct line of fire.

The two destroyers were disposed of by the 499th as we saw them both turn up their sterns and sink, bow first, leaving hundreds of Japanese sailors swimming for their lives in the sea. Several airplanes made passes and strafed the Japs until the water turned red, but I couldn't help feeling that in sinking their ships, I had carried out my primary duty. The reasoning of those who strafed the enemy in the water, was to eliminate as many as possible to keep any of them from manning other ships and other guns to shoot us down. They had a point.

Lieutenant Myers's plane in the first flight of the 498th was badly hit and lost an engine. He made it back to Lingayen on single engine after throwing everything out of the airplane that was loose and making the ship as light as possible.

The 500th and the 498th Squadrons, observing the two destroyers ably disposed of by the 501st and 499th, turned south to attack an *Asashio* Class destroyer. Lieutenant Schmidt, Squadron leader, his copilot and navigator, were wounded by an exploding shell which also hit the number two ship, flying Schmidt's wing. After scoring a bull's-eye by planting a 500-pounder in the magazine that caused a huge explosion, Lieutenant Schmidt was able to fly his crippled airplane back to base. Lieutenant Herick, his wingman, got an engine shot out and crashed in the sea with no survivors. Captain Johnson, Squadron Leader of the 498th, making a late appearance, swung into the attack with five airplanes. He dropped his two remaining 500-pounders for a direct hit, but his plane was hit with heavy *ack-ack,* caught fire, and ditched (with only one survivor) two miles from the burning destroyer. The destroyer was burning fiercely as the last plane pulled away, and was subsequently declared destroyed and sunk.

I hadn't flown with Musket again for ten days when our names were posted on the bulletin board for the following day's mission.

I was still worried about our frightened pilot, notwithstanding the fact that he had weathered a couple of missions since my talk with Musket. In fact, one of them had been pretty rough, and he had performed admirably in flying a damaged and shot-up airplane back from Formosa. Maybe more combat experience was making him into the quick, cutting and slashing strafer pilot I felt he had to be to survive. Besides, what was I doing worrying about someone else, when I had my hands full of concern for my own hide. I was not ashamed of fear; it made my adrenalin run, which in turn gave me a quickness and awareness that I knew I had to have to stay alive. There is cowardice buried in every man, as well as unknown quantities of guts and courage, and both qualities can be unpredictable. The secret, I decided, was to stay constantly alert, razor sharp, and do the job by instinct. We were all mortal, but to survive we had to rise to the occasion, fly and fight like mad men, relax and recoup our sanity, and then get it all up again for the next performance.

"Life is gettin' to be a now-you-see-it, now-you-don't proposition," remarked Blair.

"It's got to where about all we do is fly and fight and die — if the takeoffs don't get you, the gunners of the Japanese Imperial Navy will — and if the Japs miss you, the cooks and their secret weapon won't miss you," agreed Steele.

"What's the cooks' secret weapon?" asked an unsuspecting pilot replacement who had just arrived that day.

"Spam!"

That was a comic tragedy! We were all civilians taken from every walk of life, given military and flight training for a year or two, and sent halfway around the world to fight a war. We were all captive, here against our will, products of different families, nationalities, religious and regional backgrounds, but all dependent upon one another for survival. And did we have different geographic backgrounds! At times The Civil War became so real that a line had to be drawn down the middle of the bar to prevent fights by separating the Yankees from the Johnny Rebs.

But there's a strange thing about war. People with absolutely nothing in common with each other, suddenly start feeling good about each other. It was the *esprit de corps* generated from fighting, living, eating, and sleeping together in the constant struggle to stay alive — so that we could continue to fight, live, eat, and sleep together, so that we could stay alive — *ad infinitum*. We joked a lot.

"I wonder what this supper looked like in its former life?" asked Kuta, as we started down the chow line.

"It had four legs, a mane and Gene Autry rode one in all his cowboy pictures," replied Thies.

"What kind of meat is that?" inquired Kenney to the cook, who hunched his shoulders and opened the palms of his hands in a *Who knows?* gesture.

"It's all right," replied Stiles, "you never knew him!"

"Before you go to bed," said Phillips to the cook as he left the mess tent, "don't forget to walk tomorrow's breakfast!"

One night the movie was *Objective Burma,* with Errol Flynn fighting single-handedly, and defeating, the entire Japanese army in all of Burma and half of Asia. We sweated out Errol's exploits and narrow escapes with the enemy in the same manner we sweated out some of our own missions. We emerged from the movie in a wrung-out condition, and well chewed upon by the native mosquitos.

"That Burmese jungle where Errol Flynn was fightin' those Japs looked like the jungle we've got right around here, or in New Guinea," said Edmund Kasten.

"Look at the jungle over in Indochina next time you fly over there," said Hardeman, "you're only a hop, skip and a jump from Burma and it looks the same."

"I liked the realism," said Lyman, "every time old Errol slapped at a mosquito I did too!"

"Our mosquitos are bigger than his," I replied, "ours were big enough to have landing lights, but we couldn't even see his."

Our movies were shown beneath the stars and in all current elements, in a clearing between the jungle and the back of the officer's area. Seats were reserved by taking your ammunition box or food crate to the movie area and placing them in the spot where you wanted to sit. Nothing stopped the movie, and if it rained, (which it frequently did) you sat there and soaked up the entertainment as well as the rain. Although the rain washed off your mosquito repellent, it made you much cooler, and the mosquitos were not nearly as likely to bite you in the rain.

"Don't they ever show anything but war movies?" inquired Phillips.

"Naw!" replied Casky. "Fifth Bomber is trying to prove war is hell!"

"They've sure as hell proved war is hell to me," volunteered Ruchel, "and I'm ready for just a little bit of anything war ain't!"

"The opposite of hell is heaven," volunteered Edward Bina, "is that what you mean?"

"Not exactly," replied Ruchel, "heaven's my home but I'm not homesick!"

When the OD "punched" Blair the next morning at five o'clock for breakfast I awoke also.

"If you're not a beautiful, sex-crazed blonde I'm gonna knock your head off," said Blair.

"I'm not a beautiful blonde," replied Lieutenant Bell, the rancher from Oklahoma, "but I've got one for you!"

"Let's have it!" replied Blair.

"If you wanna be a man
Be a man in full
Let your balls hang down
Like a Jersey bull!"

"Oh, Bell! This early in the morning?" I groaned.

"Well, he was talking romance and I just wanted to help him out," said Bell.

"But cows and bulls!" said Blair.

"Ain't nothin' more romantic than cows and bulls," replied Bell, continuing on in the dark, to call the other pilots and crews from slumber.

I noticed my elbow was swollen; red as an apple, as a result of allowing it to rest against the mosquito netting in my sleep. Those minute vampires had a ravenous appetite and carried malaria. Doc Marcus had a mess sergeant who stood at the head of the chow line to make sure we took our atabrine. The atabrine, while preventing malaria, turned everyone a beautiful yellow, and acted much like a time bomb. We wouldn't find out if we had malaria until we returned to the states and quit taking the atabrine.

The strike was to be an airdome on Formosa, heavily defended as they all were, and we were six ships abreast across the target, leaving them strings of para-frags that cut to shreds everything within a fifty- to seventy-five yard area. I found out the pilot I worried about would be flying two ships over to my left in the attack formation.

"Remember," I reminded him as we left the briefing, "don't fly too high or too slow — keep your airplane up and even with Musket. If the *ack-ack* is too thick, keep your airplane on the treetops, and forget being high enough to open the chute to arm your para-frags. Your strafing will do enough damage to make up for any para-frags that end up duds. Besides, no telling how many Japs you'll kill when they try to dispose of any live bombs that don't detonate."

"You sound like you're trying to fly the strike for him," said Kenney, overhearing our conversation while piling into the jeep with all his maps, briefcase and navigation equipment.

"I guess I'm overly concerned about him."

"He needs some help," said Kenney, an "old" veteran of thousands of hours of flight in the Air Transport Command before being assigned to combat with the 345th Bomb Group and having observed hundreds of pilots. "I've watched him and I don't think he needs to be flying first pilot on any strike in this outfit."

The takeoff was uneventful, as well as a perfect weather flight to Formosa. As the coast of Formosa came into view, Kenney helped me with the heavy flak suit and helmet as Musket took the squadron down on the water and under the Japanese radar net. The target was thirty miles inland, and we continued to hold our V formation like a proud flock of geese.

"Kit Bag Leader to squadron," came Musket's voice over the command set, "move into attack formation!" With that command all aircraft moved up and we had six airplanes abreast, bobbing with the air currents and changes in the topography of the terrain we were flying over.

I charged my eight nose guns, as Kenney and Cronin manually charged the package guns on each side of the fuselage.

"Pilot to turret. Give me your guns firing forward as we cross the target, Warnick, keeping an eye for any *Zekes* they might have hiding up in the sun."

"Roger!" replied Warnick.

I advanced the prop pitch to 2,100 rpm and concentrated on positioning my airplane perfectly in line with Musket, leaving the throttles free to respond to my demand. A glance at the airspeed indicator told me we were hitting 290 mph as the trees and other land features became the familiar blur under my wing. The airplane was shaking from the increased speed as the airdrome came full view, with the long white runway, gun revetments and neat, white buildings to the side. Every airplane in the squadron opened up at once on the target dead ahead, and released a combined fusilade of over 50,000 rounds of fifty caliber armor-piercing incendiary steel and destruction that caused instant fires, death, and devastation. Our tracers told us where the incendiaries had gone, and we could see them erupt instantaneously in explosions, and fires, as we hit gasoline trucks and gleaming Jap airplanes with the big red circles on their wings. Everything, hundreds of yards ahead of the path of our aircraft, exploded.

I could see Jap tracers coming toward us from several different directions, meaning we were being tracked and shot at from revetments on all sides of this target, placing us in a deadly cross fire. A plane to my left was hit, and the other planes moved over one space to fill the gap, and kept firing and laying the little parachutes of destruction behind them.

We haven't changed the order and technique of battle, I thought, in hundreds of years. The English redcoats marched into battle four- and five-ranks deep at the Battle of New Orleans in 1814. When a British soldier redcoat in the front rank was shot, his replacement simply stepped into his place and kept advancing. This appeared to be an unbroken line to the American defenders under the command of General Jackson, who were enjoying the turkey shoot from behind the cotton bales. As we lost an airplane, we closed ranks and kept firing.

My gun barrels turned red, three had melted and I had only five guns still firing as we came off the target, with enemy tracers still passing over the cockpit and under the left wing. In a frenzy Warnick turned his power driven top turret. He continued to pour a steady stream of tracers and incendiaries into the Jap gun emplacements that were now to our rear, as I put the nose of *199* on the treetops. Kolodziejski and Zuber, from the tail and waist, continued a crescendo of fire back into the enemy airdrome, that was by then a holocaust.

We had hit gasoline, oil, and ammunition dumps. The target looked like a Fourth of July celebration! As I made a slow turn to port we saw airplanes, buildings, and equipment — all exploding — and projectiles were shooting skyward from out of the smoke and fire.

"Kit Bag Leader to Squadron! Piss on the fire and call the dogs! We're headin' home!"

At the interrogation and debriefing following the mission, we learned that our friend the frightened pilot, had piloted the airplane that had been lost.

"He caught a direct hit in his left engine," said Kuta, "and never had a chance."

"Was he up with the rest of the formation?" I asked.

"No," responded Kuta's copilot, "he was about the length of the airplane behind, and fifteen or twenty feet above us. He did hold the airplane straight; they skidded a quarter of a mile or more down the left side of that Jap runway burning and exploding. There were no survivors."

I looked at Musket, sitting at the next table, sipping from a canteen cup half-full of Old Grand-Dad. The expression on his face didn't change.

"He was a good man," said Musket, "and a good pilot who gave it all he had."

But isn't this the way we knew he would go? Didn't we know it was only a question of time . . . I said to myself.

Those were the things I wanted to say but couldn't. But Musket saw them in my face, in my eyes, and he understood. But he still couldn't do anything about it. And if another, and another, and another came along, he would still be sending them into battle.

"May I have a shot of that Old Grand-Dad?" I asked Doc Marcus.

"You don't drink, Blount!"

"That's right, I don't drink. But I think I'd like to try one . . . right now." I thought about the beautiful widow and the little girl with the long blonde curls.

"His luck ran out," said McGrane, one of the pilot's tent-mates, "it was just his time and he lost his rabbit's foot."

"Yeah! I guess so!" I replied, as we walked out of the interrogation tent. But I couldn't buy that philosophy. Plain, ordinary, everyday luck is when preparation and opportunity meet up. On the sole basis of luck, had he been as skillful a pilot as he should've been, after flying those day in, day out, practice missions against the old metal hull of the beached Jap freighter below San Antonio (in addition to his actual combat experience) his preparation should have been adequate to take him over the Jap Airdrome of "opportunity," and afforded him the *luck* to have made it back. We had lost so many *good* pilots, that I knew that it took more than skill and luck to stay alive.

"The way we're losing airplanes it's just a matter of time! Living is just a matter of destiny," said Stone.

But I was ultimately convinced that only an act of the Holy Spirit could safely guide any of us through this living hell. I recalled the scripture that said, *He that hath eyes let him see.* An angel stayed the hand of Abraham when he was about to kill Isaac; an angel guided the Israelites to the land of promise; an angel led Peter out of the jail and freed him from his captors; an angel sent Philip on a missionary journey. They were all influenced and led by an angel they could see. A reasonable explanation of why we couldn't see the angels might be that we were spiritually blind. Maybe we weren't spending enough time in God's presence in prayer, gaining strength and seeking answers from His Book, to be able to see the angels He was sending to us.

I helped Lieutenant Ike Baker go through the personal effects of the lost airman, sorting clothing, toiletries, towels and sheets that his buddies could use, while collecting his personal things to be returned to his wife. Inside a folder was a large photograph of his wife and daughter, like the smaller one he carried in his billfold. The beautiful young wife sat in a wing-back chair, posed with her arm around the standing eight-year-old daughter with a freckled nose, large sparkling blue eyes, long blonde curls, and with a big pink bow in her hair to match a beautiful pink dress. On the back was written in a bold feminine handwriting: *We love you — more than yesterday, less than tomorrow — always; 1944.* A letter written in scrawled letters on rough, elementary school tablet paper was folded once under the picture and was postmarked a month earlier:

> "deer daddy i am doing good in school. i have a good teacher. she lets me tel about airplanes and you. when are you coming home . . . "

The voices of Chelander and Harrah broke into my concentration and thoughts. Ike Baker was still sorting socks, pants, handkerchiefs, and shirts with his back to me. My hands started to tremble and suddenly my legs were made of putty as I sank to a sitting position on an ammo box that doubled as a stool.

"Come on, Blount!" came the voices again, as if through a long tunnel, "the 500th team is on their way and you haven't even warmed up."

"They're ready for the ball game!" spoke up Baker, not bothering to look around as he continued with his sorting.

"Yeah! The ball game."

I staggered out of the tent and into the bright sunlight. *I hope I don't look as bad as I feel.*

"What's wrong with you?" asked Harrah. "You look awful."

"Something I ate, I guess. It smelled like a football locker room, or something rotten on the beach at Galveston!"

As the afternoon and the ball game passed, my sorrow and anguish subsided, I could look upon the war objectively, and the Japanese were an impersonal enemy again. The war was increasingly complex, an endless series of heartbreaking, agonizing, anxious, gut-wrenching events involving the lives and blood of my friends. I accepted the mysterious workings of fate and destiny with an infallible, unquestioning faith. That's all I had left, and that's all, obviously, the Lord knew that I needed.

"Anybody in this outfit from Texas or the southwest?" I had asked Lieutenant Ike Baker, assistant Intelligence Officer, shortly after joining the 501st.

"We've got two or three from Texas! Does Oklahoma count?"

"Sure," I said, "unless they got here via California!"

"Lieutenant Bill Bell is a rancher from southwest Oklahoma, wears cowboy boots, chews 'Brown Mule' chewing tobacco, and talks like he should be from Texas. I think he might be your type."

Caught up in moving into a new outfit, at a new base, drawing bedding and other necessities from supply, being assigned a tent, meeting new tentmates, and generally getting acclimated and adjusting to a new military family had caused me to forget my original inquiry until a couple of days later. I had just rounded the side of the Operations tent in time to see an individual place the index finger of his left hand over his left nostril, bend slightly toward the right, downwind, and blow, repeating the procedure, with the right index finger over the right nostril, emptying his left. He was about six-foot-one, maybe one hundred ninety-five pounds and had the hands, full shoulders, and bull neck of a calf roper or bulldogger. His body could've passed for that of a football coach, topped with the crease-lined face of a rodeo performer that gave the appearance of a rub board after fifteen years of hard washings and which had been baked by a lot of hot sun. He had a big cud of tobacco in his left jaw the size of a golf ball and he looked like a red-neck version of John David Crow, of Texas Aggie Heisman fame, whom I was to observe in later years. He looked like he'd just as soon spit tobacco juice in your eye as to look at you, but I knew he had a heart of warm steel from the tone of his voice the moment he spoke to me.

"Howdy, Son!" he said, squinting his left eye and looking up at me as he ran the top of his left index finger forward under his left nostril and under his right nostril on the return trip in a continuous crosscut saw motion to make sure his nose was clean.

"Well, howdy-do to you, too!" I smiled, "you're from either west Texas, southern Oklahoma, or eastern New Mexico!"

"How'd you know?" he answered in his southwestern drawl.

"I could tell by the way you blew your nose!" I answered, "which is it?"

"Southern Oklahoma," he replied, "but I think that's the first time I've ever been recognized by the way I blow my nose!"

"You're the first son-of-a-gun I've seen who could blow his nose right in over a year and a half of this mans' army, and I want you to know I've missed you," I said, "I think this is going to be a great place!"

"Yeah, we like to call it hell!" he replied, "but you won't ever get used to it! My handle's Bell, what's yours?"

"Blount, and I'm from west Texas!" I replied, "gimme the word! Got any good country advice for me?"

"They're not unreasonable in this outfit! They just want a full ninety minutes of fighting out of every hour," he said, "and never insult seven Japs when you've only got a six-gun. Anything else?"

"I think that about covers it," I replied, not really knowing how much to believe. "How about the chow?"

"The meat's from the Civil War! It's gray on one side and blue on the other!" he replied. "In fact, the food tastes just like the food we had back home — before I ran away!"

"I understand," I laughed. "What were you doing before they got you in the war?"

"I was going to school. Oklahoma A&M at Stillwater."

"We've got Texas A&M down at College Station. My friends in the FFA and 4H Club were always telling me about the research going on at A&M. In one research project they found out that all 'possums and armadillos are not born dead beside the highways in Texas!"

"Well — so much for animal research! Let's go research some of that memory food they serve us in the officer's mess," said Bell.

"Memory food?" I asked.

"Once you eat it you never forget it. It can be prepared sixteen different ways!"

"And it can be thrown out, or thrown up, sixteen different ways too, can't it?"

"How did you know?" he asked.

"From my vast KP experience! I peeled so many potatoes in pre-flight that I was nominated to be the State Bird of Idaho!"

"The first one never has a chance," said Bell, "let's go to chow!"

I had found a friend. A kindred soul from the same part of the world I was from, and with whom I had something in common. I had much to learn from the cruel, disappointing, and devastating tragedies of combat.

To the aircrew combatant, time drags. Between strikes we had nothing to do but play Red dog, five card stud, fight insects, and sit and look at each other in endless bull sessions. We had heard the praises, (real and imagined) expressed by the native-born, and heaped upon every city, state, and geographic area of the United States. We had heard the stories of girl friends, older women, younger women, frigid women, loose women, coy women, cute women, concubines, mistresses, successful conquests, near misses, and corrective measures to guarantee success the next time. Most of the time they all ended ". . . if I'd only known then, what I know now, I'd never have been so shy." I was led to believe that no woman in the United States, of any age and regardless of social status, would be safe should any of these oversexed males make it back home alive.

We had heard the favorite and most memorable family experience of every tentmate until we could repeat it verbatim, with the proper inflection and in the appropriate tone of voice. But we regarded and respected each new telling with tolerant cynicism, knowing the shoe would be on the other foot when our own nostalgic button got punched. In combat we were the victims of a monotonous bog, marked by massive boredom and spiced with moments of excitement that would, in the words of Thatcher, "scare the shit out of you!" Endless fighting and dying made us used to repetition, and when a friend felt the need to retell his favorite memory, we'd listen. He was getting something out of it, we didn't have anything better to do, and we were not going anywhere anyway. On those rare occasions when someone told a new story, or brought up a previously undiscussed topic, it was like turning on a bright light of group mental curiosity. Doc Marcus said it was "acceptable and to-be-desired group therapy!" Father Kozlowski said, "The exchanging of ideas and opinions, among friends and within socially acceptable moral bounds, is good for a healthy mental outlook." The Chaplain didn't make all the bull sessions!

"Whatcha gonna do after the war?" I once asked Bell.

"I'm going back to Pittsburgh, Pennsylvania and get after that electrical engineering degree and go to work for Westinghouse," broke in Arky Vaughn, my old navigator who had been bumped to Squadron navigator because of the loss and normal attrition of navigators in the 501st.

"I'd hate to know that Pittsburgh, Pennsylvania, was the

only place I had to go home to," said Root Hardeman, the West Texan from San Angelo, as he shook his head.

"I'm going back to Oklahoma," finally answered Bell, when the other members of the bull session gave him an opportunity, "and raise the finest registered White Face Hereford cattle in the United States of America! I'm going to use the finest bull and breed my cows by artificial insemination."

"Now why would you do that if the bull is so valuable?" pondered Esty.

Bell smiled. "Just to show that bull that there's more to life than just fuckin', and that's something all you boys can think about!"

"I'd sooner go to hell than Oklahoma," said Lyman. "Get it? *Sooner* and *Oklahoma*?"

"What you mean," said Vaughn, "is that you'd rather be in hell than Oklahoma."

"Every man to his own country," responded Bell.

At that moment Thatcher, in tight shorts, flying boots, dog tags, and holding a hot beer in his hand, ducked under the tent flap and entered the pyramidal.

As if on cue, Lyman rose to the occasion:

"Hold it ladies! Don't despair!
Don't go crazy and tear your hair!
Look who's coming! The people's choice!
Friend of millions and the strafers' voice!
Combat problems are at an end,
Lothario Thatcher is with us again!"

There was mild applause for Lyman's poetic effort which was ignored by Thatcher.

"What's Bell doing," inquired Thatcher, "telling you a 'how to catch an Oklahoma woman' story?"

"Yeah," answered Esty, "but not the kind you're thinking about!"

"Will Rogers never met you, did he Thatcher?" asked Bell.

"Those shorts look like a cheap room in a tourist court on you," spoke up Kuta for the first time, "no ball room!"

"No respect! That's what I don't get out of this outfit!" exclaimed Thatcher, "the hottest, the finest, in all modesty, the absolute best pilot in the U.S. Army Air Corps, except maybe the 'Oklahoma Flash Gordon' — Lieutenant Wild Bill Bell, and this is the way you treat me!"

"Just how great is Wild Bill Bell?" asked Kuta, egging Thatcher on.

"Lieutenant Wild Bill Bell, the fiercest of the fearless flying *Air Apaches,* the war hawk supreme, the flying thorn in the side of the Rising Sun, the silent, stealthy nipper of the Sons of Nippon, the top gun of the Southwest Pacific, the tawny streak of death, the quick draw artist who prowls the China sea, stalking with endless patience the isolated, struggling, and straggling ships of the Japanese Imperial Navy. Then crouching, twitching his muscles like coiled steel, he releases the full, pent-up 4,000-horsepower of his trusty flying machine and leaps — Yeah! he literally flies through the flash and fire of the rockets red glare, the bombs bursting in air — to decimate, debilitate, and eradicate — not to toy, but to annoy and destroy the enemy!"

Spontaneous applause, cheering, and a heartrending, "Hear! Hear!" and "Ole! Ole!" from an appreciative audience expressing their approval of a bullshitter's "one-upmanship."

"When a dog pisses on my leg, Thatcher," responded Bell, "I don't need nobody telling me it's a thunderstorm! Don't let the tent flap hit you in the ass on the way out!"

"You're getting mighty damn familiar," said Thatcher, "and familiarity breeds contempt!"

"Without familiarity, Thatcher," answered Bell, "you don't breed anything!"

Four months into 1945, the men who flew, navigated, strafed, bombed, worked at radios, or armed and repaired B-25s in the 345th Bomb Group were in good supply. However, airplanes that allowed those specialized gentlemen to display their technical skills were at a premium. The distance to the coast of China, Formosa, and Hainan Island was only four- to five-hours but the distance to a bounteous supply of replacement B-25s was more than halfway around the world. Consequently, those who flew the airplanes to China, or maintained and repaired those the Japs couldn't send to never-never land, labored under incredible handicaps. Only the utmost resourcefulness, devotion, and courage kept the *Air Apaches* in the Japanese exterminating business. The persistent, wilting, day in, and day out, pressurized effort to meet the varied enemy strike demands of Fifth Bomber Command, became a continuous, conscious effort. Those who flew the missions had to retain their nerve, resolution, and outward sanity. They were exemplary, tough, and brave gentlemen; raucous, pessimistic, profane, fatalistic, disillusioned, as well as opportunistic, optimistic, Machiavellian, high-spirited, and debonair. If these were the *soft* Americans our enemy had publicized and exploited, (among enemy combat personnel to give them confidence and courage) they were getting an explosive and disastrous surprise with every appearance we made against them.

One combat mission, two at the outside, was all that was necessary for one pilot to evaluate another. Pilots with shared, or mutual experiences, were not strangers for long, unless the ability, talents, and judgment of one so outweighed and overshadowed the other that they silently chose to be strangers forever. On the ground, at chow, at bull sessions, in prayer meetings, and on the volleyball court, we were congenial. But from the moment the names were posted on the squadron bulletin board for a mission the following morning, the "Miss Congeniality" award was forgotten. I liked Bell and believed the feeling was mutual. He was easy with his crew, the crew chief, and the ground personnel who serviced and kept his airplane flyable. I judge a man by the way he treats all men equally, and Bell got a twelve on a scale of ten. He seldom said anything in the nature of an order to his crew, but he spoke eloquently when he had something to say. He had been generous in giving me the benefit of his combat experience, as if I had been his favorite cousin whom he hadn't seen in the last ten years. It was deeply appreciated.

"All you gotta remember," he said, "is don't fly too high, too far out front, or lag too far behind! Keep 'er up in there tight— like a hustler does the steer when you're bulldogging! Strive to be an airplane that's perfectly in line with the rest of the squadron when you go over the target, and you won't have any trouble! Got it?"

"Got it!" I answered. But it would take hours of strafing and skip-bombing runs, and several combat missions with the surrounding air full of Jap *ack-ack*, smoke, and fire, for me to be able to say *Got it!* and really mean it.

Lathrop had just returned from a courier mission to Nichols Field in Manila. To kill time while he waited for Fifth

Bomber's answer, he accepted an invitation from some of our infantry personnel to drive into Manila where the fighting was still in progress in the streets — house-to-house. His eyes continued to reflect the excitement of what he had seen and he had our attention.

"That dead Jap in the sunshine in the street," said Lathrop, "had been there for three days and was swollen up four times the normal size! It's just laying there, getting bigger every day and nobody will go out and move it."

"Ain't nothin' happier than a dead pig in the sunshine!" said Bell. "Now what they need is a flock of buzzards. They'd pick his carcass clean in thirty minutes and remove all the stink with it."

"Why didn't they move the Jap?" asked Steele.

"Nobody's gonna do that when all the dead Jap's buddies are on the other side of the street just achin' to lay out an enemy partner to keep him company," said Lathrop.

Bell's blue eyes twinkled mischievously. His wide face stretched into a grin as he shifted his cud of Brown Mule from the left to the right side of his mouth, and gave his cowboy hat a tug forward, as if he were getting ready to come out of the shute on a Brahma bull.

"Don't let it get you down, son. I use' to be kinda skittish about the deceased myself till one of my best friends went to work in a funeral parlor out in the panhandle of Oklahoma. He always smelled like embalming fluid after that, and he catnapped in the coffins during the day. They never thought to look for him there when they wanted him to work. He said those coffins are padded and really comfortable. He didn't know why they made those boxes so comfortable for those stiffs. But he made a grave error! He damned nigh got hauled off and buried one day when he was mistook for the late departed."

"Can't you talk about something else?" asked Lathrop.

"You brought it up," continued Bell, "and this is the dyin' truth! Their motto was 'you stab 'em and we slab 'em!' And they advertised all over the Oklahoma panhandle and down to Amarillo that their prices were no stiffer than their customers. Another was 'buy a grave today and we'll throw in a loved one absolutely free!' They had people coming in there from all over — standing in line!"

"Kuta," asked Lieutenant Jay Moore, "do you know the difference between a Texas cowboy and an Oklahoma cowboy?"

"No," responded Kuta, "what's the difference?"

"The Texas cowboy wears the bullshit on the outside of his boots!" said Moore, as he lit a shuck under the flap to vacate the tent. He was one step short as Bell hit his arm with a well-thrown helmet liner knocking the beer bottle from his grasp and spilling both Moore and his beer in the dirt.

"And don't forget, Moore," hollered Bell, "a bird don't fly so high that he doesn't have to light to shit!"

After flying a couple of missions with Bell, my confidence improved considerably. I didn't enjoy getting shot at anymore than before, but I approached combat with less apprehension with Bell along. Coming off the target with voluminous clouds of smoke and fire that we could see for over twenty miles, Captain Musket even used a Bell euphemism: "Piss on the fire and call the dogs! We're headin' for the house!"

"Your attention, please!" came Sergeant Franko's voice over the PA system. "Lieutenant Bell! Lieutenant Bell! Please report to Operations immediately."

"What've you done now?" I asked.

"How could they miss that B-25 I stole yesterday so quickly!" said Bell, grabbing his straw cowboy hat as he moved toward the tent opening.

"Just 'cause we've only got six left I don't know how they'd ever miss one this quick!" I answered.

Bell returned in about thirty minutes with the look of the tomcat who ate the canary on his face.

"What y'all been doin' while I've been gone?" he inquired.

"We were waiting for you to get back. We would 'preciate the pertinent poop from Group!"

"Gentlemen, you are looking at the Squadron Commander of tomorrow's mission to Formosa. None other than Bill Bell."

There was spirited applause from everyone in the tent.

"As the cow said on that cold winter morning," said Bell, "thank you for that warm hand."

"When you're tapped to lead the squadron, those railroad tracks can't be too far behind," said Kenney. "Do we start callin' you Captain Bell?"

"There's an old Polish proverb," said Kuta, "power tends to corrupt and absolute power corrupts absolutely! The first corruptible cowboy! What'll Gene Autry and Tom Mix think about that?"

"You mean, in the words of that deranged, psychotic philosopher, 'Mad Dog' Thatcher, that the fiercest of the fearless flying *Air Apaches*, the war hawk supreme, the flying thorn in the sides of the Sons of Nippon, the top gun of the Southwest Pacific, the prowler of the China sea, and Joe's Pool Hall in West Eyelash, Oklahoma, Lieutenant Wild Bill Bell is the Squadron Leader for tomorrow's mission?"

"In the flesh," Bell smiled at me.

"That calls for a prayer meeting tonight," said Moore, Steele, and Harrah in unison.

"Maybe a short one," replied Bell, "but the Squadron Commander has got to get his beauty and leadership sleep tonight — if he's gonna live up to the plaudits of his troops."

The names of the crews were posted on the squadron bulletin board shortly after Bell's conference with Captain Musket and Major Jones. Bell was listed as Squadron Commander for the strike the next morning and I was going with him.

Every prayer meeting was unique, and had, or developed, its own character, depending upon the mental and physical condition of the participants. The weather had been good, we had been flying strikes daily against the enemys' best gunners on Formosa and the China sea for the past ten days. Our losses had been heavy and those who gathered to relax on this evening more nearly resembled a sedate group of middle-aged gentlemen at the club after office hours having one for the road before catching the 5:30 home. By past standards, this gathering rated about a three on a scale of ten. Everyone's attention was focused on several replacement pilots and navigators who had joined the squadron early that afternoon. With the old-timers sitting blankly, staring straight ahead, saying nothing and starting to feel the effects of the numbing alcohol, the situation provided an appropriate opportunity for Thatcher to introduce and indoctrinate the fledgling birdmen in the customs of the 501st. Three fifths of stateside whiskey had already been introduced to the party by as many novices, in response to Thatcher's explanation that " . . . new men are expected to furnish a bottle of refreshment for the edification and enjoyment of the old-timers at the first prayer meeting they attend." As the state of collective inebriation increased, the invisible wall separating strangers dissolved and the newcomers started talking, and being accepted, as the incongruous language of the group increased.

"Do you really fly your missions at minimum altitude?" asked a new pilot who'd arrived just that afternoon.

"Lower than that!" smiled an amused, inebriated Thatcher who reveled in the shock reflected on the face and open mouth of the novice birdman.

"Whatta you mean lower than that?" came the next question.

"I mean so low that your propeller tips are green from cutting the grass! Check the tips of every airplane down on the line, that can still fly, and look at those green tips! You might look at the props on Matthews's plane particularly! They're green to the hub! He's been known to fly about two feet below the grass!" Everybody enjoyed the wide-eyed amazement of the new recruit and no one bothered to correct the eloquent bunco artist.

"Flying that low, doesn't it make it awful easy for the Jap gunners to get a bead on you?" continued the quest for knowledge.

"Oh, we make it pretty tough on 'em," answered Thatcher, "those little yellow sonzabitches have their problems trying to hit us when we're traveling at 300 mph. Their guns get blocked a lot of the time by buildings or trees as we fly by them."

What Thatcher didn't explain and what the young neophyte would learn soon enough, was that our enemy antiaircraft defenders were trained to aim the barrels of their guns straight up and hold the triggers open en masse. The effect was like trying to fly through a geyser or inverted waterfall without getting wet. That was why we got holed on every mission, daily decreasing the odds of our making the gray-haired wonder status. . .

"I'll swear," said Lyman, "this war is getting out of hand! All anybody thinks about is war, war, war!"

"Have you ever had any children?" inquired a new navigator.

"Since I'm single I thought it wasn't wise!" replied Lathrop.

"You'd rather climb a tree to tell a lie than stay on the ground and tell the truth," said Bell.

"I've got an insight into you," responded Thatcher, "you're full of horseshit!"

"I'm adrift in a sea of sour grapes!" replied Bell. "When you're born of tradition and nurtured with pride, the best never comes easy!"

"They don't like each other do they?" said a new pilot to Doc Marcus.

"To the contrary," replied Doc, "they're the closest of friends. They've been through more jams than a cooking judge at the County Fair!"

"What's combat like? Do you ever get scared?" asked a new pilot, the bottle having loosened his tongue and allowed him to ask the question he could never ask if sober.

"I've been here five months," responded Kuta, "and I haven't stopped shaking yet!"

"Honest confession is good for the soul!" said Moore, overhearing Kuta's reply. "That calls for a drink! At least!"

"What do Jap destroyers look like?" continued the inquisitive new pilot.

"All of 'em that I've seen," replied Kuta, "look like a Fourth of July celebration! All fire and explosions."

"How do you find 'em?" asked the novice birdman.

"Just watch for the flash and fire of those five-inch antiaircraft turrets and the four triple banks of .65 caliber high-velocity machine guns on each side, amidships. You'll — hic — never see a bigger fireworks display!"

"If bullshit was music," said Bell, "you'd all be a brass band!"

"History shows that most great military minds bordered on the eccentric," said Lyman.

"That's consistent with my monthly report to Fifth Bomber Command," said Doc Marcus, "I told General Kenney this whole outfit is crazy!"

"You're a real pistol, Lyman," said Major Giese.

"Only when he's loaded," responded Doc Marcus.

"I think it's time we draw the curtain on this one," continued Doc Marcus, "it's 0100 hours and those who're still ambulatory should assist those who are not." Four of the new birdmen had drunk themselves into a passed-out-under-the-table condition which was consistent with most first-timer performances. "If they survive," said Thatcher, still on his feet, "they'll get better at drinking as well as passing out!"

At 0400 hours, Steele, the OD, was punching us through the mosquito netting.

"Don't disturb the mosquitos," I said, "those little vampires have been sitting there all night patiently waiting for me to throw 'em a leg or an arm or an elbow!"

"We're missin' the boat," replied Steele, "those things are big enough to carry bombs! If we could just train 'em to fly formation we could sit back here and let them fight this war for us!"

Twenty minutes later Bell and I met near the mess tent door in the dark.

"Hark! Is that Squadron Leader Bell?" I asked.

"It is I," responded Bell, "thrust the mantle of leadership upon my shoulders, but easy on the twenty-one gun salute. It's awful early in the morning for such carryin' on!"

"I wired the Joint Chiefs last night that you were gonna merge our ability and forge our genius into an American victory today," I said, "was that all right?"

"That's a clever way of saying we're gonna be on 'em like stink on a skunk!"

"No guts! No glory!" I said.

"A masterpiece of understatement!"

"You're an extraordinary man, Bill Bell!"

"You're an extraordinary judge of character, Peppy Blount!"

"Can I persuade you to join me in the Kamikaze Kitchen?" I said, "one bite and you hit the deck!"

"Follow me," replied Bell, "here's a table for two overlooking the kitchen with a thrilling ordoriferous view of the scum on the grease trap!"

"The target for today," Captain Musket began at 0600 with all crews present, "is an airdrome just north of the town of Mato on the westernside of Formosa. Leading the Squadron today will be Lieutenant Bell. I'm sure he has a few words for you."

"Mato," mused Kenney, "is that right next to Boardwalk and Park Place?"

"Do you get $200.00 when you pass Go?" asked Cronin.

"No," said Kuta, almost imperceptibly, "but it'll get the toe of my boot about six inches up your ass if you don't shut up!"

It was obvious that Bell was somewhat self-conscious in his new role. He stood there for a moment in his yellow Mae West with radio wires, his automatic, and a jungle knife hanging from his body. In other times, in other places and surroundings, you could say he almost looked like a giant teddy bear. Taking the pointing-stick in hand, he assumed the pose of Major Jones, who epitomized what a Squadron Leader should look and sound like.

"We'll fly at 5,000 feet indicated altitude to the target area about here," Bell said, pointing to the southern tip of Formosa. "We'll fly up the west coast of Formosa, between the Pescadores Islands and the coast, to about this point. We will then turn northeast, get on the deck, and make our strike with all six ships abreast, and across the target simultaneously. I don't have to remind you not to be out front, not to lag behind, or not to fly too high. Stay in a perfect six-ship-abreast formation, strafing and bombing as we cross the target. Any questions?" There were none. We knew his speech as well as he did.

"We'll make a northeast to southwest pass across the airdrome with three airplanes on each side of the runway about one hundred feet apart. Pilots, flip your bomb release switch as you hit the north edge of the airdrome and remember, once you hit the switch all the bombs will release consecutively until they're all gone! Got it?" There still were no questions.

"Three airplanes on each side of the runway will just about cover all aircraft revetments and hardstands, gun emplacements, fuel, and ammunition dumps and buildings. In the event they're alerted and make an attempt to put *Zeros* in the air to intercept us, I will move over and fly down the runway to destroy any *Zekes* trying to take off!"

"Let's synchronize our watches; navigators, get the coordinates of friendly subs and air rescue PBYs, the weather report from Lieutenant Baker, and good hunting!"

"I'm glad I'm getting to fly the first mission you're leading," I said to Bell as we left Operations to be jeeped to the flight line.

"I'm glad you are, too," he replied, "I don't have to worry about you like I do a couple of the others who are going along today. I sure want to bring everybody back that goes out."

"Why do we have to take these damn parachutes," grumbled Cronin, getting out of the jeep as it rolled to a stop under the wing of *199*.

"Yeah," chimed in Kolodziejski, "if we got hit and had to use 'em, we wouldn't have enough altitude to bail out, and certainly not enough time for 'em to open!"

"And a nice rubber cushion would sure be a lot more comfortable," added Zuber.

"Bitch, bitch, bitch!" said Kenney. "Here the Air Corps furnishes each of you a nice, silk parachute to sit on, and to keep you awake when you walk, to protect your ass from exploding Jap shrapnel while you sit, and do you appreciate it?"

"Kenney," said Cronin, "you're just like my parachute! You give me a pain in the ass."

As the last ship joined the formation, following Bell's wide, climbing turn to the left on takeoff, I checked my intership radio.

"Hello Kit Bag Leader! This is *199*! How do you read me? Over."

"Like a comic book *199*!" came Bell's reply. He knew every pilot listening, as well as those on the squadron radio, monitoring the strike back at San Marcelino, would enjoy the answer. "Keep 'em loose!"

As we hit the coast of Formosa and turned inland, Bell took us down on the deck where the trees and other vegetation muffled and absorbed our sound, and putting us below the Japanese radar screen. Notwithstanding the inherent danger associated with flying over an enemy at a fifteen-foot altitude, totally exposed and relying completely on our speed, surprise, and audacious recklessness to preserve our well-being, the absolute, unparalleled excitement experienced brought you unhesitantingly back for another performance. It could have become addictive. Each of us had confidence in our own indestructibility. That, coupled with the enraptured exhilaration we enjoyed that fraction of a second before the gun button was depressed, releasing the unmatchable devastation of the battalion firepower equivalent of fourteen fifty caliber machine guns firing forward and four others firing from the sides and the tail turret, kept us coming back for more, although we would never admit it. The first burst of enemy *ack-ack* erased that fleeting, momentary fantasy, just as the singularly effective block of an opponent on the opening kickoff knocks the school spirit from an inspired athletic body before the last strains of the school alma mater have faded. The ever present reality that you were now fighting for your life invaded every physical and mental facet of your being and hit you like a sledge hammer in the stomach.

Without any audible or other distinguishing signal, all six airplanes moved into a combat, abreast-attack formation. Captain Musket had made it as easy as he could for the novice Squadron Commander's initial strike by assigning him Thatcher, Kuta, Moore, and Lathrop — all battle tested and proven combat pilots. At 285 mph we were now bobbing like corks in a barrel as our airplanes flew through the heat thermals rising from the earth reflecting the heat of the sun. I looked over at Kuta, a scant one hundred feet to my left, and the reassuring smile that crossed the rugged and prominent features of his Polish American face was more comforting than a mother's look of approval.

"Pilot to top turret! Strafe straight ahead with me, Warnick, and keep a lookout for any *Zeros* hiding in the sun!" *I never forget to remind Warnick at the last instant to do what he's already doing,* I thought.

"Roger!" came his reply.

"Cover us on the breakaway, Hank, and hose 'em down good, Zuber!"

"Roger, Lieutenant! Roger!"

I'd had the fifty pound flak suit pressing me into the pilot's molded steel seat for twenty minutes and was sweating freely. Only my hands and feet were free to function and perform the myriad duties necessary to fly, bomb, strafe, and maintain my position in the wing tip-to-wing tip combat alignment.

"Pilot to crew. One minute to the target. Let's give 'em a hot time in the old town tonight!"

The bomb bays opened as I depressed the gun button and pandemonium broke loose. The airplane recoiled from the simultaneous explosions of all guns as my incendiaries climbed up and disappeared into a large white building off the edge of the runway that exploded into a mushroom of fire and smoke. Three *Zekes*, with propellers idling, were poised for takeoff at the near end of the long white runway. I got two within the pattern of my fixed guns, and a short burst disintegrated one, while the other burst into flames and plowed wildly out of control, off the taxi strip and into parked vehicles at the edge of the runway. From my right and straight ahead I watched tracers arcing toward our airplanes, and black puffs of heavier *ack-ack* suddenly appeared between Thatcher and me on my right wing. Figures ran in confusion out of barracks and a headquarters building that absorbed several thousand rounds I released from the nose of my airplane. Following closely on the heels of the destruction meted out by our guns, strings of the small, fluffy white parachutes of our para-fragmentation bombs blossomed and floated almost lazily to the ground. These were the *daisy cutters* that leveled every object above ground on each side of the insignificant-looking explosive device dangling from the parachute.

Halfway across the target the gun revetments on each side of the runway suddenly erupted, and a continuous string of tracers arced across and through our formation. I silenced two revetments directly in my flight path on the far edge of the airdrome, as well as two heavily camouflaged enemy aircraft that exploded as we burst out of the hell of an infuriated nest of Japanese amid the smell of our own gunsmoke that filled the cockpit and the plane.

"Kit Bag Leader to Squadron!" came Bell's drawl. "Looks like I've thrown a shoe, I'm hit and feathering my left engine."

The words in my earphones paralyzed my senses and a combined feeling of sympathy, rage, and antagonism filled my being. *Of all of us, why Bell? How? His first mission as Squadron Leader.* I looked for him to our right and saw his left engine trailing smoke and his props beginning to windmill.

"*Zeros* at five o'clock high!" Warnick's voice was strained.

"How many?"

"I can see four!"

"*Zeros* at five o'clock high and closing!" I announced to the Squadron after switching back to command radio.

"Roger!" acknowledged Thatcher.

"Throttle back and join up around the leader and let's ease out of here!" came the voice of Thatcher as we moved in to the sides and above Bell's crippled airplane, affording the concentration of all our gunners' firepower against the attacking *Zeros*.

"Here they come!" yelled Warnick as his guns erupted, vibrating the airplane and punctuating his shout. The tracers from the first two *Zeros* passed over the top of the airplane, causing me to duck. I never could help that!

"Here comes the second two from three o'clock!" said Zuber from the waist. The six airplanes of the 501st *Black Panthers* had now reverted to sulking opossums, throttled back to 165 mph to protect our fellow warrior, and reversed our roles from aggressive attackers to sitting ducks.

Our tight formation and low altitude prevented the second two *Zeros* from diving through our slow moving aerial circus, and they pulled up short after approaching within five hundred yards, and spraying us with their twenty-millimeter cannon and machine guns. We held our collective breath as we moved down the west coast of Formosa, fearing another *Zero* attack that never came.

In the meantime, Bell's airplane resembled a Chinese fire drill, as every loose object in the airplane was thrown overboard to lighten the load. The one remaining engine was straining. Long belts of fifty caliber ammunition, the guns, boxes, control handles, levers, clothing, side arms — a steady stream of varied aircraft and combat equipment was thrown from the waist gun positions. Having come off the target at minimum altitude, and held there by the attacking *Zeros*, Bell was held to one hundred feet altitude. This was to be desired coming off the target to prevent the *Zeros* from diving on us. The advantage just as quickly became a liability. *You can't climb and gain altitude on a single engine in a B-25 strafer.* There was the weight, the modification that changed the airplane from a medium to a minimum-altitude bomber-strafer, and replaced the plexiglass bombardier's station in the nose of the airplane with twelve .50-inch machine guns, their ammunition, and the heavy steel foundation on which to anchor all that chaos. On single engine, the modifiers were not the aeronautical engineers who designed the B-25 airplane, and they built us a flying coffin!

We neared the southern tip of Formosa, cleared the south end of the mountains, and continued out over the south China sea toward Lingayen and the nearest friendly airstrip on the northern coast of Luzon. I thought we might be free of Jap fighters and enemy interception. The whitecaps of the perenially rough China sea were excessively high that day. While the weather we had to fly through to get to Formosa earlier in the day had dissipated to a large extent, it was easy to discern, by the size of the fifteen to twenty foot whitecaps, that there was a heavy surface wind above the water.

"Can you read the wind velocity from the whitecaps?" I asked Kenney.

"I already have," came the reply, "the wind is thirty-five to forty miles per hour."

"What kind of a pilot would it take to make a single engine ditching of a B-25 in that kind of sea?" came the rhetorical question from Kenney. We both knew the answer.

"Hello 057," I said to Thatcher over the Command radio, "this is *199*. Over!"

"Go ahead *199*!"

"I'm going on ahead to try and locate the *Cat* to get them back here to lend a helping hand. If you'll hold the cowboy's hand — until I find help, we will all appreciate it! Over!" Even if the Japs were monitoring this frequency maybe they wouldn't understand what was going on!

"That's good *199*! I'll stay, and you better take everybody else with you, too! Otherwise they'll be flyin' on fumes before long and we'll be looking for more help. Over!"

"Roger 057! Hang in there Kit Bag Leader! Don't let that wild Brahma bull throw you! We'll be back with the whole posse *muy pronto*! Over!"

"Thanks, Blount! I don't know how much longer this one windmill is gonna keep our feet dry! Looks like this whole deal has turned to clabber!"

"If it has, we're gonna make butter out of it! Hang in there! Over and out!"

I advanced the throttles, retracted the flaps, dialed the emergency frequency on the radio, and started my *Mayday* call to the friendly Air-Sea Rescue *Catalina* flying boat that was patrolling our area. I advanced the prop pitch to 2100 rpm and the throttles to thirty inches, and started a steady climb to 5,000 feet. The constant muffled roar of the engines took on a more urgent tone, as if they were aware of Bell's predicament and my concern for his welfare. As if they knew I was asking for increased performance. The rate of climb needle indicated we were gaining altitude at the rate of 450 feet per minute, and the airspeed had increased to 190 mph indicated. I was totally absorbed in the instruments and the emergency radio frequency to locate the PBY *Cat.* The information that the instruments silently passed on to me took my mind away from Bell momentarily. Within the next fifteen minutes I contacted the *Catalina* on the emergency radio channel.

"Will you please hurry," I admonished the skipper of the Air-Sea Rescue PBY. "He's on single engine and he can't hold his altitude much longer!"

"Roger, Air Corps *199*," he replied, "we should make contact within ten minutes! Over and out!" I said a prayer for Bell and his crew, and had Kenney give us a heading back to San Marcelino.

After landing, the photo lab grabbed our film and the jeep whisked us to the interrogation tent.

"Have you heard anything from Thatcher and Bell?" I asked immediately.

"Not a thing — but the squadron radio is monitoring the channel and the moment we know anything, it'll be reported here. What did you hit today?"

"We came across the target in a northeast to southwest pass," as I pointed to a large, aerial photo of the Jap air base we had hit only three hours before. Following the debriefing I returned to my tent and didn't get the news about Bell until an hour later when I met Thatcher coming from debriefing as I was going to chow.

"What happened to Bell?" I asked immediately and the expression on Thatcher's face told me the answer without his having to speak a word.

"The *Catalina Playmate* got there in time, but it was no use," answered Thatcher, "Bell simply could not hold his altitude on one engine and finally had to ditch her. You know how rough that water was today and he went in pretty steep, missed the top of the wave, hit in the valley between two waves, and that was it. They didn't have a chance, with surface winds of thirty-five miles per hour. Their ship nosed straight up, the top turret came forward,crushing the cockpit, and the only survivors were the two men in the rear of the airplane, the radio man and tail gunner."

"Did he say anything else after I left?"

"You heard the last thing he said," replied Thatcher, "that

it looked like this deal had turned to clabber! Sounded just like him, didn't it?"

"Yeah! Just like him." I had lost my appetite. His last words had been a *beau geste* benediction to an inevitable, even expected, plight that each of us would be in tomorrow — the day after — or next week.

Later that evening, one by one, we straggled into Bell's tent until it was full. Each of us wanted it to appear as if we had wandered in, but each of us knew it was on purpose, and out of respect for a dear friend. Ike Baker had already gathered his personal things to be sent to his family; the remaining items of clothing and toiletries had disappeared among his friends almost as quickly as they had been displayed, including a month's supply of Brown Mule plug chewing tobacco. I wouldn't have been surprised to have heard him observe: *Here I'm not dead more'n a couple of hours and already you've picked me clean, like a flock of buzzards!* Only an empty, lonesome bunk with mosquito netting, a folded air mattress, and some make-shift shelves behind the bunk that more nearly resembled an apple crate, gave moot evidence of the absence of our friend. Although the seven or eight of us who "just happened" to show up by accident after chow that evening sat on every extra stool, and overflowed on to his other tentmates' sacks — out of conscious respect, no one sat on Bell's empty bunk.

"I hate empty sacks!" said Stiles.

" Bell would've said 'Don't worry, there'll be another one in here tomorrow to take my place, just like I took the place of somebody else before me!' " said Townsley, " 'and be sure you take him under your wing, show him the ropes, and treat him right!' "

"He sure would have," I said, "he probably saved more of our necks by sharing his experience and giving us tips on how to attack a target at minimum altitude, when we were new and vulnerable, than any other individual in the squadron."

"If he heard you talking like that," said Phillips, "he'd tell you,'when a dog pisses on my leg I don't need nobody telling me it's a thunderstorm!' " Everyone laughed, but it hurt.

The small group began to break up and leave the tent in awkward silence. "Damn it! It's not right! Why Bell?" asked Julius Fisher, to no one but to everyone. "We all know some sorry, low-life, no-good bastards who wanta do nothin' but fight, carouse, and whore around! Why is it that somebody like Bell, who didn't wanta do anything but get back to Oklahoma and raise the finest Hereford cattle in the Southwest, have to get it? It's just not fair!" There was an extended silence. "It's just not fair!"

"I'm no Bible scholar," spoke up Doc Marcus, "but Job asked the same question a long time ago. He wanted to know how the wicked continued to flourish while all the good were dying. And God answered him out of a whirlwind, probably just like they have in southern Oklahoma, and said he was not indifferent to what happened on earth, or the evil and bad things that were happening to Job. God said that he didn't punish evil tyrants immediately but it was false to say He didn't hear the cries of those who were suffering, and even more false to say that he doesn't know what's going on. He does bring about justice if only we have the patience to wait for it."

"I guess so," responded Fisher, "I hope so!"

Doc's wisdom had prevailed once again. His Biblical observation had served as a fitting benediction to the life and memory of a fellow warrior, respected friend, and cowboy pilot — the fiercest of the fearless, flying *Air Apaches;* the war hawk supreme, the flying thorn in the sides of the Sons of Nippon, the top gun of the Southwest Pacific — Lieutenant Wild Bill Bell.

CHAPTER EIGHT

The Will That Says Hold On

If you can force your heart and nerve and sinew,
To serve your turn long after they are gone,
And so hold on when there is nothing in you,
Except the Will which says to them: "Hold on!"
Rudyard Kipling

"I don't believe it! I'm looking at it, but I don't believe it!" said Thatcher.

"I've never seen anything like that before in my life!" exclaimed Lieutenant Al Palace, "that belongs in Ripley's Be-lieve It or Not!" Palace was expressing the utter amazement that the rest of us shared standing there in front of the B-25 that had just returned from a strike against enemy shipping in the China sea.

"What did it feel like," inquired Captain Jay Moore, "when you hit it?"

"What did you do, Erskine?" asked Lieutenant James Johenning.

"I don't know how you taxied that thing back to the revetment," added Moore, "much less have flown it back from the coast of Indochina in that condition!"

The airplane that had our undivided attention, looked, at first glance, much better than most of our ships that returned from strikes against enemy shipping in the open China sea. Sure, it had holes in the left rudder, right aileron, "for ventilation," as Lamar would say. At first, it looked as if it was all still in one piece with no large jagged holes or frazzled, trailing edges of control surfaces evidencing the metal termite-effect of Japanese forty-millimeter pom-pom pianos. But closer examination of the left wing caused all of our lower jaws to drop. The left wing was pitched downward at a thirty-degree angle as if it had been placed in the jaws of a giant wrench and some supernatural force had given it a quarter turn.

"How did it fly? How did it feel with that wing turned down?" inquired Lieutenant Ohnemus, the expression in his voice underlining his amazement.

"One-half of the airplane wanted to take the low road, while the other half wanted to take the high road," said Lieutenant Erskine. As long as I kept the airspeed above two hundred miles per hour it seemed to be all right. It was only when we started to land and I put down the flaps, changing the shape of the air foil and the control surfaces of the wing, that it started to get hairy. I'm just glad I don't have to take it off in that condition."

What had happened was that Lieutenant Robert Erskine, in violation of the basic law of the minimum altitude strafer-bombers, had fallen behind his leader on a single element, two-aircraft attack on a Jap ship. Flying the wing of his leader, he had fallen so far behind that he was unable to catch up. As a result, the water and mist thrown into the air from the explosion of the five hundred-pound bomb dropped by the lead ship into the enemy vessel, presented an obstacle comparable to a brick wall for Erskine to fly his aircraft through. The twisted wing was the miraculous and comic result of what would ordinarily have been a tragic disaster. Enemy gunners had learned that one of the best deterrents and most effective defenses against our low level, minimum altitude attacks over open water, was to purposely shoot in front of our airplanes raising geysers of water for us to fly through which was as deadly as a direct hit in the cockpit. We lost a number of airplanes to this oriental antiaircraft ingenuity.

"You shouldn't even have followed Fisher over that ship, Erskine," said Blair, in an understatement, "when you were that far behind him."

"Now you tell me," exclaimed Erskine, turning the palms of both hands in an upward motion of helplessness, "where were you when I needed you?"

"The moral of this story," said Major Jones, driving home once again a basic, fundamental law of the strafers, "is don't fly five seconds behind a five hundred-pound bomb with a four-seconds delay fuse — unless you're at 5,000 feet! To lag behind is to stay behind." He made his point.

"You're on the hit list for tomorrow," announced Lyman, sticking his head under the flap of the pyramidal.

"There's our little ray of sunstroke," said Blair.

"You're flying, too!" responded Lyman.

"He's psycho!" I responded, "his head is so twisted that he has to screw his cap on! I'm trying to check him out as a first pilot and Musket has put me in for the DFC and the Silver Star for the two instruction rides I've had with him!"

"What you've got to do is harness that great massive amount of cowardice, and that's how Captain Musket is trying to help you with your problem," replied Lyman, "checking me out as a first pilot!"

"You're about as cute as a horned toad with the tread of a Mack truck right up your ass," said Hardeman.

"If you keep talking that way I won't tell you who else is flying tomorrow," said Lyman.

"Who else is flying?" I asked.

"In that case, Musket is leading and you, Blair, Lathrop, Thatcher, and Burg make up the rest of the strike!"

"We probably should have a short prayer meeting after chow tonight," announced Blair.

"What's the occasion?" queried Hardeman.

"Lyman's progress in getting checked out as first pilot," responded Blair. "Want all of you to come by for a couple of short ones."

"What time?"

"Oh, about 1900 hours."

"How about 1830," responded Ohnemus, "I need a half hour to warm up!'

"Come on when you're ready!"

"What's for chow?" I asked Ruchel, as he was exiting the mess tent.

"Spam."

"I shouldn't have asked!"

"No, food like that demands conversation," replied Ruchel, "a little discourse to take your mind off of the main course!"

The word spread quickly at evening chow and by 1900 Blair had a tent full of conviviality. With the free and fervent flow of intoxicating spirits, everyone was soon talking impulsively and incessantly.

"That'll clean your rifle barrel!" exclaimed Musket, after a swallow of some Australian squeezings that Thatcher brought to the prayer meeting.

"Unshaven! Out of uniform! And this tent looks like a hog wallow," exclaimed Major Jones, feigning a heartfelt disappointment.

"We thought it looked pretty good," answered Hardeman, "we modeled it after the Fort Worth stockyards!"

"Don't you ever shave?" asked Foy.

"Just my legs!" answered Kuta.

"Here's to inactivity," said Burg, leading the first toast of the evening, "the mother of inebriation!"

"Here's to free enterprise," followed Kuta, "if it's free we keep our enterprise!"

"There's a five dollar cover charge tonight," announced Blair, and was met with a round of boos and Bronx cheers, "when the shootin' starts we charge for cover!"

"They say I have a drinking problem," said Thatcher, "I have no problem drinking at all!"

"Women are like bread," Moore was saying to Pallotta, "you gotta leave 'em alone to get a rise out of 'em!"

"I'm *tougher* than a *kamikaze* pilot," remarked Hardeman, to no one in particular. "I've already flown twenty trips!"

"General Patton, leading the Third Army through France, was quoted as saying today: 'We don't want all the bacon, we only want part of the Rhine!' " said Lieutenant Ike Baker, who gave the chalk talks and kept us current on the state of the war in Europe. "How about that?"

"Just part of the Rhine should make Hitler feel fine," said Kuta.

"General Kenney was the greatest Commanding General the Fifth Air Force ever had!" said Johnson.

"Was he the same as general chaos?" asked Lyman.

Phillips and Esty got into a heated discussion and Chaplain Kozlowski, standing nearby, stepped in between them. "My sons, those who live by the sword shall die by the sword," said the Padre.

"That's all right, Father," said Phillips, "I'm only going to break the jawbone of an ass!"

"I'm applying for hardship leave, Doc," said Lyman. "Transfer me to the eastern front, say somewhere near New York — or Boston!"

"I'll work on it, Lyman!" smiled Doc Marcus, "I'll work on it!"

"Give me your attention, please!" said Captain Holtzman. "Please, gentlemen! If you please!" Everyone got reasonably quiet.

"Tonight we have a special treat! Major Bowes and his internationally famous Amateur Hour will be performing here this evening live — "

"You sure you're *live*?"

"The first entertainer tonight hails from Texas. Lieutenant "Root" Hardeman, will give his impersonation of that famous Hollywood actress, Miss Betty Davis. Let's hear it for Root Hardeman, er . . . Miss Davis!"

Hardeman had his pants legs rolled up, and his hairy legs were showing. A mop from the kitchen was hair, and his cheeks were painted red with cake coloring! After attempting a sexy walk, a couple of grinds, and a bump or two, he gave us:

Petah! Petah! Petah! I must have my Petah! And it became more obscene as he went on.

This was so much out of character for Hardeman that the costuming and staging, even without the dramatic presentation, was hilarious. His inebriated friends fell all over themselves and rolled on the floor of the tent.

"For all of you listeners out there in radioland," continued

Holtzman, "the telephone number to call to vote for your favorite act or entertainer is Murrayhill 8-9933! That number again . . .

"Our next performer tonight," said Captain Holtzman, "is that world renowned vocalist, Miss Kate Smith! Let's have a round of applause for Miss Smith! Miss Smith has just returned from Fort Leavenworth where she played a very successful engagement to the shut-ins. Some people say that Miss Smith bears a remarkable resemblance to our own Lieutenant Johnson. Let's hear it — " Applause.

Johnson came out dressed in a costume similar to Hardeman's, and while he was already on the chubby side, the makeup artists had added to it by tying a full, bulging, barracks bag around his front so that he resembled nothing so much as a small elephant. Accompanied by Lieutenant Pallotta on his concertina, he tried to sing *When the Moon Comes Over the Mountain*. The entire, well-soused audience started baying like a pack of hounds. He couldn't resist, and he joined the audience in their howling and allowed the moon to get over the mountain without any further assistance from him.

The crowd brought the entertainers back on the dirt-floor stage for a round of applause amid "Speech! Speech!" Only Hardeman responded.

"It's been a delight being with you gentlemen tonight. Just remember, if you work, study, persevere and get sent to combat, you too can achieve stardom on the stage as I have. But more important, if you live a good life, if you're lucky, say your prayers, and bathe at least once a week; when you die you might get to go to *Texas*."

This, as you might imagine, inspired the state pride of every member of the audience, who sang out, all at the same time, *California Here I Come, Back Home in Indiana, Alabama Jubilee, The Eyes of Texas, On Wisconsin, Dixie, Yankee Doodle, My Old Kentucky Home,* and a couple I'd never heard before! It succeeded in sending everyone to their tents and their sacks.

The night was short, and 0430 came around very early the next morning, particularly to those who were flying the day's mission. "Let's rise and shine, Blount!" came the friendly greeting accompanied by the nudge of a flashlight through the mosquito netting from the OD.

"I'll rise, but I'm too tired to shine," was my weak response.

Having completed our pre-takeoff routine, a ritual that could save your life and which included appropriate (and enough) clothing, Mae West life preserver, forty-five automatic with extra ammo, jungle knife, atabrine, and water purifier pills, we sat and lounged in varied positions of disarray in the Operation tent's ready room, waiting to be briefed on the day's mission. Captain Musket, leading today's strike, came in first, followed by Major Jones, and Lieutenant Ike Baker.

"Gentlemen," Captain Musket began, standing in front of a blowup of the Coast of Indochina and pointing the stick in his hand, "the target is a Japanese convoy of six merchant ships, three destroyers, two gunboats, and a cruiser last reported at 1800 hours yesterday to be located about here. If the convoy traveled steadily all night, by 1130 hours today, it should be located about here! The estimate of the situation is . . . "

All of us who had survived ten missions, could have made Musket's speech for him so familiar was the message. This didn't, however, detract from our interest in what he had to say, which had us on the edge of our seats and hanging on his every word. He neither possessed a superior eloquence nor could he express himself in the manner of a professional entertainer, and his subject matter was actually very dry. But, he could have stuttered or been tongue-tied and still retained our undivided attention. What he had to say might mean the difference in living or dying, and this had our most rapt attention. The briefing of crews before a combat strike was closely akin to hundreds of other meetings and lectures I had attended in the past, and would attend in the future, in military, university, and law school classes, where large numbers of those present would sleep peacefully. I never observed any individual, however, at the briefing of a combat strike, give anything but his undivided, sober, and complete attention to the speaker of the moment.

"The estimate of the situation," said Musket, a phrase borrowed by the Air Corps from the early Prussian military, had to start with the facts. Captain Musket now related the facts of who, where, and how many, of the enemy we were going to meet today, and how we were going to attack them in the open

China sea. It was a familiar story. Find 'em, hit 'em, and then get the hell out of there! That part of the story never changed!

The true estimate of the situation seemed to be that we had more targets than we had airplanes! We flew more suicidal missions, flying broadside at minimum altitude into the densest concentrations of the enemy's heaviest antiaircraft guns, than any pilots and their crews should be ordered to perform. Those ordering us to fly into that hell should have been honest enough to tell us they were trading our lives for time. *Like the men at the Alamo — lives for time.* They were trading our lives for the ships of the enemy by having us fly five-hundred-pound bombs in oversized rockets into the sides of enemy ships with no thought of the price we'd probably pay. I'm sure it was their sincere hope we'd make it safely back to fly some more bombs into other enemy ships with the sincere hope — and so on. The truth was, Fifth Bomber Command had lots of guts when it came to spilling our blood.

"Should we not find the convoy," continued Captain Musket, "we'll hit the secondary targets which are the railroad marshalling yards at Phan Rang, located here on the China coast — and an oil storage dump here. If we miss the convoy and have to hit our secondary targets, the squadron shall be divided into two flights of three ships each. I will hit the railroad marshalling yards at Phan Rang with Blount and Blair. Thatcher will take the second flight, with Lathrop and Burg, and hit the oil storage area!"

The convoy could have changed directions and have been out of the range of our airplanes by then, but the oil tanks and the railroad yards at Phan Rang would be waiting.

"I'd rather hit that railroad roundhouse than that cruiser and those destroyers!" whispered Kenney.

"Why?" asked Cronin, with a puzzled look on his face.

"They can never corner us there!" Cronin attempted to kick Kenney as I put my hand on his leg in an act of restraint.

Lieutenant Baker assured us the weather "all the way to the coast of China is perfect with unlimited visibility."

"Does that mean they can see us from the time we take off till we get to the coast of China?" asked Cronin.

"Yeah! That's it," replied Kenney. "But we're gonna be so low that we'll be hiding behind every wave between here and there."

"Radio gunners: check your emergency frequencies for *Juke Box* and the *Play Mate*. Navigators: get your coordinates for the friendly submarines that will be on the surface during our strike, and let's everybody get a hack coming up on 0614," said Musket. After we hacked our watches he asked, "Any questions?" There were none and we made for the jeeps and the flight line!

"Excuse me," said Kenney, standing next to the collapsible ladder that hung from the bowels of old *199*, inviting us up and inside to bring her alive, "do you have a reservation for this flight?"

"I think so," replied Zuber, carrying out the sham, "my travel agent is very responsible, in fact he's the Operation's Officer of this airline and he threatened me with a court-martial if I didn't take this flight!"

"I see your name has been scratched out," continued Kenney, "apparently you didn't reconfirm your reservation?"

"There must be some mistake," responded Zuber, "but I'm willing to return to the ticket counter to check my reservation! It's only a couple of miles and please don't feel that you have to wait. I'll catch the next flight."

"We insist that our passengers reconfirm their reservations at least fifteen minutes in advance on U.S. Combat Airlines and since it's a good thirty minutes before takeoff," said copilot Cronin, "I can guarantee that Mr. Zuber's reservation on this flight is confirmed!"

"In fact," I added, as I started my inspection walk around number *199*, "I refuse to make this flight without him! I'll confirm all the passengers on this flight, Mr. Kenney, and dare anyone of them to refuse!" I placed my hand on the forty-five automatic strapped to my side for emphasis.

"Threats, force and intimidation," Warnick said. "I'm gonna see the Chaplain—just as soon as we get back!"

"Here," said Kenney, "I'll punch your tough shit card right now and save the Chaplain his time and trouble!"

Musket started his airplane rolling down the strip and before he cleared the end of the runway, I advanced the throttles on *199* as she reluctantly, and with much vibration and shaking, accelerated toward the trees. The sun reflected off the top turret of Musket's ship right above the treetops as he made his climbing, sweeping turn toward the open sea and China. I cut inside his turn and slipped up and above his right wing, and was quickly joined by Blair on Musket's left wing. With Thatcher leading the second flight, fifty feet below and behind us, we climbed steadily to 5,500 feet.

There were needles on a dial on the panel which indicated the flow of fuel to each engine. They helped us calculate consumption and showed us when we'd flown to the end of our string — like a kite — and when we must return if we were to have enough fuel in reserve to get us back to base. Our fuel system was a hodgepodge of valves, tubes, tanks, and pumps, because the airplane was not designed to fly ten or eleven hour missions. As a result, much of the ordinarily vacant space in the airplane was taken up with auxiliary fuel tanks. When the engines coughed and spit and sputtered, we knew it was only the collection of air in the fuel system, and we tried not to allow our hearts to remain too long in our throats, until the steady hum of healthy engines returned.

Musket leveled off for a brief time at 5,500 feet, and then began a steady descent back to 5,000 feet. In so doing we had put our aircraft in a slightly nose-down flight attitude that added from five to ten mph to our airspeed. Because of the great distance we had to fly to targets along the China coast, and to achieve maximum fuel consumption, we set our props at 1,800 RPM, throttles at twenty-four inches of mercury and reduced the mixture control to cruising lean, and slightly below, until the cylinder head temperature started to ascend. We maintained 185 mph indicated airspeed and cylinder head temperature under 205 degrees centigrade. Out of habit, I constantly scanned the instruments before, to my right, and above me; absorbing their readings at a glance. When all was well, the confidence in the normal operation of the airplane was stimulating. My familiarity with the instruments was closely akin to a husband's intuitive understanding of the expression on his wife's face when he's been married to her for twenty-five years. Instantly he can recognize, in a raised eyebrow or in a minute change of expression, that all is not well and adjustment needs to be made. Usually the most insignificant, slightest, imperceptible movement of a needle, or other change in the instruments automatically transmitted the need for immediate correction of the problem without the necessity of a word being spoken.

"How far to the coast of China?" I inquired of Kenney.

"We've been paralleling the coast, which is about fifteen to twenty miles over there, for about ten minutes," replied Kenney, "and this is the general area where we should find the convoy!"

"Kit Bag Leader to Squadron," Musket broke radio silence for the first time. "Proceed with Plan Two. I say proceed to secondary. Over and out."

With the last word of the message, Thatcher and the second flight pulled away and angled to our left in the direction of the coast of China while we continued on the heading we were flying. I called for flak suits and steel helmets and Kenney wasted no time in assisting Cronin and me into the heavy steel robes.

"How far are we from Phan Rang?" I asked Kenney.

"When we turn toward the coast, if Musket sticks with a northeast to southwest attack, we should be from five to six minutes from the target."

Musket began a ninety degree turn toward the coast. "We're five minutes from the target," advised Kenney, as he started pulling on the cables between the pilot and copilot seats to charge the package guns. He had seen a topographical feature or other distinguishable landmark that was recognizable on his map.

"Watch for *Zeros* in the sun, Warnick. Be alert to pick off any *ack-ack* and gun positions to our right! Zuber: Help out with protection to our right flank, from the waist!"

"Roger. Roger, Lieutenant!"

I advanced the props to 2,300 and the throttles to twenty-six inches to keep up with Musket as we burst out from the open sea and over the beach at 285 mph indicated. Traveling ahead of our sound human figures in the surf "froze" as we passed over them while one or two, who happened to be looking in our direction in time to see us coming, dove into the waves and under the water, afraid that we would strafe them. They were already dead, had we chosen, but we were looking for bigger game and *199* did not indiscriminately strafe people unless they were recognizable enemy, or in, around, or part of, the assigned target.

The big, white, brick, and glass five-storeyed, railroad roundhouse loomed up out of the flat land a short distance from the coast. It looked as big as the Taj Mahal sitting there on the coastal plain with nothing around it. The large building, which had to have been sixty feet high and over three hundred feet long, (with three boxcar size doors in one end) was an imposing structure, and out of character for most of the buildings we had observed that were built by the enemy. Two long strings of boxcars and two engines were stationary on sidings next to the roundhouse.

Get us down, Musket! Get us down! I said to myself as we were still one hundred-fifty feet in the air as I popped the bomb bay doors open. But we had encountered no flak, and Musket must have thought we'd slipped up on them unannounced. Flying Musket's right wing I was up even with his airplane, but Blair had fallen twenty feet behind. *I won't strafe until I see Musket's nose on fire.* Flying formation on Musket, his job was to take me over the target, and he aimed my guns as he aimed his own. Before he hit his gun button the first flak burst in the middle of our three-ship formation, followed quickly by three more large, explosive black puffs of heavy antiaircraft fire. I started strafing; so did Musket and Blair. The formerly serene scene of the big, beautiful building suddenly turned into an aerial inferno. The airplane recoiled and vibrated as the guns — fore, aft, and from the side — opened their staccato message of death and destruction. The smoke from our expended ammunition filled the cockpit — as invigorating as pure oxygen.

About half a mile from the roundhouse, and while still a hundred feet in the air, Blair's plane swerved toward Musket. I saw it out of the corner of my eye, and heard Blair announce, "I'm hit in the right engine," in the same unemotional tone of voice he might have said "let's get a cup of coffee." That's the most sobering pronouncement that can be made by an airplane driver, while over a minimum altitude target. Immediately the destruction of the target was forgotten, as the welfare and safety of an injured fellow warrior took top priority. Musket's guns went silent and his bomb bays closed as he initiated a concentrated effort to fly protective formation, in an all-out attempt to shepherd the crippled airplane out of that "valley of the shadow of death."

Blair was laboring to hold his airplane straight and level at 290 mph, and I saw him struggling, across the one hundred feet separating us, and going through the single engine procedure to feather the right prop. He had to maintain enough altitude to clear the roundhouse, and ignore the flak that was now as intense as an aggravated hornets' nest and which enveloped his aircraft. The heavily smoking engine continued to draw the attention of the enemy gunners, confirming the law of the jungle, and the savage, beastly business in which we were engaged. Kill the weak and the crippled, who can't defend themselves.

With silent guns and closed bomb bay doors, Blair was struggling to hold enough left rudder to offset the massive power of the left engine, necessary to hold a straight course of flight across the target, and out of the area of danger. Despite his expertise, a chain reaction was initiated as Blair's airplane began a slight turn to the right into Musket, forcing Musket to give more airspace to the disabled airplane by easing further to the right, into me, and crowding all of us off the target.

I was thirty yards to the right of the target, but in an instinctive action, totally devoid of conscious thought, I racked my airplane up to the right — simultaneously kicking two five-hundred-pound bombs out of the bottom of my airplane. The effect was that, as luck would have it, the two bombs hit the hard surface amid the maze of railroad tracks leading into the big roundhouse, skipping through the wall or open doors to explode four seconds later. The bomb blasts momentarily illuminated the glass and brick structure like a light bulb, and then totally destroyed the building with a mushroom effect that buckled the metal roof and destroyed everything inside.

"Watch for fighters everybody!" I said over the intercom. "This is an ideal situation for them to pick us off while we're trying to protect a cripple!"

"Roger!" came three replies simultaneously.

Musket and I had throttled back to 165 mph indicated flying speed, just above Blair, like a couple of mother hens whose outspread wings protect the chicks from the hawk. Blair made a wide turn into his good left engine, back toward the open sea, and Musket and I followed. Blair's crew wasted no time in lightening the load; they were asking a lot of their one remaining good engine. Every conceivable piece of loose equipment started to be ejected from the airplane. The heavy guns in the waist, tail and top turrets, were the first to be thrown overboard, followed closely by long belts of ammunition. When Blair salvoed his bomb load, we saw the airplane ascend a good fifty feet. The wild array of articles being thrown from the crippled airplane reminded me of an excited boy going through a toy box or trunk in the attic in search of a lost toy, and discarding left and right.

"Hello *199*. This is Kit Bag Leader! Over." came Musket's voice over the radio, breaking radio silence for only the second time.

"Hello, Kit Bag Leader. This is *199*. Over." I replied.

"I'm going ahead to try to locate assistance. You stay with our friend."

"Roger," and I said no more on the radio. It would be extremely difficult for the enemy to pick up or home in on such a short message.

"Where are our friendly submarines?" I asked Kenney, who was keeper of all emergency data, including the coordinates for the subs that were surfaced, and that would remain so for thirty minutes following our strike, unless forced to dive because of enemy intervention.

"*Kleptomaniac* is approximately fifty nautical miles straight ahead," replied Kenney, "but we're out of range of the *Juke Box* and *Playmate*." *Juke Box* was the code name for the Navy PBYs that would land and rescue survivors if the sea was not too rough. *Playmate* was the code name for a PBY that had a twenty-foot boat with motor, water, and rations strapped under the airplane that could be dropped to downed personnel when the sea was too rough to land.

I looked into the cockpit where my friend Blair had trimmed the controls so that his airplane now flew smoothly, but who was in a bent-over position in the pilot's seat, as if worried with instruments, controls, or related problems of the airplane. For the first time I was afforded a long, uninterrupted view of the airplane and it more nearly resembled a sieve than an aircraft. There were gaping holes in the vertical stabilizer, a portion of the left aileron had been shot away and the rear half of the fuselage looked as if it had been hit with a massive load of grape shot. I prayed that all members of that crew were healthy and free of injury. They would need strength for the inevitable adversity they would face all too soon. I was so close, (only one hundred feet away) but it might just as well have been one hundred miles, for all the good I could do. *Why hasn't someone invented a rope, or a chute, or something!—that would allow the men trapped in a shot up airplane to be transferred in midair to another airplane?* Those and a thousand other thoughts of concern for those men went through my mind as we watched helplessly.

Out here, at the farthest, the most extreme edge of our flight range, Blair knew that he had to ditch the airplane. Whether we found our friendly submarine or not, he knew what he was going to have to do, what none of us had ever been able to ignore the possibility of doing, since we had been flying and fighting over water. Ditching was one maneuver that couldn't be practiced. Oh, we'd talked the right arms off fellow pilots who had ditched, and lived to talk about it: what they did, what they felt, how they did it. But all that we learned, was that only those who had accomplished it, knew what it was like to land in the sea; and they were the first, to a man, to admit that luck favored them more than skill. We were well aware that "the aircraft should be ditched on the top to the backside of a wave, and never in the trough," or death valley, between waves! But who was the "hot pilot" who could set an aching, agonized, sickly, eighteen tons of metal and machinery down *softly* on the top of an ocean wave, which was moving thirty-five to forty miles per hour?

What pilot genius, using a B-25 for a surfboard, could select such a desirable, pillow-soft wave, slide crosswind on single engine with it and survive to say "Would you believe I've never had a formal aircraft ditching lesson in my life? It was just natural talent!"

"Have you measured the surface wind?" I asked Kenney.

"Thirty-eight miles per hour!" he answered, already anticipating Blair's problem.

Every crewman had a specific station and position when ditching. And everyone had a better deal than the pilot when ditching the airplane! Hit the water too hard, or too fast, in the B-25 airplane, and the nine hundred pounds of top turret came crashing down on the cockpit; and that spelled *adios amigo!*

"How much gas we got to get home on?" I asked Kenney.

"We've been out six and a half hours till now," replied Kenney. "If we stay another fifteen minutes I figure we're going to be stretching it to get home without getting our feet wet, too."

Musket was nowhere in sight, out of sight in the vastness

of the China sea. If he had located help, he had not contacted them by radio, for Zuber had been monitoring the emergency channels and would have reported it immediately.

"We're surrounded on all sides, and in the slap-dab-middle of the Japanese," said Kenney. "There's no tellin' how many fighter strips, naval bases — not to mention the enemy warships — there are, right there over the horizon in every direction, all monitoring and trying to get a fix on us from everything we say."

I looked at the "needles of life" on the gas gauges that told me the painful truth of how little liquid hydrocarbons we had in our too-close-to-empty gas tanks. Gasoline, especially over water, is like an ever-decreasing bank account that can't be built back up at that time.

"How far are we from where *Kleptomaniac* is supposed to be surfaced?" I hollered over my shoulder to Kenney, to be heard over the engine noise.

"At least another ten minutes," answered Kenney, "flying as slow as we are!"

I looked across and down the one hundred feet into the cockpit of Blair's crippled aircraft. Through the plexiglass, their cockpit was illuminated like a movie set from the bright sun; both Blair and his copilot were motionless, and had the eerie look of mannequins riding a ghost ship. The red knobs of the throttles, prop pitch, and mixture controls on the column between the pilots, was in disarray, and scattered over the entire range of operation instead of reflecting the harmonious, identical-twin adjustments of the controls of my airplane.

I had tried to absorb aerial wisdom from every gentleman with whom I had flown, since I first climbed into a Stearman in primary flying school. Particularly had I learned from Blair, the anxious pilot whose wing I now flew. He was a flight leader, and among the most experienced and respected pilots in the 501st. Like all good pilots, Blair was thinking ahead of his airplane, considering every eventuality. He knew that his bag of choices had run dry! He had to find *Kleptomaniac*! All of this went through my mind as I rode shotgun for a friend who was now in dire peril.

Blair finally looked up for the first time. His face, covered with lines of worry that belied his age, was expressionless. I pointed in the direction of the Philippines, then down to the gas gauges on the panel, and exaggeratedly mouthed *Got to go home*. He pointed to his head *(I understand)* and nodded yes. He then waved goodbye, encouraging me to leave. There was so much I wanted to *say*, and the radio speaker button was under my thumb. *But I can't! I mustn't!* He could see, and feel, all I wanted to say, that was in my eyes and face. I mouthed *Good luck!* and our eye contact was broken, (I felt forever) as I made the sweeping turn for home. I took one last glance at the helpless airplane, now a speck on the horizon, flying on single engine into the vast nothingness of the China sea. I breathed a fervent prayer for their safety. That was all any of us could do. I felt so helpless. My gut hurt.

"We're really going to have to stretch the gas," Kenney told me, his voice sounding strained.

"What's your projection?"

"About ten minutes short."

"WHAT — ?" I screamed.

"Well, maybe just a mite more," replied Kenney, "we might be able to see the Philippines from where the gas runs out."

We had fought the obvious enemy; now we had to face a new enemy, a new threat — *Time*. After climbing to 5,000 feet I throttled back and set the props at 1,800 rpm. I could count the blades on the windmill, they turned so slowly; but they also required the minimum amount of fuel at that rate. I placed a maximum amount of faith in those engines, as I'd done before, and they responded in a remarkable manner.

"Give me a fuel check every thirty minutes," I told Kenney.

After about an hour we encountered a cloud buildup. "Hey! Where did the clouds come from?" I asked Kenney, "and I don't see any silver linings either."

"Baker told us about these in his weather report at the briefing this morning — except he said they weren't due until sometime tonight! Looks like the weather report wasn't accurate again," Kenney told me.

"Is it ever? How's the gas?"

"Low," responded Kenney, "just keep flyin' thataway!" He then pointed to the front of the airplane as if we were on a joy ride down to the corner drug store.

"That's what I like about you!"

"What's that?" asked Kenney.

"Your preciseness! Your meticulous, punctilious, fastidious, discriminating demand for detailed accuracy!" I told him.

"When you get off course I'll let you know!"

"Gee, thanks! But promise me one thing!"

"What's that?"

"Give me corrections in course headings only if it won't inconvenience you any." I received an irked and painful look from the best navigator in the United States Army Air Corps who was now writing, figuring, and turning the wheels on his E-6-B "confuser" (computer) like a mad professor working on Einstein's theory of relativity.

"Put the food in the oven," I said to Cronin. Soon the K-Rations, from breakfast through dinner, were passed over the bomb bay and deposited on top of the instrument panel under the plexiglass, where the rays of the bright sun peering through the clouds warmed them. My philosophy was — if we went down, we went down on a full stomach.

Three hours later we'd been in and out of spotty rain squalls, but fortunately the weather had not closed in, forcing us to go on instruments. I would not touch, or change, the engine settings that would cost us a thimblefull of gas unless I was absolutely driven to it as a last resort in order to save our necks.

I'd learned to never doubt or dispute the instruments, follow those flight practices that were odds-on favorites to be successful, never relax, but be constantly alert while in the air. As Moore said, "strive to be a cautious pilot rather than a dead hero!" To be constantly alert implied that a pilot must know what he should be aware of and that could only come from experience. Learning the dangers, and potential dangers of flying was like working high voltage conductors with the kilowatts flowing.

"Is there anything you'd like to tell me?" I questioned Kenney.

"Yes. Warnick and I, after a close inspection and detailed study of the situation, estimate that we have thirty gallons of gasoline remaining for each engine!"

"What's your prognosis?"

"You better start looking for a place to land!"

"How do you figure we have sixty gallons left?"

"Warnick says that half of that is the additional gas he added when he topped off all the tanks just before takeoff!"

"Warnick?" I said on the intercom.

"Roger, Lieutenant!"

"Remind me to recommend you for the Nat Kenney Award if we fly this airplane back to base!"

"Yes, sir!" replied Warnick. "Does that Kenney Award cover an increased pay check at the end of the month?"

"Not necessarily," I responded, "but it does mean you're Number One in the hearts of everyone of us on this airplane and we love you like a brother!"

"One more question, sir!" Warnick intoned on the intercom.

"What is it?"

"If we make it back can I have your ration of Old Grand-Dad?"

There was instant pandemonium on the intercom as everyone got his two cents in. "Hush," I said, "— Listen! Now hear this! This is the pilot! We're gonna make it back and I'm gonna try to get Doc Marcus to give all of you, who want it, a canteen cup full of Old Grand-Dad! In the meantime, ride light and take deep breaths!" We carefully avoided talking about Blair and his men on the plane we'd had to leave behind.

Ten minutes, fifteen at the most, was all the flying time we had left in the fuel on board. We hadn't even seen the coast of Luzon. Another fear. Even if we made it back to the island of Luzon, how far would we be from San Marcelino? *If we're off three minutes and have to correct . . .* After seven more minutes of watching the clock on the instrument panel I was barely touching the pilot's seat, unconsciously trying to assist the airplane to stay in the air. Cronin and Kenney looked like zombies as they stared straight ahead through the plexiglass, straining to catch a glimpse of shoreline through the mist and rain.

We had flown the seven minutes in total silence with only the steady hum of the engines lending moral support, anticipating momentarily their last coughs and sputterings before giving up the ghost. I had already made mental plans and calculations for a long, extended glide ending with a dead stick landing at the last possible moment. My mental preparation "for the worst" had probably surpassed my better judgment, but I had full faith in my ability to ditch the airplane safely.

Even a dead stick landing in water, of the B25J! I wasn't going to give fate, or death either, one foot of that 5,000 feet I now had and if those windmills quit turning we were going to find out just how far a B25J with an overloaded nose might glide.

"Are we close enough to swim to shore if we go down right here?" asked Warnick.

"How about that Kenney, are we?" I asked.

"If you could swim well enough to pass your first class merit badge in the Boy Scouts," said Kenney, "you'd have no trouble making it from here."

"But I'm not trying to be a Boy Scout!" said Warnick.

"You've got your Mae West and the inflatable dinghy back there," I added, "we could row into shore and be there in time for chow!"

"If I have to go to chow I had just as soon stay in the water." said Warnick. This nervous conversation was only wishful thinking. We had neither sighted land nor did we know when we would — if ever.

How long we could continue to kid each other, and maintain this pretense of calm, and how much the steady hum of the engines unconsciously sustained our confidence, we would never know. Perhaps the comradery and the presence of all of us, confined in such a small space together, smothered the fear that we all felt, but which we suppressed and refused to acknowledge in the presence of one another. The minutes slipped quietly away, and the needles of life on our fuel gauges moved inexorably toward the big red E. We retained our cool. I watched, imperceptibly, the sweeping second hand of the clock on the instrument panel and hoped the others hadn't noted my anxiety.

"There! There it is!" shouted Cronin. Sure enough, through the darkness and patches of rain we made out a thin, dark line on the horizon that was unmistakably land.

"Tell me you see three mountains," I said to Kenney and Cronin. Three mountains — the landmarks of our base at San Marcelino.

"I see 'em Lieutenant!" responded Warnick, who had climbed into the top turret for a better view.

"I see three mountains," whooped Kenney, "and we're right on the button!"

I flipped on the IFF switch, so that our own *ack-ack* batteries would know we were friendly, and headed for the south end of the landing strip.

We were still in a precarious situation and I refused to touch the throttle, props, or mixture settings until the very last moment. The fuel supply should have been depleted fifteen minutes before by every standard of judgment known by all of us, and while I still couldn't understand it, I was not going to push our luck any further than was absolutely necessary to get that baby on the ground. And hopefully in one piece.

"Pilot to Engineer! Give us a red flare, Warnick, so everybody will know we're emergency and can't go around to make another approach for landing!"

"Roger!" came the reply.

In that kind of weather we were not jockeying with other aircraft for the runway. No pilot in his right mind would have been flying in that weather, but I wanted the ground, as well as other aircraft, if any, to know our true situation and give us the right-of-way!

I had been easing the airplane down at five hundred feet per minute from 5,000 feet since we had positively sighted land and the three mountains surrounding San Marcelino. I turned slightly left to line up with the runway for a straight-in approach and landing, and had worked my way down to 2,500 feet. I ran the GUMP check, (gas, undercarriage, mixture and props) preparatory to bringing the aircraft back to *terra firma*.

"I've gotta wheel!" shouted Cronin from the copilot's side after making a visual inspection of the right wheel down and locked into position for landing, verifying the green light on the instrument panel. I repeated his performance from the left side and verified the left wheel down and locked. The adrenalin was pumping and I was hyper as a result of the previous seven hours strike, the aftermath with Blair along the China coast, and the subsequent trip back to base sweating every drop of gas from China to the Philippines. The rain had increased in intensity and I called for Cronin to turn on the windshield wipers.

"Oh, hell! There's no windshield wipers!" exclaimed Cronin. I didn't take his word for it. I reached across the cockpit to the instrument panel and wiggled the switch three or four times. Unable to see anything in front of the airplane, I made an unforgivable error in judgment that could have done us in, as we tottered on the brink of the cup. Reaching forward with my left hand I threw open the sliding window to my left with one continuous motion. The fresh air, even if mixed with rain, felt good and filled the cockpit with new life. I now saw the landscape, the tents, the motor pool and activity off to the side and about halfway down the muddy, practically inundated, landing strip. But the runway was hidden behind the liquid curtain that covered the windshield in front of me. I had landed Stearman PT-19s and Vultee BT-13s during my flight training days, with my head extended to the side from behind the windvisor, and into the slipstream, to gain a better view of the runway. Those training aircraft, slow flying, aerodynamically sound, and designed to allow students to make certain flight mistakes (and live to tell it) didn't land any faster than sixty- to sixty-five miles per hour. I was approaching the end of the runway at 170 mph and in an instantaneous decision I thrust my head through the side window and into the full force of a wind traveling at tornadic speed — and I was momentarily blinded. The high velocity wind struck my eyes with such force that I thought they'd been torn from their sockets. Cronin had been glued to his side of the cockpit, concentrating on staring away the water thick against the windshield, and trying to locate the runway in relationship to our airplane.

Dear Lord, I thought frantically, *I can't see.*

"I'm blinded. I can't see," I said in a tone loud enough to be audible but calm enough, I hoped, not to frighten anyone.

"You want me to take it?" asked Cronin, in something less than a persuasive, confident voice. Fortunately, we were still a half- to three-quarters of a mile from the end of the runway, pursuing our straight in approach.

"Follow me through on the controls," I answered, knowing that I had been perfectly aligned with the runway, and our glide path had been established when my eyes suffered the shock of the windblast, "and cut the power when we come over the end of the runway. We've gotta land this time if it takes all this strip and a mile of jungle on the other end!"

I felt the controls tighten as Cronin gripped somewhat tighter than simply placing his hands on the wheel and his feet on the rudder pedals. The copilot's most important job in a strafer, was to turn on the camera switch as we went over the target, and to pull the airplane out of the trees, the sea or other obstacle, when the pilot became more intent on strafing and bombing, than flying the airplane. His job was to keep me from flying the airplane into the target we were attacking. I had told him that he trusted me too much, that I might not really be as good as he thought I was, which I really hadn't meant, but which I hoped would free him of any hesitancy in taking the wheel and pulling us from sure death should an emergency ever present itself. He did allow me to mow the tops out of the trees in northern Luzon, but I felt my copilot was adequate for any task, including landing that airplane blind, at that moment, if necessary.

Suddenly and miraculously, just as swiftly as I had lost my sight, it returned. "I've got it!" I whooped in relief to Cronin. "My eyesight's back."

"You sure?"

"Yeah! Hold up three fingers and ask me how many!"

"That wouldn't be fair! You'd already know how many I had up!"

We were down to one hundred feet, and the rain was torrential; but I had my bearings, and could judge my speed and height by the trees, tents, trucks, and other objects out to the side and far up the runway. I leveled off, the tires touched down and it sounded like a pep rally behind me. I used all the runway, letting the airplane roll the complete 5,000 feet, and turned off to the right, behind a jeep that was waiting. I retracted the flaps and increased the throttle on the left engine to make the right turn, and it coughed and sputtered —. We rolled another fifty yards, and the right engine coughed, and I caught it with additional throttle and momentarily brought it back to life. Both engines then coughed, sputtered, belched smoke — and died a natural death. *We were out of gas!* We sat in prayerful silence, looking and smiling at each other as if we had good sense, while the rain beat a crescendo on the plexiglass above us.

"Get that shit-eatin' grin off your face," Warnick said to Zuber, "you didn't do anything but sit back there and add weight to the airplane!"

"What did you do?" asked Zuber.

"I was figuring the fuel consumption with Lieutenant Kenney," replied Warnick.

"Well, I picked up two Jap messages and decoded them,"

replied Zuber, "they were listening to us up there today and trying to figure out where we were!"

"Were you watching the clock?" I asked.

"Yeah," answered both Cronin and Kenney simultaneously, and then both looked rather embarrassed since they had not wanted to show their concern, but knew they had blown it with their quick answer to my question.

"Don't feel bad, men," I replied, "I was, too. Particularly knowing that every time that sweep second hand made a revolution around the face of the clock another one- and three-quarters gallons of gasoline had gone out the exhaust stacks."

The jeep turned around and came back to the airplane. The driver shouted, "Lieutenant, if you'll just follow me I'll take you back to your hardstand."

"Unless you've got some gasoline, Sergeant, or a tow line," I yelled through the window, "this is as far as we're going in this airplane. We're out of gas."

"That's cuttin' it a little close, Sir," he replied.

"Too close!" I nodded.

"Let me get you some transportation. I'll be right back."

"Take your time. We're not going anywhere!" And, I added, as an afterthought, "Don't *want* to go nowhere!" I closed the side window, sealing the rain out. In about ten minutes, a weapon's carrier pulled up under the left wing and we loaded in and were taken to the interrogation tent.

"You're the last plane in from today's strike, Lieutenant Blount," said the interrogating officer, "we thought you were down."

"I hope nobody else is out behind us. We were out a little over eleven hours," I replied. "Do you have any word on Lieutenant Blair?"

"We were hoping you'd bring us information on Lieutenant Blair and his crew."

"Have you talked to Captain Musket? I stayed with Lieutenant Blair on the China coast while he went for help."

"He was unsuccessful. And when he couldn't find *Juke Box* or *Playmate*, he came on back to base."

I drew our path over the target, told him we had gotten two bombs into the roundhouse and logged just over eleven hours on the mission.

"I don't think B-25s were intended to fly eleven-hour missions," said the Captain.

"I think you're exactly right," I replied, "and you might tell Fifth Bomber that, too. I'm asking for time and a half."

Years later, I could appreciate and better understand General George Patton's dream, that he would achieve immortality in war after he'd been reinstated by Eisenhower and given command of the Third Army to help General Omar Bradley following the invasion of Europe. He had a dream that he could take the entire German 3rd Reich if he had only had "a few gallons of gasoline" to keep his tanks operative. "I'm precisely at the right place, at the right time, to win the biggest battle, in the biggest war in history! It depends only on a few gallons of gasoline!" he said.

I didn't have one dream about a few gallons of gasoline; I had a bad dream about the shortage of a few gallons of gasoline almost every night. It wasn't on the grandiose scale of General Patton's "win the biggest battle in history," but was on the relatively insignificant reason and concern for the personal welfare of my crew and myself. We were dead in the China sea if the gasoline ran out not just once but on every strike to the coast of China. Therein lies the basic difference between Generals and Lieutenants. Generals think about making history while Lieutenants and enlisted men, on the cutting edge of combat, think about living and going home.

After two days we had received no word on Blair, and Lieutenant Ike Baker came around to perform "the last rites." He collected all of Blair's personal things to send home and all his shorts, pants, jackets, underwear, toilet articles, sheets, and towels were gone within an hour after being laid out on his empty sack.

"How much longer do you think we can continue to play this game of elimination?" I asked Ike Baker. "I don't think I can hold on much longer!"

"You can hold on," replied Baker, "because you can do that little extra, do whatever it takes, to survive."

"I try," I replied, "and I'll keep trying."

"I know you will," said Baker, "survival is the real, the only glory of this business!"

How right he was.

CHAPTER NINE

Too Close To The Grim Reaper

The reports of my death are greatly exaggerated!
Mark Twain

"At Command and General Staff school they teach two rules," said Major Giese. "Rule Number one is young men die and get killed! Rule Number two is you can't change Rule Number one!"

"Never let the Jap attack you," was the general order that came down the chain of command from General MacArthur. "When the Japanese soldier has a well planned and coordinated plan of attack he carries it out efficiently and smoothly. It's when he's attacked, when he doesn't know what's coming, that he's vulnerable!"

"I agree with that," said Thatcher, "I don't ever want any of those little yellow sonzabitches attacking me. It's bad for my nervous system not to mention my life expectancy!"

Yesterday we had lost Blair and his crew. Today the strike

was back to the coast of China in pursuit of the same convoy we failed to find yesterday. Counting the ships as they returned, we were one short.

"Who was it today?" I asked.

"McGrane." said Fisher who was on the strike.

"Any survivors?" the standard second question.

"They think they saw three or four in the Goodyear inflatable life raft after they ditched!" Palace was his copilot and Groves his navigator. Did they make it? Would we ever know?

"Did you find the convoy?"

"No, they must've split up. We found this big tanker that had holed up in a little cove at Phan Rang bay. You know what that means. They had *ack-ack* set up every ten feet surrounding the ship along the shoreline."

"Did you get the tanker?"

"Yeah. But if we'd've caught 'em out in the open sea, I don't think the price would've been as high!"

"Who got credit for the ship?"

"Root Hardeman! He got the first bomb into her. He's in for the DFC."

The first ship that gets the first blow in usually gets the credit. A month or so earlier Fisher had gone over the largest ship in the convoy, got in the first blow, and he went in for the DFC. I had made the second pass, along with some of our other pilots. We did more damage, and the ship probably sank as a result of our follow up — but we got nothing. At the time it seemed so important. Six months, a year later, it made no difference. Who cared? As Thatcher said, "Nobody cared if you were a 4F or sunk every ship in the Japanese Imperial Navy. The important thing is that you survived!"

The following morning we were sent on a strike to Canton.

"I didn't think we had enough airplanes to fly a strike," said Stiles.

"The service squadron got on the ball yesterday and last night," replied Kenney, "and they came up with six that might make it."

"We'll fly this route to the target," said Musket, who was leading the strike. He pointed to a large map of the coast of China. "We'll fly just off the coast, past Hong Kong, and inland here, flying up to the west of Canton. When we reach the city of Canton we turn south down the Canton River, hitting targets of opportunity all the way out to the coast — approximately seventy-five miles. This is a river sweep to seek and destroy everything that aids the enemy's war effort, from river shipping to military installations. We're carrying two hundred and fifty-pound para-demolition bombs and they should be dropped from fifty to sixty foot altitude. They have a much greater explosive potential than the ordinary para-frags we've been utilizing against Jap airdromes. Any questions?

"Pilots: We shall position ourselves about a mile apart. On this one we're all on our own, so keep your eyes peeled for *Zeros*. We will be particularly vulnerable to fighter interception, but we're counting on our minimum altitude, speed, and our ability to hit and run to get us in and out of there safely. When we get to Canton I'll lead. Blount, in the number three position, will be the second ship. Position yourself," he said, "a mile or so behind, and to my left. Lathrop, in the number two position in the first flight, will position himself a mile behind Blount, and to his right and so forth for the remainder of the squadron. In this manner we should cover everything on, and to the sides of, the river — all the way out to the coast. At the speed we're traveling we won't see everything, but what I miss, you should see, Blount. What Blount doesn't see, Lathrop and those following should pick up. Any questions? Good hunting!"

"This should really be a good one," said Kenney, "I can feel it. A seventy-five mile buzz job, shootin' and bombin' the hell out of 'em!"

"You're really just an agitator. A hell raiser at heart, you know it?" I said.

"I feel the same way I used to feel just before we kicked off to A&M," replied Kenney, "and if that's being a hell raiser I've got to plead guilty!"

"That's bein' a hell raiser," I replied, "and that's the only kind I want flyin' with me!"

"Musket's utilizing the 'flushed quail theory' on this strike," I added, "and we're the quail."

"What's the flushed quail theory?" questioned Kenney.

"Haven't you ever hunted quail?" I asked, "if you had you'd understand. When you flush a covey of quail the birds go in all directions. A hunter follows the direction where the majority of the birds fly, but usually half- to two-thirds of the covey get away and are never shot at again. It could get pretty hairy if a squadron of *Zeros* jumps one or two of us, but the rest of us would be out to sea and gone before they could find us!"

"I hope we're among the one-half to two-thirds who get away," replied Kenney.

As the tempo of strikes against Jap shipping in the China sea and inland targets along the coast of Indochina increased, we were issued brightly colored silk flags bearing the China-Burma-India Theater patch and an American Flag stating in Chinese: *The bearer is an American flyer. The party or parties who help, aid, or assist the person in possession of this silk Chinese message, to escape the Japanese, will be rewarded with the equivalent of $5,000 American dollars.*

"What if we run into someone who can't read Chinese?" asked Warnick, enroute to the flight line after we had received the silk flags, "or don't understand $5,000 Yankee dollars?"

"You better start learning some Chinese — and fast," volunteered Zuber, "and I'm willing to help anyway I can. I'm a real asset."

"You're off by only two letters," replied Warnick, "and a real pain in the neck!"

"Try three feet lower," responded Kolodziejski.

The weather thickened as we approached the coast of China three hours later, and the ceiling was 3,500 feet. "How long till we turn inland?" I asked Kenney, as we flew by the entrance to the harbor into Hong Kong.

"It'll be another fifteen minutes," said Kenney.

"Better hand me that hardware then," and he started helping me into the flak suit and helmet.

As we turned into China from the coast, Musket took us down to 1,500 feet. "How far are we from Canton?' I asked Kenney.

"Another ten, eleven minutes," replied Kenney.

"Pilot to crew! Let's be alive and alert. Warnick, you and Hank, keep a lookout for fighters. You should have some good shooting out the side today, Zuber. We'll try to let you know what's up front so you and Hank get a shot on the breakaway. Let's lighten the load so we don't take any ammunition home. Let's leave it *all* here."

As we approached Canton, black puffs of heavy 90-mm *ack-ack* greeted us about one hundred yards off our left wing. I advanced the props to twenty-one hundred rpm, and the throttles to twenty-six inches. "That's too accurate for comfort," said Cronin with a straight face. Musket made a sharp, diving turn to the right, and I followed in a diving — but wider turn — to place my airplane outside, to the left, and staggered behind Musket. Now we were right on the water, below the level of the trees, and free of the flak; ready to go to work. In twenty seconds, Musket was out of sight and we were alone. It was us against the Japanese war machine, and a feeling of elation swept over me. *This,* I thought to myself, *is my kinda war!*

The water of the Canton River was placid and free of traffic, except for native fishermen in small boats, which were not military targets. I pulled up to one hundred-fifty feet to gain a better view of the river, its turns and meanders. The river is wide, from two hundred- to six hundred-yards, the water appearing very still, indicating considerable depth. I saw smoke dead ahead, heavy and black, coming from something that was obviously laboring under, or pulling, a great load. At 285 mph the distance closed fast, and in a matter of five or six seconds I saw a one-stack river steamer with five or six barges in tow, coming up the river to meet us. Musket had evidently gone too far to the right and missed the river steamer. I dropped back down to the treetops, to assure our concealment and preserve the stealth of our approach.

"River Steamer with barges dead ahead," I spoke into the intercom, alerting the crew. "Strafe straight ahead, Warnick, and be alert on the breakaway, Hank. The boiler room is what we want to hit."

In a swift, fraction-of-a-second decision, I decided to "skip it in" instead of trying to "float it in." Better this time to skip-bomb, rather than pull up to sixty or seventy feet and allow the two hundred-fifty-pound para-demolition bomb to float down and explode on or near the river steamer. A floater stands a better than even chance of missing at 285 mph. *I've never dropped a two hundred-fifty-pound para-demolition bomb before, so I better drop it the way I know how,* I told myself. I made this brilliant, tactical decision on the basis of a limited knowledge of aerial explosives proving once again the truth of the old axiom: a little knowledge is a dangerous thing! *If I fly the bomb into the river steamer,* I thought, *and treat the two hundred-fifty-pound para-demo as if it were a free-falling missile and eliminate the parachute effect by dropping it so low and fast that it has neither the height nor the time to open, it will maintain all the characteristics of a free falling bomb including the higher percentage of accuracy.* However, one minor detail, embarrassingly consistent with such hasty decision, had completely escaped my mind. Unlike the one thousand and five hundred-pound bombs I ordinarily dispensed at minimum altitude, with five- to ten- second delay fuses, this two hundred-fifty-pound para-demolition number didn't have a delayed fuse of *any* duration. It traveled at the same speed, exploded on contact, and directly under the airplane that dropped it. I would never again drop another para-type bomb except in the conventional manner for which it was designed. We were in for a rude awakening!

I popped the bomb bay doors open. Then I eased the airplane slightly right, and flew over the rice paddies, instead of following the winding of the river; that way we would get a better angle of attack to strafe the river steamer and its barges. As I hit the gun button, releasing the twelve forward firing fifties, the airplane recoiled, shook and vibrated. Warnick was strafing from above the plexiglass covering the cockpit, and the fourteen streams of incendiaries and tracers into the ship brought it to an instant stop. The trees along the west bank of the river, which appeared forty to fifty feet high at that point, had hidden us until the very last moment. I was over the trees — on top of and even with — the top of the smoke stack of the steamer when I released the para-demolition bomb. The bomb had been accurately dropped, (too accurately) and evidently dropped into the boiler room. There was an explosion that threw our airplane into the air, like a child would throw a toy! The concussion from the bomb, when we were directly over the exploding river ship, increased our altitude a good hundred feet. For a moment the controls of the airplane were neutralized and it felt like we'd been simultaneously hit with heavy, explosive flak from at least five guns.

"What happened?" yelled Kenney over the sound of the engines and exploding machine guns.

"How're things back there, Zuber!" I asked on the intercom. "We're not hit by *ack-ack* that I didn't see are we?"

"The river ship blew up," answered Zuber, "and I went to the top of the fuselage back here for a couple of seconds!"

"Half of that river ship has just disappeared," said Kolodziejski, from the tail turret, "and what's left is burning furiously! I don't know what's under the tarps covering those barges but whatever it is it's smoking from our incendiaries!"

"Do you see any damage to the airplane from back there?" I asked. I was looking through patches of Canton River mud that had splotched and spattered the windshield in front of me.

I thought back to an overseas training experience I'd had while shooting the seventy-five millimeter cannon at Myrtle Beach, South Carolina. I remembered the cracked plexiglass I had, after flying through the water spray kicked up by a projectile that had hit in the water short of the target.

I was impressed that the 75-mm was the largest gun ever fired regularly from an aircraft even though rivets continued to be blown from the nose of the fuselage that held the airplane together and the airspeed dropped about ten miles per hour from the recoil. The cannon was arranged so that it was loaded in the well behind the cockpit and the pilot straddled the barrel of this monster, the end of which was pointing out the front of the airplane. The gun was loaded by the navigator who crawled into the well behind the cockpit and inserted the rounds of ammunition that were stacked like bottles of wine around each side of the wall of the fuselage. The cannon had a recoil of twenty-four inches which was almost the exact length of the well in which it was seated. When the cannon was fired there was no room for anything else in the well wider than a piece of paper, so the navigator, after loading, had to jump out of the well and also straddle the cannon while it was being fired. If he failed to remove himself from the well as the cannon was fired — you immediately had a navigator without legs. To prevent an accident the navigator loaded the cannon, jumped to his straddling position, and then reached up and tapped the pilot on the shoulder when he was clear. This was the pilot's signal to fire. I was real impressed with the fact that everyone who had anything to do with firing the cannon had to straddle it, *trust extraordinaire* for the male homo sapien.

In those initial training sessions Arky Vaughn had a devoted audience. Both Zuber and Kolodziejski were atop the bomb bay peering forward, and Warnick was seated in the top turret looking down on the agile performance of the navigator as he strained to lift the heavy round of seventy-five millimeter ammunition from the fuselage, slide it into the breach, jump to his straddling position of the cannon, and tap me on the shoulder. After the first couple of passes over the target I heard this cheering from the voices in the back of the airplane! *That's nice*, I thought, *the crew's showing their appreciation of my shooting the cannon!* Later I learned they were cheering the agility, dexterity, and derring-do of our fighting navigator.

"I saw an acrobat in the circus one time," said Warnick, "that didn't have half the moves of Lieutenant Vaughn!"

As with a rifle calibrated for one thousand yards, a shot inside this range must be aimed below the target to compensate for the shortage of distance.

The first time I fired the seventy-five I nearly jumped out of the cockpit as a forty-foot length of flame enveloped the front of the airplane, and momentarily obstructed all vision of the target area. Next, an enormous explosion (accompanied by a violent shaking and shuddering of the airplane) with a massive cloud of smoke filled the cockpit immediately. After what seemed an eternity, of five or six seconds, the smoke cleared sufficiently to observe the shell exploding on or near the target on the beach. The frequency with which the human animal participates in a thrilling, quasi-dangerous endeavor, (no matter how scary or breathtaking the first experience might have been) subsequent repetition tends to make the experience less exciting. The adventurer is destined to increase the dose or magnify the thrill. So it was with firing the seventy-five millimeter from the B-25H.

After making 25 passes over the target to fire twenty-five rounds and consuming more than an hour of time, we devised a plan whereby we were able to get off three-rounds in one pass by firing the first round from a mile out and then increasing the efficiency and teamwork between the navigator loader and the pilot. For variety, to break the boredom, I decided to try firing a round at the target at point-blank range of fifty yards or less at top speed. I told the crew on the intercom what I was going to do and to hold on. Putting the nose down I allowed the airplane to pick up speed until we were indicating 300 mph at the bottom of our dive. With the wings starting to vibrate from the excessive speed, and, with the target coming up fast and filling the entire plexiglass windshield, I fired the cannon. At such point-blank range I had to aim at least ten feet under the target and I was anxious to see what I had done to the target! I didn't have long to wait! As is usually the case in such ill-advised and ill-conceived ventures, I miscalculated and fired too low, the fifteen-pound projectile hitting in the water in front of the target and throwing up a fine mist of sea water. Of course, just as sure as night follows the day, the airplane followed the cannon shell hitting the "mist" that had been thrown into the air by the projectile. Instantaneously, like magic, the one-half inch plexiglass windshield, that stretched the entire width of the cockpit, cracked into a thousand jagged and crooked lines resembling a spider's web. And just as instantly I broke into a cold sweat that saturated my shirt, filled my leather flying gloves and necessitated my taking a swipe to remove the salty beads of sweat from my forehead. After that experience I was content to fire the seventy-five millimeter cannon from one thousand yards expending one round, and one round only, on each pass if it took all day!

With removal of the cannon from the B-25J, they also put the copilot back in his right-hand seat with dual controls to pull the pilot and airplane out of strafing dives when he became too intent on destroying enemy targets and would fly the airplane into the ground. I never heard a B-25H pilot express regret at having that cannon taken from between his legs, now that I think of it, and I'll assure you this one never missed it. Replacing the 75-mm cannon with 12 forward-firing .50 caliber machine guns was the most destructive firepower that I saw in World War II. It could only be matched, in intensity, by the collective firepower of a warship of the destroyer or larger class. Of course, attacking warships in open sea was the nearest thing to suicide in World War II, and not even those of us who ultimately perfected the technique and procedure of such specialized warfare even had an inkling that to seek out and sink the Japanese war and merchant fleets would be our lot.

"Nothing but mud under the wings and along the sides," Zuber was saying. That brought me back to reality.

The airplane was functioning properly; all of the engine instruments told me at a glance that *199* was now feeling her oats in a normal manner, and if we sustained damage, it would be structural rather than mechanical. We were streaking across rice paddies that became an instant blur under our wing. As far as I could see there was nothing more of interest on the river after we'd climbed to two hundred feet. I moved over to the left bank so that any land or river target would be more accessible. I definitely decided to drop the remaining two hundred-fifty-pound para-demolition bombs as floaters rather than free-falling missiles. The mud on the windshield was a constant reminder, should I think about changing my mind.

The river made a wide turn to the left, and I cut across the delta that was divided into endless rice paddies. The paddies were divided into small squares — each an acre or less — and there were coolies wearing big round hats. Some had only pants on, and the legs were rolled up above the knees. I pulled up to keep from decapitating those workers who did not see us coming. Those who happened to be looking in our direction, and who saw us coming, flattened out in the muddy water that appeared to be two or three feet deep, and dug deeper into China.

At that moment we spotted a figure on top of the dam between two rice paddies, a mile or so in direct line with the path we were flying. As we got closer we could make out a female figure in a full length sack-like dress that covered her body to the ankles. The striking feature about the figure, however, was the full, long black hair that hung loosely down her back, and which was at least five feet long. At the last moment she saw us, and she started running down the dam separating the paddies. I moved away from her and to the left, hoping she would not throw herself into the dirty water.

"How would you like to have a premeditated romp in the rice with that?" Cronin asked Kenney.

"Get your mind on the war. Besides, you could never catch her," Kenney laughed.

Dead ahead, across the remaining four or five miles of rice paddies, a small hill of about three hundred feet jutted out of the edge of the river that curved lazily across the countryside back to the southeast. To avoid any surprises I zoomed the airplane up to five hundred feet to see what was on the other side. What I saw caused me to immediately put our nose back down to three hundred feet, to avoid detection.

"Pilot to crew! Just over the hill dead ahead is a concentration of military barracks with a flagpole flying a big Jap flag. I'm strafing the barracks straight ahead and will drop two or three bombs. Warnick, you and Zuber be particularly aware of buildings or targets to the side and Hank, it's all yours on the breakaway."

"Roger! Roger!" came the replies.

As we approached the steep hill, I pulled the airplane up and even with the top, and, at the last instant, climbed an additional two hundred feet so that I could depress the nose with all twelve guns firing into the first barracks at the base of the hill on the other side, and rake all of them through to the end.

A more placid and serene military base you've never seen. It looked like a 20th Century Fox movie set, with whitewashed stones around the base of the flagpole, along each side of the walkways, driveways, and marking the outlined areas of the barracks. The grounds were landscaped and immaculately clean. The big Japanese flag waved in the easterly breeze from the top of a forty-foot, white, flagpole. This must have been a permanent installation that had been there at least since the Japs first arrived in China in the 1930s.

Now indicating 285 mph, I treated the Japanese picture of military serenity in the only manner such a beautiful oriental panorama should have been treated. I pointed the nose of the *Touch O' Texas* down at a thirty degree angle, hitting the gun button simultaneously, and releasing nine thousand rounds per minute of incendiary and tracer ammunition into the first barracks. Frantic and frightened soldiers erupted from the barracks immediately, running wildly in all directions; not knowing where to run because they didn't know from where, or from which direction the destruction was coming. Being careful to remain at least seventy feet above the barracks, I continued to fantail the airplane so as to equally distribute the incendiaries and tracers from my guns, and I dropped three para-demolition bombs in a row among what I could then see were seven barracks in perfect alignment. The incendiaries did their job well. The wooden barracks and buildings to the side, that Warnick and Zuber had worked over, burst into flame. Well past the barracks and out over the river again, we continued to feel and hear the bursts from Kolodziejski's and Zuber's guns. What Warnick and I had stirred up, they were bringing to a successful conclusion by adding the icing to the cake.

"Those barracks looked exactly like ours in the states!" exclaimed Warnick.

"They've copied everything else of ours," I replied, "why not our military barracks. I like the nice way they lined 'em up so we didn't miss a single one of 'em on the strafing and bombing run."

"I missed a truckload of Jap soldiers," exclaimed Zuber, "we were just going too fast and I couldn't get a bead on 'em till we were out of range."

"I'll slow down for you if you'd like," I answered over the intercom.

"No, sir," answered Zuber, "you can't fly fast enough for me! But if I'd been a little quicker, I'd have gotten 'em."

"If the dog hadn't stopped to shit he would've caught the rabbit, too!" added Warnick.

The closer we got to the China coast the wider the river became. What looked to be a major highway came in toward the river from a northeasterly direction, and there were three big block houses with large Jap flags flying from the top of each.

"Block houses dead ahead," I barked into the intercom, "complete with slits, peepholes, and big flags waving on top to attract our attention. Let's tatoo 'em! Warnick, strafe with me straight in; Hank you get 'em in the afterglow; and Zuber, keep your eyes open for anything on either side."

Big chunks of cement came flying off the tops of the sides as we opened up on the block houses with the armor-piercing and incendiary ammo. The walls would have had to be two to three feet thick to have withstood our onslaught. They had been hit badly, and they did not return our fire.

As we saw the coast, I climbed to one thousand feet looking for other members of the squadron. There was no time to be lost, this far from home and having used so much fuel. I turned to Kenney to request a heading for San Marcelino.

"*Bandits* at seven o'clock high and closing fast!" said Warnick.

"How many?" I started climbing toward the cloud cover, which I hoped was solid stratus at thirty-five-hundred feet. Lower, I might have taken our chances at minimum altitude on the water where they couldn't dive at us. But my split-second decision was the overcast! If we could make the overcast, slip into the stratus sealing out the *Zeros*, and conserve precious gallons of fuel that would be wasted at full throttle down on the waves — then we might escape with our skins! We moved to get away.

"There's six, seven, eight *Zeros*! About a thousand feet above us!" he shouted.

"Hello Kit Bag Leader! This is *199*! Over!" No answer.

"Hello Kit Bag Leader! This is *199*! Come in Kit Bag Leader! Over!" I repeated.

"Hello *199*! This is Kit Bag Leader! Go ahead!"

"Roger Kit Bag Leader! Have picked up eight *Bandits* coming off the coast! They're closing fast! We're heading for the clouds to play hide and seek. Pass the word. Over."

"Wilco, *199*! Give 'em a goose chase and hide well! Over and Out."

"Where are they now?" I asked on intercom, climbing at five hundred feet per minute with the props set at 2300 rpm, and the throttles at twenty-seven inches of mercury.

"They're about two miles back now, and should be in gunnery range in about a minute!" replied Kolodziejski. If they were flying at three hundred-fifty miles per hour and we were indicating one hundred-seventy-five in a climb, it didn't take an Einstein to figure we had better get lost or get ready to fight.

"How much ammo do y'all have? Everybody?" I asked.

"I'm covered for a couple of passes!" stated Warnick.

"Me too!" said Kolodziejski.

"Me too," added Zuber, "although I can shoot longer from the left gun than from the right!"

"I'll keep turnin' left so you can keep shootin' left." I was now about five hundred feet from the base of the overcast and if they held off for another minute I felt as if we would have it made.

"Here they come!" said Kolodziejski, as his and Warnick's guns fired simultaneously. I tried to look back over my shoulder and to the left in the direction the *Zeros* were coming in. At that moment I saw fifteen holes open up in a straight line across the left wing, about five feet outside the engine. I saw the big red meat ball on the *Zeke* as it split S's out and down to our left, showing us its belly after the Jap pilot made his gunnery run. On the deck they weren't able to dive or split S's through us and were forced to fly up and slug it out. They seldom did this unless we were crippled, or they vastly outnumbered us, which was now the case.

"I got some tracers into him!" yelled Kolodziejski.

"Shoot low sheriff he's ridin' a shetland!" exuded Warnick out of the top turret.

At that moment we entered the dismal, dark, gray mass of stratoform cloud and could see absolutely nothing. The gloom never looked so bright. We were safe! I continued to climb, totally and completely on instruments, and hoped that the *soup* was five thousand feet thick. The *Zeros* couldn't follow us into that! I continued to climb to five thousand-two hundred feet, leveled off and then nosed the airplane down slightly to five thousand feet. With a nose-down attitude, I throttled back and reduced the props to 1800 rpm. I pulled the mixture knobs back to cruising lean, watched the cylinder head temperature start to rise, pulled them a fraction below cruising lean and locked them in. We were rid of the Jap peril and had shifted our attention to another life and death game: Sweat the Gas!

"What's the damage?" I asked into the intercom.

"None in the tail!" stated Hank.

"Waist is clear," said Zuber, "but my feelings are hurt about missing that truckload of Japs!"

"Nothing but those fifteen or twenty ventilation holes out there in the left wing, as far as I can see," said Warnick.

"Do you think they could've nicked a wing tank?" I asked.

"Maybe if they'd been another ten- to twelve-inches closer to the engine," answered Warnick, "but I think they missed everything that far out!"

"What do you project on the gas consumption?" I asked Kenney.

"Give me a minute on that," he replied, "I've been pretty busy the last five minutes."

"You haven't been doing anything but taking up space and adding to the weight of the airplane," said Cronin.

"If that's not the pot callin' the kettle black," said Kenney, "and what've you been doin'?"

"I closed the bomb bay doors, turned the camera switch on and off, and checked Blount to make sure he didn't put the landing gear down after nearly blowing us up over that river steamer!"

"You've quit preaching and started meddling," I responded.

Kenney, tapped me on the shoulder; "Want a dinner K-Ration prepared 'specially for your dining pleasure by our super European chef, Jean Claude Warnick?"

"Yeah," I responded, "but give me one that Zuber hasn't been sitting on. How're we doing on gas?"

"Looks pretty good!" said Kenney, "we've got some left!"

"That's fine," I agreed "but how much have we got left?"

"Well — ," and he paused amid his calculations.

"That's what my grandmother fell into!" I added.

"Who?"

"My grandmother."

"Your grandmother! Did what?" he hollered to be heard over the engines.

"Fell!" I said.

"Fell where?"

"In the well! Isn't that what you said? Well?" He gave me a dirty look but Cronin smiled in appreciation.

"We've been off the coast of China for two hours and forty-five minutes and I estimate we have enough fuel for at least another two hours," said Kenney. "We're in good shape, if we can fly straight into San Marcelino!"

The stratus, if anything, had become thicker and darker since we entered it at about 3,500 feet just off the coast of China and just ahead of the *Zeros*. I thought, for the first time, of letting down through the billowy fog without full radio facilities. Not only were we minus any radio navigation assistance but we were under strict orders not even to speak to one another except in dire emergency.

I motioned for Kenney and Cronin to listen. "Do either of you recall Ike Baker saying anything about this stratus moving in, or how thick it is, at the briefing this morning?" Both shook their heads in the negative.

"This has to be something that's come up fast and unexpected," said Kenney.

"We better start our letdown through this stuff right now," I said. "We don't know how thick it is."

"Roger," exclaimed Cronin.

"We're going down," I spoke into the intercom so that everyone could be apprised of what we were doing, "it's more expedient to make an instrument letdown out here over open water than any closer to Luzon."

I set *199* into a slightly nose down attitude, although we couldn't feel it. The only indication that we were losing altitude was reflected in the altimeters that were steadily unwinding. The little airplane on the autogyro was slightly under the artificial horizon and the rate of descent read five hundred feet per minute. The further down we went the more concerned I became, for a pressure altimeter is not accurate unless it has been recently set to the barometric pressure of the area in which you are flying. If a front, or other weather disturbance, (common to that area of the world) had blown in since we'd left that morning, it would have brought common changes in barometric pressure. Our altimeters could have been off four hundred, seven hundred, or a thousand feet.

"I'd give a month's pay for an altimeter setting right now," I said out loud.

"I'll add another month's pay to that," responded Cronin.

"If that'll do it I'll make it two months pay," added Kenney.

The stratus that had given us such reason for joy and celebration, that had rescued us from the enemy, became the source of nervous concern. What had been a blessing was now a curse! One door opened, another one closed! We were confronted with a new crisis: Sweat the Weather! This problem must be solved without the assistance of ILS or other radio aids! The same radio beam that would bring us back to San Marcelino and place us safely on the end of the runway for landing would also furnish a direct flight path for the enemy to home in on, to blow us to Kingdom Come. On instruments in combat we were flying literally, by the seat of our pants.

I maintained the descent with everyone staring through the plexiglass windshield, willing dark gloom to turn into brightness — but it didn't happen. There was total silence — no humorous repartee from anyone at all; the exuberance and enthusiasm generated from losing the *Zeros* drained from us. We were comforted only in the thought that the sea, no matter how rough and windy, was a flat surface. Surely this stratus didn't extend right down to the water's surface. I determined, by positive thought, that I would see greenish whitecaps in time to level off.

The altimeters read five hundred feet and I made up my mind that we'd only let down another one hundred feet — maybe one hundred-fifty — and no more. If this failed to produce more light and clearer weather underneath us, I'd just have to make another decision at that time.

"You look just like an old chicken sittin' perfectly still and squattin' in the grass to catch the worm," Kenney teased Cronin.

"That's all right," replied Cronin, "just as long as I *catch* the worm I'll be all right!"

I decided to descend another one hundred feet and with three hundred feet indicated on the altimeter I squirmed in my seat. We were still in heavy gloom and there was no silver lining in sight — anywhere.

"Pilot to radio! Over!"

"Roger, Lieutenant!" responded Zuber.

"We've got a problem and you can help! How long is that trailing antenna you've got back there?"

"Ninety — a hundred feet! Why?"

"I want you to let it out! All the way! Right now!"

"Roger! It'll only take a minute!" The trailing antenna had a fifteen-pound weight on the end that kept the wire cable from flying up into the tail.

"Now what?" asked Zuber.

"Can you put your hand, or rest your hand, on the wire cable after it leaves the airplane?" I asked.

"Roger!"

"We've got to get through this stuff and we're going to letdown until we can see something! I want you to feel or hold on to your end of the antenna cable as we descend. If you feel a jerk, the weight will have hit the water and let me know quick! Got it?"

"Roger! But remember the fish doesn't hang straight down for a hundred feet, Lieutenant! Maybe sixty-five or seventy feet because the wind blows it back!"

"I know," I replied, "but sixty-five or seventy feet is that much between us and the water below us. Wherever it is. You might help him back there, Hank, if you can."

I could not see Zuber because of the top turret directly behind me as well as the bomb bay that hid him from view. At this moment I was thankful for the intercom radio.

I took a deep breath, (I don't know why) advanced the props to 2100 rpm and started the airplane imperceptibly toward whatever was beneath us. When the altimeter read one hundred feet I determined not to look at it again. Almost simultaneously with my glance at the altimeter, Zuber yelled into the intercom! "It's gone!" He had lost the fish from his antenna just as he had lost a similar antenna weight on a low level mission we had flown out of Columbia, South Carolina down into Georgia in our oversea's training. The first time by accident. This time on purpose and we were all deliriously happy.

"You lowered your trailing antennae into my well of despair, Zuber," I said into the intercom, "and raised me into relieved happiness."

"You made me feel pretty good, too!" added Cronin.

We were twenty feet off the tops of the whitecaps that were ten to fifteen feet high in the perennially rough China sea. The waves were literally licking at our underside and, under other circumstances, would have been reason for concern. At that moment, however, they were beautiful and I was suddenly overcome with the feeling that I had never really observed how truly beautiful they were. We were picking up some intermittent rain showers and squalls at the sea base of this five thousand- to seven thousand-foot cloud thickness which presented no problem. We could see where we were going and we were on the deck where we were used to traveling anyway. We continued happily at such altitude for another thirty minutes, when the ceiling miraculously ascended to seven hundred feet over the coast of Luzon. We made a straight in approach and the good earth had never felt better under our feet, when we crawled from the airplane.

"If the ground *ack-ack* doesn't get you the *Zeros* will," remarked Kenney, gathering all his navigational charts and paraphernalia.

"And if both the flak and the *Zeros* don't get you the weather still makes for a rather formidable opponent in itself," added Cronin.

"Not to mention no gas, and flying this baby on the fumes for the last hour- and a-half!" added Kenney. I just kept writing up the Form I and listening to the merry music of the gyros (that had saved our lives) winding down.

"Where did you get that mud on the underside and around the engine nacels of the airplane?" asked Sergeant Albright, the crew chief.

"That's Canton River mud," answered Kenney, "we got a little too close to an explosion up there this morning!"

"That's a great farming country up there around Canton. They raise a lot of rice," I added, "and I couldn't resist trying my hand! I got my plow stuck and when I gave 'er the full throttle, turnin' all those horses loose to help me pull it out, it just slung dirt and mud everywhere!"

"That sounds like the west Texas wind blowing to me!" said Cronin.

"You keep talking that way and I'll crank up *199* and fly you right back to Canton," I replied, "*Zeros,* bomb concussions, river mud and all, blindfolded and drunk!"

For the next few days a moratorium was declared against the war by the 501st *Black Panthers* Squadron of the 345th Bomb Group *Air Apaches*. It is true that all of us had experienced enough war to do us a lifetime, but that wasn't the reason for our delay.

Thatcher told Musket he was tired of flying "because of illness, fatigue, and the threat of oriental lead poisoning." Musket asked Thatcher to explain his feelings in greater detail. "I'm sick and tired of flying and being shot at by those little yellow oriental sonzabitches!" stated the indomitable Thatcher, "and I want to go home. Is that detail enough?"

Our delay in fightin the war was brought about by a shortage of airplanes, so we took a welcome vacation to lick our wounds, and drove down to the beach for a swim, while the service squadron worked night and day in an all out effort to repair enough aircraft to put us back in the war.

Two weeks later, during a mid-afternoon siesta, a weapons carrier drove up in front of the Operation's tent and four very tired and weary figures crawled out. Nobody paid much attention until someone yelled, "It's Blair and his crew! They made it! They're back!" Everyone within hearing came running. It was if they had returned from the dead.

"I knew you were too onery to die!" I pounded Blair on the back, "or did the devil reject you?"

"I don't know which, but in either case I'm sure glad to get back!" replied a smiling Blair, obviously happy and ecstatic just to be alive.

"I just count four of you!"

"We lost Richardson, the tail gunner," said Blair, "we found the submarine, ditched the airplane, and everybody got out. We were all in the water together, but Richardson, our tail gunner, disappeared before the sailors could get to us. Boland, my radio gunner, said Richardson couldn't swim and he had his jacket zipped up over his Mae West! You can't believe how high those waves are and how rough that sea is!"

"This calls for a prayer meeting tonight!" said Thatcher.

"And let it get as drunk as you can get it!" agreed Blair.

"Tonight is New Year's eve for the first time this week," announced Thatcher, "and we want a prayer meeting to remember!"

"Give me your attention, please," came Thatcher's voice a few minutes later over the Squadron's scratchy loudspeaker, "everybody, give me your attention! Do I have your undivided attention?"

"You've got everybody's attention from here to Bataan, to Corregidor and in between," boomed Musket's voice in the background, but through the PA system. "Get on with your announcement!"

"Thank you, Sir!" responded Thatcher. There will be a wake in the Mess Hall tonight to celebrate the passing of your good friend and mine, Lieutenant George Blair! The mess hall is the most appropriate place since so many have already died there! The wake will be followed by a prayer meeting in Lieutenant Blair's tent at 1930 hours. Admission is by invitation and/or the return of any clothing, toiletries, or other property any of you might've prematurely latched on to before Lieutenant Blair returned from the dead. Over and out!"

An hour- and a-half later, as Blair entered the Officer's Mess, the assemblage already gathered burst forth spontaneously: *For he's a jolly good fellow,*

For he's a jolly good fellow!
For he's a jolly good fellow-w-w-w-w-w!
That nobody can deny!

This was followed by shouts of: "Speech! Speech!" Blair was assisted to a chair where he stood on the seat so that he could see each and every face beaming with joy and appreciation, for this one who had cheated the Grim Reaper. One of us had accomplished the impossible and lived to tell it; a fellow warrior had been successful in ditching his airplane in the monstrous waves of the China sea, had defeated death, and was back among his friends.

"I don't want to interrupt your dinner!" he started, his opening statement being met with mixed boos and laughter.

"What dinner?" asked McGowan.

"I couldn't even pick it up with my fork!" said Wilky.

"You didn't have to!" added Thatcher, "it'll come to you when you call it!"

"Shut up and let him speak!" said Johenning.

"All of this has been a big mistake!" said Blair, "I was much too young to die!" There followed cheers and loud support with someone saying: "Ain't we all!"

"Any man who thinks he won't be scared when it comes time to ditch a B-25 in the open China sea doesn't know cowshit from wild honey! I never thought I'd ever be so glad that I'm even glad to see this mess tent and whatever there is to eat!"

"He's not rowin' with both oars, Doc!" observed Erskine, speaking to Marcus.

"Talking like that he doesn't even have 'em in the water!" replied Doc Marcus.

"But it's great to be back and I can't say enough for the *Kleptomaniac*," continued Blair, referring to the code name for the submarine that had been his benefactor. "We owe 'em our lives! I'm looking forward to the prayer meeting tonight and, I hate to have to ask it, but I hope all of you who got my clothes, sheets, air mattress, toilet articles, and everything else will bring 'em back!"

The prayer meeting that followed that evening provided the most sober and contradictory setting for an otherwise ordinary imbibing and drinking session that I had ever seen. The guest of honor occupied a prominent seat in front of the entrance, while friends entered Blair's tent with the widest assortment of hangdog, sheepish, humiliated expressions I'd ever observed on human countenances. Particularly on these otherwise and ordinarily irreverent, wild, "flying hell to leather," uninhibited extroverts! With much embarrassment they entered the tent with their contraband tucked under their arms and folded, if possible, in a beleaguered attempt to hide the article they were returning. Almost without exception, each beneficiary would have the trace of a grin of embarrassment on his face, and would sidle up to Blair's bunk and quickly deposit a pair of pants, a shirt, underwear, socks, a jacket, soap, shaving lotion, cap, boots, shoes, sheets, towels, pillow cases, wash rags, and even an extra pair of first lieutenant's bars, as unobtrusively as possible!

"I knew you were gonna make it," said Cavins, in a shy, apologetic manner that belied his true feelings, "and I took real good care of the things I got!"

"He sounds like the guy who buried his talent in the parable of the talents," said Kuta to the Chaplain.

"There is a similarity, my son!" replied Father Kozlowski.

"I was just trying to help Lieutenant Baker get rid of your stuff," explained Jeans, "and I'm sure glad you made it so I can give it back to you!"

The greatest entrance, and most appropriate statement, was made by Thatcher who carried a fifth of Canadian Club. "Dang you, Blair," he started, "this fifth of Canadian Club is the only thing that I almost got off of you, and it's so damn good don't ask me right now which one of you I'd rather see if I had to make a choice! But here it is and I was thinking I might still get a drink or two out of it!" Nervous laughter and applause followed this confession, which broke the ice and made it much easier for those profiting from Blair's "demise" to return his property.

"Pop the cap on that Canadian Club, Thatcher," said Blair, "I'll never have a better reason or more favorable occasion to kill that bottle! But what happened to the *other* bottle? The fifth of Jack Daniels?"

"It got broken in the handling," said Lieutenant Baker, "without a drink ever having been taken from that seven year old bottle!"

"The good always die young!" added Thatcher.

"A toast!" yelled Thatcher. "Here's to a good ditching and less bitching!"

"Johnson," said Pallotta, "you gonna inflate your barracks bag and do your Kate Smith imitation again?"

"A toast!" said Thatcher, "here's to blood that runs into our boots and turns our socks red!"

"What kind of toast is that?" exclaimed Hardeman.

"Okay, you don't like that one," said Thatcher, "here's to World War None!"

"I'll drink to that!" answered Hardeman.

The prayer meeting was now well underway and everybody was at least three sheets in the wind, and collected in little clusters of two and three individuals as it assumed its regular format, its reason for being lost in the reverie of alcohol. The largest group still huddled around the honoree, and he fielded questions in a state of uninhibited relaxation, frankness and total veracity.

"It's rather cliche at this point but we're really glad to see you back," I told Blair, "and having to leave you alone and turn for home the other day up there on the China coast was one of the toughest things I've ever had to do!"

"I understand," responded Blair, "and I knew you were really cutting your fuel close to make it back after staying with us as long as you did!"

"You fooled 'em," exclaimed Phillips, barging up and patting Blair on the back, "you're supposed to be dead but you fooled 'em!"

"The reports of my death have been greatly exaggerated," replied Blair, "I think Mark Twain said that! Really he stole it from me!"

"What did it really feel like," asked Steele, "flying on one engine, all by your lonesome up there on the coast of China, knowing that you couldn't make it back across the China sea and that your only hope was finding that sub that neither Blount nor Musket had been able to locate before they had to turn for home?"

"Do you really wanta know?" responded Blair in a quiet, serious manner.

"Yeah!" responded Steele, the question getting the attention of everyone in the group as everyone stopped talking to listen.

"It was like the country dog in the city," replied farm boy Blair. "If I stood still I got fucked and if I ran I got bit in the ass! So I decided to keep running and here I am!

"But I'll tell you one thing," continued Blair, "I don't ever want to make another tour of duty on a submarine! We were attacked twice by Jap destroyers dropping depth charges trying to sink us. Those ash cans exploding just outside that sub, make the lights flicker and knock you to your knees; makes you look at your hole card! I'll take my chances in the air, on top of the water, and on single engine in preference to what those swabbies have to take down in Davey Jones locker!"

Lieutenant Arthur J. McGrane, from Max Meadows, Virginia, would be the only other pilot in the 501st Squadron shot down along the coast of Indochina who would ditch, be picked up by one of our subs, and survive. McGrane, who got a broken arm in the ditching, his navigator, Joe Groves, from Clarksburg, West Virginia, and two gunners, spent four days in a life raft before one of our submarines, purely by accident, happened upon them. The sub first thought it an enemy trap and fired a couple of rounds near their rubber raft before deciding they were genuine American Air Corps personnel. Lieutenant Al Palace, from Chicago, Illinois, was McGrane's copilot and, like Blair's tail gunner, cleared the airplane after the ditching and was in the water with the rest of the crew. He was lost in the rough sea before they could get into life rafts.

"We didn't know whether you were late, Blair, or the late Blair!" said Major Jones. "You had a close one! We're all glad that you made it!"

"Comin' close only counts in horseshoes, hand grenades, and an occasional five hundred-pound bomb," replied Blair, "but I was wearing my lucky bunion pads!"

"It's not how you drive but how you arrive!" said Major Jones.

"All I want the Air Corps to do is validate my parking ticket so I can go home," answered Blair.

"I think that can be arranged," replied Jones, "when a pilot is called upon to perform double duty, particularly serve a tour on a submarine, almost without exception he's on the first plane home!"

While we hated to see him go, we rejoiced with Blair in his good fortune. Within three days he had cleared the base, checked out, and we said goodbye. We all agreed that the only thing better than seeing Blair go home would have been for each of us to have been going home with him. The Lord willing, that day would come.

CHAPTER TEN

A Leap In The Dark

Now faith is the assurance of things hoped for, the conviction of things not seen.

Hebrews 11:1

War! I don't know how to talk about it or explain it. The politicians glorify it; the veterans defend it; the religious condemn it; the old men discuss it; the kids play it; mothers cry about it; wives live in fear of it; generals worship it; while those fighting it just want to go home!

"The word has it that we're moving to Clark Field," said Thatcher. "They've cleared the Japs and retaken the field." This was good news, for the rainy season, which we had moved out of when we left Tacloban, Leyte, and moved to San Marcelino, was starting in Luzon.

"I don't care about Clark Field! I just want to go home!" responded Lyman.

"Me, too!" said Kuta, "I've got a great lookin' girl to go home to, not to mention my wife!"

"I'd just as soon stay right here as move to Clark Field," said Kenney. "We've got our tent fixed up and it's a nice place!"

"And if you ain't where you are you're no place," said Lyman.

"I'm tired of always being wet and everything mildewed," said Mathews, "and now I'm gettin' the jungle rot and athletes foot!"

"I knew it! Pain is no stranger!" said Thatcher, "you've had athletes' foot all your life!"

"The advanced detail to Clark Field found the graves of one of our crews shot down on one of our strikes from Tacloban," said Esty, immediately getting the serious attention of everyone in the pyramidal.

"One of the native Filipinos said they beheaded the crew before they buried them! They wrote an inscription in English on the cross at the head of the graves that said: 'Even though they be devils, the Japanese Imperial Army erects this cross.' "

"Probably written by a little yellow sonofabitch who graduated from Southern Cal!" said Moore.

"They also got the story on what happened to one of our other crews! Lieutenant Buffington's airplane was shot down and crash-landed near Clark Field in January and all of the crew were murdered by Jap soldiers. The radio-gunner, Sergeant Walter J. Nelson, was the only one who escaped and he was rescued by friendly Filipinos!"

"What makes the Japanese do these terrible things?" asked Lathrop. "They're human and made in the image of God!"

"Seems like I remember some scripture: 'an eye for an eye, and a tooth for a tooth,' " responded Thatcher. "After what the Japs did to our buddies at Clark Field, ain't nobody gonna tell me to turn the other cheek to these — Japs!"

It had been raining for a week and every strike that had gotten off the ground during that time had returned to base because of the weather. As the names went up on the bulletin board, announcing the next day's mission, there was a low volume buzz of voices and a soft, alarmed whistle. When I was finally able to work my way through the stationary bodies surrounding the board to read the names and the mission, I understood the surprise. The mission was rolling-stock to Formosa, which was to be expected, but a takeoff time of 0200 in the morning was the concern of all who read the strike announcement. Of even more immediate concern, I was one of the six pilots listed to fly the mission.

"As you are aware, gentlemen," said Captain Musket, in the strike briefing session in the Operation's tent following evening chow, "there have been two stationary fronts between Luzon and Formosa for the past week!"

"Yeah, and those two fronts are what've turned back every mission flown out of here for the past week too!" whispered Cronin.

"And while the weather has given us some trouble for the past week, we have reason to believe it has dissipated enough that you'll have no trouble tomorrow morning!"

"Why doesn't he fly out an hour or so early and check it out for us?" whispered Cronin again, "if it's bad, he could radio the OD to let us sleep!"

"He figgers what we can't see won't hurt us!" whispered Kenney.

"You guys shut up!" came a voice a couple of rows back.

"The enemy knows that it takes us three hours to fly from here to Formosa. If we take off in daylight at 0700 hours we can't make it to Formosa before 1000! To land in daylight, after a strike to Formosa, we must leave the target no later than 1530 hours! As a result, all trains, truck convoys, and any other activity stops between the hours of 1000 and 1530 on Formosa. By taking off at 0200, we can make it around the southern end of Formosa, up the west coast and hit the enemy in a rolling-stock sweep from the northern end of the island to the southern end, beginning at 0700 hours when the enemy should be out in full force, very active and very vulnerable! Are there any questions?" There were none! Only an Operation's tent full of worried, puzzled expressions on the faces of the lucky six crews flying the strike.

"Whew!" sighed Kenney, bending forward and speaking softly in my ear, "we're being treated like mushrooms!"

"Mushrooms?" I inquired.

"Yeah! Keepin' us in the dark and feedin' us horseshit!"

"The navigators will pick up the names and coordinates of the friendly subs, where they'll be located off the west coast of Formosa during the strike, as well as the *Jukebox* and the *Playmate*! Radio men will pick up the frequencies of the emergency craft! I would suggest everyone hit the sack! The OD will get you up at 0100 hours and that will come pretty quick!

"One other reminder to the pilots," said Musket, "the enemy has started stringing wire and cable between the trees and on poles from seventy-five to one hundred feet in height around optimum targets to try to catch us! Keep your eyes peeled for these aerial booby traps!"

"If they're seventy-five feet high we'll fly under 'em," said Kuta, "won't we Blount?"

"What ever you say, Kuta," I answered, "we'll do what's gotta be done!" What had to be done was to miss the wire and cable! Should I be able to see any at twenty feet altitude, I reserved the right to make my decision at the time of sighting.

"If Morton can bring a chicken back in his engine and Mathews a fifteen-foot piece of one of those little two-foot high oriental fences they have around the houses up there on Formosa wrapped around his vertical stabilizer," I added, "surely we can maneuver under a cable strung twenty feet in the air!"

"I'm one of the more experienced pilots! One of the old-timers now, wouldn't you say?" I asked Musket, following him off to the side.

"Right!"

"Tell me, who thought up this mission anyway?" I asked in a low voice, insuring our privacy. *If any of the other pilots hear my inquiry,* I thought, *and stop to think what we are being asked to fly into, there may be a mutiny.*

"Whatta you mean? It came down from Group and probably from Fifth Bomber before that! Why?" he asked.

"If it came from you I just wanted to be sure you were still on our side!"

"Only the weather can prevent us from really striking a damaging blow to the enemy's transportation and supply lines on Formosa today."

"Yeah! And only the weather can do to us what the enemy's guns and his *Zeros* can't do! Destroy, annihilate, and eliminate all of us by flying us into those cumulo nimbus stationary tornadoes that'll do a better job on an airplane than the combined firepower of two cruisers and three destroyers. And, to top it off, you're asking us to fly into this stuff, at night, that has turned back at least four strikes in the past week! In the daytime we'd at least have the pleasure of seeing what got us.

You're forcing us to wear a blindfold while some of us would prefer to keep our eyes open during our execution!"

"Have a little more faith in Fifth Bomber's intelligence reports!" answered Musket.

"I would prefer to have a little more faith in Fifth Bomber's weather report, as well as a psychiatric examination of the pin-headed general who thought this one up. Better still, call up Fifth Bomber and tell them I want the architect of this strike to fly as my observer! An early morning mission is a good idea but why today? What's so important on Formosa that this couldn't wait for a couple of days till the weather clears?"

"I was born at night but I wasn't born last night," mumbled Thatcher leaving the tent, "this whole damn mission smells like suicide! They're gonna kill us!"

"I don't want to send you out on this wild goose chase any more than you want to go," replied Musket, "but I only do what I'm told!"

"I want a letter from you saying we were ordered to make this strike!" I requested.

"Why?"

"In the event none of us make it back!"

"Are you serious?"

"No," I replied, "if we don't make it back what difference would it make!"

"Good luck!" he said, as he started to turn away with a trace of concern on his face.

"Don't wait up for me," I added, "I might be a little late coming in!

"But you can do one thing for me."

"What's that?" he asked.

"Leave the porch light on and tie up the dog!" He smiled.

I had no sooner completed the ritual of tucking in my mosquito netting and stretching out in a sound sleep when the OD was nudging me in the ribs with his flashlight.

"Piss call! First piss call of the morning from your friendly Officer of the Day, Lieutenant Vernon Townsley! It is a beautiful morning, the temperature is a delightful seventy-nine degrees, with a wind out of the southeast at ten miles per hour, two solid fronts of thunderheads between here and Formosa and, to the lucky airplanes who make it to the target, there is anticipated a rather warm oriental reception otherwise celebrated in native song as 'There'll be a hot time, in the old town, tonight!' "

"Townsley," I mumbled, still half asleep, "you remind me of that old Chinese philosopher: On Too Long! And his younger brother, Tai Wan On!"

"Can't you clowns draw the curtain on this pre-dawn vaudeville show!" said Lathrop.

Twenty minutes later I was walking to breakfast. "Would you care to accompany me to the mess tent?" I asked Burg, coming out of Operations. "I'll show you where it gets its name!"

"What's for breakfast?" I asked, picking up a metal tray.

"Chateaubriand on a shingle," answered the sergeant at the head of the line.

"Would you care for some canned peaches?" he asked.

"Yeah! But cut the rust!"

"How about some marble cake left over from last night?"

"No, thank you," I replied, "I forgot my hammer and chisel!"

It was 0130 hours as we boarded the weapon's carrier to be ferried to the flight line. "You look sleepy and tired, Kenney!" commiserated Cronin.

"I was born tired and had a relapse," answered Kenney.

Arriving at the airplane the dutiful and responsible Sergeant Albright, crew chief extraordinaire, was waiting for us. "She pre-flighted perfectly, Lieutenant," reported Albright. Warnick was up on the wing topping off the gas tanks, cramming the last possible drop of the life-sustaining fluid into the wing tanks.

"Is this a nonstop flight?" asked Cronin facetiously.

"On occasions such as this that's the only kind I fly," I answered, "and it stops only when I bring this baby right back here later today."

"We've got some mighty funny people running this war," I said later, as I turned on the blue phosphorescent lights and started to run the checklist.

"Yeah! Sometimes I'm sorry I bought tickets for it," said Kenney.

It was a tumultuous, dark, and sinister night and I could smell rain behind the fog and mist already in the air. *Back in west Texas,* I thought, *we'd be jumping up and down, and the farmers and ranchers would be overjoyed with the prospects of thunderstorms and the attendant showers. I am underjoyed, to say the least, with the order to blindly fly this airplane into two solid weather fronts that couldn't be penetrated by the same aircraft in daylight for the past week.*

A thunderhead is the nemesis of all aircraft, containing up-and-down drafts, side by side, of tornadic proportions, that literally disintegrates an airplane. In daylight I'd at least have been able to see, and possibly circumnavigate, menacing and explosive pockets of weather. But under such weather conditions, and at night, I felt I wouldn't have a cut-dog's chance. Oh, what I wouldn't give for just a plain, every day, bright, sunshiny mission against the Jap Imperial Navy, where the only worry would be the broadside guns of a cruiser or a destroyer. Joys were only relative.

Any other flying field in the world would have been officially closed to operations. Fog and mist, so thick that you couldn't see the distance of one hundred yards, held the strip and revetments in its grasp.

"Do you think we can see the tail lights of the jeep to get us to takeoff position at the end of the runway?" asked Kenney.

"If he doesn't drive too fast!" I growled.

Instrument takeoffs with fully lighted runways on modern, asphalt strips in the United States were hazardous enough, but such takeoffs from a chuckholed jungle path, with a couple of ground crewmen holding flashlights somewhere out of sight down the runway, was absurd. The last instrument takeoff I had made was back in Columbia, South Carolina, and that under perfect conditions, and for practice only, while sitting in a blacked-out cockpit. But this was for real and there was no flight instructor or copilot, sitting in the right seat, having perfect visibility, to pull me out of any mistake.

Cronin could see no more than I could see. The fog and mist and eerie darkness of the night was unreal. The engines were running smoothly with their unique, flat *splat splat* idling sound. The jeep turned away, its tail lights fading out of sight, swallowed up immediately in the fog and mist after leading us to the end of the runway. There was no rush on the part of the aircraft to assemble for takeoff, it seemed, either from pilot reluctance or the fact we were taking off at three minute intervals. The first airplane started its roll down the runway, picked up speed, and the fire of the twin exhausts vanished immediately in the darkness. I lost no time in centering my airplane in the middle of the jungle path, pointing it in the direction we were taking off, when the magnetic compass finally stopped its gyrations and became stationary. After setting the altimeters, I carefully set the gyrocompass to match precisely the reading reflected in the magnetic compass, and prepared to hold that exact heading until the airplane became airborne.

"Pilot to radio," I spoke into the intercom.

"Radio to pilot! Over!" came the response.

"Zuber, look and see if your Saint Christopher has his eyes open?"

"Yes, sir," came the reply from that devoted Catholic, "they're wide open! He's not scared! I always thought Saint Christopher had magnetic feet!"

"How's that?" I asked.

"We always stood him up on the dashboard of the car and he'd stand there."

"Keep him awake and standing up on this takeoff."

"Roger!"

We were ready. Cronin's face reflected the phosphorescent glow of the cockpit light on the instruments. Kenney was standing behind me, his left hand on the back of my seat and one foot in the edge of the cockpit with the other back in the well. With the signal I pushed the throttles forward with a steady, easy touch as far as they'd go. The airplane shook, rattled, and rolled down the runway, into the fog, mist, and darkness, picking up speed as it accelerated. The gyrocompass began to move one degree left and I corrected it quickly with the brakes. The gyrocompass heading remained constant as the controls came to life, losing their mushiness as the speed increased. I saw a light flash by, indicating only one-third of the runway remained, and flying speed must be attained *muy pronto* to avert disaster. I gave the wheels up signal, removing the excessive drag that bound us to the earth, and twenty tons of aluminum, steel, and explosives left mother earth. I kept the little airplane, glowing in the phosphorescent light, slightly above the artificial horizon, and held a steady rate of climb, still concentrating on the gyrocompass heading which I had to maintain to fly us safely between the mountains that were on each side of us in the darkness. As we hit 5,000 feet altitude, I throttled back to cruising speed and, under my breath, whispered a prayer of thanks.

"How long until we get to Formosa?" I asked Kenney over my shoulder, never taking my eyes from the instrument panel.

"Do you want the time or the odds?" he answered.

"Don't get funny with me! Would you ridicule and berate the man who holds your life in the palm of his hand and the seat of his pants?" I asked.

"Only if it would get a laugh and put him in his place," said Kenney.

"You know what Confucius says?" observed Cronin, listening to the conversation.

"I'm not gonna bite," answered Kenney.

"I'll bite," I said, "what does he say?"

"Confucius says 'Show me a man who can laugh and I'll show you a man who is either 4F or too old for the draft!' "

Suddenly and without warning we hit turbulence that threw the airplane upon its side and straight down nine hundred feet before I could right the plane and return it to straight and level flight.

"Did you see what this airplane just did?" rhetorically wondered Cronin aloud and to no one in particular.

"Wait'll you see what Warnick just did!" exclaimed Kenney, "and he's got to clean up his own mess."

"Pilot to crew!" I said into the intercom, "keep your safety belts fastened if you value your hide. There's no telling what else we're going to hit before the night is out. Everybody might say a prayer in their spare time. Over and out."

In another moment we hit an updraft and regained five hundred of the lost nine hundred feet of altitude! And just as quickly as we lost the nine hundred. I figured we'd passed through the first front, although the turbulence continued as we were alternately up and down and up and down, three hundred to four hundred feet, like a giant yoyo.

"What's our ETA (estimated time of arrival) to Formosa?" I asked Kenney again.

"I was working on that when you asked me the first time," he answered. Of course, an ETA was all that we could fly, and without radio or other navigational aids, the weather conditions only compounded our problems.

"I'm saying 0515 hours, give or take a couple of minutes," he answered.

"Kenney, what's the couple of minutes? The time we're spending going up and down instead of straight ahead?" I asked.

"That's about it."

I became absorbed in the instruments as we hit a relatively smooth stretch of air. I asked Cronin to turn down his cockpit light. With some of the glare removed from the right side of the cockpit my eyes returned to the instruments, as my left hand held the wheel very loosely, while my right hand wound in a half-turn of vertical stabilizer trim. I had been forced to change the throttle settings several times, costing us excessive use of gas which would "kick us in the fuel-consumption ass later," as Warnick said. At that point in time, I looked forward to having the "later" factor to worry about.

The information being passed to us by the luminous dials of the instruments was reassuring, and I gazed back with an unblinking stare. I'd been conditioned to never question their honesty and that was the way it should have been. The only way it could be. I was attentive, and ordinarily would have been lulled by the perfect readings reflected by the instruments, but the turbulence and the black void that surrounded us had me sitting on the edge of my seat.

"Are you steering us well off the west end of Formosa?" I asked Kenney. "We don't want to risk flying into those 13,000 feet mountains!"

"We're flying a good three to four degrees west of the heading that should take us west of the southern tip of the island," he responded. "Sure wish we had a radio range to check my navigation."

With a radio range we would not need a navigator. A radio range was simply a broadcasting station which was on the air twenty-four hours a day broadcasting a *dit dah* and a *dah dit* which told the pilot using it where he was. The signals formed the four spokes of a wheel, usually equidistant from each other at ninety-degree intervals around the circle, which intersected at the hub of the wheel. The hub, or center of the circle, was *the cone of silence*, and you could tell when you were directly over it when everything went silent. The closer you got to the hub, the stronger the signal became. *My kingdom for a radio range station,* I thought wistfully to myself, *anywhere on Formosa!*

We were indicating 185 mph when a sudden increase in turbulence alerted my suspicion. I pulled back on the throttles, and reduced our airspeed to 175 mph indicated, and Cronin, in obvious disapproval, did everything but advance the throttles to their previous settings. I called for carburetor heat, which Cronin delivered, as we suddenly hit a head wind that stopped us in midair as the bottom fell out. We were weightless, as if suspended in space, and the instrument panel had gone crazy! When the instruments became readable, I couldn't believe what I saw. The altimeter showed us descending at the rate of one thousand feet per minute. I shoved the prop pitch full forward with increased power right behind it. We had flown into the ocean, it would seem, as an avalanche of water inundated the airplane, followed by the staccato noise of rocks hitting the fuselage.

"What's that?" said Cronin.

"That's hail!" I answered.

"Sounds like we're in a barrel with somebody throwing bricks at us!"

The altimeters slowly stopped unwinding, as I was able to pull the nose of the little airplane above the artificial horizon in the instrument on the panel, and we started a slow ascent from three thousand feet. I was thankful we hadn't lost the artificial horizon instrument completely. I breathed a sigh of relief as I readied myself for the next onslaught of Mother Nature. Fortunately, it didn't come, as seemingly, we'd found another pocket of semi-calm air.

"Radio to Pilot. Over!" came Zuber's voice over the intercom.

"Pilot to Radio. Go ahead."

"There's a red light that appears to be about one hundred yards to the right and behind us, Lieutenant, and flying at exactly our same altitude. Whatta you think I should do? Over."

"It might just be the reflection of our own engine exhaust on that side of the airplane, Zuber," I responded, "or it could be one of the other airplanes in the squadron. It could also be a Japanese night fighter, so keep your guns on it and stay alert."

"Roger!"

We flew for another five minutes in relatively still air and Zuber came back on the intercom.

"This red light seems to have moved in closer to us, Lieutenant, whatta you think? Over!"

"If you don't think it's a reflection in the clouds we're flying through give it a couple of bursts from your fifties! Over."

"Roger! Wilco!" he replied. In a moment the airplane vibrated as Zuber squeezed off a couple of bursts from his guns.

"Did you get him, Zuber? Over!" I inquired.

"I don't know, but at least he's not shooting back and the red light seems to come and go now. Over!"

"Just keep your eye on it, and should it move quickly toward us let me know. Warnick will be tracking it from the top turret should you need any help. Over and out!" The red light finally dissipated or disappeared, and we chalked it up to an apparition, on a Halloween-kind of night.

At the precise moment when I allowed myself the luxury of thinking *we've got it made*, we collided in midair with a giant net, swung by the hand of an unseen force of preposterous size, and the altimeters registered our ascent at 1,500 feet per minute, notwithstanding the little airplane in the instrument was below the artificial horizon. I advanced prop pitch and power as I, putting the airplane in a nose-down attitude, attempted to dive the plane at full power. The altimeters laughed at me, I felt, as we continued to gain altitude. The Wright engine corporation never designed those engines to overcome that type of aerial emergency, or that kind of celestial phenomena. At 8,500 feet our ascent slowed, and I breathed easier.

"Think we oughta turn back?" asked Kenney.

"And fly through those thunderheads again?" I replied. "It's probably safer on this side of Luzon right now, than the side from which we came. Besides, give 'em a few hours, and they might dissipate, and we'll be looking at 'em in daylight coming back!"

"I guess so," said Kenney. "I was just asking! I agree with you."

"How much longer to Formosa?" I asked.

"Another hour, if I'm right!"

"I'd bet my combat pay you're right!" I told him. "That last elevator — let's just hope it was the Formosa side of the last weather front we just went through!"

Fifty-eight- and-a-half minutes later, just before dawn and in clean, pure air under a cloudless sky, we arrived over the southern tip of Formosa. The 13,000-foot, foreboding looking mountain range rested in the early morning darkness fifteen miles off to the northeast. After flying up the west coast of Formosa, past the Pescadores Islands, and nearly to the northern tip of Formosa where our assigned mission was to begin, we still had not seen another aircraft from our squadron.

"Pilot to crew!" I said into the intercom, "has anyone seen another airplane from our squadron?"

"Negative!" came the reply from the tail, side, and top turret.

"We are five minutes from where we start the fightin' side of this mission. Today this is our own, private, personal war and I hope in later years you can take pride in telling your grandchildren about the day you carried the war to the enemy, in their own backyard, on their ground, and, single-handedly, fought the entire Imperial Japanese war machine on Formosa!"

"Don't you want your flak suit?" asked Kenney, after manually charging the package guns from the handles between the pilots' seats.

"I think I'll dress informally at the office today," I replied, "and enjoy myself!"

At 0710 hours I advanced the prop pitch to 2100 rpm and put the nose of the *Touch O' Texas* down toward the beach at the northern tip of Formosa, simultaneously hitting the button on my wheel that charged the eight fifties in the nose. The slipstream from our airplane screamed a crescendo as I accelerated, hugging the treetops in the shadows as the first rays of the early morning sun made their appearance in the sky above us. What appeared to be a large, luxurious, white, ranch-style residence or officer's club, came into view on a hillside. My tracers disappeared into the building, followed by the incendiary and armor-piercing ammunition that set the building on fire.

"I bet that woke the general up," said Kenney.

"His aide and the buckass privates on KP, too! And the Geisha girls," added Cronin.

We were over the hill and back on the treetops as Kenney, standing behind me, yelled in my ear, pointing wildly off to the right.

"Right back there! Right back there! We gotta go back! There's about three hundred Jap soldiers in formation and stripped to the waist, taking early morning calisthenics! We can annihilate 'em! We gotta go back!" he said jumping up and down.

"I saw 'em when we were right even with 'em but too late to do anything about it," I answered.

"But we've gotta go back!" continued Kenney, half pleading and half crying.

"It hurts me as much as it does you," I told him, "but we can't go back."

"We can duck around the edge of this hill and come in from a different direction! They'll never see us!" said Kenney.

"But if they saw us, which they very well could have," I answered, "they'd be waiting for us and we'd have lost our personal war today. Those are the three hundred luckiest Japs on Formosa, and it's best we leave 'em that way — and live to fight another day!"

As I pulled up over a little knoll, to climb up on a plateau, I sighted a twin-engine airplane, with single fin and rudder, flying straight at us at about eight hundred feet altitude. I recognized it immediately as an enemy *Tess*-type transport aircraft comparable to our C-47. The rate of closure of two aircraft meeting each other head-on is only a matter of seconds and, being on the deck and in the shadows, our concealment was complete until the very last instant. While still a quarter of a mile apart, I pulled the nose of *199* up, and I could see the tracers from the first burst of my twelve fifties disappearing into the enemy aircraft. My second burst caught him flush and head-on, from point-blank range, and the airplane gave the illusion of coming to a stop in midair, as both engines were shot out and the propellers started to windmill, turned only by the wind. As he started a turn to the left, the bright sun illuminated the big red meatballs on the fuselage and the wings, and I followed, flying a curve up and to the right, and gave him a third burst which was slightly in front of his nose. Relaxing the pressure on my controls and allowing the enemy transport to move further in front of me, I gave him a fourth burst, after which the right wing caught fire, then the left, and finally the whole ship was enveloped in flames as he made a steep approach into a rice paddy and exploded. Having followed him all the way in I realized, too late, that he was in the traffic pattern and on the downwind leg, preparatory to landing at a big Jap airdrome. I was suddenly flying down the middle of the main runway of their airdrome at fifty feet altitude! The enemy flak was everywhere. We had shot down one of their aircraft in full view of every person on that enemy base, who was outside and watching! But there was no doubt that we were not expected, and had caught them with their pants down by coming in so early. I saw every conceivable facial expression from surprise to pathos reflected in the oriental faces staring at me along the runway, in the revetments, and near the hangers! I also saw the flash from the ends of rifles and pistols, fired by ground personnel who were alert enough to respond. That caused me to duck instinctively!

"Let's get outta here!" shouted Kenney, "shootin' down one of their planes in a traffic pattern must be right next to spittin' at Tojo on the Japanese Insult Scale — the way they're shootin' at us!"

I put the nose of *199* on the treetops and wasted no time in leaving the inhospitable reception.

"Three fighters at nine o'clock high!" said Warnick into the intercom.

"Do you think they see us down here in the dark and shadows?" I asked.

"Maybe they haven't — they're continuing to fly formation right on over us — going in the opposite direction, at about six or seven thousand feet I'd judge."

"Keep your eyes peeled for 'em, or any others! In four or five minutes we'll be long gone and they'll probably never find us at this altitude, even if they're told we passed through. And its still dark."

I came upon a railroad, running generally in a north and south direction, so I followed it just above the treetops on either side of the rails.

"Look at that," said Cronin, "telegraph wires along this railroad just like back home!"

"You better hope some sharp Jap telegrapher hasn't wired ahead and told 'em we're coming!" I told him.

Dead ahead, a couple of miles, was a town still asleep. The depot, to the left of the railroad we were flying, could have passed for the sleepy railway station of a thousand small towns and hamlets back in the states, complete with matching brown and yellowish-orange colors. I opened the bomb bay and there was still no sign of life anywhere. We made a sieve out of the station with our fifties and left it exploding and burning, after the para-demolition bomb had done its work.

Eight or nine miles, or a couple of minutes the other side of town, we hit pay dirt! An enemy train of six cars and an engine was chugging up the track and approaching us head-on! The steam engine, laying down heavy black smoke, labored up a slight incline with its load in tow. With all twelve of my fixed guns, and Warnick's twin fifties from the top turret concentrated on the engine, it exploded like the Fourth of July when the armor-piercing incendiaries hit it. Our immediate concern was our safety, as the air ahead of us was filled with smoke, steam, and pieces of metal scrap from the engine. I held my breath, and my heart skipped a beat, until we safely cleared the explosion. I managed to drop one para-demolition bomb that derailed two freight cars. People dove, ran, and were blown from the train on both sides of the tracks. Zuber cleaned up with the fifties from the tail turret.

"Another trip or two on the explosive express and I think we should put a train whistle on this airplane," said Kenney, "we've sure left a lot of evidence back there that we've been working on the railroad!"

"We can't go back?" asked Kenney, knowing the answer before he asked it, "there's still a lot of target that we could work on back there."

"No, we can't go back." I responded, "they might be waiting for us the next time around."

"Around the bend came Number Ten,
Loaded down with Tojo's men.
The boiler burst and the engine split,
And all you could see was Japanese shit!" recited Cronin, smiling.

"Thank you, Ralph Waldo Cronin! Poet Laureate of old *199*."

"Pardon me boy!" sang Kenney, "was that the Chattanooga Choo Choo?"

"This is Track 29," answered Cronin, "but it's the incendiaries from those fifties that shine!"

"There you go! You've done it again! But while you've been reciting all that poetry you better have taken pictures of that transport we shot down and the train we've just blown up." I laughed, "Or you might be the last bomb we drop today!"

Now indicating 285 mph and streaking five feet above the telegraph wires, a maze of wire and steel on the horizon suddenly developed into a huge electrical power plant. I pulled up to five hundred feet to get a better view of several ultra-modern, steel-towered high lines of multiple conductors that dead ended into the big plant from several directions. By the size of the steel towers, the conductors they carried and the oil switches in the sub-station yard, this facility probably provided all, or a major part of, the electrical energy for the entire Island of Formosa.

As the son of a foreman of a line crew that maintained high voltage power lines for Texas Electric Service Company in West Texas, a child who was born in the company cottage of a Texas Power and Light sub-station yard in Ferris, Texas, one who had been taught all his natural life that shooting out a street light or an insulator on a light pole was an unforgivable sin punishable by something just less than death, I was overwhelmed by the sight of that gigantic electrical power plant displayed in front of me. I strafed the power lines, the oil switches, and electrical structure in the sub-station yard, and deposited a para-demolition bomb in the center of the big power plant. The results appeared unimpressive since the enemy probably had killed the power, shutting down the plant anticipating our presence in the area. We received no enemy flak, as Cronin observed "they're either asleep or out on piss call!"

"What did you do that for?" inquired Kenney.

"Oh, just say it's something that I've wanted to do all my life," I replied, "and something I want to tell my Dad about."

We continued to fly the railroad for another one hundred-fifty miles, strafing and bombing three more railroad stations, three cities, and two large factories until all our bombs and ammunition had been expended. I turned out to sea, climbed to eight thousand feet and headed back to Luzon.

"Look at that!" said Cronin, pointing to a clear sky in the

direction of Luzon as we reached the southern tip of Formosa. The nightmare of turbulence, rain, and thunderheads we had flown through blindly, a few short hours before, had now dissipated, leaving only gale-force winds in their wake on the surface of the China sea.

"You've been livin' right," I said to Cronin.

"Naw," answered Kenney, "it's got to be Warnick!"

"Whatta you mean?"

"He's been squeezin' his left nut for luck ever since we hit that first downdraft when we lost nine hundred feet altitude about 0300 hours this morning," responded Kenney, "and he hardly turned loose of it long enough to do any strafing!"

"You see how good it worked though, don't 'cha?" said Warnick, "we made it through those thunderheads we couldn't see and the Japs didn't touch us today did they?"

"But that's just because Blount didn't listen to Kenney and make a second run on those Japs taking calisthenics, or go back to strafe that train again," added Cronin.

"How much gas we got left?" I questioned.

"We've got one hundred-sixty gallons indicated," he replied. "That'll get us back to Lingayen, but I'd sure hate to know we had to make it back to San Marcelino!" Lingayen was the northern most airstrip on Luzon where we could refuel.

When the wheels of the *Touch O' Texas* touched the metal landing strip at Lingayen, we had fifty gallons of gasoline left in the tanks. The airstrip on this desolate, sandy stretch of real estate was laid through the middle of a Filipino cemetery. The marble grave markers and headstones had only been removed from the area where the engineers had laid the steel matting. It was the first time I'd ever landed in a graveyard!

"People are dying to come here!" remarked Cronin.

"Yeah! A place of last resort!" answered Kenney.

"What's the name on that big marble statue?" asked Warnick, pointing to a marble angel six feet tall.

"It doesn't make any difference," answered Cronin, "as long as it's not mine!"

We made arrangements for the gasoline, as Warnick crawled up on the wing to oversee the refueling operation. This northernmost landing strip on Luzon was very popular with all types of aircraft making strikes to Formosa and the China sea. The weather earlier in the day, plus the two hundred miles of full throttle, twenty feet above the railroad for nearly two hundred miles or the length of Formosa, had really depleted our fuel supply.

"They say we're the first airplane that's dropped in short of gas for a week," said Warnick.

"That figures," I replied. "With the weather we've had between here and Formosa for the past week."

I taxied to the end of the strip, checked the mags, got the flashing green light from the makeshift jungle tower, and gave her the throttle. As we cleared the end of the runway I gave Cronin the wheels up signal and never bothered to gain altitude. I trimmed her up, rolling in a half-turn of elevator and a three-quarter turn of aileron trim, and the airplane flew itself on the treetops of that Philippines virgin jungle. We flew back to Clark Field in the brilliant sunshine of a beautiful, early spring afternoon. What a contrast, I thought, between the perfect, unlimited visibility of the present as compared to the ghastly, death-dealing turbulence of the thunderheads we had flown through, and that had been only five thousand feet above us, ten hours earlier.

In an hour's time we were on the ground, and I was writing up the Form I to the background music provided by the winding down of the gyros. We had been in the air nine hours and forty minutes, of which five hours and thirty minutes had been an instruments and four hours and ten minutes had been contact or visual. Kenney was waiting for me next to the ladder as I climbed down out of the airplane.

"Ole Musket is a real huckster, a real promoter, isn't he!" stated Kenney.

"Whatta you mean?" I asked.

"The way he tried to sell us on this strike at last night's briefing," he replied.

"Yeah! He has the entrepreneurial instinct," I said, "when he's ordered to sell us on a strike that he doesn't, or can't, believe in himself.

"Did you say this strike stinks?" inquired Cronin.

"Yeah! Now that we're back on the ground, it stinks!"

"I agree," replied Cronin, "it stinks and I don't want no more like it!"

The weapon's carrier finally arrived and we piled in, to be ferried back to the interrogation tent. "That's the roughest night flying weather I've ever been in," confided Zuber, leaning over and speaking into my ear to be heard above the wind and engine noise of the weapon's carrier.

"That's the roughest I've ever been in, too," I answered, "day or night."

"You've gotta have a lot of faith in those instruments don't you?" he asked.

"Absolutely! Unwavering faith!" I nodded my head.

"It's like the story I read about in the early days of the heavy bombings of London, when a father and his little boy ran out of their burning home one night. Trying to find any kind of shelter, the father jumped into a deep bomb hole in the yard. Then he held up his arms for his son to follow. The little boy heard his father's voice in the darkness urging him to jump, but he froze in his tracks. 'I can't see you!' he cried. But the father could see his son outlined clearly against the night sky and the flickering flames, and he hollered, 'You can't see me, but I can see you. Jump!' I got to thinking that was kinda what we were doing early last night. Your faith in those instruments was like a leap in the dark!"

"You're right, Zuber," I answered, "that's exactly what it was like!"

"But it wasn't an empty darkness. Lieutenant," said Zuber, "He was there, His voice in the darkness, saying 'You can't see me, but I can see you. Jump!' "

"It was an act of faith! You're right," I said, "and that's the only way to explain flying on instruments in a thunderhead. I'm glad you're the radio man on this crew!"

"Me, too," he said, as the weapon's carrier pulled up in front of the interrogation tent.

Only Doc Marcus, a fifth of Old Grand-Dad, and six empty interrogation tables with only two interrogation officers behind them, met us.

"Where's the rest of the squadron?" I asked. "Were we so late gettin' in that every other crew has been interrogated and gone to the showers?"

"There aren't any other crews!" responded Doc Marcus. "You're it!"

"Whatta you mean there's no other crews? You mean not another plane got through? Not another plane made the strike today?"

"That's right!"

"Didn't I tell you," I said, turning to the rest of the crew, "didn't I tell you this was our own personal war today! It was us against the whole Island of Formosa!"

"That made the odds just about right," said Kenney, "five to two million!"

After the interrogation, after everyone carried off nearly the whole fifth of Old Grand-Dad in canteen cups dispersed by the benevolent doctor, after we had recited in detail how we shot the Jap transport down; what we had strafed, bombed; and after we marked the route of our attack on the big map of Formosa, we straggled out of the interrogation tent as total exhaustion started to catch up with us.

"Did you see the copilot in that Jap transport salute us just after you gave 'em the third burst, when they started their turn to the left?" asked Warnick.

"I didn't see that," I said, "I had my hands too full of airplane, shootin', and tryin' to miss 'em I guess!"

"It was a kind of 'you got us, good luck, and we're happy to die for the Emperor' salute, I thought!" said Warnick. "I had a great view from the top turret and I not only saw the salute but I could see the expression on his face as well! He looked kinda proud and satisfied that he was gonna die!"

"In their religion they're supposed to die happy when they die in combat in service to the Emperor," said Kenney.

"Cliff Wiley, the Chevrolet dealer back home, has a business motto that fits this situation ideally," I said, "Cliff says 'When you're pleased we're happy!' I'm pleased and they're happy!"

Musket was sitting behind his desk as always, in deep thought, when I walked into Operations. "You made it back!" he said, looking up from the list of pilots and crews he was studying. "Congratulations!"

"After we didn't return with the rest of the squadron you figgered the weather got us didn't you?" I asked.

"Naw! I knew it would take more'n a high wind to stop you!"

"Believe me, it was more than a high wind. Try *tornado!* Like four or five in a row," I said. "You fouled up and I handled it perfectly! Oh, the power of well-intended incompetence!"

"I did what you told me though!" he replied.

"What's that?" I asked.

"I left the front porch light on, but I couldn't find the dog."

"He's gone," I responded, "he was afraid you'd send him up next. And not even a dog should be sent out in weather like that!"

"Congratulations," said Major Jones, coming into Operations. "I understand you flew your own personal strike against the enemy up at Formosa today and shot down a Jap transport."

"Yep! Four more will make me an ace!" I replied.

"How do you spell that ace?" asked the Major.

"No respect! No professional appreciation for an exemplary, if not an absolutely brilliant, magnificent, superlative, single-handed, crushing blow to the enemy," I replied, trying to keep a straight face while feigning insult, "and you have the audacity to ask how do you spell ace!"

"You keep talking and you'll leave no doubt in anybody's mind how to spell that ace," responded Major Jones, as we left Operations.

"Where you going?" asked Kenney.

"There's nothing like a good wet shower after a morning in downtown hell," I replied, "and the sun should've warmed the water in those P-51 wing tanks to a relaxing and soothing temperature by now!"

"I used to play water polo but my horse drowned," said Kenney, "so I take nothing but showers now! I'll join you!"

A good shower, now that I think about it, was about the best thing we had in that war.

CHAPTER ELEVEN

Preparation For Suicide

It is better to know some of the questions than all of the answers.

James Thurber

"Doc! Doc Marcus!" Lyman, three sheets to the wind and reverting to his favorite topic when under the influence: "if you wet the bed, isn't that grounds for a medical discharge?"

"I don't wet the bed, Lyman," answered Doc Marcus.

"I don't mean *you* wet the bed," replied a frustrated Lyman, "I mean *I* wet the bed. Isn't that right, Townsley?"

"That's right," added Townsley, equally drunk and coming in on cue, "Lyman wets the bed so bad, Doc, that we call him the midnight sailor."

"I can't stand this," said Doc, "I think I'm going to cry."

"I do that too, Doc," added Lyman, "I cry myself to sleep every night."

"That's right," chimed in Townsley, "he cries himself to sleep all the time. Between his crying and bed wetting he has to wear water wings to bed."

"Doesn't all that water make your tent floor rather muddy?" inquired Doc Marcus.

"My eyes are bothering me, too, Doc!" added Lyman, "can I come in and get 'em checked?"

"I don't like checked eyes," replied Doc, "I like your eyes blue, just like they are!"

"Why do you always see the olive drab side of things, Doc?" queried Lyman.

"What's the matter, Lyman," asked Doc Marcus, "did somebody sew up your fly again?"

"That's it, Doc," said Townsley, about to split, "how'd you know? When he couldn't unzip his fly he had to drop his pants to piss and he mooned all the Japs on Formosa!"

The first prayer meeting in four days, to celebrate promotions (including Thatcher's captaincy) was starting to warm up when Lyman became concerned about being separated from the service, for any reason he could think of and in any manner he could talk Doc Marcus into helping him. Snatches and pieces of boisterous, convivial conversations could be heard above the din of the festive gathering of men who were alternately singing and laughing loudly.

"That whiskey's so bad it would raise a blister on a rawhide boot," said John Hamner.

"Now look," said Thatcher, to a new, young pilot who'd only made two missions, "you're not murdering anybody. You don't murder animals, you kill animals. General Kenney said, a long time ago, the enemy are just vermin, and that's all you're doin', killing rats!"

"All you have to worry about is to get him back in his coffin before the sun comes up," said Kuta, overhearing the conversation.

"Just remember," continued Thatcher, "hate makes you grow up quick. Hate makes you strong."

"What's his rank?" questioned the confused novice pilot in a low voice when Thatcher, attired in his usual skimpy shorts and dog tags, turned to acknowledge the pat on the back and congratulations of Chester Phillips.

"Now he's a Captain," replied Kuta, "but he made it the hard way! He started as a Colonel!"

"A toast!" shouted Pallotta, mounting a chair with the assistance of Kuta and Phillips who held him upright to keep him from falling. "Here's to swimmin' with bowlegged women!"

"What kind of pissy-assed toast is that?" exclaimed Mathews, "Bowlegged women! He doesn't know cowshit from wild honey!"

"I've got one," said Thatcher, coming to life. "Here's to that mean, sonofabitchin', explosive Jap shrapnel that ventilates and perforates us and our airplanes!"

"I'll drink to that!" said Kuta, and all joined in agreement.

"His brain has a charley horse," said Doc, "kick him in the shins and you'll give him a headache!"

"Here's to Myrna Loy and Betty Grable!" toasted Major Giese.

"Add Lana Turner and I'll drink to that," said Hardeman, and there was majority agreement.

"Thatcher, you have rosy red cheeks and eyes to match," mused Doc.

"Just my natural color, Doc," responded Thatcher, "just my natural color."

"And when you've seen one nurse you've seen 'em all," said Kuta. "Her perfume was *Moon Over Formosa*."

"And I said, 'I have an affliction that'll keep any lengthy relationship from enduring.' " Thatcher was saying. "And she said 'What?' And I said, 'They call it terminal marriage.' "

"Whiskey and war don't mix! General Grant kept throwing up all over his bugler," stated Lyman.

"And Phillips throws up all over his copilot," added Doc Marcus.

"Have you gotten any word about my appointment to West Point?" I asked Major Jones.

"I've sent inquiries all the way up to Fifth Bomber," replied the Major. "I've got more brass in on this than John Philip Sousa's trombone section, but we've received no word!"

"Just wondering," I told him. At that time I was wondering if I'd be alive to accept the appointment if it did come through.

"This stuff's not champagne," said Musket, "champagne tickles my nose! This stuff is eatin' it away!"

"One last toast," announced Major Jones, "before lights out around here! Here's to the national landmark of the Philippines, the drinking memorial, our honoree, Captain Charles Thatcher!" This quietly drew the curtain on another prayer meeting, as everyone staggered, stumbled, and fell toward their tents in the early morning hours.

The next morning found the 501st sleeping in, or sleeping it off, and with no mission scheduled there was no hurry on the part of anyone to become ambulatory.

"Where's Kenney?" I asked Stiles, who had moved in with us after our move to Clark Field.

"You mean the Royal Sultan of Scrounge?"

"Don't tell me." I shook my head.

"He took off early this morning with a bottle of Jack Daniels to do a little *midnight requisitioning* with the quartermaster. They have just received a load of plywood and screen that'll make this pyramidal into a penthouse! He's wheeling and stealing."

"Don't tell me my trusty navigator would bribe the quartermaster for a little plywood and some screen?" I said.

"For just a little plywood and screen? I hope not!" answered Stiles, "but for enough plywood to floor up this tent and enough screen to completely go around it making it mosquito proof, yes. He better not let that fifth of Jack Daniels go for any less!"

Thirty minutes later, Kenney pulled in with a weapon's carrier loaded with plywood and screen. "Just back it up right here," I instructed, "and Lieutenant Stiles and I will be happy to assist in unloading this contraband which you so thoughtfully secured from the Quartermaster Corps, and our comrades in arms. You epitomize the 'free enterprise' economic theory that we're all fighting to preserve."

"Free Enterprise!" said Kenney. "They drink free and we keep our enterprise!"

On the way to chow, Mathews told me my name was on the bulletin board for a strike the following day, ". . . and it looks like something big."

"What's he talking about?" asked Kenney.

"I don't know, but I've got a feeling we'll find out soon enough," I answered.

"What kind of meat is that?" I asked wonderingly.

"I don't know," said Esty, "but it tasted pretty good after I combed it!"

"At least the gravy is better today; you can cut it with a fork."

Leaving the mess tent we met Pallotta coming in. "You better report to the Big Top. I think the circus is about to begin."

"Yeah, I know."

"How'd you know?" he asked.

"Trouble rides a fast horse."

Entering the Operation's tent I could tell immediately that something special was in the cooker. Sergeant Franko was busy behind his desk, as were all other enlisted personnel, and there was no lost motion, or any extra bodies in sight. Looking to the back of the tent to the area that doubled as a briefing and ready room, I found the reason for the picture of peak efficiency. Before a big map of the China coast that had Saigon prominently displayed, stood Colonel Chester Coltharp, CO of the 345th Bomb Group, talking with Captain Musket in hushed tones. Kenney and I joined the other pilots and navigators seated informally in front of the two figures at the map board, and awaited their pleasure. I saw Jay. W. Moore, from Kirkwood, Illinois. There was Lieutenant Andrew J. Johnson from Cadillac, Michigan, flying his first mission as first pilot; Lieutenant Vernon M. Townsley, Jr., who had flown a couple of missions as copilot on our crew, and whom I had helped check out as a first pilot, from Salt Lake City, Utah; Lieutenant Milton E. Esty from Hartford, Connecticut; the indomitable Captain Charles Thatcher; Lieutenant James Harrah, from Caldwell, Idaho; Lieutenant Bob Burnett from Batavia, Iowa; Lieutenant Aubrey Stowell from Indianapolis, Indiana; Lieutenant Paul E. Langdon from Cincinnati, Ohio; and Lieutenant Leonard H. Miller from New York City, all relaxed and in various states of attire.

"Gentlemen," said Colonel Coltharp, turning around from the map to face us, "you have been selected to fly the most important strike in the history of the 345th Bomb Group. The target is Saigon harbor, on the coast of Indochina where the enemy has a large concentration of shipping, and which our photo reconnaissance people have photographed hiding under cover of land *ack-ack* positions. Our job is to get in there, quickly, wipe out the shipping, and get out in a minimum length of time. We will be carrying five hundred-pound demolition bombs. This will be a coordinated attack; I'll lead the 501st Squadron with Captain Wiley leading the 499th, and we'll be joined by two squadrons of B-24s, who will hit the target five minutes ahead of us, and twenty-four P-38s. Eight *Lightnings* will fly close aerial top cover for us over the harbor area, while sixteen P-38s will assist us in strafing the target."

"That's good," said Kenney, whispering in my ear, "that should take some of the sweat off of us, and give those enemy gunners something else to shoot at besides us."

"We are to stage out of Palawan, Puerta Princesa, about seven hundred-fifty miles south of here. In addition to a full load of bombs and ammunition, each of you shall fly all of your flight, as well as take ground personnel with you to Palawan. That will include bedding and cots for everyone. All crew chiefs have been alerted, your aircraft are being loaded, and we take off at fifteen hundred hours. We will have a detailed briefing of the target tonight after chow at Palawan. Are there any questions? I'll see you at the flight line and good hunting."

"Ole Fuzzy Balls is leading this one!" said Kenney, as we walked from the Operation's tent, "it must really be important!"

"What's the pertinent poop from group on this Saigon strike, Ike? We've just heard Coltharp's pitch, but what's the real scuttlebutt?" I asked Ike Baker, the assistant Intelligence Officer who knew everything, official and unofficial, as we exited Operations.

"The story out of Group Headquarters is that MacArthur has had a gut-full of the Thirteenth Air Force — based at Palawan — and the Thirteenth's failure to complete a strike against Saigon. After aborting, and turning back from three or four missions, they're claiming their B-25s can't fly the seven hundred-fifty miles round trip and hit Saigon without running out of gas. Even though they have three hundred gallons more gasoline than you do with a one hundred-fifty gallon tank slung under each wing."

"That doesn't sound like gasoline, somebody's been running out of! Sounds like they're running out of guts. Somebody's got shit in their neck!" responded Thatcher, overhearing Ike Baker's explanation.

"But why us?" I asked. "Why have we been chosen to be the guinea pigs?"

"It's not only their B-25s," answered Baker, "their B-24s, as well as their fighters, claim they can't make it to Saigon and back without running out of gas. MacArthur told General Kenney to pick some of his best minimum altitude people out of the 345th and send 'em down to Palawan to show the Thirteenth how it's done."

"Their B-24s and their P-38s damn sure better get to Saigon on this trip, or I'm liable to mistake the whole Thirteenth Air Force for the enemy and burn their asses," rumbled Thatcher.

"If you get back," I told him.

As we neared the tent, Cronin came running over. "What's up? I heard we're on the board for tomorrow and the Colonel is leading the strike."

"You got it right," I answered.

"Where we goin'? What're we hittin'?"

"Let's see! Did the Colonel tell us, Kenney?" I asked.

"The Colonel didn't tell you?" asked Cronin, impatiently.

"Guess he forgot," I innocently replied, "maybe he's going through the menopause!"

"It's Saigon!" Kenney put in.

"And don't forget your toothbrush, overnight bag, and mad money," I added, "we're spendin' the night!"

"In *Saigon*?" Cronin had a funny look on his face.

"I hope not," said Kenney, "that could sure get embarrassing! Gettin' caught in Saigon after dark might just be a permanent lights-out kinda experience!"

"Embarrassin' and lights-out?" murmured Cronin.

"Yeah! Like goin' to cash in your chips, and findin' that the gunners in the harbor at Saigon are the bankers."

After collecting our gear, folding cots, bedding, and a toilet kit for toothpaste and toiletries, we loaded everything into a weapon's carrier parked at Operation's and started for the flight line.

"If I'd ever seen an overloaded Model A truck headin' out of the Oklahoma dust bowl during the depression that would do the *Grapes of Wrath* credit," said Kenney, "this is it!"

"Well, Sergeant, this is one time that you're going with us," said Warnick, the aerial engineer to Albright, the ground crew chief engineer, "you're going to have to *fly* your mistakes — if any!"

"I'd fly in this airplane to Timbuctoo," replied Albright, "or anywhere else."

"You tell him," I responded, "and I'll fly it there, too."

I walked around the airplane, patted the fuselage of *199* as I ducked under the belly behind the open bomb bay doors, where the armorers were still winching the five hundred-pound bombs into their receptacles. I observed the patchwork of new, shiny aluminum applied to the underside to cover flak holes of such recent vintage that there had been no time to apply camouflage paint, and I kicked one of the big tires supporting that massive weight.

"Think you might buy this airplane, Lieutenant?" laughed Sergeant Albright, observing me kick the huge tire.

"I don't think so," I replied, "this one's been wrecked! Not just once but several times, and the body shop didn't even bother to paint over the damage, much less blend it in with the old paint!" We both laughed.

Cronin was already in the cockpit filling out the Form I and listing the names of the passengers, as I squeezed through the small space separating the pilot and copilot's seats. The list of our passengers looked like the roster of a Notre Dame football team.

"Kolodziejski, Abramovich, Sinko, Zuber, Smith," I read aloud, "how did he slip in there?"

"It's gotta be a mistake," said Cronin, as he kept on writing.

"We can't get that many people in this airplane," I said, "much less all their bedding and personal gear needed to spend the night."

"They're back there," replied Cronin. "Making like sardines — but they're there."

"Is the ark loaded?" yelled Warnick, the last person aboard as he pulled the collapsible ladder up behind him, sealing the bottom of the airplane.

"No," answered Albright, sitting behind Kenney, "we have room for one more monkey. Come on in."

As we taxied toward the end of the runway for takeoff I motioned for Kenney to lean forward. "What's the weight of this airplane?"

"I thought you'd never ask," he replied, "I figure forty-two thousand, maybe forty-three thousand pounds."

"That's just a four thousand-pound overload! If we had another one thousand-pounds, that would be exactly a one-pound overload for every foot of runway which we have for takeoff." I had a strange sensation in my midsection.

"I don't think it works exactly that way," said Kenney.

"I'd like to have another four thousand feet of runway instead of the additional four thousand pounds of weight."

The runways at Clark Field were the nearest thing to stateside facilities we'd seen and enjoyed since leaving the States, with long, well-surfaced runways and no surrounding obstructions. There were only the mountains to the north, and the enemy that our ground forces were still fighting practically off the end of the runway.

"Give me ten degrees of flaps," I said to Cronin, after revving the engines, checking the mags, and running the checklist. We splashed through puddles left from a midday shower, as we were the second airplane to takeoff. The moisture was so heavy that configurations of vapor played along the wings, and about the propellers, in a swirling demonstration of the basic principles of mechanical flight. Due to the excessive weight, *199* was slow to respond to the full throttles, and I got anxious after we had covered half the distance to the end of the runway.

Come on baby! I whispered under my breath, *make like a bird!*

The engines were working harder, it seemed, as the momentum of the aircraft built. The airspeed increased dramatically, the controls lost their mushiness, and the feeling of lightness slipped over the ship as it started to fly. Over the end of the runway I gave the wheels up signal, and we hung on the props momentarily, until the tremendous drag of the wheels folding into the fuselage was removed. I milked the flaps up, a degree at a time, as we picked up speed and stayed only a few feet above the jungle below us.

We climbed back to the west, over the mountains, and over San Marcelino along the west coast of Luzon. I was delighted this overloaded takeoff wasn't made from the pock-filled runway of San Marcelino, our old home. Without conscious thought, I looked for a forced landing area, a habit left over from the flying instructors who would reach over, kill the power in a single engine trainer, and yell "forced landing!" With that load it was comforting for a moment to know that San Marcelino was down there. That was notwithstanding the continued, steady, purr of the two Wright-Cyclone engines that were now pulling us through the pure clean air of the Luzon coast.

"What's our ETA to Palawan?" I asked Kenney.

"I'd say 1810 hours," he replied, "give or take a minute or two."

The real significance of the mission had not really soaked in. Until then it had been something of a lark: flying down to Palawan — seven hundred-fifty miles south of Clark Field — with all ground and flying personnel; to stage out of this jungle island base to hit a target further south along the China coast than any other. After a couple of hours of flying in the featherbed-smooth and calm air at five thousand feet above the placid China sea, I was almost lulled into serenity. All the instruments before me reflected the perfect, collective operation of the airplane, the Wright-Cyclones emitted the gigantic purr of two engines in perfect synchronization, and the setting sun on the western horizon reminded me of home, in West Texas.

"Look at that sunset! Isn't that something?" exuded Cronin, the Alabama native.

"That's just what I was thinking," I said. "Have you ever seen a west Texas Sunset?"

"Sure haven't," responded Cronin, "have I missed something?"

"Sunset on a Texas prairie is a sight to behold," I exclaimed. "The sky in west Texas is incredibly blue and the purest color you'll ever see. And then far away out there, where the earth meets the sky, the sun rests like a great ball of liquid fire, its rays spreading out and upward, in a thousand directions into the heavens it has just left. In that high, clear altitude, where you can see Lamesa forty miles from the top of Scenic Mountain, the sun seems close and far away at the same time. The mare's-tails clouds, like those right up there at about twenty thousand feet, are rose and gold and every imaginable shade of the rainbow. And out there on the prairie, like up here, there's nothing to break the view, no tree, nor house, nor hill; only the free sweep of the prairie that shimmers in the reflected light. Over at the horizon's edge there's burning splendor of that setting sun. It seems the whole world should stop and view the beauty of God's handiwork! Like right now, I feel as if we should take off our hats before this pageant of a world on fire. Back home, with the west Texas desert as a stage, the only spectators that usually observe this phenomenon are coyotes, indifferent prairie dogs, and maybe a skunk and a screech owl!"

"That's about like up here," replied Cronin, "nobody but a bunch of indifferent goats and jackasses are looking on today."

"Speak for yourself," said Kenney, overhearing the conversation, "I appreciate the view mighty fine!"

"Radio to Pilot! Over!" came Zuber's voice from the waist.

"Pilot to Radio! Go ahead."

"The whole side of the airplane back here is covered with oil!"

"Where's it coming from?"

"Out of the number one engine!"

"Keep an eye on it and let me know if it increases. Pilot to Engineer. Climb up in the top turret and tell me if you can see anything!"

"Roger!" came a quick reply from Warnick.

I had a more reassured feeling because Sergeant Albright was aboard. *I don't know why. He can't crawl out on the wing, remove the nacelle cover, and facilitate an oil leak repair in flight.* Still, I felt better because he was aboard!

"How far are we out of Palawan?" I asked Kenney.

"An hour — fifty-five minutes — give or take five minutes."

In an hour's time we could not only lose the engine, we could lose the airplane. A strafer didn't fly on one engine without a bomb load, much less a full bomb load plus nine extra personnel and all their sleeping gear. This went through my mind as I watched the oil (our life, our blood) slowly being blown from the engine. Without it the engine could freeze solidly in a matter of seconds.

"What's your diagnosis?" I asked Albright, who had just stuck his head in the cockpit.

"Could be a broken or cracked oil line. Or a fractured main bearing, a hot piston, a sticking valve — a hundred things, Lieutenant!"

I looked ahead. There was nothing but water in sight. I started mentally reviewing the ditching procedure and the speech I was going to make to the crew.

"The oil pressure is holding so far," said Albright.

"But the temperature has risen a couple of degrees," I added.

I looked at the instruments to the good engine. *Everything perfect. Thank the Lord. We may be giving it the test of its life very shortly.*

"Cylinder head temperature on both engines is normal and only the oil on the bad engine is a few degrees hotter," Albright said.

I nodded approval. He hadn't needed to say that! All of us had our eyes glued to the instruments, and I wouldn't have been surprised to see Zuber from the back of the bomb bay nodding as well. From experience I knew that twenty drops of oil could look like twenty gallons, spread over the side of the fuselage by the slipstream of an airplane indicating two hundred-ten miles per hour. I hoped it was the former!

In fifty minutes, Palawan was in sight. I asked Warnick to fire a red flare from our *Beri* pistol, giving us the right-of-way for a straight-in approach and landing. On the ground I cut the engine at the end of our landing roll, and turned the airplane over to Sergeant Albright and his crew.

"Whata you think?" I asked later, after Albright made a cursory inspection.

"I don't know right now, Lieutenant," he replied, "but we've got all night and she's gonna be ready for takeoff in the morning!"

The relationship between the men who flew the airplanes and those who fixed them was harmonious, because it was based upon a mutual admiration and appreciation. In a manner of speaking, it was unfair that the pilots were covered with confetti, got pats on the back and other hero treatment, while the airplane mechanic wasn't given a second look by anyone. But nowhere did the aircraft grease monkeys enjoy more respect and fame, than in combat. In this live or die atmosphere the crew chief enjoyed the prestige and genuine appreciation of the pilots and aircrews who won or lost on the turn of his wrench, the wisdom of his mechanical judgment, and the insight to anticipate and remove engine parts before they failed. A mechanic had to have the intuition to replace a fatigued bolt, and the perceptive ear that told him an engine wasn't running properly, when all the rest of us thought it was making beautiful music.

The B-25 airplane was a mass of orderly, structured, electrical, hydraulic, and mechanical combinations, scientifically designed and arranged to function in harmonious reliability. If one area failed to function there was a backup or substitute system, that might save the day. This multitude of devices encompassing hydraulics, electronics, plumbing, radio, and engines, easily surpassed the mental ability of any one individual, demanding experts in each field to assure normal operation. However, the one man who came closer than anyone else in mastering all of these things, was Sergeant Albright.

The 499th Squadron, who was making the strike with us the next morning, and who had been able to muster only seven flyable aircraft, lost two of their airplanes to mechanical failure enroute to Palawan. The next morning I learned that Albright and his ground crew had accomplished the impossible under the most trying conditions: completely tearing down and reassembling the number one engine of *199* overnight, in what proved to be a major aircraft mechanical miracle. Neither of the two 499th Squadron aircraft could be repaired by their crew chiefs and ground personnel in time to make the following day's strike.

"Albright is *too* damn good," Cronin would say later. "If he wasn't so good, we could fly this mission sunning ourselves on the beach, like those two lucky 499th crews who lost their airplanes to mechanical troubles. Instead of getting our ass shot off!"

"But you wouldn't have our buddies flyin' this mission without us now, would you?" asked Kenney.

"Try me!" replied Cronin. "My mama didn't raise no halfwit!"

Within half an hour, a couple of weapons carriers arrived at the airplane. The officers loaded into one, while the enlisted men loaded themselves and their sleeping gear into the other. We quickly learned that only half of this southernmost island in the Philippine's group was secure, and free of the enemy. "They're still fighting for the northern half right up the road," our driver informed us.

"Would you like the General MacArthur suite overlooking the motor pool?" asked Kenney.

"I'm from Missouri! Give me the Harry Truman Presidential Suite with the dancing girls," replied Thatcher, "you've gotta show me!"

All of the pilots, navigators, and other officers were assigned to a pyramidal tent on the north side of the metal landing strip, that the engineers had dug out of the sand. We were in a palm grove, and the floor of the tent was deep sand, which was actually an extension of the beach and the open sea, only two hundred yards to the east. After assembling our cots and rigging our mosquito netting, the impact of the rumors we had been hearing concerning the mission we were to fly tomorrow began to soak in.

"Anybody know anything about what we're doing here?" asked Lieutenant Johnson.

"Only what the Colonel told us earlier today before we flew down here," answered James Harrah.

"This is probably the brainchild of some over-the-hill, 4-F General in Fifth Bomber Command who couldn't fight a fly off his ass!" said Townsley, "and who's looking for a little vicarious glory before being shipped home for hemorrhoids and flat feet!"

"What about us? The sonofabitches who have to fly this damn mission? We don't share in the plan of glory of some armchair general. We're the poor bastards out here at the end of the line who have to fly their senseless, nitwitted plan with death riding in the cockpit and tugging at our elbows! Every man who flies into the hell of that harbor tomorrow, and makes it back alive, is gonna miss the best damned chance he ever had of becoming a lost in action statistic on Harold Timmerman's engineering report!" said Lieutenant Johnson.

"The only glory in this whole, wild nightmare is to stay alive!" said Harrah, speaking now in a soft, rhetorical tone. "We're the edge of the sword of victory who gets sacrificed in the winning of the war! So what if we don't make it? We lose a few airplanes, a few flying personnel. What difference does it make to the generals so long as we ultimately win the battle . . . and the war?"

"Horseshit!" exclaimed Esty. "Let that fuckin' General, smoking those thick Havanas and sippin' that stateside Scotch up there in FEAF Headquarters come up here and take my place on the edge of the sword of victory! He's so far away from the fightin' end of this war, that he has to read the wire reports in his hometown newspaper to find out what's going on. I'll damn sure put on his fresh, starched shirt, date a different nurse or Red Cross female every night, eat his T-Bone steaks, sip his fine Scotch whisky, and sleep on his comfortable innerspring mattress. I'll show up at his desk promptly ten minutes before 0900 hours every morning, if he'll come out here and take my place as the prime target in this Japanese shooting gallery. He's the bastard I'd like to put out in front of a twenty-one gun salute!"

"You're a bunch of pessimists," exclaimed Townsley, speaking with a gleam in his eye. "Think of it this way! We're helping some Bird Colonel make his first star. In a brilliant display of the military tactics he learned at the Point, he decided that he, meaning you and me, should do something nobody else has done. Of course it came to him in a blinding flash in a moment of blood and guts discussion with a fellow General. He's reacting to the frustrations accumulated from flying a desk, and being denied his only true desire, of being a combat, front-line pilot like you and me. Just think how lucky you are."

"Yeah! The mental pain and suffering they go through in anticipation of receiving their next star must be almost more than the human body can endure," said Jones.

"And enduring all that blood and guts back there at Far Eastern Air Force Headquarters," added Johnson. "Their guts and our blood!"

"Today we might even write a new paragraph in the *Air Tactics Manual* they use to teach the junior birdmen at the Point!" added Townsley. "And think how good we're gonna make that General feel, if we pull it off!"

"And if we don't?" inquired Harrah, with a quizzical look.

"Then it's back to the drawing board, and some other birdmen will get a shot at the next suicidal target attempt," replied Esty.

"But think how bad we're gonna feel if we don't!" added Johnson.

"If we don't make it, we won't have any feelings about it anyway," said Jones.

"Of course nobody in their right mind, including the enemy, would even think about sending a *kamikaze* after this target. Much less a bunch of fun-and-freedom-loving, red-blooded

American boys! But some funny decisions are made by Generals over a Scotch and Soda at the Officer's club after a hard day at the office!" said Esty.

"Yeah! They mistake booze for courage!" said Jones.

"— and inebriated, and paralyzed stupidity for good judgment!" added Johnson.

"But would you miss it? Even if you could?" inquired Townsley.

"Maybe! Before I was invited!" replied Moore. "But since they've aroused my curiosity I gotta see for myself!"

The brakes of a weapon's carrier screeched, as it ground to a stop outside the tent, and a small cloud of sand and dust rolled under the raised flaps of the tent. Captain Wiley of the 499th alighted from the vehicle, ducked under the flap, and entered the tent.

"I'm here to pick you up for evening chow. After chow Colonel Coltharp wants to use your tent for the briefing of the crews making the strike tomorrow," said Wiley.

"You tell the Colonel he has my permission," replied Thatcher, "only because we're all heart — and we have the biggest tent."

"And also because this is where the Colonel wants to have it," I added. "And where the Colonel wants to have it, we want to have it. Isn't that right, Captain Thatcher?"

"I couldn't have said it better, Lieutenant Blount, and I thank you."

"What is that smell?" asked Vaughn, as we arrived in front of the Officer's mess five minutes later.

"That's the mess tent," replied Captain Wiley. "Come on with me and I'll show you how it got its name!"

"We had a rendering plant in San Antonio that smelled just like this," remarked Kenney, getting a tray and starting down the serving line.

When we returned to our tent, we found a large board with a map of the coast of Indochina and the city of Saigon prominently displayed. Colonel Coltharp was standing in front of the map and drawing lines across the city of Saigon, its dock area, and drawing circles around obvious targets.

"Gentlemen, tomorrow we fly the most important mission in the short, two-year history of the 345th Bomb Group. Our objective is to plug one of the few remaining holes in our blockade. The last, open shipping lane of the Japanese from Singapore to Japan — Saigon!"

There was an audible hush among the combat crews present. Reflexive breaths were unconsciously drawn in and released by experienced combat personnel who could appreciate the significance, and the inherent danger, of the Colonel's statement. The avid, as well as the nervous smokers held lighted cigarettes between their fingers that were momentarily forgotten. Even Captain Thatcher, ordinarily aloof and nonchalant in his approach to a strike briefing, was now alert, and soberly hanging on every word.

"A large concentration of enemy shipping has been photographed hiding out, and camouflaged under cover of land antiaircraft guns and emplacements, in this largest of enemy ports along the China coast. Our job is to seek out and destroy this enemy shipping, in the manner that's given us the reputation of being the best in the United States Air Corps, and — at minimum altitude and with five hundred-pound demolition bombs. Our job has been made even more difficult by the lack of serviceable aircraft needed to make this strike, but we will do what we have to do, with what we have to do it with."

"A man's gotta do what a man's gotta do!" whispered Cronin in Kenney's ear.

"Yeah," added Kenney, "as often as he can, but especially when old Fuzzy Balls says to — even in a B-25 that has only one good engine!"

I nudged Cronin to be quiet, as several dirty looks were directed in our direction from point-blank range.

"This will be a combined strike, including heavy bombers and fighters, which will join us in hitting the target. A concentration of high altitude B-24s will bomb the target five minutes before we make our strike. There will be twenty-four P-38s joining us, eight of whom will provide close aerial cover to intercept any enemy fighters, while the remaining sixteen *Lightnings* will assist us in strafing the target!"

This statement of heavy bombardment and fighter assistance, a luxury we had never before experienced in combat, brought nervous laughter of appreciation that almost erupted into applause from the combat crews being briefed. Any kind of aerial assistance was great; particularly other aircraft who would share the mast-height flight down the gun barrels of the enemy. Not to mention friendly, protective fighters, to keep the *Zeros* off our tails, during and after the mission. We rejoiced in this message in the same manner a destitute man, dying of thirst, would welcome a cup of water.

"The B-24s will soften 'em up with thousand-pounders, principally in the dock area, at eleven hundred hours. We shall fly inland a short distance and make a north to south attack. I will lead the first flight with Lieutenant Johnson on my right wing. Captain Thatcher will lead the second flight with Lieutenant Harrah flying his right wing. Lieutenant Blount is leading the third flight with Lieutenant Townsley on his right wing. And Lieutenant Esty will lead the fourth flight with Lieutenant Jones on his wing. I have drawn on the map the approximate strafing and bombing run of each flight, and the targets we anticipate hitting. We all have enemy ships that the latest high altitude photo reconnaissance pictures show to be located as we have marked them on the map. However, the Japanese have been known to move their shipping to different moorings every twenty-four hours, and the harbor at Saigon is conducive to easy shipping movement, with varied locations. If the enemy ships remain where the latest photos show them to be located, the prize target is the six thousand-ton *Fox Tare Baker*-class freighter assigned to flight number three, led by Lieutenant Blount. Pilots should stay flexible, and be ready to attack any target that's more accessible than previously ordered, should the enemy have moved any shipping targets. Do you understand?" We all understood!

"He means get anything you can see!" whispered Esty.

"You bet your ass!" replied Jones.

"That's what you're bettin'!" added Moore.

"The weather is reportedly going to be clear, with unlimited visibility and scattered cumulus at the time of our strike. Navigators get the bearings and locations of our friendly submarines, the emergency radio frequencies, and we'll synchronize our watches before takeoff in the morning. Are there any questions?"

There were none!

"Then good hunting tomorrow, gentlemen. I would remind you again that in two years of continuous combat with the Japanese this strike is the most momentous in the history of the 345th! I am honored to lead you on this occasion."

As Colonel Coltharp started to leave the tent somebody yelled, "Attenshun!" All combat personnel popped to attention until the Colonel had exited the tent, and then it sounded like a beehive come alive as everyone spoke at once.

"Shades of Hainan Island and Yulin Bay, where the guns line the shore and every ship is a floating gun platform," said Johnson. "He doesn't care if we get our ass shot off!"

"He'll be out front flying point and the first over the *ack-ack!*" answered Thatcher. "He'll probably trade places with you if you'll ask him!"

"Those B-24s and P-38s are the best news I've heard in this war since we came overseas," said Johnson.

"I've never shared Tojo's shooting gallery with so many friends," said Esty, "I don't know if I'll know how to act! But I'm damn sure looking forward to it!"

"Me too," I said. "Anybody who can take some of the heat, or make like a clay pigeon for those Jap gunners, is my friend, and welcome to fly over any enemy target with me at any time."

We walked down to the beach where most of the crews were swimming in the surf. The moonlight was so bright that you could recognize familiar faces as far as you could see them. It was as if the sun had never gone down. Stepping from the shade of the palms into the moonlight was like stepping on to a well-lighted stage.

"What's war without death, casualties, and forgetting the hell of tomorrow with a stroll along a beautiful white sandy beach like this tonight?" I asked.

"That's peace!" answered Kenney. "Peacetime."

"And that's a good thought to turn in on!"

We hadn't been asleep over an hour, when the siren announcing a Jap air raid brought us to instant, rigid attention in our sacks. As the antiaircraft crews at the east end of the strip started limbering up with their *Boom! Boom! Boom!* we lost no time in scrambling through sand and palm trees to the safety of the bunkers provided by our hosts which were about fifty yards from our tent. After fifteen minutes the *All Clear* signal sounded, and we all returned to our sacks. The various group melodies, grunts, and sleep-talking was once more under way. An hour later, the same routine was reenacted as the siren once again signalled a fifty-yard race to the bunkers, to the accompaniment of the fusillade of the antiaircraft cannon. Down at the end of the strip, they were shooting at the *Bandits*.

"I wouldn't've volunteered for this trip if I'd known they weren't gonna let me sleep!" said Kenney.

"This used to be fun when I was ten years younger," I replied, sitting with my head between my knees, dug into the sand.

"You did this when you were ten years old?" queried Kenney, spitting the sand from his mouth that was the result of an over-zealous dive into the bunker.

"It was down at my grandmother's! They had a tornado one spring that nearly blew the town away, and put the fear into that community like you wouldn't believe. Every family had a cyclone cellar that became the most popular part of central Texas-living each spring and summer — every time a cloud came up with a little lightning in it."

"But you lived in west Texas where they really have some electrical storms! Why did you go to the storm cellar?" he asked.

"When in Hill County we did as the Hill Countians did and went to the storm cellar. The storm cellar always doubled as a pantry and was full of mason jars full of peas, corn, figs, peaches, and a lot of other fruit and vegetables that had been put up during canning season. But the jars also provided a resting place for dust, spiders, and an occasional chicken snake that usually livened up the dash to the storm cellar that soon resulted in a retreat back to the house. Some of the women folk were known to take an immovable, positive, stance. Staying in the house and braving the fiercest cyclone, in preference to entering the storm cellar where the friendly old chicken snake was coiled up in the corner. A chicken snake is a dead ringer for a cottonmouth water moccasin and was never known to harm a soul! But coming face to face with one in a storm cellar, lit with only the light of a coal oil lamp, has been known to hazzard life and limb. I've seen many a man, caught in such a predicament, break his leg, skin his arms and elbows, and set the place on fire while enlarging the door out of the cellar."

"Well you should enjoy this run to the bunker in the middle of the night!" said Kenney, as the noise got louder.

"I did enjoy the visits to the storm cellar. All the kids carried quilts and pillows and it was like a slumber party. If the storm turned out to be a driving rain you could end up with water running down your back and the floor of the cellar could fill up with three or four inches of water. By the time I was a teenager, when some of the adults would take off for the storm cellar in the middle of the night, my family and I would stay in the house and sleep soundly. But the old-timers, who religiously took to the hole in the ground with the first drops of rain, would look at us skeptically through bloodshot eyes the next morning!"

"We've got to get some sleep," said Thatcher as the *all clear* sounded and we retreated back to our sacks. "Or we're damned sure going to have bloodshot eyes."

Forty-five minutes later the siren *Alert* had us dashing for the bunker once again. I watched as the last scantily-clad body hit the tent opening, running and diving for the bunkers as the *Boom! Boom!* of our heavy *ack-ack* opened up.

"I'm not going to the storm cellar again tonight!" I recognized Thatcher's half-asleep, mumbling voice in the shadows from the far side of the tent.

"No," I answered, turning over and putting the pillow over my ears to shut out the sound of the heavy *ack-ack* fire, "I'm not either! My sleep is more important, and they've yelled *Wolf* one too many times tonight!" However, the antiaircraft crews didn't stop their shooting, and the other *ack-ack* crews surrounding the strip opened up. After ten minutes, other (and worse) sounds interrupted the steady *Boom! Boom! Boom!* of our antiaircraft crews. It was the sound of a string of bombs being laid down the side of the nearby runway, accompanied by the staccato *Splat! Splat! Splat!* of machine gun ammunition striking the palm trees, *our tent,* and other objects in the immediate area.

"What in the hell is that?" screamed Thatcher from the sand under his sack across the tent.

"We're being bombed and strafed!" I yelled back, trying to dig a little deeper in the sand floor of the tent.

At once and at the same time, Thatcher and I independently reached the conclusion that the bunker, fifty yards away, was the place we should be. We met in the exit of the tent, running at full speed. We burst through the opening as a bomb exploded through the palm trees, a hundred yards from us—with accompanying flash and explosion, as the screaming, whining, whistle of the Jap machine-gun projectiles struck everything around us like giant hail stones!

"Get behind a palm tree!" I shouted to Thatcher, as I crouched behind the nearest tree trunk. The enemy strafer continued to pour a steady stream of machine gun fire into our immediate area.

"How do you know if you're behind the *right* side of this tree, smart ass?" yelled Thatcher, making like a mole intent on digging through the sand to China. *By heaven,* I realized, *he's right!* Confused and half-asleep, I didn't know from which direction the enemy fire was coming. The more intense the strafing, the more confused I became. I promised myself that if I lived through this strafing encounter, I would sleep the remainder of this night, and any other night when an air raid *Alert* was sounded, in the protection of the bunker provided for such emergencies. Very little sleep was accomplished by anyone for the remainder of the night, and we all got the OD's call a couple of hours later for breakfast, with frazzled nerves and bloodshot eyes.

"Nothing like an all-night Chinese fire drill to prepare you for a Japanese outing to Saigon," rasped Johnson.

"Don't mention the sleepless experience we've just endured," replied Thatcher, "and don't you *ever* tell me about staying in the house instead of going to the storm cellar like wise, rational, and ordinary people do when a storm comes up, Blount!"

"I didn't tell you not to go to the bunker," I replied. "In fact, I didn't even suggest that you not go to the bunker."

"Tell me you didn't tell me to get behind a tree! But which side?" said Thatcher, now ranting and raving. "You could've gotten me *killed*!"

"It's almost as bad as you taking me in on that Jap convoy — out of the clouds, without a radio, and starting a run on that destroyer without my guns charged and bomb bay doors open — isn't it?" I asked.

There was silence.

"Yeah. Last night was almost as bad, wasn't it?" I asked again.

"Okay, okay!" said Thatcher. "We're even! But that being strafed scared the shit out of me!"

"Remember that when you're strafing those Japs this morning," I said.

"I will, I will," replied Thatcher with a gleam in his eye, "and I'll enjoy every burst I give 'em! I've got a fifty caliber incendiary enema for every little yellow asshole in Saigon harbor!"

We picked up metal trays and started down the chow line.

"If those are powdered eggs I don't want any!" said Cronin. "Just give me two pieces of that burned toast and an urn for the ashes!"

So breakfast didn't take very long. Between the low-quality food, and the impending mission, our appetites were ruined. Most of us were on the first weapon's carrier back to our tent. Every combat soldier, in the air or on the ground, developed a certain ritual, encompassing everything from dress and equipment to good luck charms, and a religiously-followed routine of getting ready for battle.

"We've got some nervous cats today," I said to Thatcher as we stepped from the weapon's carrier, "a couple of these guys will hardly speak to you this morning!"

"When they're young, in age or experience, they're afraid! And when they're afraid it comes out arrogance!" he replied.

"And when you're old," I questioned, "in age or experience?"

"You're either damn lucky, smart as hell, or the good Lord loves you an awful lot!"

"Wait just a minute! Do I detect a religious affirmation from that self-proclaimed, worldly agnostic, Captain Charles Thatcher?"

"That Japanese *ack-ack* at minimum altitude is having an increasingly persuasive Christian influence in my life," agreed Thatcher.

"Amen, Brother! Come right on in and join the congregation!"

Fifteen minutes later everyone was dressed in full battle gear, and ready to be jeeped to the flight line.

"Where's that weapon's carrier?" said Johnson, walking nervously back and forth.

"Sit down and rest your ass," said Esty, "we're gonna get there soon enough anyway. The war's not going any place."

"What are you doing, Harrah?" asked Johnson.

"I'm writing my wife. What else would I be doing? Writing my Congressman to bitch about the chow?"

We all knew what he was doing. In the event he didn't make it back this afternoon, his wife would receive a letter telling her his last thoughts were of her and his family. From the look on his face, Johnson was sorry he had asked the question.

"What in the hell are we doing?" asked Kenney, in a suppressed tone of voice that only two or three sitting on nearby bunks could hear.

"Whatta you mean what are we doing?" asked Cronin, loud enough that the rest of the tent could hear.

"Here we are, scraping the bottom of the barrel to get eight good airplanes in flyable condition at the same time — and we don't even know yet whether our's is gonna be ready to fly or not — to hit Saigon, the biggest, most important, and most heavily defended target in this war!" said Kenney.

We don't need to be sitting here killing time, I thought to myself, *when we're ready to fly. This gives people time to think, and people going into combat don't need to think.* Where was our transportation to the flight line?

"What I wouldn't give for just twenty-five of those two hundred B-25s that are in perfect condition sittin' back there on the ramp at Columbia Army Air Base," volunteered Cronin with a far-off look in his eye.

"Yeah," added Esty, "and the pilots, navigators, and gunners to fly 'em."

"What kind of wish is that?" I asked. "If this is the time and the place to cash in our chips, then we're enough of a loss without taking no telling how many more airplanes and crews with us. Too many airplanes, and we'd be gettin' in each other's way. And if we live, the fewer the airplanes, the greater the accomplishment, and the bigger the honor."

"You can have the honor, Blount," responded Harrah, "I'll settle for my hide — in one piece."

"I don't wish for one more airplane or one more crew. And if it's a fight — and it's going to be a fight — " I went on, "well if I shouldn't make it back, then I've had the greatest honor that can be bestowed upon one man — to have flown, fought, and died with the finest and bravest men I've ever known."

There was silence in the pyramidal tent as everyone either gazed at the palm trees, or toward the beach and open sea from under the tent flaps. Some stared blankly at nothing, from reclining postures. No one looked at anyone. Only Cronin exhibited any movement as he traced aimless circles in the sand with his jungle knife.

"And those of us who live today and survive this war," I added, "are really gonna have a story to tell their grandchildren!"

"You're a damn romanticist, Blount," said Johnson, breaking the spell, "and you sure as hell better do more than romanticize that airplane in the harbor at Saigon today."

"No, he's not!" interrupted Thatcher, in a low, soft monotone, "and he's right! I've never wished for one more pilot, or one more airplane on any strike I've ever flown with this outfit. Sure, we've gotten the shit shot out of us, and we've had to hustle and scrounge to come up with eight battle-wearies to make this strike. Not even all the airplanes we flew down here yesterday held together long enough to make this strike today. But you are my friends, my buddies, and the best damn pilots in this man's Air Corps. I'd fly through hell with any one of you on my wing, and don't ever let me fly with the bastard who doesn't have the stomach to fly down the Jap's gun barrels! I wouldn't even want to die with that kind of a faint-hearted sonofabitch lookin' on!"

I would think of Thatcher's words as I eased the throttles forward and felt the surge of power from the Wright-Cyclones that brought old *199* to life, one more time, in response to my call, as she shook and shuddered down the metal runway and began the gradual climb toward Saigon!

CHAPTER TWELVE

Coup De Grâce At Saigon

True heroism consists in being superior to the ills of life in whatever shape they may challenge man to combat.

Napoleon

The weapon's carrier was overloaded and it paused briefly in front of each airplane to deposit its cargo of aerial artisans, who would make each aircraft an instrument of death and destruction. At the end of the line was *199,* showing her age (and tenacity) with her patched aluminum fuselage offering sobering testimony to the accuracy of the Jap gunners of earlier missions. Sergeant Albright, the ground crew chief, sat in the pilot's seat, with his left arm resting in the open window of the cockpit.

"If that's not a classic picture of a hot pilot, I'll eat your dog tags!" I said to Cronin.

"Clear left!" shouted the crew chief to a corporal who echoed the pronouncement while standing to the left, and in front of, the number one engine. The Wright-Cyclone engine belched smoke and thundered to life, shattering the otherwise peaceful dawn. Red streaks of the early morning silhouetted the palm-studded runway, and shimmered on the pilots' canopy and the top turret of the B-25. That airplane exuded character. A composite of the dedicated individuals who flew, repaired, serviced, and fought in her. She looked menacing and lethal sitting there at the edge of the runway, with her "doctor" giving her his last check before releasing her to her crew. All the ground crewmen were underneath and to the side of the engine, to make doubly sure no oil was leaking from the engine. The engine was revved to such a high pitch that we were forced to cover our ears. After about five minutes, Sergeant Albright cut the engine and climbed out of the airplane.

"You timed it just right," he said, "and we've completely reworked and overhauled that engine since our arrival last night. We made it in nine hours and forty-five minutes."

"We'd better hurry if we're gonna test-fly it before takeoff,' said Cronin, the careful copilot.

"We haven't got time to test hop it," I said, "if we're gonna get to Saigon with the rest of this outfit and rendezvous with those B-24s and P-38s."

"You're gonna take off and fly this airplane, that's had a major engine overhaul, across the China sea, and into nobody knows what kind of hell at Saigon, fifteen hundred miles over nothing but water, and you're telling me, that you're not gonna test-fly it to make sure it doesn't fall apart? Are you crazy?" yelled Cronin.

"What do you say, Sergeant Albright?" I asked.

"She's ready! I'd fly'er and never look back. In fact," he added, "I'll go with you if you'll let me."

"That's not necessary," said Warnick, monitoring the conversation, "when you fly with us, just on a joyride, we develop oil leaks. No telling what might go wrong if you flew a strike with us."

"Top off those tanks, Warnick, and let's make like a bird!" I said, while Cronin shook his head.

"When you start to look death in the face you start to notice and enjoy the simple things in life," mused Kenney, with his head turned so that his facial expression was hidden. "Simple things, like a leaf, or a sunset, a sunrise, the blue sky, or —"

Cronin couldn't believe what he was hearing and he gave me an incredulous, puzzled, look.

" . . . A well-turned pool cue, a full house when you've been losing all night, or fourteen straight passes without changing the dice . . ."

"I almost gave you credit for having some sense but I was mistaken," muttered Cronin, "as I usually am about you!"

When I ducked under the underbelly to climb into the airplane, Warnick was pulling the arming-pins on the five hundred-pound bombs in the open bomb bay. The bombs hung, two on each side of the fuselage walls, on bomb racks, and they looked ominous and foreboding. They were situated under the Tokyo tank that filled the top half of the bomb bay.

"If we didn't have to carry this extra gas in the Tokyo tank," said Warnick, "we could double our bomb load in the bomb bay and give Tojo twice as much fun."

"Four will be enough," I answered, "if we make each one count."

I stepped up into the cockpit, turned sideways, and squeezed into the solid steel "executive seat" reserved for the first pilot. The bright-colored knobs, levers, switches, the faces of all the instruments with their red and green lines, the ever-present smell of hydraulic fluid, the throat mike and headset, all welcomed me into a world I loved. (I can understand George Patton's mystic glee when he wrote his wife from Europe that "peace is going to be a hell of a let down.") Running checklists, setting altimeters, starting engines, taxiing to the end of the runway past the ground crewmen of other aircraft, who were all waving encouragement much like the groomsmen and stewards wished well their "Knights of Yore" as they rode into battle, was enough excitement for any man, and the ultimate in adventure. And this one was the biggest. Saigon! The Colonel had said so, and we had the B-24s and the P-38s to help us carry it out. I hoped I would feel the same at seventeen hundred hours that afternoon.

Flying the Colonel's left wing in the first flight, we were the third ship in line to take off. While we were stacked up on the end of the runway awaiting the signal for takeoff from the crude wooden control tower supporting a metal water tank that would've looked more natural next to a west Texas windmill, Cronin leaned over from the copilot's seat and made a motion with his hand to his left ear to listen in on the intercom.

"Radio gunner to the Navigator."

"Go ahead, Joe!" responded Kenney.

"Is this a round trip flight, Sir?"

"I don't know," replied Kenney, "I forgot to validate my ticket at the ticket counter before we left Operations. That's what happens when I get tied up with meaningless details of where we're flying, the distance, the target, location of *Lethal Dose,* our friendly submarine if we ditch, the compass headings, location of the enemy *ack-ack* positions, the wind direction and velocity, the weather report, and all my navigation equipment."

"My ticket says round trip," interrupted Warnick from the top turret, "and I'm ready to assist in any way possible to see this airplane delivered back to this airfield."

"Pilot to crew," I interrupted, "I don't fly 'em unless they're programmed for a round trip. And since we're not equipped with pontoons I'm planning on bringing this baby back to this very spot, just like a homing pigeon, about 1630 hours this afternoon."

"You're supposed to be on intership communication," chimed in Kenney.

"Our intercom must be acting up," I replied with tongue in cheek, clicking the mike in their ears a couple of times, "we better check it out when we get back, Zuber!"

"Roger, Lieutenant," said Zuber, from back in the waist at his radio position.

Colonel Coltharp, immaculate in his starched khakis, sat poker-faced, looking straight ahead, awaiting the signal to takeoff. "Kit Bag Leader to Squadron!" came his voice over the command radio, "I'll make a slow climbing 180-degree turn to the left. Follow me!"

"Roger! Roger!" came the replies.

Old "Fuzzy Balls" was Colonel Chester A. Coltharp, Jr., commanding officer of the 345th Bombardment Group, *Air Apaches* (medium bombers), V (Fifth) Bomber Command, Fifth Air Force, and he never personally led a strike unless it was something special. Colonel Coltharp, a native of Newport, Arkansas, had started out as CO of the 498th Bomb Squadron, and subsequently became commanding officer of the *Air Apaches* following the normal attrition of 345th Bomb Group COs. I judged the Colonel to be in his early thirties, very quiet, (even retiring) blond hair, observant eyes and always immaculately groomed; a real trick I was never able to accomplish with only Filipino houseboys and native women to do the laundry (with G.I. soap on the rocks and in the river) for a pack of cigarettes. He seemed exceedingly ambitious, but, when you were "the Colonel," with everyone falling over himself for you, and with no one above you except Fifth Bomber, you really couldn't prove positively or with certainty what a man was or what he felt. Perhaps all bird colonels just naturally wanted to become one-star generals even more than first class privates wanted to become corporals! What's more, his uniform was always free of perspiration, soil, and wrinkles when we returned from a mission, as if he had just returned from a reception for the general and hadn't even sat down. My uniform would be wet through and through from being plastered to my body with the fifty-pounds of flak suit and steel helmet. Maybe, like Superman, he didn't wear a flak suit. I'd been taught that men and mules sweat while ladies and women perspire. The colonel, seemingly did neither!

"What *is* he?" I voiced aloud.

"He has a sergeant who sweats for him," volunteered Nat Kenney.

"It might be," said little Ken Cronin, my copilot from Sheffield, Alabama, "that he stays cool and unwrinkled by not going after the biggest ship in the harbor!" Ken was alluding to the fact that we had been assigned the Number One target while leading the third flight.

On the steel mat runway there was no dust, as the propellers, in high pitch, started to whine, striking the air with a deafening, throbbing, roar. I gave Johnson, the second ship to take off, a thumbs up signal across the sixty feet that separated us, as Colonel Coltharp's aircraft rolled down the runway. Johnson returned the thumbs up gesture and his airplane followed in close pursuit, as Coltharp left the far end.

"Give me five degrees of flaps," I told Cronin, when Johnson reached the halfway mark, "and help me watch this number one engine for any sign of oil!"

As Johnson hit the three-quarter mark of the runway, I thrust the throttles forward and the *Touch O' Texas* came to life. The thundering sound of the Wright-Cyclones, with all thirty-five-hundred horses straining to overcome the forces that bound us to the earth, was deafening, but gradually faded to a steady roar as we picked up speed. The sound subsided into a steady hum as we rocketed off the end of the runway, overtaking, and passing our sound. The early morning air over the China sea was calm and it seemed we were motionless, sustained in midair and floating on a giant feather pillow. We were on Coltharp's left wing at thirty-five-hundred feet, and by the time we hit five thousand, all the squadron was in formation and headed for Saigon.

"Pilot to Engineer and Radio. Over."

"Roger! Roger!"

"Can y'all give me a reading on the number one engine? Over."

"I can't see anything. She's operating perfectly thus far, Lieutenant," replied Warnick.

"Not a trace of oil anywhere on the engine, Lieutenant!" reported Zuber.

"She's looking good from up here also," I replied. "Keep your eyes open and let us know something the moment you detect anything!"

"Roger! Roger!"

"What's the weather?" I asked Kenney.

"Generally good. Visibility about ten miles. Four- to five-tenths cumulus cloud coverage with the wind from two hundred-seventy degrees at about five knots."

"Navigation?" I asked.

"Dead reckoning and pilotage from reefs with log entries kept every thirty minutes."

"I thought we'd just home in on Saigon's *Tokyo Rose* Imperial radio show featuring Snotty Mitsubishi and his nine nasty nose pickers!"

"Wish we could latch on to a good, strong, Saigon radio beam," answered Kenney. "It'd sure save me a lot of work and worry looking for and trying to discover the Great Discovery Reef about two hundred and forty-five nautical miles out here in the China sea!"

"What's your fuel consumption estimate?"

"We're startin' with one thousand three hundred and thirty-nine gallons, and I figure two hundred-thirty gallons the first hour, one hundred-thirty gallons the second hour, one hundred and twenty-five gallons the third hour, one hundred gallons the fourth hour, and ninety gallons for the last five hours making a total of one thousand and thirty-five gallons for a nine-hour mission. Then, allowing two hundred gallons for any fluctuation, like flying full throttle over the target for fifteen minutes, we'll still have over a hundred gallons reserve, plus Warnick's extra forty gallons he claims he gets every time he tops off the tanks but which you can't count on."

"We're gonna be out here longer than nine hours today," I said, "you better figure on ten hours!"

"Ten hours will be no sweat, Lieutenant!" contributed Warnick, overhearing the discussion, "when I top off those tanks we pick up at least another thirty minutes!"

After we were out for an hour and a half, Kenney tapped me on the right shoulder. "Look over there," pointing off to the left side of the airplane, "that's a water spout!" Sure enough, there was a seldom seen weather phenomenon, a whirlwind-shaped tube of water extending vertically from the water's surface to two thousand or twenty-five-hundred feet into the air.

"You might fly the airplane through it if you'd like a quick wash job," said Kenney.

"I think I'll pass." I replied. "What's our ETA to Saigon?"

"Looks like 1105 hours if the wind stays constant."

At 1045 I asked Kenney to help me with the flak suit and helmet.

"How's the left engine?" Kenney looked toward it.

"Oil pressure, cylinder head temperature, and all other instruments normal and running like a clock! You can depend on Albright!" I replied. "Anyway, if it's not all right now, we're really up the creek!"

The coast of Indochina came up on the horizon as a thin line that grew quickly into a shoreline, and then the details of the countryside, with buildings, roads, and railroads, became visible. It was then 1107 hours, and I heard nothing on the intership radio from B-24s or P-38s! By then we should have been seeing smoke and fire from the target area, as a result of the B-24s high altitude assault, if not a visual sighting of the heavy four-engined airplanes. But everyone could be playing their cards right, for once, by maintaining absolute radio silence. Coltharp had taken us down gradually to fifteen hundred feet but we were getting too close to the target area to maintain this altitude, and preserve the element of surprise.

The peace and serenity of every target approached at minimum altitude, free of detection and catching the Nips asleep, afforded a beautiful and intimate observation of the enemy. At twenty feet you see the expression on a face, the fear in the eyes, the frantic dive for cover, the figures sprawling and crawling in the mud, all in the streaking fraction-of-a-second's-glance at an enemy taken completely by surprise. The feeling was good! It was when we had waited too long to get down on the deck, when we had blown our surprise, when the enemy knew we were coming and we felt all hell about to break loose with no place to hide — that's when we got sick! I had started to get sick!

Why doesn't the Colonel take us down on the deck? We're sittin' ducks up here! I said to myself. I had learned quickly that the ground, the trees, the natural or man-made obstacles, the topography and terrain were the best, closest and most appreciated friends of the strafers. This was a game of the quick and the dead and only the quick were still alive!

I had been amazed at the similarity of the flat, coastal plain and general appearance of Saigon and Houston, (Texas). With the flatness of this oriental coastal countryside, the 6,000-ton Japanese freighter I was looking for would have been as difficult to hide as the Shamrock Hotel, when it was first erected as an isolated edifice on the west plains of Houston by Glen McCarthy. These thoughts had been interrupted by ugly black puffs of heavy Japanese *ack-ack* that told us we had blown our surprise and that we were expected.

"Hello, Ping Pong Leader! Hello, Ping Pong Leader! This is Kit Bag Leader! Do you read me? Over!" It was Colonel Coltharp's voice breaking radio silence for the first time. This was the first inkling that the master attack plan for this strike had gone *kaput*. This entire blue-ribbon mission, suddenly and dramatically, started to smell.

"Hello, Ping Pong Leader! This is Kit Bag Leader! Do you read me? Over!" came Coltharp's second try.

"Hello, Kit Bag Leader! This is Ping Pong Leader! I read you loud and clear! Over!" came the P-38 leader's reply. I almost swallowed my heart that had lodged momentarily in my throat, when I thought we were alone with a hostile enemy harbor now alerted to receive us.

"Hello, Ping Pong Leader, this is Kit Bag Leader! We're five minutes north, northwest of the target at one thousand feet closing at two hundred-twenty miles per hour indicated. Where are you? Over!"

"Hello, Kit Bag Leader! This is Ping Pong Leader! We're at fifteen thousand feet, about twenty minutes from the target, running low on gas, and returning to base! Repeat!"

He didn't have to repeat that message. Everyone of the eight planes of the 501st Squadron, as well as each aircraft of the 499th Squadron hitting another target just north of the Saigon harbor, heard this sickening and gut-wrenching message.

"Repeat! We're running low on gas and must return to base! Over!"

"Running low on gas . . . or guts?" asked Cronin, monitoring the conversation and yelling in my ear.

"Roger, Ping Pong Leader! This is Kit Bag Leader! Over and Out!"

At that moment an unidentified voice of one of our 501st pilots broke in: "Hope you pea-shooter bastards have enjoyed drawing your combat flight pay today! Do a barrel roll and go on back home while we win the war!" Eloquent silence. He very definitely had supporters from all other seven squadron pilots.

Coltharp had taken us north of the target and we now turned south toward Saigon and destiny. There were no B-24s to soften up the target, there were no P-38s to help strafe, share the enemy flak, or fly top cover! This was just another mission, with just us against the entire Japanese world of war in the Saigon area! Ordinarily we would have the element of surprise but we had been flying around the area for ten minutes advertising our presence and alerting every enemy gun within fifty miles while waiting and trying to locate our help! At that moment I started sweating profusely from the heat and the fear! The name of that mission could now be spelled s-u-i-c-i-d-e!

As we approached the city of Saigon from the north, Colonel Coltharp gave a hand signal and everyone went into battle formation. Johnson stayed on Coltharp's right wing, I moved over to the far left, and Townsley moved up from the second flight on my right wing. Thatcher, leading the second flight, moved to the right of Coltharp with Harrah flying his wing, and Esty lead the fourth flight, bringing up the rear, with Jones flying his wing.

Arriving over the city at two hundred feet altitude the

flak, small, medium, and heavy, from every direction and location, was so intense you could have walked on it! Coltharp strafed and dropped two bombs destroying a heavily camouflaged two-hundred-ton engine-aft freighter on the north bank of the Saigon River. His next attack was on a five-hundred-ton freighter transport anchored off the west bank of the Saigon River. He dropped one bomb which hit the ship on the deck amidships, and skipped off into the water on the other side; but it still destroyed the ship. He continued south, and made a run on one of two freighter transports docked on the south bank of the River. Coltharp dropped his last bomb, scoring a direct hit and sinking this ship. The Colonel sustained flak damage that severed the right rudder control cable and removed him from the fight.

Captain Thatcher, leading the second flight, started his run by strafing the five big Socony Oil tanks that set them afire and caused an explosion with large sheets of fire and black smoke. He then strafed a flak tower just past the oil tanks and dropped two bombs for near misses at a small engine-aft freighter in the Saigon Navy Yards. As he proceeded off the target, he sank a five-hundred-ton freighter transport near the north shore of the Saigon River mouth.

Lieutenant Harrah, flying on Captain Thatcher's wing, started his run by heavily strafing the Socony Oil tanks and the flak tower to the south. He was hit head-on by a blast of forty-millimeter flak from the south bank of the Saigon River. This flak blew a hole eighteen-inches in diameter in Harrah's plane, just behind the auxiliary gas tank, which cut the left aileron control cables, destroyed all aileron trim tab control and shot off half the flaps. Lieutenant Harrah salvoed his bombs and kept right on strafing everything in his path, until he crossed the Dong Nai River and rejoined the formation.

It was impossible to determine what a target would look like, and be able to recognize landmarks, from a vertical profile perspective — when you'd only seen them through a magnifying glass on a high altitude photo reconnaissance picture, taken from twenty thousand feet. At ground level all perspective changes. Even a bend in the Saigon River (as large and wide as it can be) was difficult to ascertain at twenty feet and at high speed. Add to that the confusion of approaching a large city at treetop level, and at three hundred miles per hour.

Seeking out, finding, and destroying one particular target, even one as long as a football field, can be difficult. This was my problem as I veered left, giving Townsley plenty of room to move up on my right wing. Now it was my war, my strike, my business, and my own ingenuity as to how I carried it out. This was the way I wanted it! This was the only way we had a chance!

"Pilot to crew! Everybody alert! Watch for fighters above and coming out of the sun, Warnick, and strafe everything straight ahead with me. Cover our tails, Zuber, and pay particular attention to everything we go over after strafing and bombing it! Make 'em keep their heads down and don't give 'em a chance to track us on the breakaway! Treat everything like it's a coiled rattlesnake. We're flying out of here just like we came in — in one piece. Kick 'em in the balls!"

I saw the big oil tanks, with Socony on the sides in giant letters, bearing moot testimony to our free enterprise system that the enemy was now enjoying. I could see Thatcher and Harrah working them over with their forward guns, and I hoped they would totally destroy them. I derived a special kind of satisfaction from the destruction of anything that had originally been ours, and that the enemy was now using for their own purposes.

Townsley was now on my wing. I opened the bomb bay doors, and simultaneously opened up with all twelve nose guns on a small, camouflaged, engine-aft freighter. The armor-piercing incendiaries did their work well as I used our first bomb. I pulled up to seventy-five feet altitude, still looking for the target that was designated as Number One, although it could have been halfway to Singapore by then, or hidden in another part of the harbor. I sighted it at the same moment Townsley took a burst of flak.

There she sat! Precisely where the high altitude photo-reconnaissance pictures, taken less than 24 hours before, showed the 6,000 ton Japanese freighter to be moored.

That was April 28, 1945, and the 6,000-ton freighter of the *Fox Tare Baker* class, the Number One target of the first low level, minimum altitude strike against Saigon, Indochina, in World War II, rode the waves in silent splendor.

The big ship, empty and moored in the bend of the river about two miles in front of us, looked like she was sitting on the wide open, sprawling river plain at least forty feet out of the water, and she looked as big as the Settles Hotel, ten stories high in the center of downtown Big Spring, Texas. The enemy *ack-ack* continued to track and haunt us as I took evasive action to the left and went back down on the treetops in an attempt to protect my wingman.

How bad was Townsley hit? What should I do? The assigned target was only seconds away and I was moving at three hundred miles per hour! Indecision, at such a moment, is the wrong decision. I glanced across the short airspace that separated us, and the expression on Townsley's face was one of determination. Both fans of his airplane were turning with no visible smoke, although there was plenty from the enemy flak that was concentrated all around us. Two strings of tracers, now joined by two more from different directions, started to converge on the cockpit, but passed over the top of the airplane at the last moment! Our target was anchored against the west bank of the river, in exactly the same position our latest high altitude reconnaissance photos had showed it to be. It didn't take an Albert Einstein to understand that if a ship of that size remained in the same location for twenty-four hours, inside or outside the Saigon harbor, you could bet your life that every antiaircraft gun within twenty miles was zeroed in above that ship.

If it's to be, it's up to me, I thought, *and if I don't make it, no one has ever been blessed with a finer, richer twenty years of life.* That was the moment of truth that I had thought through, had prayed through, many times before — and I was ready!

As fate would have it, there was a quarter-mile or more of trees, fifty to sixty feet in height, growing in a perfect line along the east bank that followed the meander of the river, turned slightly north, and across the river from where our target was moored. Those trees, which could never be located or identified on the photo reconnaissance pictures, were miraculously, and directly, in our line of flight, and could provide the cover behind which we could hide to keep us from detection until the last possible moment. *If they can't see you, they damn sure can't shoot you!* was an old strafer truism of Bill Bell's that came to mind. This could give us those precious last three or four seconds, before we exposed ourselves to the Japanese gunners. The only critical aspect of that plan was that from those trees to the ship, there was a quarter- to- one-half mile of open water, and during that time we would be a big sitting duck, with nothing to hide behind but our fear!

As we pulled up to clear the trees, I glanced at Townsley out of the corner of my eye, and I said *You're too high! Get it down!*

I pointed the nose of our airplane down to within twelve inches of the placid, dirty water of the Saigon River, and hoped he would follow. That was the last time I saw Townsley, as the most intense antiaircraft fire I'd ever experienced opened up. Then I knew how a quail must feel, flushed from its cover of the brush it was using as protection when it flies into the open. As we exploded from behind the trees and made our appearance over the River, the antiaircraft fire met us with such intensity I jerked, and ducked instinctively, to miss the explosion I thought would hit me. The heavy flak was fired in front of, and around us, raising huge geysers of water, which, should we hit one of these gigantic columns of water, would be every bit as fatal as flying into a brick wall. I pushed the throttles to the firewall in an attempt to get all the speed possible from the engines. From the water's surface the ship looked larger than before, and I determined to fly the bombs into this ship, to make absolutely certain that it would no longer remain in the service of Hirohito. If, in fact, I made it to the ship before being shot down.

I pulled up to twenty feet altitude about eye-level with the deck, and dropped my first bomb one hundred twenty-five- to - one hundred-yards short. The bomb skipped up and into the side of the transport on the starboard side, opposite the bridge. Four seconds later it opened a hole the size of a cavern in the side of the ship. As I started to pull up I dropped my second bomb. It fell directly into the well deck between the bridge and the engine room and exploded four seconds later, after we'd traveled into the inland harbor. It completely gutted the huge freighter, with the third and last bomb exploding in the water between the ship and the shore. The ship was sunk and totally destroyed.

Warnick and I had been strafing the ship continuously from the time we pulled up over the trees. With my bombs dropped, I was so low that I dipped my left wing to pass between the twin masts, simultaneously pulling up the nose of the airplane to avert flying into the ship. At full throttle, this rocketed the airplane five hundred feet into the air. As a result, the major portion of a fusillade of heavy antiaircraft fire that would have otherwise blown us out of the sky, passed under our tail. Enough of the flak, however, found its mark, and half of the right elevator and right trim tab were shot off completely.

Lieutenant Johnson, flying on Colonel Coltharp's wing, dropped his first bomb at a five hundred-ton freighter, and his last three bombs at a twenty-three-hundred ton freighter transport, docked at the main wharves on the south bank of the river. The first fell short, the second skipped up to the waterline, and the third bounced up on the deck. The ship was loaded with ammunition or other explosives, and it blew up with a violent explosion, and immediately disappeared as if it had never existed. Lieutenant Johnson was hit by a massive flak burst of heavy calibre coming off his attack on this ship, and his right engine caught fire. The crippled airplane climbed to one thousand feet altitude where it drew the attention of every enemy gun in the Saigon harbor! At that moment a *Zero* got on his tail, and had fired three long bursts at the airplane before I could come to his rescue.

"Warnick! You and Zuber take care of the *Zero* on Johnson's tail!" I yelled into the intercom as I came up on his left wing. The flak continued to explode above and to the sides of us in heavy black puffs as the *Zero* was driven off.

"Johnson! Johnson!" I yelled into the intership radio. "Get out! Bail out! Get out of that airplane!" As I closed to within fifty feet of the cockpit, we could not see anyone at the controls. Like a ghost ship that seemingly was flying itself, both the pilot and the copilot had taken a direct hit from a massive round of explosive flak, that either blew them out of their seats or caused them to slump over and out of sight.

"Get out! Bail out Johnson! Do you hear me? Over!" I continued to try to reach someone, anyone, in the doomed plane. The fire that started in the right engine, had now spread over the length of the entire wing and into the fuselage, so that the airplane was now completely enveloped in fire. I stayed with the intensely burning B-25 down to two hundred feet, at which altitude a crewman attempted to bail out. The plane was so low that his chute never had a chance to open.

We were being tracked with heavy and accurate *ack-ack,* having exposed ourselves at such altitude for such an extended period of time. I put the airplane in a dive for the river, and the safety of the trees or other cover. Immediately in front of me was a small boat at the river's edge, and the figure of a man broke and started to run up the steep bank. Infuriated, angry with the fate of Lieutenant Johnson and my friends, I turned the wrathful firepower of all my guns on the figure, and he disintegrated.

"How are things back there, Zuber?" I asked, as the *ack-ack* continued to track us.

"I'm all right, Lieutenant!" replied Zuber, "but that last burst of flak shot off the right elevator just twelve inches from my head here in the tail turret! I'm glad it wasn't an explosive round. AND HERE IT COMES AGAIN! Do something QUICK!"

I put the nose down and back on the deck, as three heavy bursts appeared where we had been, and from where we had just removed ourselves!

Lieutenant Esty, leading the fourth flight behind me, was hit by a heavy burst of *ack-ack,* and a stream of tracers was seen to converge on his plane as he opened up all his guns on the first target he attacked. He probably saw the guns, as we frequently did, that got him before he could get them. He simply didn't fly down their gun barrels quickly enough. *A fate that ultimately will befall all of us,* I thought, *if we continue to fly these suicidal sorties.* His plane caught fire immediately, exploded, and crashed with no survivors.

Lieutenant Jones, flying Lieutenant Esty's right wing, opened up with all his guns on the revetment from which had come the heavy *ack-ack* that shot down his flight leader. Crossing the river, he spotted a two hundred-fifty-ton, engine-aft freighter, which he strafed and dropped one bomb into, destroying that vessel. Lieutenant Jones then dropped a bomb among *ack-ack* positions located in a group of buildings on the south bank of the Saigon River, and heavily strafed a patrol craft. He dropped his last two bombs for near misses, at a five hundred-ton freighter transport that had previously been put in a sinking condition by Coltharp. He continued strafing warehouses and buildings across the remaining part of the target.

My flight path, following my attempt to assist Lieutenant Johnson, took me over the main part of the Saigon harbor. Suddenly, there were six huge warehouses on the south bank of the river in front of me. Once again I pushed the lethal nose of *199* down, and strafed the warehouses heavily, leaving them burning from my incendiaries. Dropping back to the treetops, I spotted a large ship which appeared to be in dry dock, and under construction or repair. With the first burst of the lethal fifties, a human figure suddenly appeared on the deck of the ship as the fifty caliber incendiaries continued their relentless march up and into the target. Like a developing snapshot, the image frozen into mind and memory, the figure appeared to be transformed into a grotesque mannequin, suspended in air, with arms hanging limp and a massive, bloody hole where a stomach and chest had been only a moment before. The incendiaries had exploded through the figure at point-blank range, and the aircraft, now travelling in excess of 350 mph, passed over the ship before the figure could crumple and fall.

Walking the rudder pedals to fantail the airplane and cover a greater area with my fifties, I pulled back on the steering column to gain the necessary altitude to clear the ship upon completion of my strafing run. No matter how much muscle I gave it, too much of the elevator controls had been shot away to facilitate the climbing maneuver I was trying to initiate. The distance was too short, the speed too great, and the damage to the control surfaces too massive. I was still frantically wrestling with the controls when a dull *thud*, accompanied by a sound like a jackhammer on steel plating, announced our collision with the mast of the target. What I was soon to learn, was that I had knocked out two cylinders, had torn the cowling from the right engine, opened a hole a foot in diameter in the lower left side of the right engine, caved in the right side of the right engine nacelle, and had also torn a ten-inch jagged hole in the leading edge of the right horizontal stabilizer. The stabilizer was now holding a seven-foot section of the mast that I had just hit, and there was only twelve inches of metal in the stabilizer to hold the entire right side of the tail section onto the airplane! This damage, coupled with half the right elevator that had already been shot away, left me with an airplane that more nearly resembled, and handled, like a bucking horse.

We left Saigon harbor, and the landing strip at Palawan was only seven hundred-fifty nautical miles straight ahead, over nothing but the water of the China sea. The vibration was so intense that it threatened to tear the airplane apart. The racket of loose objects banging around inside the airplane and bouncing off the sides of the metal walls of the fuselage and flight deck, reminded me of the uncontrolled ambulation of the friendly drunks of the 501st, three hours into a prayer meeting. I almost laughed at the thought of Phillips or Thatcher, suddenly thrust into the cockpit of this wild and violent beast, while deeply under the influence — and the comical, sobering effect I knew it would have upon them!

"What's so funny?" asked Cronin, leaning over with a strained and worried look on his face.

"Nothing!" I replied, "I just had a thought."

"There's not a damn humorous thing about any of this," answered the obviously nervous copilot who, like the rest of us, was still in a state of shock from what we had been exposed to for the last fifteen minutes.

"Aren't you scared?" asked Cronin.

"Always!" I answered. "And I still am!"

"Pilot to crew! Let's have a damage assessment!" I spoke into the intercom, still wrestling a steering column that had a case of the Saint Vitus dance.

Everyone spoke at once.

"Wait a minute!" I said. "One at a time. What do we have in the right engine, Warnick?"

"I think we must've hit the mast of that last ship with the propellers on the right engine. It threw that three-bladed five hundred-pound fan out of balance — otherwise we wouldn't be vibrating and bucking the way we are!"

"I think a lot of that is our speed," I answered. "I'm trying to dissipate that slowly, to relieve the tension on those damaged control surfaces. That should help the bucking and smooth out the ride considerably!" Sure enough, when I had slowed the airplane to one hundred-sixty miles per hour indicated, the slower airspeed cured a lot of the roughness, but it was still flying with a porpoise up-and-down motion and the controls were visibly jumping in my hand.

"Everyone stay awake! We're still vulnerable to enemy fighters and they'd love to jump on this cripple.

"What else, Warnick?" I asked.

"That's all I can see from the top turret for the time being."

"Stay up there. Keep your eyes peeled for fighters. We need you more as a gunner now than as an engineer. Until we get more of this air and water between us and Saigon!" I added.

"What do you have in the tail, Zuber?"

"Just the right elevator shot away, and all the trim tab controls!" came the answer. "We also have a seven-foot length of that mast we hit. It's back here lodged in the right horizontal stabilizer — which is doing a great job of filling up the hole it made."

"You can have it as a keepsake. Something to remember this mission by, if you want it!"

"I wouldn't touch it, even if I could," answered Zuber. "When it comes out I don't know what's gonna hold the whole right side of the tail section on the airplane!" We didn't have long to wait to find out! The airplane continued to vibrate and shake so intensely that the length of Jap ship mast was shaken from its mooring and fell into the China sea below.

We were an airplane flying a tightrope. The rope was swaying, back and forth, and if we lost our balance for even a second, all could be lost.

"I hate to ask, but do you have a heading for Palawan?" I asked Kenney.

"Thought you'd never ask," he replied, "try ninety-five degrees. Think you can hold the heading?"

"I should be able to hold it within five degrees!"

"You and Teddy Roosevelt have a lot in common, you know!" said Kenney.

"Yeah! How's that?" I asked, still battling the controls.

"The way you're flyin' this rough ridin' son-of-a-gun!"

Cronin looked out the window with a pained expression on his face.

"You're gonna have to loosen up, Cronin," I said, "you can't stay tense and nervous! Airplanes are like horses, if they know you're nervous they're gonna try to throw you everytime! You gotta relax and let 'em know you're not scared!"

"You're both wacky!" exclaimed Cronin. "Both of you are out of your heads!"

"Will this heading help us rediscover the Great Discovery Reef?"

'Yeah! It better! If this thing holds together that long," he answered, "that's just two hundred nautical miles straight ahead!"

"I think I was right!"

"How's that?" said Kenney.

"We're gonna be out on this one longer than nine hours!"

"I don't care if it's twelve hours, just so long as it's not for eternity and you don't get our feet wet!" he said.

Once again I weighed and analyzed our situation. I thanked the Good Lord that we were over the open China sea, the weather was good, ten to twenty miles visibility, and very little turbulence to aggravate further a dismal situation. What if we were nursing that ruptured duck through the mountainous jungles of Luzon, playing hide and seek with mountain tops, and flying instruments through pea soup. Call it fate, call it luck; but I chose to call it what it was — the answer to prayer!

For the next two hours it was touch and go as the airplane defied the smooth flight that skill can ordinarily remedy. The engine instruments continued to reflect efficient operation, and the original trouble experienced with the left engine, had been forgotten hours ago. Trouble, I realized, was relative. The full significance of the suspected loss of my wingman, the control surfaces shot away by the Jap *ack-ack,* and the damage sustained as a result of hitting the mast of the enemy ship began to soak into my consciousness. I didn't really mind the anxiety produced by the jumpy controls which, at times, called for both my hands to hold the airplane on a steady course. Such activity demanded my constant attention, and prevented any conscious thought about what we had endured only a few hours before. It was just as well that I didn't know there were only two threadlike wires that remained operative and were continuing to carry the spark from the magnetos to two of the cylinders in the right engine, as the result of the collision with the enemy mast. If both of these last, minute, wires failed, the two cylinders would have filled with oil and then burst, with the resulting loss of the engine. I didn't learn about this disastrous flight condition for another two- and a-half hours, at which time apoplexy almost rendered me helpless at the realization of how quickly our damaged aircraft would have been swallowed by the China sea, if it had been forced to attempt flight on a single engine.

I was filled with a great awareness of our airplane; it had become a projection of my personality, my determination, my spirit, and myself. As that haggard and damaged collection of steel and aluminum limped through the clear air above the China sea, I realized how much I loved her. That airplane, in which we had missed a midair collision climbing out of a socked-in valley in northern Luzon by less than fifteen feet. That airplane, that sustained a burst of flak from an enemy ship on the China coast, had then flown us home across the seemingly endless expanse of water of the China sea — smoking all the way, but never giving up. That airplane, that had flown through the tops of the tall trees guarding the extremely high bank of a river where the Japs were dug in, on a ground support mission north of Manila; the airplane that had sustained flak holes on every mission, and increasingly looked like a patch-work quilt with all the bright, unpainted aluminum squares that covered the flak holes all over her. Then, on that day, she had survived the fiercest, most accurate antiaircraft fire ever seen in the history of the 501st squadron; the airplane with a heart so big that even when she could not pull up, and collided with the mast of an enemy ship, her propellers kept turning, and she kept flying! She had to be a very special lady. How did she do it? What special powers did she possess? These thoughts went through my mind as I continued to guide and assist her through the calm air as she continued to struggle in her damaged condition, like something alive and breathing, to take us home.

We had been out nine hours and thirty-eight minutes when we sighted the strip at Palawan. There was much rejoicing. I hadn't realized how tense and concerned everyone had been until a shout or two went up, barely audible above the roar of the overworked engines. There were smiles on the faces of everyone.

"Fire a red flare, Warnick," I said into the intercom, "so that we can make a straight in approach!"

My problem was to line up with the runway and be right the first time. There would be no going around for a second try if we missed. For the last three hours I had flown at one hundred-sixty miles per hour indicated to relieve the vibration as much as possible. Approaching the end of the strip for landing, I accelerated my airspeed to one hundred seventy-five miles per hour in a maneuver I thought necessary to hold the nose up and, hopefully, to prevent snapping off the nose wheel thereby standing us on our ear halfway down the runway.

I had never flown an airplane so damaged before. By experimentation from Saigon I knew what was necessary to satisfy the demands of flight in a straight and level attitude. What was going to happen when I put the nose down, lowered the wheels and flaps, increased the airspeed, and changed the aerodynamic conditions? The only thing we would be assured of was that the vibration would increase and the rolling, porpoise effect would probably return. We didn't know.

When the landing gear, along with the flaps, came down what would happen? What would the tremendous drag of the wheels do? One hundred-sixty miles an hour was normal approach speed, with touchdown to the runway at one hundred-twenty. But now? How much warning would there be if the elevators were not effective and operative? Should I make a steeper descent on my approach?

I forced the crippled airplane into a slipshod descent that I felt not even a Primary flying student would take pride in. I tried to ignore the vibrating and buffeting. This was just another approach, I tried to tell myself. Things were just going to happen faster and more radically.

The Palawan strip was cut through the palm trees and jungle, and making a straight in approach. I didn't know whether I was coming in downwind, crosswind, or into the wind. At any rate, there was no choice. One runway — and you landed coming in from the open sea; the Saigon end. From a thousand feet I began my approach.

"Wheels down," I told Cronin, never taking my eyes from the runway and the instruments, "and twenty degrees flaps." As the wheels and flaps started down, the airplane went crazy as it attempted something I recalled from the dim dark past of my earliest flight experience: an aborted snap roll. With nerves that were frayed and reflexes drawn tighter than a bowstring, my hands and feet moved by instinct to make physical corrections that reduced the emergency from a damaged airplane in a steep bank, to one in a lesser bank, but still heading for the palm trees to the right of the runway at eight hundred feel altitude.

"Wheels and flaps up. *Everything up!* QUICK!" I shouted. Changing the shape of the damaged air foils made the airplane glide like a rock. As I eased back to the left, banking ever so slightly to realign the airplane with the runway, I decided this landing would be made hot without any flaps. Our speed was up to one hundred seventy-five miles an hour, with the increased vibration and shaking threatening to tear the airplane apart. It was less speed and less vibration or more speed and more control. I feared the inability to control the airplane without sufficient airspeed. I elected the latter,which I felt was the lesser of the two evils.

"Wheels down!" I yelled, and held my breath. I concentrated on the controls like a stalking cat poised to pounce on a mouse.

"Wheels down!" parroted Cronin from force of habit, but with a hesitancy in his voice, like he was tiptoeing on egg shells.

Our airspeed dropped off alarmingly to one hundred fifty-five miles an hour as the massive drag of the wheels took effect, and the airplane became a giant pendulum; a body suspended in space, swinging freely to and fro under the partially controlled action of gravity. I quickly advanced the throttles to full power, increasing our airspeed to one hundred-seventy miles per hour and simultaneously leveled the wings, neutralizing the pendulum rock, and getting lined up with the runway. At that speed I didn't know if there would be enough real estate to handle this runaway bowling ball down the ever-narrowing, telescoping, bowling alley ahead.

I flew the airplane onto the metal runway and the tin roof racket was the sweetest music I'd ever heard. We hit hard and the *Touch O' Texas* belched and backfired as she stayed there with no further objection. I cut the power immediately and got on the brakes. I was thankful for the transition that changed that nineteen tons of vibrating, shaking mass of metal from a bird to a groundling. I used all the runway and finally braked her to a stop just short of the jungle!

"Good afternoon, Palawan!" said Cronin, in a half-whispered, prayerful tone of voice.

"Wave your magic wand in Palawan!" crowed Kenney. Although the vibration had stopped, I continued to sweat, vibrate, and tingle. I didn't know if this was a carryover from the airplane's condition for the past five hours, or whether it was the result of fear and frayed nerves. I decided it was a combination of both.

When a final assessment was made by A-2 at Fifth Bomber Command of reconnaissance photos taken following our strike, it was shown that this had been a great blow struck for our Allied Forces in their war against Japan. The 501st Squadron *Black Panthers* had buried their fangs in the Nips for a total kill of six merchant ships destroyed, and had badly mauled and damaged an additional three vessels.

"I knew we would make it!" stated Cronin in a confident tone of voice that he hadn't exhibited since we had begun the run on the target at Saigon.

"Your vicissitude amazes me," I remarked.

"My what?"

"Your vicissitude," repeated Kenny.

"Whatsit mean? Confident?" asked Cronin.

"That's it! You got it! Brave! Unafraid!" I replied, and winked at Kenney.

"Listen! I was plenty scared! My life started to pass before my eyes!" said Cronin.

"That's good! I love a parade!" responded Kenney.

"You had lots of company," I said, "and now I know how old Joshua and Jerusalem felt!"

"How's that?" asked Kenney.

"Like a burning stick pulled out of the fire! Surely that was covered in chapel at Baylor at some time or another?"

"I'm sure it was, but maybe I slept through that one," he answered. "But I can tell you one thing! After today I'll never go to sleep in church again!"

The engines were quiet. The tow truck, like an aerial funeral hearse, quickly attached itself to the front wheel of *199* and began a slow, mournful, pace toward the parking area. The silence and stillness of the metal monster that only moments before had been a wild, violent mastodon, was now a silent, affectionate friend for whom we had inexpressible appreciation. That which might have been our coffin had now become our liberator; that which could have destroyed us, had now delivered us.

Unknown to me we were the last airplane to land. I

counted five airplanes of the 499th. *They all made it back,* I said to myself. As we were towed past four airplanes of the 501st I saw Sergeant Albright waving us to the end of the line. As *199* was swung around and pulled up in line on the end, a sober-faced Sergeant Albright dropped his hands, signaling the truck to stop. The ground crew was immediately all over the airplane, assessing the damage and making ready to put her in the service squadron for repair. I reached for the Form I in the pocket next to the pilot's seat and started to fill it out to the sweet music of the whirring gyros starting to wind down. Whirring gyros, which couldn't be heard when the engines were running, were always a beautiful sound, signalling the end of a mission. They had never sounded more beautiful, nor been more appreciated than that day.

"What's the official time?" I asked Kenney.

"1605!" he replied.

"This one was nine hours and forty-eight minutes."

"Seemed more like nine days," responded Warnick.

As I climbed down the ladder and touched the ground, I felt an overwhelming desire to get on my knees, kiss the ground, and say a prayer. I'd already been praying for five hours, and I controlled the urge to kiss the sandy ground on which I stood, although it didn't make me appreciate the *terra firma* any less.

"How did the number one engine operate?" inquired Sergeant Albright.

"Like a fine watch! But it was the number two engine that I was afraid of!"

"I've seen it. What happened?" asked Albright.

"We tried to turn a Jap ship over with the right engine!" interjected Cronin.

"Yeah! We were out of bombs and decided to just ram it, but the mast broke in two," added Kenney. "We thought the prop would chew it up but we couldn't even hit the mast with the propeller! Blount put that mast right between two of those three blades on that right propeller!"

"Truth is, I'm such a dern sorry pilot that I couldn't pull the airplane up to get over the mast," I added.

"Truth is, it was my fault," chimed in Cronin, "that's what the copilot is s'posed to do, pull the airplane out of anything the pilot is about to hit!" Everybody tried to share the blame as if it made any difference. The bottom line was, pure and simple, we were thankful to be alive!

"You're in better shape than the three we lost today!" said Albright.

"We lost three airplanes today?" I echoed in disbelief, "then we're the last and final plane?"

"And we didn't know whether you were gonna make it or not, according to what the other ships had to report," said Sergeant Albright, "until we saw your red flare and the airplane coming in!"

"Who did we lose?" I inquired.

"Lieutenants Esty, Johnson, and Townsley," replied Albright.

"We stayed with Lieutenant Johnson until he crashed in flames, but we didn't know about Esty or Townsley for sure," I said.

"Lieutenant Townsley was with us going in on the big ship," spoke up Zuber, "but I think he got that big burst of flak in one engine that we missed most of when we pulled up to miss the masts. Townsley's plane did a snap roll right on the deck when they lost the engine, and they went in on their back. That burst of flak that shot off half of our right elevator and all the trim tab just missed my head in the tail turret by about twelve inches."

Of the eight B-25s of the 501st that had taken off from the Palawan airstrip at 0635 hours, only five had returned. Of the five, flown by Colonel Coltharp, Captain Thatcher, and Lieutenants Harrah, Jones and myself, only Thatcher's and Jones's airplanes were still flyable. The five aircraft of the 499th had faired much better, hitting a target north of Saigon and all had returned intact. Colonel Coltharp quickly determined that the two flyable airplanes, along with the five 499th aircraft, would be serviced immediately and would proceed to return to Clark Field, providing transportation for all flying personnel of damaged and unflyable aircraft.

"I'd like you and your crew to fly with me, Lieutenant Blount," said Colonel Coltharp, who had commandeered one of the 499th Squadron's airplanes. "Get your gear together and meet me back here as soon as possible!"

"Thank you, Colonel!" I replied, "we'll be right back!"

We all climbed into the waiting weapon's carrier to be ferried to our temporary double pyramidal tent, where we had slept the night before between dashes to the bomb shelters. The empty bunks and personal items of clothing and toiletries of Lieutenants Esty, Johnson, Townsley, their copilots and navigators, bore stark evidence to the fact they were gone, never to return. All of them, who had been there only last night, all of us walking barefooted along the sandy beach in the brilliant moonlight like school kids, discussing this mission, right here in this tent this morning, now gone forever. An extra pair of boots under Esty's bunk. *Did he change his mind and decide to wear another pair?* A khaki shirt on Coyle's bunk. This one looked clean and unsoiled. *Did he decide to wear the shirt he wore yesterday, flying down from Clark Field?* All the toiletries, razor, shaving cream, toothbrush, toothpaste, shaving lotion, laid out in neat order just as they had been left by Townsley that morning. He had left them there laying on his towel where they could dry, where they could be easily gathered up and placed in his toilet kit, before returning to Clark Field in the afternoon. *How desolate. How lonesome. How grievously sad.* I hurried to gather my gear together, to get into the weapon's carrier, and to get back to the flight line. As if distance would erase the sadness of the memory of those friends.

Back at the flight line both Zuber and Warnick had returned with the first load of enlisted personnel and were busy storing their gear in the back of the B-25 in which we were flying back to Clark Field. Zuber was standing under the tail, as Warnick disappeared into the interior of the airplane.

"Did you ever finish that book on fear?" I asked Zuber. I was speaking about a book I had accidentally seen when it fell out of his duffle bag, when we boarded the SS *General Anderson* troop ship in San Francisco bay before coming overseas.

"No, I've been too scared!" he answered, "and I haven't stopped shaking since we got our right elevator shot off this morning!"

"I thought maybe I'd ask you to loan it to me for a day or two," I said, "I really need it after today!"

"There are some things I'll never understand, Lieutenant!" he said.

"What's that, Joe?"

"Tech Sergeant Henry Wreden! My good friend and the engineer gunner on Lieutenant Esty's crew that got shot down almost before they even reached the target today. Last night we were swimming right down there on that beautiful beach in the moonlight together. And he was so confident that nothing was gonna happen to him, that he made me confident too! He was indestructible! He had ditched, he had bailed out, he had suffered a concussion from a bomb explosion. And now, they finally got him at Saigon today! How? Why?" asked Sergeant Joe Zuber, with a concerned, confused, and strained look on his face.

"I don't know, Joe! I don't know why!" I answered.

"Whose fault was it, Lieutenant?"

"Nobody! Everybody!" I answered.

Warnick returned from the inside of the B-25. "Did you top off the tanks of this airplane after the ground crew finished fillin' her up?" I asked.

"Yes, sir! Any airplane our crew flies in, the tanks get topped off by me!"

"We're still seven hundred-fifty miles from home, so we want to be ready for any emergency!" I said. With the arrival of Colonel Coltharp, we were airborne, and we tolerated the easy flight back to Clark Field. I was oblivious to the engines' roar, while consumed by the massive sorrow over lost friends, and with an introspective examination of my nervousness and feelings as I said a fervent prayer of thanks.

As we were unloaded, with all our gear, in front of Squadron operations tent at Clark Field, Lyman came running toward the weapon's carrier.

"Your orders came through this morning sending you back to the States and West Point!" he said, excited to be bearing glad tidings.

"There are times I don't think your elevator goes all the way to the top," I responded, "so don't kid me about something this important."

"I'm dyin' if I'm lyin'!" answered Lyman.

"I guess that cancels our rest leave into Manila," I grinned.

"I'll sure understand if you'd rather go home than go to Manila on a three-day rest leave with me!" answered Lyman.

"I would've thought you'd have figgered some way to get Doc Marcus to send you home with me!" I replied.

"I've tried everything I know, but that old sawbones is too damned smart!" he responded. "But I'm not gonna stop trying!"

Confirming with Operations that Lyman had in fact told me the truth, and that I had been ordered stateside "on the earliest air transportation available," I set in motion the checking out process to leave the first thing the following morning. It was a mad dash — checking in bedding, my .45 automatic, distributing my sheets, toiletries, and other hard-to-obtain items to Kenney, Stiles and friends, and saying goodbye.

"We're glad to see you go," said Sergeant George Blackwell, Operations Clerk in charge of the Combat Points records of all flying personnel. "You know you've set a new record, don't you?"

"You've accumulated your one hundred combat points by flying the fewest number of missions — thirty-one — of any flying personnel in the history of the 501st Squadron!" The record would stand for the remainder of the war and never be broken.

"That's only because he doesn't drink or smoke, and was always sober and ready to fly!" added Captain Fisher, overhearing the conversation.

"Yeah!" I added, "All I did was chase women!"

"Remember," said Fisher, "you can go to hell for lyin' just the same as fornicatin'!"

"Are you sure they didn't hold up on my West Point appointment in Group, or here in the Squadron," I asked Sergeant Blackwell, "until they'd gotten all the combat mileage and a hundred points out of me?"

"They wouldn't do a thing like that to you, Lieutenant!" he answered.

"Well, it's history now, but I'm not gonna drag my feet gettin' out of here! If Musket sees me he'll have me on his hit list for just one more mission for old times sake!"

There was no prayer meeting or other gathering to celebrate my leaving. Just the shaking of hands, an exchange of good luck wishes and a lingering gaze when our eyes met, for the last time, that said it all. Other times, other places, and under different circumstances, we would forget military protocol, rank, custom and openly embrace each other. That's what brothers do! But that was war. Agonizing, relentless, perpetual, gut-wrenching, suicidal war, and those who must go on dying, as well as those who had been given a reprieve, simply did not exhibit any emotion, no matter how strong the feeling in their hearts.

"Promise me one thing, Doc," I said to Doc Marcus, in the presence of ten or fifteen officers who had gathered to say farewell, "donate at least two fifths of Old Grand-Dad medicinal spirits to the next prayer meeting in my name!" My suggestion was met with wild applause and approval.

"For you, Blount," replied Doc, "I'll do it! The United States Air Corps has saved more than five cases of Old Grand-Dad by having you as a pilot in this outfit!"

As I picked up my records and walked from the Operation's tent, I ran into Thatcher.

"You lucky bastard! I just heard the good news. You'll be in San Francisco or Los Angeles day after tomorrow, livin' it up! But you've earned it."

"I'm gonna miss you, Thatcher. I'm gonna miss all of you."

'Yeah! 'Bout like you'll miss Yulin Bay, Saigon, or Formosa."

"No, I mean it!" I replied, with a genuine sincerity.

"I know," said the crusty Thatcher, showing the carefully guarded and seldom seen softness of the real man, "and we'll miss you too! You're one of the happy endings who's beat the odds of this hellish game of aerial suicide we're playing! When I think of Bell, Johnson, Townsley, Esty, Miller, Coyel, Thies and all the others who won't be going home it makes me proud when anybody beats the odds! It gives the rest of us hope that we can beat the odds and get home too!"

"I never got to go to Sydney with you! And you were going to show me the town, too!"

"You sure didn't," he replied, "and I'm glad you didn't! Down deep inside I admired you for not going. When it's all said and done, all that any of us have left are our values, and you stuck by yours! And I respect that, you big Texas bastard!"

"With all your stories about all those naked women you almost sold me!" I replied.

"If one of those Australian women had gotten in your pants you'd have become a lover, and this outfit would've lost one of the finest, flying-est, fighting-est pilots that ever shit 'tween two boot heels!"

"That's not yours! That's not you speakin'!" I replied. "That's a west Texas or southern Oklahoma expression!"

"Yeah. You're right. That was about the highest compliment Lieutenant Bill Bell could pay anyone," said Thatcher, "and damn it to hell — I miss him!"

"I do too," I replied.

"Who're those?" I asked, as four young, eager new faces approached us with the anxious, strained looks of confused and worried replacements. Their bright, clean appearance, compared to the haggard, atabrine yellow look of the veterans, gave them away, and even the most dramatically inclined individual of the four was finding it difficult to swagger with conviction. They were cocky, but behind their nervous laughter I recognized the earliest evidence of worry and fear. I had been there! Like the rest of us they were boys when they arrived but they would mature quickly, so that when they left, if they survived, they would leave as men.

"They're four new pilots," replied Thatcher. "When the word got to Fifth Bomber Command that you were leaving, General Whitehead said it would take at least four to replace Blount!"

"You're as full of it as a Christmas turkey," I responded, "but take care of 'em and show 'em the ropes!"

"Have no fear! Mother Thatcher'll be near!" he said as he met the recruits at the corner of the tent and put an arm around the necks of two of them. "Welcome to downtown hell!" he said. "Have I shown you men where the 501st has suffered most of its casualties in this war? Come with me to the Officer's Mess! I think we're just in time for tea and crumpets! Incidentally, did any of you by chance bring any stateside drinking whiskey with you? We have little Squadron get-togethers every week or so we call prayer meetings, and new men are expected to furnish a bottle or two of good drinking whiskey!"

His voice faded in the distance, and I shook my head and smiled, as Thatcher and friends disappeared from view around the corner of the tent.

A light rain began to fall, as it did early every morning, and the low-hanging clouds covered Clark Field like a dark, fluffy comforter. My B-4 bag with the big, menacing Apache Indian head, the proud insignia of the 345th Bomb Group painted by Sergeant George Blackwell on its side, sat just inside the Group Headquarter's tent with my Japanese Samauri sword leaning against it. Having said my goodbyes to the rest of the crew back at the Squadron area, only Warnick accompanied me to my rendezvous with the jeep that would carry me to the flight line for the last time, to meet the Troop Carrier DC 3 transport that would take me back to the States.

"I'll be sweatin' out every minute of every mission that I have to fly without you as my pilot," he said in a grim and determined tone of voice, "until I get my last mission in! You're the best damned pilot in the U.S Army Air Corps and I'd fly to hell and back — on one engine — if you were flying the airplane!"

"We have flown through hell," I replied softly, "and we made it back 'cause we had the best Flight Engineer top turret gunner in all of west Texas, the United States, the north American continent, the world, or anywhere else!" We laughed, shook hands, and looked at each other for a fleeting moment, with a feeling and understanding that comes only from having flown, fought, been shot at and up, averted catastrophe, been pulled from the jaws of death, and experienced the gut-sick feeling together of watching our friends shot down in flames. Ours was a closeness that grew from the coordinated effort of a flight team in which each individual delivered a split-second performance of a necessary duty that guaranteed the normal operation of a complex instrument of destruction, to the dependence of each of us on each other for the collective preservation of our lives. Few brothers ever share or experience this kind of closeness, much less this kind of concern, for each other!

Warnick lifted my B-4 bag into the back of the jeep, we shook hands, and the sergeant driver turned the little olive drab vehicle toward the flight line. As the jeep made the last turn around the Headquarter's personnel tents, I looked back for one last glimpse, and I was glad that I did. Harold was still standing there, in the light Philippines jungle rain, waving goodbye, and saying *Don't go* at the same time. I waved back until he was out of sight, and then said a prayer for the bravest men I had ever known — my crew!

Epilogue

Those were the bravest, the most absolutely fearless men that I have ever known! Boisterous, irreverent, joyous, rambunctious, wild, unmilitary civilians on the ground but *Hell on Wings* when in the air, they were the kind of men the Air Corps loved in wartime but feared in peacetime — a special breed. Typical of these renegades was the parting shot of Major Theodore Wright, CO of the 498th. Having finished his combat missions, his last unofficial act was a buzz job of the strip and the squadron area that was so low that not a man was left standing. All the tents were blown down by the propwash of his B-25! Those impish rebels neither feared nor backed down from death, the enemy, their superiors, courts-martial or the Fifth Bomber Command. They held *all* in contempt.

Lieutenant Lum Lamar, and one gunner, Staff Sergeant Harold M. Balonier, were taken prisoner after being shot down by a Jap destroyer off Hon Noi Island, Indochina, on March 21, 1945. After ditching the airplane near the destroyer, other pilots had reported seeing three or four survivors in a life raft. Both Lieutenant Lamar and Sergeant Balonier were beheaded a month later by the Kempei-tai (Japanese Military Police that were the equivalent of the Nazi Gestapo) in Saigon, Indochina.

Lieutenant Everett W. Thies, one of my tentmates and copilot for Lieutenant Lum Lamar, died from wounds received in a gunfight resisting capture. He was buried behind the Kempei-tai barracks in Nha Trang, Indochina.

Captain W.A. Johnson was shot down attacking the enemy destroyer *Amatsukazi* off Swatow-Amoy, China, on April 6, 1945. His body washed ashore at the Chinese village of Kulei, five miles from the crash scene, where it was found by Chinese fishermen.

First Lieutenant Chester Phillips survived the war, returned to radio broadcasting, and retired as a television news anchor man in 1976. His grandson, now in the Air Force at Lackland, heard much about Tokyo Rose referring to the *Air Apaches* as the "Yellow-Nosed Butchers" who strafed and bombed only children and non-military targets. Chester retired as a Major in the AF reserve serving his last fifteen years in a special information Squadron in the Southeast United States.

First Lieutenant Melvin "Wild Bill" Bell, after having an engine shot out over Formosa on February 20, 1945, ditched off North Island. He had a bad ditching, hit in the "valley of death" between two big waves that broke the fuselage in two, causing the 1,000-pound top turret to crash forward into the cockpit killing both pilots, navigator and engineer gunner. Only the radio and tail gunner, in the back behind the bomb bay, survived the crash and were rescued by the *Playmate* PBY.

Colonel Chester Coltharp, CO of the 345th Bomb Group, died as a test pilot in the midair collision of two B-47 bombers on a training flight east of Wichita, Kansas, on the afternoon of September 1st, 1951.

As the best and most combat experienced engineer-gunner in the Squadron, Major Giese moved Staff Sergeant Harold E. Warnick up to his crew when he succeeded Major Jones as CO of the 501st. While flying with Giese, the Japs finally drew a bead on Warnick that made him a casualty when a 90-mm enemy antiaircraft shell exploded under his turret. Most of the shrapnel was removed from his legs in the M*A*S*H Unit hospital at the Laog airstrip on Luzon, where his aircraft made an emergency landing. It was twenty-nine years from the time he suffered the wound in 1945 before the one- and one-half inch-long sliver of Jap hardware, lodged in the bone and muscle of his left leg, could be surgically removed with safety. It took that long for medical science and neurosurgery to advance to the point that the operation could be performed without the exceedingly high risk of losing his leg to amputation or paralysis. The war was over for him! He had beaten the odds!

I once wrote a letter to Warnick's parents in 1945. I would not have occasion to write another letter for Harold Warnick for over twenty-five years and the occasion would be another Warnick in another war — Vietnam!

"Long distance calling Peppy Blount," said the operator as I picked up the telephone, "Is this Mr. Blount?"

"This is he," I responded.

"Go ahead," said the operator, "Mr Blount is on the line."

"Hello, Peppy!" came the voice, the same, down-to-earth, West Texas, flat, nasal twang that sent my mind racing back over the years searching to remember where I had heard that familiar, but now misplaced, voice before. *Big Spring, Sterling City . . . Coahoma . . . Odessa . . .* I couldn't remember.

"Yeah, this is Peppy," I replied, "who's this?"

"This is Harold Warnick . . ." That's as far as I let him get.

"Warnick . . . you son-of-a-gun, where are you? How've you been?"

"Not too good," he said in his even, straight-forward, slow voice; just as he had stated matter-of-factly on several occasions returning from a strike on the China coast: "we only have about ten minutes of gas left . . . we better start finding some land mighty quick or we're sure going to get our feet wet."

"It's my son, Mike," he continued, "we've just been notified by the War Department that he's missing in action in Vietnam and we can't get any information from anybody!"

"Oh, Harold!" I responded, my heart reaching out, comprehending his agony, "have you tried your United States Senators, your Congressman?"

"I've tried 'em all. But nobody can — or at least they won't — help us and I'm calling on you as a last resort. I've kept up with you and I'm sorry this had to be the reason for me to talk to you for the first time since — "

"This is the best reason I know of for you to talk to me," I cut him off again, "and don't you ever hesitate to call if you need me . . . I'd do anything I could for you . . . we've been through too much together! Now, tell me about Mike."

He filled me in with the sketchy information given him by the War Department.

"Let me contact my senator, Harold, and give his office this information. Each United States Senator has a privileged contact with the War Department regarding war casualties and can order an immediate investigation into the status of any service man and I'll guarantee you, if the War Department doesn't know what happened to Mike, I kinda' feel like they're going to find out right away! I'll call you the moment I know something. Our thoughts and prayers for his well-being are with you and your family."

I hung up and called my Senator in Washington, D.C., relating all the information about Mike Warnick to his executive assistant and explaining the worry and anguish of his parents and my deep concern.

A long, detailed telegram from Senator Ralph Yarborough a day later confirmed the fears of Harold Warnick and his wife. Sp/4 Michael G. Warnick died while serving his country on active duty in another war. While his Dad had received the Purple Heart in World War II, catching a Jap antiaircraft missile in his leg, and had been a member of a closely knit team that laughed at the grim reaper and cheated death time after time while constantly giving thanks to an all-powerful, ever-present God, Mike was not as fortunate. I knew that Harold would have traded places with his son, if that were possible, just as I or almost any other father would . . . to give him a chance in life. When you live with death long enough, I remembered that you could accept it, even grow to expect it, for yourself. But after all these years, to have to face it again through your own flesh and blood. How many generations, I wondered, have gone through this. Could that vibrant, unquestioning, totally dedicated Christian faith of one's youth still see one through? After one's personal understanding of "though I walk through the valley of the shadow of death I will fear no evil" and having gained a reprieve by the grace of a loving God, can our faith remain solid as a rock, and undergird our weakness? Once again I thought it would . . . it has . . . and it shall always, for our God is a constant, unwavering, and permanent source of strength as near and as close as your next prayer. I wondered if Mike knew his pilot, the other members of his crew, and his God? I hoped, and prayed, that he did.

The luck of Nat M. Kenney Jr. and Claude J. Stiles, my friends and last two tentmates, would finally run out — but both would beat the Grim Reaper and survive the war. Kenney, as the navigator for a new pilot, ditched off the shore of northern Luzon when his airplane ran out of gasoline on a strike to the coast of Indochina. Stiles would subsequently bail out, returning from a mission to the Japanese mainland, and would swim around in the Sea of Japan, fighting off sharks, before finally being picked up and rescued by a United States Navy Destroyer.

Now it's been almost two score years since we were so very young, so very cocky, so very eager, so very scared, yet so very dedicated to our task! Those of us who outlived those days, and who came safely home, now stand a little middle-aged taller. But we feel a slight chill of excitement, and still experience a hesitation in our breathing when someone mentions Rabaul, Guadalcanal, Morotai, Biak, Dulag, Nadzab, Hollandia, Tacloban, Corregidor, Bataan, San Marcelino, Subic Bay, Clark Field, Manila, Formosa, the China sea, Yulin Bay, Canton, and Saigon; for these are the far away places where we fought and where we left so many brothers!

Colonel Jay W. Moore (Retired), Lieutenant Colonel R.H. Ohnemus (Retired), Captain George H. Musket, Lieutenant John T. Hamner, Captain Don E. Marcus (Flight Surgeon), Lieutenant William M. Mathews, Lieutenant Rico F. Pallotta, Lieutenant Isaac (Ike) E. Baker, Colonel Ed L. Bina (Retired), Tech Sergeant George M. Blackwell, Captain Julius B. Fisher, Major Thomas D. Giese, Lieutenant Virgil L. Gross, Lieutenant Chester J. Kuta and Lieutenant Arthur G. McGrane, all beat the Grim Reaper and have lived to tell it!

Now, as the years pass with the ever increasing speed and acceleration of a fighter peel off, rocketing us ever closer to eternity, we unashamedly keep the vigil. Telling and retelling the exploits and brave deeds of these long since departed comrades in arms. Old men forget, it's true, but a few will never forget the feats they did that day at Saigon. Their names, familiar on the lips of these few, flow endlessly, as with glasses raised, we salute Lieutenant Andrew J. Johnson, Cadillac, Michigan; Lieutenant Paul E. Langdon, Jr., Cincinnati, Ohio; Lieutenant Aubrey L. Stowell, Indianapolis, Indiana; Corporal Lester F. Williams, Burkesville, Kentucky; Sergeant Alfredo P. Paredes, Del Rio, Texas; Lieutenant Vernon M. Townsley, Jr., Salt Lake City, Utah; F/O Hilbert E. Herbst, Webster City, Iowa; Corporal Seymour Schnier, Brooklyn, New York; Corporal Harry Sabinash, Milwaukee, Wisconsin; Lieutenant Milton E. Esty, Hartford, Connecticut; Lieutenant Marlin E. Miller, Minot, North Dakota; First Lieutenant Joseph M. Coyle, St. Clair, Pennsylvania; Tech Sergeant Henry C. Wreden, San Francisco, California; Sergeant James L. Golightly, Melbourne, Florida.

This story will the father hand down to his son and he to his son's son, so that these few will never be forgotten, so long as Freedom's Holy Light shall illuminate this land. As Shakespeare said of men like this:

We few, we happy few, we band of brothers;
For he to-day that sheds his blood with me
Shall be my brother . . .

And they were, they are, and they will forever be!

[*Editor's note*: Captain Blount received fifteen military decorations including the Distinguished Flying Cross, Air Medal with three clusters, and six battle stars. He married Eva Jean Finch of Longview, Texas, and the Blounts have three sons: Ralph Finch, John Eugene (Jeb) and Stephen Howard Blount.

R.E. Peppy Blount has been a public figure in Texas since he returned from the South Pacific. He was an outstanding athlete at The University of Texas serving as an end on championship Cotton Bowl, Sugar Bowl and Orange Bowl teams in 1946, 1948 and 1949, and as a member of the varsity basketball team.

He served as the youngest member ever elected to the Texas House of Representatives and later as County Judge of Gregg County.

The author makes his home with his wife in Longview, Texas, where he is a practicing attorney and an independent oilman and rancher.]